The
Tsarist Economy
1850–1917

PETER GATRELL

St. Martin's Press
New York

For my mother and father

First published in the United States of America in 1986

Printed in Great Britain

ISBN 0-312-82191-3

Library of Congress Cataloging-in-Publication Data
Gatrell, Peter.
  The tsarist economy, 1850–1917.
  Bibliography: p.
  1. Soviet Union—Economic conditions—1861–1917.
2. Soviet Union—Social conditions—1801–1917.
I. Title. II. Title: Czarist economy, 1850–1917.
HC334.5.G38 1986   330.947'08   85-25014
ISBN 0-312-82191-3

Contents

Preface

My aim in writing this book is to explore aspects of the economic history of late tsarist Russia. I have not attempted a comprehensive treatment of the Russian economy, which would have resulted in a different and much longer book. Instead, I have chosen to concentrate upon a number of significant issues. Needless to say, it is not self-evident which issues are significant and which are not. Different people will identify different issues as significant, depending upon the underlying assumptions they make.

Three major analytical traditions – liberal, populist and marxist-leninist – crystallized in Russia during the second half of the nineteenth century, giving rise to prolonged and often acrimonious debate about the desired and actual progress of the tsarist economy. Each tradition identified a series of significant issues, which are indicated in Chapter One. Modern scholars have in turn frequently addressed themselves to problems of Russian economic development that first surfaced in those contemporary debates. I have thus organized much of what I have to say in the form of critical examination of the issues posed by these three traditions of thought. I believe that this approach will serve to convey as much of the present state of knowledge of the tsarist economy as is feasible within the confines of a short textbook.

I have been fortunate to receive assistance from many quarters during the preparation of this book. I am grateful to the University of Manchester for allowing me study leave and for helping to defray travel costs. Financial support was also forthcoming from the British Academy. Among the librarians who have helped me at various times, I should particularly like to thank the staff of Inter-Library Loans at the John Rylands University Library and Jenny Brine of the Centre for Russian and East European Studies, University of Birmingham. I am also grateful to Constantine Brancovan for the loan of books.

I am happy to have the opportunity to thank Theo Balderston, Malcolm Faulkus and Mark Harrison. Each of them read large parts of the manuscript, helped me to clarify my ideas and saved me from blunders. Whatever merit this book possesses owes a great deal to them. Stephen Wheatcroft allowed me to draw upon his as yet unpublished research on Russian grain production. John Salter gave me much-appreciated intellectual support. Cambridge University Press has kindly given permission to draw upon material contained in the path-breaking work by Paul Gregory, *Russian National Income, 1885–1913* (1982).

My parents gave me much practical assistance in the preparation of this book. The dedication acknowledges a much deeper debt to them both. I should also like to thank Kate and David Shoenberg, whose friendship, support and kindness I have been privileged to enjoy for more than a decade.

Jane and our children, David and Elizabeth, have helped me to appreciate how much more there is to the present than the study of the past. I thank them for making it all worthwhile.

Transliteration

In transliteration from Cyrillic, I have decided in the interest of simplicity to omit all diacritical marks: thus, Danielson (not Daniel'son), and *kustar* (not *kustar'*).

Abbreviations

Footnote references to journal articles are abbreviated thus:

E.E.H.	*Explorations in Economic History*
Ec.H.R.	*Economic History Review*
Ist.zap.	*Istoricheskie zapiski*
J.E.E.H.	*Journal of European Economic History*
J.Ec.H.	*Journal of Economic History*
J.P.S.	*Journal of Peasant Studies*
S.R.	*Slavic Review*

Glossary

barshchina	Labour-service, or corvée.
black-earth	One of the major soil types in Russia, found to the south of a line drawn between Kiev, Tula and Kazan. The top layer of the soil (sometimes several feet thick) is very fertile.
chetvert	A measure of capacity, equivalent to a quarter (2.10 hectolitres).
dessyatina (pl. *dessyatiny*)	Square measure, equivalent to 1.09 hectares (2.7 acres).

European Russia	In 1913 European Russia comprised 50 provinces. It excluded the Grand Duchy of Finland, the Kingdom of Poland, the Caucasus, Central Asia, Siberia and the Far East.
guberniya	Province; the major administrative subdivision of the Russian Empire. In 1913 there were around 80 provinces in the Empire.
kulak	A rich peasant; literally 'a fist'.
kustar	Cottage or rural industry, undertaken by *kustari*.
mir	A peasant community, which regulated the affairs of its members through an assembly of heads of households; see *obshchina*.
non-black earth	Land to the north of the black-earth (q.v.), consisting in large part of forest. In the far north, the forests merge into desolate tundra.
obrok	Quitrent; sum paid by serfs to the lord in lieu of labour-service (*barshchina*).
obshchina	Term used to denote a group of peasants who held allotment land communally, and who periodically redistributed it.
otkhod	Literally 'going away'; term applied to temporary migration or tramping by peasants (*otkhodniki*), in search of employment.
otrabotka	'Labour-rent'; a system whereby peasants were obliged to work land owned by the gentry after 1861.
pomeshchik	Landlord; member of the Russian gentry.
populism	An ideology espoused by self-styled populists (*narodniki*); it takes its name from a belief in the primacy of the needs and interests of the Russian 'people', i.e. the peasantry.
promysly	'Trades' or 'Crafts'.
pud	Unit of weight, equivalent to 16.38 kg. (36.11 lb.).
ruble	Unit of currency; in 1913, 9.55 rubles exchanged for £1 sterling.
steppe	Undulating plains in the southern part of the black-earth.
uezd	District, subdivision of *guberniya*.
verst	Unit of length, equivalent to 1.06 km. (0.66 miles).
zemstvo (pl. *zemstva*)	•Organ of local government in rural Russia, introduced in 1864; operated at the level of the province and the district. By 1878 *zemstva* existed in 34 provinces, but not in western areas, nor outside European Russia. The *zemstva* were responsible for a range of services (public health, poor relief, roads, prisons, agronomic advice, etc.).

The Russian economy in 1900

European Russia, regions and provinces, 1850–1917

Map labels:

Barents Sea
Grand Duchy of FINLAND
ARCHANGEL
OLONETS
VOLOGDA
PERM
ST. PETERSBURG
ESTLYAND
LIFLYAND
KURLYAND
PSKOV
NOVGOROD
YAROSLAVL
KOSTROMA
VYATKA
KOVNO
VITEBSK
TVER
VLADIMIR
NIZ.-NOV.
KAZAN
UFA
VILNO
SMOLENSK
MOS-COW
ORENBURG
Kingdom of POLAND
GRODNO
MOGILEV
KALUGA
TULA
RYAZAN
TAMBOV
PENZA
SIMBIRSK
SAMARA
MINSK
CHERNIGOV
OREL
SARATOV
VOLYN
KURSK
VORONEZH
Dnieper
KIEV
POLTAVA
KHARKOV
PODOLYA
BESSARABIA
KHERSON
EKATERINOSLAV
DON
ASTRAKHAN
TAURIDE
Volga
Black Sea
Caucasus Mts.
Caspian Sea

NIZ.-NOV. NIZHNII-NOVGOROD
1 North
2 Baltic
3 North-West
4 Central Industrial
5 Urals
6 Lithuania
7 Belorussia
8 Central Black Earth
9 Mid-Volga
10 Lower Volga
11 South-West
12 Little Russia
13 New Russia

0   500 Miles
0   800 Km

ix

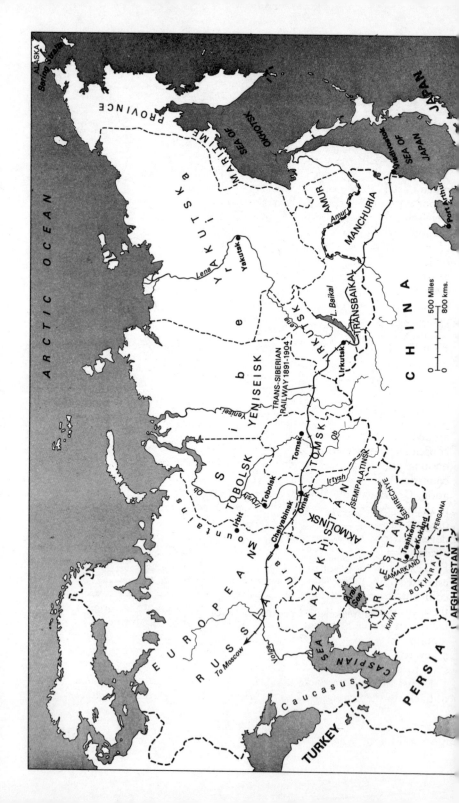

Introduction

The wealth of interpretation of the economic history of tsarist Russia, much of it available only in Russian publications, is testimony to the importance of the subject. Historians continue to be interested in the development of the economy before the Bolshevik Revolution, either because they seek to compare its performance with that of the Soviet economy or because they wish to establish a link between the economic development of tsarist Russia and the Revolution itself. Some historians have also sought to interpret Russia as a prototype of less developed countries in the modern world, and have suggested that Russia faced similar problems of economic backwardness in an earlier period. For these reasons, historians in East and West have generated a substantial body of interpretation.

Of the scholars who have contributed to the interpretation of the tsarist economy, none has been quite so influential in the English-speaking world as the late Alexander Gerschenkron. Gerschenkron did not confine his attention to the tsarist economy, and was concerned to locate Russia in the context of nineteenth-century European economic development. To make sense of that development, he argued, one had to recognize that each country became increasingly conscious of the relationship between its economic base and its international status. In order to secure their power and prestige, European countries had to address themselves to the question of industrialization. Gerschenkron dismissed any suggestion that successive industrializing countries in nineteenth-century Europe simply emulated the original British experience. As each country industrialized in turn, it developed not in accordance with a British blueprint, but rather in accordance with the legacy of accumulated economic backwardness. For example, Germany in the middle of the nineteenth century espoused the cause of industrialization, but at the same time confronted an uphill task of mobilizing the required resources. In these circumstances, it was necessary for 'substitutes' to be found for factors of production that had been relatively abundant and easy to mobilize in Britain. In Germany, the new investment banks fulfilled a key role; elsewhere, the task could be sufficiently onerous for the state to act as a 'substitute' for private initiative.[1]

Tsarist Russia offered an illustration of a country where the legacy of backwardness weighed heavily upon society. The clearest manifestation of economic backwardness was the preponderance of an unproductive agricultural sector, which failed to generate the resources needed for economic development. Until 1861, agricultural progress was hampered by serfdom. Yet the form taken by the emancipation of the peasantry was no more conducive to economic development. Peasants remained wedded to an outmoded system of agriculture, typified by the institution of the village community. Resources were consumed by the rapidly growing rural population.

Industrialization offered tsarist Russia the opportunity to escape from poverty and economic backwardness. The tsarist state also looked upon industrialization as a means of regaining the international leverage that Russia had lost during the course of the eighteenth century. However, Russia was in no position to industrialize without the intervention of the government, which fulfilled the functions that elsewhere had been appropriated by the private sector. The government transferred savings from peasant agriculture, by means of a stringent fiscal policy which, during the 1880s and 1890s, forced peasants to release their grain for export and urban consumption. Other fiscal and monetary devices (a high tariff and the stabilization of the ruble) encouraged the inflow of capital from western Europe, which laid the basis for investment in large-scale industry. The government also constituted a market for the products of industry, such as railway equipment.

Once the process of industrialization had been initiated, the Russian government could play a less active role. Indeed, after the government had engineered a transformation in land tenure at the beginning of the twentieth century (the Stolypin land reforms), the peasantry – no longer constrained by the commune – became more dynamic and prosperous. Peasants began to save more out of their growing income and to create a market for the products of manufacturing industry. Industry itself was able to seek credit from the developing commercial banking system, rather than to depend overwhelmingly upon state support. According to Gerschenkron, only the unfortunate impact of the First World War on the tsarist economy frustrated the process of 'westernization' upon which the economy had embarked in the decade preceding its outbreak.

The arguments that Gerschenkron put forward have been immensely provocative and influential. They must, nevertheless, be treated as propositions to be tested, rather than as assertions that can be accepted uncritically. The researches of other scholars have challenged many of Gerschenkron's original contentions.

In the first place, Gerschenkron maintained that tsarist agriculture proved incapable of improving the productivity of land and labour during the nineteenth century. In the light of research by Paul Gregory and others, this view must now be modified. Aggregate agricultural production and labour productivity in agriculture both emerge from Gregory's study in a more favourable light.[2] His research also has significant implications for Gerschenkron's hypothesis about peasant living standards. Gerschenkron maintained that higher rates of indirect taxation intensified the burden on peasant incomes, imposed as a result of the compensation paid to the former serf-owners.[3] However, Gregory has demonstrated that per capita consumption of grain in the Russian village did not decline during the period of rapid industrialization, and other scholars have argued that peasant incomes were not adversely affected by the fiscal policies pursued during the 1890s.[4]

Gerschenkron's insistence upon the extent and positive impact of government economic intervention has also come under critical scrutiny. Olga Crisp has pointed to the fact that Russian manufacturing industry developed in an autonomous fashion, especially where sectors such as textiles and processed foodstuffs were concerned. Her argument suggests that it is more appropriate to think of the tsarist government as one element only in the formation of a market for manufactured goods. Arcadius Kahan questioned the degree to which the tsarist government had a positive effect on capital investment. He raised the possibility that the government hindered the process of industrialization, by competing for funds with the private sector.[5]

A third example of the revisions that have been made to the interpretation advanced by Gerschenkron concerns his remarks about 'westernization'. Reduced to simple terms, Gerschenkron maintained that the Bolshevik Revolution was brought about by the pressure of war upon an economy that was struggling to find its feet. Had it not been for the First World War, the tsarist economy would have continued to grow and to release the energies of private farmers and businessmen; tsarist society would have continued to develop along stable lines. There are several problems with this interpretation, not least the assumption that the 'pattern' of economic development changed decisively around the time of the 1905 Revolution. The main difficulty, however, concerns the notion of 'stability' in tsarist Russia. The work of historians such as Leopold Haimson and Victoria Bonnell has disposed of the idea that relations between the Russian working-class and the tsarist state were more stable in 1914 than they had been a decade earlier. Nor can it be said that the relationship between the state and other social classes (notably, of course, the peasantry) was any more reassuring for the survival of tsarism.[6]

The relationship between economic and political change in tsarist Russia has been explored by many historians. Gerschenkron, as we have seen, took the view that economic development had been engineered by the tsarist state and that the history of Russia demonstrated the 'subordination of economic policies to the exigencies of power'.[7]

The tsarist state, in his opinion, reaped the benefits of economic progress, but succumbed to the challenge of total war. Other historians have insisted that economic progress in late imperial Russia had devastating political consequences. For instance, Theodore von Laue had emphasized the persistent pressure on the living standards of peasants and workers, the disintegration of traditional rural society, and the failure of the political system to respond to social change. As a result, he argues, the Russian masses were alienated from the regime.[8] Marxist historians point to the intensification of class conflict in Russia, as the inevitable outcome of the development of capitalism. The contradiction between the dominant capitalist mode of production and the feudal state could only be resolved by revolution.[9]

The interplay of economics and politics in tsarist Russia also pre-occupied contemporary observers, whether they be government officials, intellectuals or political activists. The political aspirations of contemporaries passed away, of course, with the collapse of the tsarist regime and the transfer of power in October 1917 to the Soviet government. But those aspirations are of more than fleeting interest, because the divisions of opinion among contemporaries have profoundly influenced the historiography. The interpretations advanced by contemporaries revealed very different approaches to the tsarist economy. To be aware of this fact is to acknowledge that there is more than one way of conceiving the 'problems' of Russian economic development.

We may distinguish three major approaches to the tsarist economy, which crystallized during the later nineteenth century. They are, respectively, a liberal, a populist and a marxist-leninist interpretation. The adherents of each school of thought held decided views about the desired course of tsarist economic and social change, as well as providing an analysis of the actual course of development.

The liberal opponents of tsarism argued that political and economic change should proceed hand in hand. Russian liberals took England or the United States as models for their country to emulate. The liberal historians Paul Vinogradov and Paul Miliukov believed that economic development would create a more dynamic and wealthy society, which would provide the basis for a democratic system of government. Political change would in turn create the climate for further economic expansion. Russia could then take her place in the community of parliamentary democracies and in the front rank of advanced economies.

Liberals were conscious of the efforts that tsarism had made during the 1860s to reform its institutions. That decade had witnessed the emancipation of the serfs and of other categories of peasants, as well as reforms in local government, the legal system, education and the army. However, the momentum had not been sustained. Reaction set in during the 1880s. In addition, the government appeared to be incapable of overcoming problems of poverty among the mass of the population. These problems required measures to stimulate and reward private enterprise. In so far as the government promoted industrial growth and embarked, after 1905, on a reform of land tenure, its measures were to be welcomed. But only a fully democratic political system could, in their opinion, unlock all the resources that Russia possessed in abundance.[10]

Scholars who have worked within this liberal tradition have diagnosed the tsarist economy in the following terms. First, the central 'problem' was that of economic backwardness. Second, the chief obstacles to be overcome were the concentration of the population in traditional peasant agriculture and the restrictions placed by government on private enterprise. Finally, the 'solution' to the problem lay in land reform and in capitalist industrialization. Gerschenkron belonged to this tradition, even though he differed from many historians in ascribing a positive role to government and in denying the necessity of land reform as a necessary condition of economic development.[11]

Russian populists (*narodniki*) pinned their hopes for political change on the peasantry. Populism was a diffuse tradition; to call it a movement is to exaggerate its coherence. But populist ideology was extremely influential in nineteenth-century Russia, especially among the intelligentsia.[12] Broadly speaking, populists shared a basic belief in the possibility of social progress in Russia by means of the reaffirmation and extension of the land commune. The populist idealization of the commune went hand in hand with a belief in the undesirability and even impossiblility of capitalism in Russia. Hence, populists parted company with those who endeavoured to promote capitalist industry: their aversion to it distinguished them from liberals, marxists and many government officials. Populists devoted numerous books and articles to the case against capitalism. After 1901, the new Socialist Revolutionary party took up these themes. Its chief spokesman, W. M. Chernov, stressed that the struggle of peasants against economic and political exploitation was in essence a struggle for the redistribution of land, from the state and landlords to the 'people'.[13]

The populist analysis of the tsarist economy took the following form. First, the central 'problem' was the poverty of the people. Second, the chief obstacle to be overcome was the exploitation of the people by landlords, merchants and the state. Finally, the solution to the problem lay, not in the abolition of the commune and in industrialization, but rather in the redistribution of privately-held land. Put in these terms, the populist analysis has had relatively little impact on the historiography. But because the populist argument invites us to reflect upon the supposedly specific features and dynamics of Russian peasant society, this tradition has by no means been exhausted.[14]

Russian socialists who followed the ideas propounded by Karl Marx anticipated that the growth of capitalism in Russia would generate new forms of class conflict, which were destined to sweep away tsarism and eventually to bring about socialist revolution. Marx had argued that capitalism would dig its own grave by creating a class of wage labourers, whose interests were directly opposed to those of the bourgeoisie. But Marx had illustrated his argument with particular reference to Britain, already an advanced industrial society in the middle of the nineteenth century. How could his analysis apply to an economically backward society, such as Russia?

In answer to this question, Russian marxists such as Plekhanov, Lenin and Trotsky maintained that capitalism had made great inroads in the Russian economy by the end of the nineteenth century. By 1900, peasants were being deprived in ever greater numbers of access to the means to production, and compelled to become wage labourers. These proletarianized peasants had a common class identity with the small but growing numbers of Russian industrial workers. Together with the Bolshevik Party (formed in 1903), they would challenge the tsarist state and the propertied classes which supported it.[15]

The marxist-leninist diagnosis of the tsarist economy may be summarized as follows. The central economic problem was the need to release the potential for the development of the productive forces. The obstacles derived from the failure to sweep away the remnants of feudalism after 1861. The abolition of serfdom had not dealt a sufficiently decisive blow to feudal relations in society. At the same time, capitalism had made rapid inroads into the post-reform economy. In the long run, however, the productive forces could only develop fully if the tsarist autocracy were overthrown and – along with it – the feudal landlords.[16]

This introduction has sketched in some of the central problems in the historiography, and has argued that those issues cannot be reduced to a single formula. What was a 'problem' for one school of thought was part of the 'solution' for another. For example, liberals looked to the development of private enterprise in the tsarist economy, whereas populists regarded this as a symptom of the exploitation of the 'people'. Furthermore, the issues addressed by historians have not emerged out of the head of this or that scholar. Historians themselves adhere to distinct analytical traditions, which define particular issues as significant. In the following chapter, the economic arguments of each tradition will be scrutinized more closely. The remainder of the book is designed to examine these arguments more fully.

1 Russian Economic Development: Models and Issues

The aim of this chapter is to set out more formally the different models of economic development that have been adopted – often implicitly, rather than explicitly – in the interpretation of Russian economic history. The first section is devoted to what is termed the liberal economic viewpoint. Here the emphasis falls on the characteristics of a backward agricultural sector and on dual-economy models, which pinpoint the interaction between the backward sector and a dynamic industrial sector. The section also outlines the way in which such models have informed historical study of the tsarist economy. The second section looks to the populist tradition of economic analysis. Populist economics rejected some of the assumptions and most of the values of liberal economics, in particular challenging the desirability and necessity of a transfer of labour from countryside to city. The third section introduces the main propositions advanced by marxist-leninist analysis, which has also informed much historical scholarship on the tsarist economy. Marxism-leninism is counterposed to populism (for instance, in its rejection of populist assumptions about the peasant economy) and to orthodox liberal economic analysis (in its assumptions about the reality and outcome of class struggle). The chapter concludes with some brief observations that constitute an agenda of topics to be treated in the remainder of the book.

1.1 The Liberal Interpretation

We may begin by imagining an economy in which the bulk of the population is engaged in the production of foodstuffs for its own consumption. We may further assume that the rural labour force works on a limited supply of land and uses a stock of primitive techniques. As the population and thus the rural labour force increases

in size, land of increasingly inferior quality is brought under cultivation. The marginal productivity of labour in agriculture declines;
that is, each additional worker contributes marginally less to agricultural output. The existing economy is unable to offer the new workers
any productive employment; their additional labour may at a certain
point have no net effect on total output (economists term this zero
marginal productivity). Given the assumptions of this simple model,
there appears to be a 'surplus' labour force. The labour surplus can
be reduced only by finding productive employment outside the
traditional food-producing sector. The only other alternative, barring
of course a sudden increase in the supply of land, is to find a way of
overcoming the obstacles to technical stagnation and to introduce
technical changes that will increase the productivity of rural labour.
In the absence of such opportunities, the population will become
impoverished and subject to the Malthusian positive checks of malnutrition and starvation.

The argument can be presented in diagrammatic form, as in Figure
1. In graph A we see the growth in output with successive amounts
of labour applied to the available land. The gradual flattening of the
curved line indicates the progressive decline in the marginal
productivity of labour. As the total workforce grows from L_1 to L_2
so an extreme position is reached where the marginal product of the
additional labour is zero. In the next graph, B we introduce an element
of technical change (the forms this might take are discussed below).
In this case, technical change is sufficient to offset the effects of
'diminishing returns' and, although the rural population has
increased, the total output of food per capita is higher than before
(compare the position of the straight lines OX_1 and OX_2 in Figure 1
B). However, it is also conceivable that technical change will be
insufficient to offset diminishing returns to labour; the problem would
be compounded if population growth were still more rapid. In graph
C, technical change takes place, but it is not enough to improve output
per person. Put another way, at the new level of rural population there
is less food available per head.

One may next conceive of a more modern sector which will be able
to absorb the labour surplus and in which the marginal product of
labour would be higher than in traditional or subsistence agriculture.
This possibility was explored by W. A. Lewis in his famous model of
economic development with 'unlimited' supplies of labour.[1] Lewis
argued that the capitalist in a modern industrial sector could recruit
the labour surplus by offering a wage equivalent to the subsistence
'wage' that already obtained in the traditional sector (more realistically, wages will be somewhat higher in order to offset higher living
costs in the city). Lewis took for granted the prior existence of an
industrial sector that drew upon an elastic labour supply. What inter-

A

utput

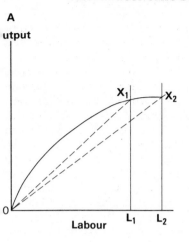

B

Output

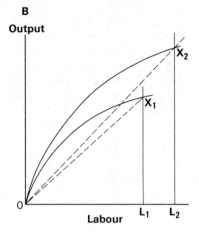

C

utput

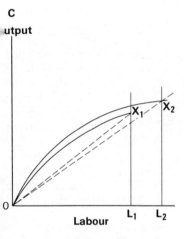

Fig. 1   The 'traditional' sector

ested him was the mechanism that facilitated further expansion of the modern sector.

In Figure 2 we see the situation in the industrial sector as understood by Lewis. The curve NR is taken to represent the marginal product of labour engaged in industry. The prevailing wage rate in industry is indicated by point W on the vertical axis. The capitalist employer will recruit workers up to the point where their marginal product is equal to the wage rate: this level of employment is given by OM in the figure. Other workers have to fend for themselves in the traditional sector. The area represented by OMPN indicates the

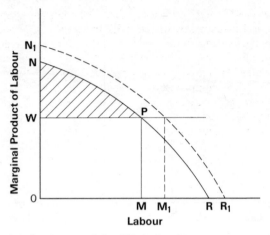

Fig. 2   The 'modern' sector (after W. A. Lewis)

total product of the industrial sector, comprising wages and profits. The share of output paid to workers is given as OMPW while the surplus, or profit, is given by the shaded area PNW. Lewis then assumed that these profits will be reinvested. Accordingly, the capital stock in industry increases and additional workers will be taken on at the prevailing wage rate in proportion to the growth in capital formation. The assumptions of a constant real wage rate in the traditional sector and of a proportionate increase in labour and capital are both crucial to Lewis's argument. With the reinvestment that takes place, the labour force grows from OM to OM₁, and this process continues until all surplus rural labour is absorbed. When this stage is reached, the modern and the traditional sectors compete with one another for available labour.[2]

Lewis went on to argue that the process he described could be halted prematurely, because real wages might increase to the level where the capitalist surplus disappears and nothing is left over for reinvestment. One cause of increasing wages might be organized pressure by the working class. Another might be a shift in the terms of trade in favour of agriculture, occasioned by an increase in the demand for food or raw materials relative to the growth in agricultural productivity. In this case, the capitalist sector finds that the price of inputs rises relative to the price of the manufactured goods it sells in exchange. Real wages in industry have to rise to take account of rising food costs. Lewis said that this possibility could be outweighed by an improvement in agricultural productivity, but discounted the likelihood of this in practice.[3] In these circumstances, the government might come to the rescue of capitalist production in the industrial sector by taxing farmers' additional incomes and providing resources for new capital investment. In the long term, growing commercialization in the agricultural sector will bring benefits to the economy as a whole: producers can generate an additional surplus for export, thereby earning foreign currency to pay for imports of capital goods, while the creation of new money incomes in agriculture ensures a source of taxation that can be devoted to expenditure on transport, housing and education.

Let us see next how some of these arguments have underpinned the work of economic historians. To begin with, it is necessary to return to the assumptions of population growth in a traditional agricultural sector and of the fixed supply of land. One of the distinguishing features of the tsarist economy during the second half of the nineteenth century was the rapid growth of the rural population, from an estimated 50 million in 1858 to 80 million in 1897. This increase in peasant population manifested itself in the fragmentation of holdings, soil exhaustion and periodic harvest failures, problems that were most acute in the Central Black Earth Region. Historians have been much less concerned to account for the rapidity of population increase than they have to document its effects. Some historians simply treat population as an exogenous variable. In the words of Richard Pipes, for instance, the increase represented a 'devastating natural pressure ... outside human control'. But to say that people have no control over their fertility is distinctly odd.[4] As we shall see in Chapter Three, other historians have related population growth to the high rate of marital fertility among peasant women, which has been linked in turn to the pattern of land allocation and distribution.

In what sense is it realistic to maintain the assumption of a fixed supply of land? A distinction may be drawn between natural or geographical constraints on the supply of cultivable land and institutional constraints. Large parts of Russia were either completely uninhabitable or not conducive to a reasonably secure existence. In the early twentieth century the Russian Empire comprised around 2,200 million hectares of land, only half of which had been surveyed. Less than half the surveyed area could be regarded as suitable for cultivation.[5] Much of this land had not been settled, because it was inaccessible. The problem of access diminished with the construction of railways in the 1860s and 1870s, and the fertile lands of western Siberia began to be settled more extensively during the 1890s and 1900s, when the construction of the Trans-Siberian Railway commenced and the government promoted migration. But those who adhered to the concept of a labour 'surplus' believed that it could not be absorbed by internal migration alone. Colonization was put into context by the American historian G. T. Robinson in the following

way: 'the natural increase of the rural population of the fifty guberniyas (of European Russia) was nearly fourteen times as great as the
net loss which these guberniyas incurred through emigration to
Siberia' between 1861 and 1905.[6]

The system of land tenure that prevailed during the second half of
the nineteenth century also exercised an influence on the availability
of cultivable land to peasant farmers. Before 1861, peasant access to
land was largely determined by serfdom. Land was divided between
the state, Church, royal family and the landed nobility (*dvoryanstvo*).
Peasants were attached to each of these categories, with around one-
half belonging to noble landowners. These peasant serfs had no title
to land of their own and worked on the lord's demesne or, with the
approval of the lord, discharged their feudal obligations by providing
him with a quitrent, of money or goods. Peasants' farmsteads were
located on the estate and were provided at the lords' pleasure. Peasants had no freedom of movement; gone were the days of mass flight
from feudal oppression to sparsely settled land to the south and east.

Emancipation gave these serfs personal liberty and an allotment of
land. For this allotment (*nadel*) they had to compensate the lord by
means of redemption payments, spread out over almost half a century
from the date of the agreement between the two parties. Redemption
gave the peasants a communal title to the land. A distinction thus
emerged between peasant allotment land and the privately owned
estates of the former serf owners, although this was a legal distinction
that the Russian peasantry could neither understand nor accept. If
the peasantry required additional land to support increasing numbers,
it would have to be rented or purchased from the landed gentry, or
from other private sources. The emancipation settlement did not
provide for adjustments to the total pool of allotment land that might
be necessary if the rural population grew rapidly. With the subsequent
growth in population, rentals and land prices moved upwards. Emancipation had an even more immediate effect on the supply of land, in
so far as it tended to reduce the effective amount of land occupied
by peasants compared to their situation under serfdom. How this
situation came about is traced in more detail in Chapter Four. In the
fertile black earth provinces, peasants lost around one-quarter of the
land they had previously worked. Ultimately, peasants would be
driven to redress these wrongs in the revolutions of 1905-6 and 1917.[7]

An integral part of the liberal explanation of Russian economic
backwardness is the concentration of the rural population in a
traditional agricultural sector, where the marginal productivity of
labour was very low. This adverse situation might have been alleviated
by improvements in the stock of techniques, but it is normally
assumed that such improvements did not take place. Peasant farming
was typified by the use of traditional implements to prepare the soil

for cultivation, to harvest the crop and thresh the grain. The symbol of technological conservatism was the old wooden plough (*sokha*), which simply scratched the surface of the earth, rather than turning it over. No attempt was made to improve the quality of seed. Low and stagnant yield ratios dictated that a high proportion of the crop had to be retained for the next planting. Fluctuations in the cereal harvest introduced a serious element of uncertainty into such calculations and reduced the potential marketable surplus.

The use of the available land revealed the inability of the peasantry to innovate. Arable fields were worked in accordance with the three-field system, in which one-third were planted in winter, one-third in spring and the remainder were left for the soil to recover its moisture and fertility. Where other societies, notably in western Europe, had moved towards new rotations involving grass, clover and legumes (pulses), Russian agriculture retained a cereal monoculture. Indeed, the growth in numbers compelled the peasantry to plough up precious pasture, thereby exacerbating the problem of maintaining adequate livestock herds. This in turn had serious repercussions for the supply of manure and contributed to the failure to improve yields.

In addition, units of production were peasant households, organized into communes, each of which customarily claimed an entitlement to part of the land at the disposal of the commune (*obshchina*). This resulted in the sub-division of land into narrow strips, in order to satisfy the claims of new numbers of people and thus new households. Since the commune stipulated that each household should be given access to land of similar quality, the strips farmed by any one household were scattered over a wide area, creating problems in the allocation of both time and land (because some land had to be set aside to mark out boundaries between the strips). Finally, it was traditional in Russian peasant society for these strips to be reallocated periodically in accordance with demographic changes, that is the formation of new households, changes in household composition and the disappearance of others. A farmer hardly had any incentive to improve the quality of land at the disposal of his household, when he knew that the long-term benefits of any innovation would not accrue to its members. As a result, to quote the poignant words of Robinson, Russian peasants had not found 'an exodus from their economic Egypt'.[8]

The main conclusion to be drawn from the standard liberal economic interpretation of Russian peasant agriculture is that technical change was very limited, at least until the early twentieth century. Certainly, it is assumed that such limited technical change as may have taken place was insufficient to prevent a reduction in food output per head (as in Figure 1 C). But why were changes in technology and organization so few and far between? It seems silly to argue that

Russian peasants were inherently incapable of making the necessary innovations, and more plausible to locate any aversion to change in terms of the risks involved in change. In some specific instances, such as the adoption of new varieties of seed or breeds of livestock, the problem may have been lack of complementary inputs of credit and of agronomic advice. More generally, the explanation could lie in the overall economic climate of tsarist Russia, which did not afford the agricultural producer a reasonable return on his investment. One approach has been to suggest that the main obstacle lay in the under-development of the market in agricultural commodities, and thus the lack of an appropriate market stimulus.[9] Another is to ask whether the rewards for innovation would not have been captured by other hands, be they gentry or government. In the meantime, the distribution of strips of allotment land may have been perfectly rational, given the likely differences in land quality and accessibility; and the reallocation of strips was rational from the point of view of matching changing household labour and consumer patterns to the available land.[10]

Turning to the notion of a dual economy, particularly as formulated by Lewis, a number of interesting observations and qualifications suggest themselves. Some historians of tsarist Russia have expressed serious doubts about the potential for the labour 'surplus' in peasant agriculture to be absorbed in a 'modern' industrial sector. The most familiar form of this argument is that constraints on the supply side served to limit the migration of labour. In other words, the interpretation centres not so much on the failure of an industrial sector to exert the appropriate pull on rural labour, as upon the failure of the Russian commune to release labour.

The detailed case for this assertion is set out in Alexander Gerschenkron's survey of tsarist agrarian policies and industrialization. Gerschenkron emphasized the restrictive impact of the 1861 emancipation settlement. The statutes made it possible for a peasant household to leave the commune only if its head agreed to forfeit for ever a share in the allotment lands administered by the commune, and provided that he settled all outstanding debts, including his share of the redemption debt. Gerschenkron also argued that an individual member of the household who wished to leave would have to obtain the permission of the head of the household, permission that was unlikely to be granted, in so far as the loss of one member had repercussions on the overall entitlement of the household to a share of the allotment land. Temporary migration was possible, but according to Gerschenkron this was hampered by the need to have the approval of the commune as a whole, which until 1894 controlled the issue of internal passports. Thus, 'if industrialization required the formation of a labour force which had accepted the discipline of the factory and had acquiesced in the life-long exercise of a non-agricultural occupation, the reform (of 1861) certainly tended to retard the process of formation of such a labour force in Russia'.[11] In terms of Lewis's model, labour supply was inelastic and the price at which labour was made available to industry did not reflect rural 'overpopulation'. This bottleneck resulted, in Gerschenkron's view, in a substitution of capital for labour in industry, which took the form of new investment in labour-saving technology. The tsarist government encouraged this process by opening the door to foreign capital and by purchasing much of the product of this capital-intensive 'heavy' industry.

Gerschenkron's argument about the contraints on labour supply may nevertheless be called into question. To begin with, the number of passports issued to members of the commune assumed large dimensions towards the end of the nineteenth century. Nor did this process simply indicate an increase in the number of peasants who sought short-term employment during slack months in the agricultural calendar. Many peasants left the village on a long-term basis and gained several years' or even decades' income and experience in urban employment, before returning to their native villages. In short, the supply of labour was more fluid than Gerschenkron's 'legalistic' approach allows. The interesting question is to what extent and why the labourer chose to look for work on agricultural estates – for example in south Russia – rather than to seek employment in the towns. This calls for more extended discussion of the labour market (see Chapter 3, section 3.4).

Lewis assumed that capitalists in the modern sector would invest the surplus and contribute to a continued expansion in industry, but that pressures tending to increase real wages in industry would frustrate this process. Applying this model to Russia, the pressure was more likely to have come from increases in the price of foodstuffs, caused by the failure of agricultural productivity to grow sufficiently fast, rather than from organized labour, which the tsarist regime banned until after the 1905 Revolution. However, the relative prices of agricultural and industrial goods in the late nineteenth century did not conform to the expectations of the Lewis model; in other words, the terms of trade moved in favour of industrial rather than agricultural producers. Why did this happen? One reason was that the last quarter of the century witnessed a prolonged agricultural depression in the world economy. Russia did not escape the effects of the slump in cereal prices. The tsarist government appeared to encourage the adverse movement in the terms of trade for agricultural producers, by levying indirect taxes on basic commodities purchased by the peasantry, thereby forcing them to yield up more of their agricultural output in order to obtain manufactured goods in exchange.[12] In theory, the effects of such a shift in the terms of trade could be offset by an increase in agricultural labour productivity, but – as we have seen – the conventional view of Russian peasant agriculture rules this out in practice.

One of the weaknesses of the simple dual-economy model is its assumption that the agricultural sector was synonymous with the production of foodstuffs by peasant households. Applied to the tsarist economy, this assumption is erroneous in two respects. In the first place, peasants engaged in a wide range of productive activity, which included the manufacture of handicrafts for domestic consumption or for sale. The scope for additional rural labour to be allocated to the production of manufactured goods clearly complicates the simple model of a traditional sector with a fixed supply of land and diminishing returns to food producers. The question of the circumstances under which peasant households might opt to allocate labour to handicraft production has attracted considerable attention in recent years, though not with any special reference to tsarist Russia. As we shall see in the next section, some contemporary commentators argued that the government frustrated this potential by promoting instead the development of a competitive factory industry.

The second complication with regard to the agricultural sector is that peasant farmers comprised only part of the overall scene. The emancipation settlement of 1861 left the private gentry landowners with large estates to manage. It has to be established whether the assumptions made about the absence of technical change in peasant agriculture also apply to these estates. For example, while some private estates were farmed on modern capitalist principles, contemporaries noted that others were leased to peasant farmers. Many of the conventional liberal strictures about 'irrational' and primitive farming methods on peasant land thus pertain to lands that formally belonged to the gentry.[13]

This argument can also be incorporated into the liberal approach to the problem of capital formation. One may suggest that the pressure of population on land led to an increase in rents received by private landlords and thus transferred income from peasants to gentry. The question then arises as to the use to which this additional income was put: was it consumed by the *pomeshchiki* (gentry) or invested and, if so, how? The overwhelming impression created in the literature is that landowners as a whole were incapable of productive investment and that they frittered away the increment in their income on luxuries or other conspicuous consumption. This standard observation needs to be tested against the evidence. If it is confirmed, it could be regarded as another justification for the interventionist role of government in the investment process, which Gerschenkron believed to be of paramount importance.

Many elements in what is here termed the liberal analysis of the tsarist economy were first adumbrated by economists and other public figures in Russia towards the end of the nineteenth century. During the late 1890s, for example, liberal spokesmen for the *zemstva* called for the commune to be dismantled, in order to release the energy of the more dynamic peasant entrepreneurs. The Minister of Finance, S. Yu. Witte, himself by no means a liberal in his political convictions, also came to espouse the anti-commune cause.[14] With regard to the capital market, Russian businessmen and liberal academics constantly voiced their opinion that steps should be taken to ease restrictions on the supply of credit for industry. They coupled this with an insistence that industry itself should increase the productivity of labour and reduce manufacturing costs. This would then boost trade between agriculture and industry and would improve the competitive position of Russian manufactures on world markets. The continued expansion of industry that resulted would in its turn facilitate the further absorption of the labour 'surplus'.[15]

We may consider, finally, the analysis Witte himself made of the economic situation in Russia in 1899. Witte took a quintessentially classical view of the need to transfer the labour 'surplus' from agriculture to industry. He justified this on the grounds that the marginal productivity of labour in agriculture was low and falling. In his opinion, the advantage of a programme of rapid industrialization was that 'national labour, which is at present extensively employed only for a short agricultural season, will find full application and consequently become more productive. This, in turn, will increase the wages of the entire agricultural population'. The agricultural sector would become commercialized, exchanging food and raw materials for domestic manufactured goods.[16]

There is much here that would be echoed fifty years later, by W. A. Lewis! The main difference is that Witte pinned his hopes on a massive injection of foreign capital investment in industry. 'We have at our disposal cheap labour, abundant natural resources, and only the high price of capital now stands in the way of obtaining cheap goods.' Foreign investment provided the key to future economic expansion. Accompanied by an influx of foreign skills and technology (as Witte anticipated), capital imports would shorten the period of industrial transformation.[17]

An assessment of the costs and benefits of this policy has been essential to economic historians who have worked in the liberal tradition. But it is important to recognise that the programme Witte outlined, and its underlying assumptions, were challenged by his contemporaries. Foremost among his critics were men of a populist persuasion, who argued that Witte's policies had proved detrimental to the Russian peasantry and that the policies themselves were based on false premises. Accordingly, it is upon the populist analysis that attention will focus next.

1.2 The Populist Interpretation

At the risk of oversimplification, populism can be distinguished from liberal economic analysis in its rejection of the concept of a labour 'surplus' in peasant agriculture. Liberal opinion, as we have seen, regarded the agricultural sector in Russia as the Achilles heel of the entire economy. An inert peasantry were barely able to provide for the growing rural population. Liberals argued, therefore, that the peasantry had to be forced out of their sloth, for example by government action (land reform) or by attracting rural labour into modern capitalist industry through the offer of a wage. From a populist standpoint, the question of a mechanism to transfer labour from a 'backward' agricultural to a 'modern' industrial sector did not arise. The notion of an agrarian 'problem', as understood by liberals, was fundamentally misconceived. Agriculture was not a sector to be modernized; it was a way of life that had to be respected.

This section begins with a discussion of the views put forward during the later nineteenth century by leading adherents of the populist viewpoint. It then outlines the interpretation of the peasant economy formulated by so-called 'neo-populists' during the years immediately before and after the Russian Revolution. As in the previous section, attention will be paid to some of the instances in which the populist interpretation has been reflected in the work of historians.

Russian populists believed first and foremost in the vitality and viability of the traditional peasant commune (*obshchina*). The commune was the cornerstone of Russian economic development. It allocated land to all households in the community, and periodically redistributed that land in accordance with the households' need and ability to work it. The commune enabled all its members to secure the resources for their subsistence. The Russian peasant was therefore guaranteed the key factor of production, namely land, and ran no risk of being expropriated by other peasants. It followed that Russia could not experience capitalist development along the lines of western Europe, because the preconditions for capitalism (the expropriation of the producer from the means of production) were absent.[18]

During the middle years of the nineteenth century, these views were widely held among the Russian intelligentsia. What is more, they were held by radical and conservative thinkers alike. For instance, famous radical thinkers such as Herzen and Chernyshevsky argued that Russia could skip the capitalist stage of development, with its attendant social inequality and unemployment, and proceed to socialism, in which the commune would be an essential feature. The suggestion that the commune maintained peasants on the land, and thus frustrated capitalist development, was no less dear to conservatives. A well-known Prussian nobleman, August von Haxthausen, had taken this line in a book published in 1852. Conservatives put forward the argument that the commune served to maintain social stability and respect for authority. Thus the notion of a largely homogeneous peasant society, comprising households that coexisted within the framework of the village community, found favour with people of different political persuasions.[19]

The emancipation of the serfs lent a particular urgency to the question of peasant social organization. In the aftermath of emancipation, some intellectuals imagined that the peasantry would be deprived of the plots of land that they had hitherto held of the feudal lords. In principle, the government's decision that peasants should be freed with a plot of land seemed to make those fears unfounded. But in practice things might not be so simple. Some populist writers actually detected a strong whiff of economic individualism in the post-reform village, which ill accorded with previous assumptions about egalitarianism and with the radical vision of a new social order founded upon the *obshchina*. The exiled Russian landowner A. N. Engelhardt came to the conclusion that 'the ideas of the kulak reign among the peasantry; every peasant is proud to be the pike who gobbles up the carp. Every peasant will, if circumstances permit, exploit every other.'[20]

Nevertheless, populists adhered to the view that the commune was a bulwark against the dispossession of the peasantry. They argued that the peasantry would only be driven from their plots if the government intervened to abolish the commune, or if it were undermined through intolerable fiscal exactions on the peasantry. In fact, it became increasingly clear to Russian populists that the tsarist government was doing just that. In particular, tsarist fiscal policy made it difficult for peasant households to pay their dues, and this forced many of them into the hands of rural exploiters (kulaks and petty merchants). Eventually, peasants were being forced off the land. The government, therefore, artificially created a labour surplus. Left to its own devices, the commune would have been perfectly capable of finding work for all its members. Even though the increase in population led to an apparent deterioration in the ratio of people to land, the commune could have coped. The commune could allocate labour to the production of rural manufactured goods, or to the production of more intensive crops, such as flax or sugar-beet. As will be seen, however, the first of these possibilities was, in the opinion of the populists, frustrated by the government.

The populist argument about 'artificial' measures taken to destroy the organic association between peasants and land took as its starting-point the emancipation settlement of 1861. The abolition of serfdom initiated a process of peasant impoverishment and potential expropriation, which it was the historic task of the valiant commune to oppose. According to two of the most well-known exponents of populist economics, N. Danielson and V. P. Vorontsov, the poverty of the majority of the peasant population reflected inequalities in income distribution which the 1861 decree had intensified, by endorsing an unequal pattern of landholding. Peasants were compelled to purchase or rent land from the *pomeshchiki*, on top of the compensation ('redemption payments') that they had been forced to pay for the land allocated them from the old demesne. In addition to these burdens, the government levied extortionate taxes on articles of basic necessity, largely in order to force grain exports from agriculture and thereby to finance interest payments on foreign government loans. The artificial monetization of the peasant economy in order to pay taxes and rents afforded plenty of opportunity for a small number of speculators to enrich themselves at the expense of the majority. Financial burdens were thus threatening to throw peasants off the land, in the name of a perverted notion of progress.[21]

The populist ethic also insisted upon the moral superiority of peasant farming, as against the large-scale factory industry of western Europe. For the 'legal' populist N. K. Mikhailovsky (so called, because he did not argue for the overthrow of the state by force), the experience of western Europe was entirely negative, in that it destroyed the integrity of the individual and compelled him to specialize in a narrow field of endeavour – of which Adam Smith's famous pin-makers could be taken as archetypal. At the level of the peasant farm, so Mikhailovsky thought, the division of labour hardly existed, and peasants were the happier for it.[22] One of the main threats to this Arcadian existence emanated from the new factory industries. However, Russian populists evolved a theory to account for the future non-viability of factory industry in Russia. They used this theory subsequently to justify the allocation of resources to rural industry.

Russian populist theory assumed that the prospects for the creation of an indigenous factory industry were poor, in the first instance because of the lack of an internal market for its products. Vorontsov took as his starting-point the poverty of the peasantry, and he attributed their poverty to a complex amalgam of high rents, rising taxes, high rates of interest, low food prices and dwindling opportunities for craft work. The gap between living costs and rural income served to prevent the formation of a sustained market. In particular, fiscal pressures on the peasantry compelled the majority to market their modest surplus during the autumn, when tax demands were due and when grain prices were at their lowest. At other times of the year the peasant producer had to borrow from the landlord or the village money-lender (kulak). This process simply transferred income from the productive to the unproductive members of the rural population, and reinforced the effects of capitalist penetration of the rural economy, which turned the surplus over to speculators in grain and to an irresponsible government.

Vorontsov proceeded to argue that the output of industry in a given year had to be consumed in its entirety, either by domestic income-earners (peasants, workers, capitalists or landlords) or by foreigners (consuming Russian exports). He discounted the possibility that part of the annual industrial product could be invested. Why Vorontsov overlooked or discounted this possibility is not entirely clear. He may have believed that capital was expensive, relative to labour, and that industrialists – left to themselves – had no incentive to invest. Of course, Vorontsov could not deny that investment had already taken place, and he attributed this to the role played by the government. The government encouraged investment by offering attractive subsidies to capitalist entrepreneurs, and also purchased capital goods on its own account, such as locomotives and grain elevators. In minimizing the element of autonomous investment in the private sector, Vorontsov at the same time denied the potential for factory industry to reduce its costs of production. He alluded specifically to the high overhead costs imposed on industry by the need to heat, light and secure the factory in the inhospitable Russian climate. More generally, Vorontsov held the opinion that the manufacturing sector in Russia was inherently incapable of improving labour productivity, for example, by technical change. Thus, the possibility that capitalists might cut costs, and pass on lower costs to the consumer in the form of lower prices, never received adequate consideration. One major means of enlarging the market for manufactured goods went by the board.[23]

Danielson was less representative of mainstream populist thinking on the subject of the internal market than was Vorontsov. Indeed, Danielson thought of himself as the person who modified the analysis made by Karl Marx, in such a way that it could be applied to the conditions in tsarist Russia. He had, after all, helped to translate *Das Kapital* into Russian. Unlike Vorontsov, Danielson did not discount the possibility of autonomous investment (in Marx's scheme, 'enlarged reproduction'). Danielson concentrated on the constraints imposed on the development of mass purchasing power in the urban sector, arguing that this was curtailed by the substitution of capital for labour. Capitalists tended to reduce aggregate employment, the pressure to compete leading them to innovate and substitute unskilled and cheap labour for skilled. The failure of employment and thus total urban purchasing power to grow placed upon the shoulders of the capitalist class the main burden of consumption of manufactured goods. But the capitalists and their families were insufficient in number to consume the entirety of the increase in the industrial product. So far as the peasant market is concerned, Danielson's analysis is close to that of Vorontsov: the first effect of factory industry was to reduce the scope among peasants for craft industry and thus their supplementary income. Peasants were forced to market grain in order to purchase manufactured consumer goods, but the profits from the grain trade, like the taxes, rents and industrial profits, simply ended up in the hands of a small minority. Thus the unequal distribution of wealth and income undermined potential purchasing power. Capitalism could only 'solve' its internal contradiction by a large-scale redistribution of resources in favour of the working-class and peasantry.[24]

The other constraint on the long-term possibility of factory industry in Russia originated with the relative lateness of Russia in joining the club of industrialized nations. Far from regarding this, as did Witte, as an opportunity to tap foreign technology and capital, populist observers tended to despair at the advantage western Europe had already secured in cornering markets in Europe and further afield. The competitive advantage such countries had already reaped also allowed them to dominate the Russian market, whether or not it was protected by a tariff (if the tariff were completely prohibitive on an entire range of goods, this would simply bring high-cost Russian firms face to face with impoverished consumers and the economy would grind to a halt). Yuzhakov, writing in the main populist economic journal, *Russkoe bogatstvo* (Russian wealth), suggested that Russian industry could escape the dilemma by establishing its own protected markets elsewhere: Asia seemed the obvious candidate. As we shall see, Witte himself espoused the cause of Russian imperialism in the Far East. But anyone could see that Russian expansionism would do no more than encourage the appetite of her competitors.[25]

In these circumstances, Russian populists argued that the only long-term factor which favoured the development of factory industry was the Russian government, upon whose shaky foundations an 'artificial' industrial revolution had begun to be built. The main weapon in the government armoury was its fiscal policy, allowing it to transfer funds to industry by means of loans and subsidies, normally concealed in the form of generous orders for railway track, rolling-stock and armaments. This was the other side of the coin in Russia: peasant tax-payers indirectly supported capitalist factory industry. By the same token, any threat to the government's fiscal health – or any sudden need to curtail spending, such as might be induced by the withdrawal of foreign credit, on which the regime also depended –

would undermine the entire basis on which Russian factory industry had come to depend. In proving unable to market goods among the bulk of the population, industry would simply go bankrupt.

The 'crisis' in industrial production at the turn of the nineteenth century seemed to populist critics of government economic policy ample justification for their viewpoint. Those branches of industry – engineering and metallurgy, above all – which had experienced a 'hothouse' growth during the boom of the 1890s, thanks entirely to the government promotion of a railway network, had been the first to suffer. Peasants did not have any need for locomotives; but neither could they afford other products which manufacturing industry might more realistically be disposed to supply to them. The depressing circle of Russian industrialization was now complete. Peasant purchasing power had been eroded, and the only goods on offer were priced out of their reach. In the words of one of the leading critics of economic policy within the government, 'an entirely sound basis for industry is guaranteed only by a corresponding development of the domestic market, representing a sufficiently broad and constant demand for manufactured goods'.[26] This argument was thought to be just as valid after the 'crisis' had passed.

The final element in the populist analysis of the tsarist economy emerged from both ethical and economic considerations. Populist observers favoured the development of rural or cottage industry (in Russian terminology of the time, *kustar*), which would both reassert the 'wholeness' at the level of the peasant economy and be able to respond more directly to the needs of the peasant consumers. Populists were not opposed to industrial development. Rather, they regarded the particular form it had taken in Russia to be undesirable and short-lived. The superiority of rural industry lay in the close and organic association between the agricultural and the industrial producer and the lack of an artificial division of labour in society. The craft worker and the food-producing peasant retained control over the means of production and together defended the village against the unwelcome and exploitative intrusion of capital. Populists held out the prospect of a future social system in which peasants cooperated with each other in the production of goods for use rather than profit.

Interestingly enough, the disposition on the part of populist economists to support *kustar* production also found favour among mainstream economists in the liberal tradition. There were two reasons for this convergence. In the first place, in so far as liberal economists maintained that the scarce factor of production in Russia was capital, then rural industry fully deserved to be supported, having as it did a lower capital: output ratio than modern factory industry. Industry could expand gradually on the basis of progressively reinvested profits, which might or might not lead to the eventual consolidation of the factory in the Russian context. In addition, many economists in the classical tradition, ranging from P. P. Maslov (a social-democrat) to I. Kh. Ozerov, argued that no policy of rapid industrialization could hope to absorb surplus labour from the countryside and that resources would be more rationally devoted to the encouragement of labour-intensive rural industry. This appeal could be appropriated by populist economists to demonstrate still further the futility of any policy of rapid industrialization. They coupled this with a suggestion about the need for the development of more diversified agriculture, designed to improve the supply of raw materials, such as flax or leather, to the *kustar* producer. Such ideas about the optimal strategy for Russian economic development reappeared during the 1920s. They have also entered into much mainstream thinking about the economic development of low-income countries during the 1970s and 1980s.[27]

The populist prescription for Russian economic development and the populist analysis of the process of development were elaborated by a new generation of writers in the early twentieth century. Foremost among these writers, who were inevitably christened 'neo-populists', was the famous economist A. V. Chayanov (1888–c.1932). Chayanov belonged to the populist tradition, because he concentrated his attention upon the organization of the peasant economy which, he maintained, had to be understood on its own terms.

One of the consequences of this approach was that Chayanov, like his predecessors in the populist tradition, refused to accept the concept of a labour 'surplus' in peasant agriculture. The peasant farm, in Chayanov's words, was a 'family labour farm in which the family as a result of its year's labour receives a single labour income and weighs its efforts against the material results obtained'.[28] Household labour was not employed or shed in accordance with standard neo-classical arguments about the marginal productivity of labour, whereby labour was employed only up to the point at which its marginal product equalled its marginal cost (or wage) in money terms. The peasant household worked on different principles. What were they?

At the level of the individual household, a constant tension existed between the 'drudgery' of labour and the marginal utility to the peasant of the income that he obtained for his labour. What mattered was the subjective valuation of this labour income, and this depended above all on the relationship within the household between workers and consumers. A moment's thought suggests that a new household comprises two workers (and two consumers), that is husband and wife. Over time, children are added to this unit and increase the number of consumers, without adding to the labour force as yet. In these circumstances, the able-bodied peasant, assisted by his wife, will be compelled to work harder in order to provide for his family.

Eventually, there comes a time when the worker–consumer ratio (or 'balance') changes and less labour time needs to be devoted by the individual to the support of his family, because the family's labour resources are now swelled by able-bodied children. The individual calculates that the marginal utility of work (and income) is sufficiently offset by the 'drudgery' of labour to make it worth his while to take more time in leisure. From his point of view, this is a rational calculation, dictated by the circumstances of the household at that particular time. To the outside observer, who sees a peasant doing nothing, this represents 'surplus' labour or disguised under-employment in agriculture. But to the neo-populist observer, there is no evidence of a labour surplus, still less of a surplus waiting to be rescued from its enforced torpor by the *deus ex machina* of modern industry, as in the classic dual-economy model of the previous section.

Chayanov also emphasized that the peasant economy was engaged in a broad range of activities, non-agricultural as well as agricultural. By implication, any action taken outside the peasant economy that would affect the potential for craft work had clear repercussions for the freedom of manoeuvre of the household. Chayanov thus echoed one of the basic themes of nineteenth-century Russian populism, namely the effects of government economic policy on rural industry.

Chayanov defended his analysis on the grounds that it was 'created, not out of the head of some theoretician, but as a result of observing features in the economic conduct of the masses of peasants'.[29] The particular evidence on which he drew comprised a series of budget studies of peasant households, a tradition of data collection that extended well back into the nineteenth century. Needless to say, the conclusions to be drawn from this data were by no means self-evident, and a continuous debate took place during the 1920s about the neo-populist challenge to other, more conventional notions of peasant society.[30]

Many of the central ideas of populist economics have exercised an influence on the work of economic historians of Russia. The suggestion that a 'sound basis' for industrialization did not really exist and that factory production depended largely on the steady – if ultimately unreliable – flow of government orders has often been expressed. A recent general survey of European industrialization concludes that Russia 'had its modern industry implanted ready-made from abroad in a social system which did not provide a favourable soil for it'. The government substituted for the lack of an adequate internal market.[31] As we have already seen, this view of government is central to the interpretation advanced by Gerschenkron, but in his case the intervention of government is seen in a much more positive light than it is by populists. Other economic historians have alluded to the 'industrial crisis' at the turn of the century as an illustration of the erosion of domestic mass purchasing power under the regime of Finance Minister Witte, arguments that echo Vorontsov and Danielson.[32]

The interpretation of peasant society advanced by Chayanov has attracted particular attention in recent years. Teodor Shanin has stated that historians need to understand the Russian peasantry in terms other than those of the liberal or marxist-leninist tradition. Closely echoing Chayanov, Shanin argues that the Russian peasantry found various mechanisms for adjusting available land to the labour of peasant households, and that class divisions were absent from peasant society. We shall discuss this argument in greater detail in Chapter Three. Suffice it to say here that the recent emphasis upon peasant society is of the utmost significance; for, if the 'neo-populist' interpretation is accepted, 'basic problems of Russian economic history, such as the accumulation of wealth, capital formation in agriculture and key migratory processes appear in a new light'.[33]

1.3 The Marxist-Leninist Interpretation

Most of the scholarly work on the tsarist economy has been undertaken by Soviet historians. This may seem an obvious thing to say, but it is important to realize that marxism-leninism has informed the bulk of historical output on Russian economic change. The issues discussed by Soviet historians belong to a tradition of scholarship that dates back to the nineteenth-century analyses made by Marx, Engels and Lenin. To ignore the questions raised within this tradition and the results generated by a century of enquiry would be foolish and shortsighted. The final section of this chapter is accordingly devoted to a consideration of Marx's approach to social and economic change, paying particular attention to his views on development in Russia, and to Lenin's analysis of the development of capitalism. This section concludes with a brief discussion of the pertinent issues that have been taken up by Soviet scholars.

Marx and Engels maintained that human society evolved progressively from lower to higher stages of existence and that each stage was characterized by different sets of relations between human beings. Evolution also comprised a series of periodic crises during which conditions were created for a decisive change from one form (or mode) of production to a more advanced mode. Such epochal changes were manifested by the emergence of new social relations which both corresponded to and facilitated changes in the level of productive forces in the economy. The economy registered gains in productivity as new social relations came into being. The shift from one mode of production to another was achieved through the generation of contradictions between the productive forces and existing social relations, which came to restrict the development of the former. Under feudalism, for example, the growth of output was achieved through the exploitation of serf labour by landowners. Feudalism set limits to the further expansion of output, because a privileged minority enjoyed a monopoly power over land, capital and labour and prevented the mobility of these factors of production. The accumulation of capital could go only so far and no further. Capitalism, which was unlocked by a struggle between the emergent bourgeoisie and the old feudal landlords, proved much more dynamic. But capitalism also generated its own internal contradictions, given that the majority of the population lost ownership and control over their means of production; peasants were dispossessed, in order that capitalists could freely exploit their labour and extract what Marx termed 'surplus value'. This expropriation created the potential for rapid expansion as the surplus was reinvested in capitalist enterprise by men who had to compete with each other in order to stay in the market. At the same time, capitalism created a class of dispossessed workers who came to feel a sense of solidarity with one another and who articulated their grievances in the form of class struggle. This struggle would, according to Marx, lead eventually to the overthrow of capitalism and the emergence of a communist system, based not upon exploitation but on production from each according to his abilities and distribution to each according to his needs.[34]

Central to the marxist interpretation of capitalist development, therefore, was the notion of a universal expropriation of the traditional producer (peasantry) from the means of production (land, equipment, livestock). The model with which Marx operated drew upon the experience of Britain, but he offered it as broadly applicable to the experience of other countries, maintaining (in an oft-quoted phrase) that 'the more developed country industrially shows to the less developed an image of the latter's future'.[35] The problem arose, however, that in Russia there existed institutional arrangements that helped to keep peasants on the land, even after serfdom had been formally abolished in 1861. Interestingly, we have some indication as to how Marx himself dealt with the dilemma posed for 'Marxism' by the Russian experience.

The Japanese scholar Haruki Wada has shown how Marx's views on Russian development were initially a mixture of ignorance and contempt. When he published the first volume of *Capital* in 1867, Marx had little idea of what was taking place within the tsarist Empire. The possibility put forward by Alexander Herzen a generation earlier, that a specifically Russian socialism could emerge on the basis of the commune, was treated with derision. Within a few years, however, Marx had read the work of populist writers such as Chernyshevsky and was reading some of the empirical data for himself. Chernyshevsky had concluded that Russia could move from communal landholding to socialism without the need for the creation of an industrial proletariat. By the last years of his life (he died in 1883), Marx was prepared to take this view seriously. In 1878 he felt able to announce that 'if Russia continues along the road she has followed since 1861, she will forego the finest opportunity that history has ever placed before a nation and will undergo all the fateful misfortune of capitalist development'.[36] The option to which Russian populists had drawn attention was not yet foreclosed. Marx clarified this point further in a series of draft letters to the Russian socialist Vera Zasulich in 1881 (the final letter was not published until 1923 and the drafts only saw the light of day in 1924). He suggested that the *obshchina* might provide the means for the 'regeneration' of Russia. The commune could become an association of free producers in which the means of production were owned socially and in which production was geared towards collective use rather than profit. By means of production he understood the possibility of joint ownership of animals and equipment and not just land. The key qualification Marx made was that the tsarist government had to relieve the peasantry of the burden of taxation, and that 'the poisonous influences that attack (the commune) from all sides must be eliminated and the normal conditions of spontaneous development ensured'.[37] We should note that Engels later insisted upon a second condition being met, namely a parallel socialist revolution in the West, which would facilitate the international division of labour among new socialist states.[38] Marx appears to have been less insistent upon this. In sum, we may conclude that the future development of Russian society appeared to Marx much more ambiguous than might be deduced from a reading of the major theoretical writings.[39]

Lenin was not aware of Marx's detailed and anguished reflections on Russian development. To Lenin, the hallmark of economic development in Russia was the slow but steady movement along the path of capitalism. Before 1861 the feudal system had acted as a brake on the growth of internal trade and accumulation of capital; after 1861 there were still remnants of feudalism, but capitalism had made rapid strides. The economy was being progressively transformed by the application of new techniques of production, economic activity was becoming more specialized and commodity circulation was expanding. Underlying these trends at the end of the nineteenth century was a change in social relations, marked by the disintegration of traditional peasant society and the emergence of a landless proletariat. Unlike Marx, Lenin believed these processes to be unstoppable and unconditional.[40]

Lenin's analysis of the changes that were taking place in Russian society was presented in his famous and path-breaking work on *The*

Development of Capitalism in Russia, first published in 1899. As the title suggests, Lenin took as his main purpose the need to challenge the belief of populist writers that Russia could not follow the path taken by western Europe. In this respect Lenin was stating a view articulated before him by Russian marxists such as Plekhanov, but the depth of treatment and evidence in his book placed it in a special category.[41] According to Lenin, evidence showed that the agricultural sector displayed an increasing tendency to produce for the market. But this could not be attributed to the intervention of the government, as the populists argued. Studies of peasant household budgets and the distribution of land also revealed that peasants were differentiated with respect to access to the means of production. Although previous commentators had shown that there was inequality the differences were becoming more pronounced. A growing number of households disposed of less draught animal power and smaller plots of land, while both land and capital became concentrated in the hands of rich kulaks.

As traditional peasant society began to disintegrate, so the conditions were created for the formation of a 'home market for capitalism'. This process occurred in two ways. Rich peasants required additional capital goods to develop their ability to produce a market-able surplus, as well as consumer goods to maintain their living standards. Poor peasants had to purchase the goods that they were no longer able to produce themselves, having been deprived of their independent access to the means of production. This manifested itself, argued Lenin, in the paradoxical fact that the rural proletarian 'consumes less ... *but buys more*'. For this reason, he said, 'the Russian commune peasantry are not antagonistic to capitalism, but on the contrary are its deepest and most durable foundation'.[42]

The main obstacle to economic progress, according to Lenin, comprised the incomplete reconstruction of social relations in agriculture. Emancipation had not fully transformed the relationship between peasants and landlords. Thus, although capitalism had begun to take root in the countryside (as marked by the production of commodities for exchange and the transformation of labour itself into a commodity), there remained important indications of 'semi-feudal' institutions and practices, such as debt peonage, labour-rent and sharecropping. The only effective way of achieving a more productive capitalist organization of agriculture was to abolish the current distri-bution of land, which reflected the political power of the feudal nobility after 1861, and to create a free market: 'In order to establish really free farming in Russia, it is necessary to "unfence" *all* the land, landlord as well as allotment land'.[43] The context of this analysis was the consideration of tsarist agrarian reform in 1905 and 1906. Lenin sketched out two potential paths of rural capitalist development. He termed the first the 'Prussian' path, which involved dismantling the peasant community and the creation of a pool of labour that could be employed largely by a dominant class of landowners. Those who did not find employment on large estates would move to urban areas. Lenin had in mind the Stolypin land reforms as a clear illustration of the Prussian path, since they attempted to break up the *obshchina* without affecting the economic and social position of the nobility. A second possibility involved the abolition of unequal land distribution, the dissolution of the commune and of privileged noble landholding. The advantage of this 'American' path lay in the creation of a free market in land. Economic growth might then take place on the basis of extended peasant purchasing power, increased labour productivity and the greater mobility of factors of production.[44]

Within the manufacturing sector, the development of capitalism was to be understood as much more than the appearance of large-scale factory production, even though this was its most dramatic and ultimate expression. To begin with, Lenin noted that there still remained elements of traditional artisanal production, which he defined as the production of goods for household use or for a personal client. The term 'artisan' was thus largely reserved for craftsmen whose work was commissioned. This form of production increasingly yielded to commodity trade in manufactured goods, whereby the rural producer took his goods to market and accepted the risks involved as well as the opportunities to profit from the transactions. At the same time, the trade in manufactured goods was gradually being taken over by merchant middlemen who bought up the product and dictated the final sale price. Eventually, such men were able to dominate rural producers entirely by putting out raw materials and controlling the process of production as well as distribution of the finished product. The capital accumulated by merchants allowed them to establish workshops and factories in which the worker ceased to be engaged in the entire production process and was compelled to specialize in a particular function. He became a wage-earner. The development of capitalistic forms of industry and the formation of a class of expropriated peasants were thus inextricably related. Hand in hand with the emergence of modern industry, which had already taken deep root in Russia, went the creation of a working class that had severed its links with the land. The labour of this proletariat provided the source of further capital accumulation in industry, while workers' wages were translated into the consumption of marketed goods from the agricultural and the industrial sectors.[45]

Lenin adjusted his analysis of the tsarist economy to take account of concrete developments in the early twentieth century. By 1917 he continued to draw attention to the maturity of large-scale industry in Russia, while at the same time manifesting a still greater consciousness of the backwardness of Russian agriculture. In his work on *Imperialism, the Highest Stage of Capitalism* (written in 1916 and published on the eve of the Bolshevik Revolution), he alluded to Russia as a country 'which is economically most backward, where modern capitalist imperialism is enmeshed, so to speak, in a particularly close network of precapitalist relations'.[46] Precapitalist relations were confined largely to the Russian village; by contrast, Russian industry had reached an advanced stage of concentration of labour and monopoly. The import of capital had helped to accelerate the development of Russian industry. By 1917 the ground had been prepared for a socialist revolution, without the need for a sustained period of bourgeois development, because of the maturity of industrial enterprise (whose apparatus could be appropriated by the new workers' government), and the concentration in a small number of units of a class-conscious proletariat, which made up in revolutionary commitment and potential what it lacked in numerical strength.[47]

Soviet scholars have followed the broad outline laid down by Marx in *Capital* and in his other major writings, and by Lenin. As far as the situation before 1861 is concerned, scholars have argued that feudal social relations defined the potential for the development of the productive forces. The production of cereal crops and iron did indeed increase during the eighteenth century, as did inter-regional trade. But further expansion of output was frustrated by the immobility of labour and by the control exercised by a privileged elite over land, labour and capital. The nobility defended its privileges and had little interest in the accumulation of capital; its members devoted themselves in the main to the consumption of the product of the servile workforce. The growth of an urban population and overseas demand for food gradually stimulated a shift towards the production of marketable products, and this led to an intensification of exploitation which allowed landowners to bring new land into cultivation. But the old regime was unsuited to the task of increasing the productivity of labour in the long run. The emerging crisis of feudalism demonstrated the incompatibility of serfdom with sustained commodity production. During the period of transition, which some Soviet historians consider to have lasted for more than a century, but which most now ascribe to the period from *c.*1800 to 1860, the use of hired labour became more widespread. This was partly encouraged by the willingness of some feudal landlords to commute the customary service obligation and to require in its place a money quitrent. This occurred on a large scale in the Central Industrial Region, and by 1800–50 the peasantry there had developed a familiarity with industrial production and distribution. The contradictions of feudalism revealed themselves in peasant protest against increased levels of exploitation (the greater burden of labour service, higher rates of quitrent). The weakness of the economically backward Russian state was exposed during the Crimean War, and the threat of widespread peasant rebellion convinced the Tsar that the time was ripe to abolish serfdom. Serfdom, however, was doomed by objective circumstances, not by the voluntaristic impulse of the autocrat.[48]

A central question in Soviet historiography has been the formation of commodity markets in post-reform Russia. I. D. Kovalchenko and L. V. Milov have recently provided a new quantitative foundation for the debate, in their extended study of price trends and relationships between economic variables over the period 1750–1914. Their main purpose has been to correlate prices of the basic factors of production in agriculture and of cereal crops in European Russia. They conclude that regional price differentials narrowed over time, suggesting the integration and unification of the market. However, this process was only completed towards the end of the nineteenth century. Until then, a national market arose only in respect of oats, which was the major fodder crop for horses. The process of market integration was stimulated by the development of new forms of communications, by merchant capital and, above all, by the abolition of serfdom. By the 1880s social relations had changed profoundly, such that a class of specialist agricultural producers now marketed a surplus and traded with far-flung corners of the Empire. These authors thus give a quantitative dimension to Lenin's original argument. Furthermore, they show how, by 1900, the economic development of Russia synchronized with the international economy, the evidence for this being the close correlation between rye and oats prices in Russia and western Europe during the 1890s.[49]

Contrary to popular opinion, there is no monolithic Soviet historiography and no consensus about all major issues in tsarist economic development. Such uniformity undoubtedly existed during the Stalinist period, but no longer exists. Old Stalinist stereotypes (for instance, about the semi-colonial dependence of tsarist Russia upon western imperialism) have been abandoned. The new atmosphere was conducive to the articulation of controversial views about the level of economic and social development in Russia at the turn of the century.

One illustration of this feature of modern Soviet historiography was the furore created by the argument put forward by A. M. Anfimov, to the effect that Lenin had overstated the development of capitalism in Russia. More orthodox Soviet historians argued that this interpretation had serious implications for the leninist notion of a class alliance or *smychka* between the working class and the poor peasantry.[50] Other historians have built upon the suggestion that late tsarist Russia cannot be fitted into a neat mould – 'capitalism' – and that Lenin himself acknowledged that the economy was characterized by interlocking modes of production. To describe this complex characteristic of Russian society on the eve of the 1917 Revolution, historians have coined the term *mnogoukladnost* (literally, 'multi-structuredness' or 'multi-modality'). To these historians, this is no more than a development of some of Lenin's central contentions about the parallel evolution of capitalist and pre-capitalist relations in both town and country, although to others it comes too close to undermining the evidence for the economic preconditions of socialist revolution.[51]

The outstanding Soviet economic historian I. F. Gindin has been pre-eminent in challenging established orthodoxy. For example, he traced the role of government as an agent of industrial development, in a way that lends itself to a semi-populist analysis of late nineteenth-century Russia (emphasizing the weakness of the mass market and the widespread use of government subsidy to heavy industry). Gindin has also been outspoken in his criticism of Soviet historians who have assumed that Russian industry was dominated by large firms and characterized by high profits: in the case of 'heavy' industry, neither of these propositions is seen to stand close scrutiny.[52] All of these arguments suggest that the development of capitalism in Russia was more complex and ambiguous than was thought by an earlier generation (though Lenin himself gave plenty of ammunition to anyone who wanted to argue the case for ambiguity and complexity in Russian economic development).

Conclusion

Each of these analytical traditions, liberal, populist and marxist, has generated its own agenda and methods of enquiry. The fundamental assumptions and implications of each ideology were forged in the heat of contemporary debates about the desired direction of change in the tsarist economy: whether towards 'modern' industrialism, with rewards for individual enterprise; towards a society of autonomous peasant communities; or towards a developed socialist society. The historiography has in its turn been shaped by the obsessions of contemporaries, in a way that justifies the definition of three distinct historiographical traditions.

The liberal interpretation of the tsarist economy concentrates upon the obstacles to economic growth and upon industrialization as the 'solution' to the problem of economic backwardness, which was typified by the retention of labour in traditional peasant agriculture. In the historiography, the question of the mechanism for the development of industry has been especially prominent. Gerschenkron argued that the tsarist state intervened to rescue the Russian economy from the crisis of backwardness to which it had been reduced by unproductive agriculture. Other historians have queried this emphasis upon the state. The populist interpretation rejects the concept of a labour 'surplus' in peasant agriculture and thus denies the need for investment in large-scale factory industry. Indeed, at first, Russian populists maintained that industrialization was not merely unnecessary: it was doomed, on account of the lack of a 'home market' for its products. In the historiography, attention has focused particularly upon the organization and dynamics of peasant society. Historians of a populist persuasion have maintained that peasant society was characterized by internal solidarity and stability, rather than class division. Finally, the marxist-leninist interpretation emphasizes that capitalist development and its attendant class divisions were manifest in tsarist Russia by the end of the nineteenth century. A 'home market' for capitalism most certainly did exist, contrary to populist insistence that it did not. The central theoretical and empirical underpinning for the marxist-leninist view was the progressive differentiation of the peasantry. In the historiography, it is the progress of capitalism and the development of class struggle that have received most attention.

2 The Dimensions of Poverty and Economic Growth

The majority of Russian people were peasants and the majority of peasants were poor. This observation satisfies the popular notion of the tsarist economy, but how accurate is it? As a very broad generalization, it is undoubtedly true, but further reflection suggests a number of important qualifications.

In the first place, the term 'peasant' is less straightforward than it appears. At the beginning of the period, peasants in Russia were assigned to different categories, according to whether they fulfilled obligations to noble landowners, the state, the royal family or Church. Differences of status could have important implications in determining living standards: for example, state peasants were generally better off than their serf counterparts.[1] By the end of the period, long after these different groups of peasants had been emancipated, the tsarist administration fostered the concept of a unified peasant 'estate'. This convention had the effect of identifying as peasants many thousands of factory and other workers, including those with only the most tenuous connection with the land. In other words, the official mind of imperial Russia persisted in labelling large numbers of people in a perverse manner. Most important of all, the emphasis upon a mass of impoverished peasants tends to suggest homogeneity and uniformity. Crucial social and economic differences within the peasantry are thereby overlooked.[2]

In so far as the term peasant suggests a basic link with agriculture, it can be misleading. Throughout this period, including the era of serfdom, peasants engaged in non-agricultural economic activity. On the farm, this involved the production of handicrafts for sale or for domestic consumption. Other peasants resided full-time in the village, but engaged in production on behalf of factories. Off-farm employment included work in trade, transport, personal service or in industry, which could take the peasant away from the village for weeks or even years at a time. Nor would it be correct to imagine that peasants, where they cultivated the land, were engaged in agricultural production simply for their own subsistence.[3]

The initial characterization of Russian economy and society captures something of the unequal distribution of income and wealth. After all, if the majority of people were poor, then it follows that a minority were not. But the original blanket statement fails to indicate that wealth was unevenly distributed geographically, as well as socially. Given the size of Russia, and its regional geographical and cultural variations, generalizations about poverty or economic backwardness can be extremely hazardous.

Finally, the observation with which this chapter began lacks a chronological perspective. In particular, it fails to mention the dimensions of economic growth and social change that took place between 1850 and 1917. The tsarist economy did not stand still, although the rate at which growth took place is a matter for debate. On one level, this meant that the environment was no longer the same in 1917 as it had been in 1850. The tsarist economy had been changed by the settlement of new regions, by industrialization and by urbanization. On another level, it meant that social relations – that is, the way in which people conceived of their relationship to one another – had changed as well.

The historian cannot escape the need to assess an economy in aggregate terms, even at the risk of oversimplification. Accordingly, the first task is to decide upon the criteria that may be used to gauge the level of economic development in Russia, and to ask in what sense the tsarist economy may be considered to have been poor.

Aggregate poverty can be expressed in a number of ways. Conventionally, economists measure it in terms of national income per head of population. Comparisons of income per head can then be made to yield information about the relative economic backwardness of a given country. But national income measurements are only one way of gauging aggregate poverty or wealth. Poor countries are likely to suffer from low levels of calorific intake among the population, and severe malnutrition will occur during periods of dearth. Rates of infant mortality will be high. The bulk of the population is also unlikely to be able to read and write.

Approximate calculations of national income in Russia did not become available until after the October Revolution. Some rather crude guesses had been made before then, but it was the eminent economist S. N. Prokopovich who published the first serious set of estimates in 1918. His estimate of 'material product' in 1913 did not make allowance for areas of the Empire other than European Russia (see Map, p. x), and on methodological grounds must be revised upwards, as M. E. Falkus has shown. Even so, these qualifications do not alter the fact that, according to this criterion, tsarist Russia was

– in Prokopovich's dismissive phrase – 'the poorest of the civilized nations'.[4]

Recent computations of national income by the American economist Paul Gregory confirm this verdict. Gregory's methods differ from those of Prokopovich: Prokopovich estimated the value of production contributed by each sector of the economy, whereas Gregory has calculated national income by end-use.[5] But Gregory's painstaking computation of national income per head of population in 1913 also suggests that Russia lagged well behind Mediterranean countries, such as Italy and Spain. The gap was greater still when Russian income per capita is compared with that of the four developed countries, Britain, France, Germany and the U.S.A. (see Table 2.1).

What of the situation in an earlier period? Gregory has attempted a rough calculation of Russian income per head of population in 1861. As the evidence in Table 2.1 suggests, the position of Russia in relation to other countries was unfavourable in 1861. Germany and France, for example, were twice as wealthy in per capita income, and Britain was around five times better off. If we then compare Russia's relative position in 1861 and 1913, we can see that the gap between Russia and Britain, France, Germany and the United States had actually widened during the half century (relative to Italy, Russia's position had improved slightly).

The arithmetic of Russian economic backwardness should thus be clear. In 1861 Russian total output did not diverge greatly from that of other continental economies; and in 1913 total output was on a par with that of Britain and was well ahead of output in France and Italy (though not Germany). But this is not the issue that is at stake. Russian output in 1861, in terms of the *size* of the population which it supported, was unimpressive, when set against the achievements of other economies. That the gap between Russia and most other countries widened during the years 1861–1913 was partly a function of the *growth* of population.[6]

How did the tsarist economy perform relative to other countries, according to other criteria? The rate of infant mortality (that is, the number of deaths of babies under one year, per thousand live births) also marked Russia out as a poor country, in absolute as well as relative terms. As Table 2.2 shows, more than a quarter of children born to mothers in European Russia were unlikely to survive beyond their first birthday. During the second half of the nineteenth century, substantial improvements took place in infant mortality in western Europe, but the gains in tsarist Russia were hardly noticeable.

Literacy is a further criterion of economic backwardness, and the statistics of literacy tell something of the extent to which individuals are able to fulfil their potential in society. In Europe at the turn of the nineteenth century, wide disparities existed from country to country in

Table 2.1

National Income in 1861 and 1913: Russia and Other Selected Countries

	1861				1913			
	National Income (million rubles, 1913 prices)	Population (millions)	NI per head (rubles)	Russia = 100	NI	Population	NI per head	Russia = 100
Russia	5,269	74	71	100	20,266	171	119	100
U.K.	6,469	20	323	455	20,869	36	580	487
U.S.A.	14,405	32	450	634	96,030	93	1033	868
Germany	6,313	36	175	246	24,280	65	374	314
France	5,554	37	150	211	11,816	39	303	254
Italy	4,750	25	183	258	9,140	35	261	219
Spain	n.a.	16	n.a.	n.a.	3,975	20	199	167

Source: P. Gregory, *Russian National Income, 1885–1913*, C.U.P., 1982, pp. 155–7.

Table 2.2

Recorded Rates of Infant Mortality in Selected European Countries
(deaths of infants under one, per thousand live births)

	1867–1871 (annual average)	1907–1911 (annual average)
European Russia	267	245
England and Wales	156	116
German Empire	234 (1871–80)	174
France	193	128
Italy	227	151
Spain	197	157
Sweden	140	76

Sources: A. G. Rashin, *Naselenie Rossii za 100 let*, Gosstatizdat, 1956, p. 194; B. R. Mitchell, *European Historical Statistics*, Macmillan, 1975, pp. 127–34; W. R. Lee, ed., *European Demography and Economic Growth*, Croom Helm, 1979, p. 187.

the proportions of people who had (or claimed to have) some ability to read and write. The comparisons of national literacy rates may be drawn from Table 2.3.

The estimation and interpretation of literacy statistics are fraught with difficulty. These figures conceal the fact that many people in Europe were probably barely literate. Perhaps individuals qualified as literate by being able to do no more than write their name or read a simple phrase. Nevertheless, whatever the possession of such basic skills represented in practice, it is clear that a significant gap existed in 1900 between Russia and the Mediterranean countries. Between Russia and more advanced countries, such as France, the gap was enormous. The figures given here are, of course, national averages and conceal regional differences; literacy also varied according to age and sex. But as a guide to aggregate poverty, Table 2.3 provides graphic testimony.[7]

The Russian Empire was a vast geographical entity, comprising a multitude of ethnic groups and cultures, as well as distinct soil types and climates.[8] For these reasons, it is necessary to draw attention to the regional dimensions of poverty and backwardness. Once again, the quantifiable criteria will be income per capita, infant mortality and literacy.

Table 2.3

Juvenile and Adult Illiteracy in Russia and Selected European Countries c. 1900 (percentages)

	Total*	Male	Female
Russian Empire (1897)	72	61	83
France (1901)	17	14	19
Belgium (1900)	26	23	28
Austria (1900)	23	21	25
Spain (1900)	56	45	66
Italy (1901)	48	42	54

* The rate of illiteracy is expressed as a percentage of the population aged ten and over, except in Italy, where it refers to the population over the age of six. 'Illiteracy' is defined according to the conventions of each national census; but, generally speaking, the enumerators took the individual's declaration of his or her ability to read and write as an indication of literacy (see Source).

Source: C. M. Cipolla, *Literacy and Development in the West*, Penguin, 1969, pp. 126–8.

Regional variations in income per head of population may be assumed to have been substantial. The descriptions of contemporary travellers and writers lend credence to this view.[9] So, too, does the knowledge that extractive and manufacturing industries – especially the more dynamic – were concentrated in particular regions. Finally, variations in regional population density will be reflected in the geographical distribution of income per head. Falkus has calculated that the peripheral provinces outside European Russia were around one-third more wealthy than European Russia itself. In the 50 provinces of European Russia in 1913, income per head amounted to 107 rubles, compared to 136 rubles in other provinces.[10] The disparity reflected the extent of manufacturing industry in Russian Poland, the location of the oil industry in the Caucasus, and the growing diversification of agricultural production in western Siberia. In most of these regions, furthermore, population density was low by comparison with central European Russia. Siberia looked to pre-war observers as if it was on the verge of becoming a second Canada; but the central black-earth provinces seemed destined to become the equivalent of Bengal.

Further disaggregation of income per capita is unfortunately not possible. However, data on infant mortality and literacy were collected province by province, and they can serve as a proxy for income differences. They are also significant in their own right. The provincial differences in both are represented on the accompanying maps.

Clearly, provincial variations in the levels of economic development could be substantial. In south Russia, for example, close on one in five infants in the later nineteenth century was destined to die before reaching his or her first birthday. As we move from south to north-east, the proportion rises considerably. In Nizhnii Novgorod and Perm provinces, more than two out of five infants would on average fail to survive their first year. Generally speaking, the Urals stand out as an economically underprivileged region, characterized by high rates of infant mortality and illiteracy. By contrast, the Baltic provinces constituted a region of advanced economic development. In terms of literacy, for example, they appear to have been on a par with western Europe in 1900 (see Table 2.3). Elsewhere, however, the correlation between literacy and infant mortality is less clear, and this makes it difficult to label such regions either backward or relatively advanced. In the south-west and in most of Belorussia, for instance, rates of infant mortality were low, but so too were literacy rates.

These inter-provincial differences (which could be multiplied, if further disaggregation were carried out) are explicable partly in terms of the degree of urbanization and industrialization, and partly by differences in culture. Assuming that income per capita varied from province to province in the same way as other indicators of development, disparities could be explained by the fact that dependency ratios were higher in rural than in urban areas. In other words, the income generated in the former had to be spread over a large number of non-working inhabitants. We have already indicated that industrial development did not extend uniformly to all parts of the Empire. Within European Russia, specific areas were industrialized: the Ukraine (Kharkov and Ekaterinoslav provinces), St Petersburg and parts of the Baltic region, and the area in and around Moscow.

Urban areas were rather better provided with educational facilities, although disparities in the availability of primary schools were declining in the late nineteenth century. For this reason, it might be more appropriate to explain rural and urban literacy variations by remarking that urban life placed a higher premium on the acquisition of basic literacy skills, however they were attained. The situation with regard to infant mortality was more complex. At the start of the period, urban rates of infant mortality were higher than those in rural Russia. By 1913 this differential had been reversed, but this did not reflect a real reduction in age-specific mortality rates in the cities, so much as changes in the age structure.[11]

Literacy rates in European Russia, 1897

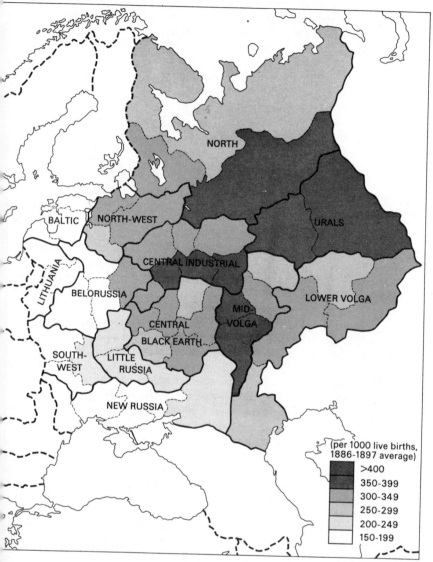

Rates of infant mortality in European Russia, 1886–1897

Urbanization did not have a significant effect on *national* literacy and infant mortality rates. The scope for urbanization to have an impact on either was limited by the weight of the rural population. In 1913 the urban population comprised no more than 15 per cent of the total population.[12] Urbanization thus created or reinforced provincial and regional inequalities in economic development; but it hardly affected the national picture at all.

Aggregate measures of income or of other indicators of development fail to disclose the extent of social, as well as geographical inequalities. However, inequalities in the distribution of income are not easy to quantify in continental Europe prior to 1900, and tsarist Russia is no exception. The ownership of land provides a valuable proxy for the distribution of wealth, and this crucial aspect of Russian society is explored in greater detail in Chapters Three and Four. The data on income distribution are much less satisfactory. The tsarist government levied no income tax. A projected income tax was shelved on several occasions before 1914, and only on the eve of the Revolution did legislation actually reach the statute book.[13] Like the wartime prohibition of alcohol and the change of name of the capital city to Petrograd (both in 1914), the introduction of an income tax seemed more of a gesture than a serious innovation. However, some data were published in advance of the new law.

Using this information, which enumerated the individuals in Russia who had an annual income of 1000 rubles and over, Paul Gregory has provisionally calculated that one per cent of families in Russia accounted for 15 per cent of total income in 1905. This calculation may, as he says, underestimate the extent of inequality. One reason is that the incomes of members of the royal family and the Church appear to have been discounted (presumably because they were not to be liable for income tax); another is that there was an element of double counting, which therefore overstates the actual number of individuals who earned more than 1000 rubles. Finally, the relevant statistics on which Gregory draws appear to indicate that income from land generated less than 20 per cent of incomes over 1000 rubles, and this hardly seems plausible in a predominantly agrarian country.[14]

The distribution of income and wealth was unequal *within* broad categories of society, as well as between nobles and peasants, factory owners and workers. We can observe something of intra-noble inequalities of wealth in the mid-nineteenth century by examining the statistics of serf ownership. On the eve of Emancipation, the leading noblemen (those who owned more than 1000 'souls') comprised no more than one per cent of the total noble population. More than two-fifths of the total owned fewer than 20 serfs. As Pipes has said, 'the Rostovs, Bezukhovs and Bolkonskys of *War and Peace* are in no sense typical: they were members of an exclusive club of some 1,400 grand seigneurs in an Empire in which a million persons claimed 'noble' status of some kind'.[15] To this observation, it must be added that inequalities in noble landownership persisted through to the 1917 Revolution.[16]

Resources were also distributed unequally amongst the Russian peasantry, although contemporaries disagreed about the significance of inequality and about its trend.[17] There could be no doubt about the manifestation of social and economic differences in the peasant village. Peasants themselves drew attention to inequalities, by giving the name 'kulak' to rich peasants, who loaned money or seed and who sought thereby to retain power and status in the village.

Were differential rates of infant mortality and of literacy associated with the manifest inequalities of wealth in peasant society? As far as infant mortality is concerned, the available data are scanty. The pre-revolutionary statistician, F. A. Shcherbina, compiled data from six districts in Voronezh during the late 1880s. The average rate for these districts was 183 per 1000 live births (suggesting, amongst other things, that these districts were well above the provincial average rate of infant mortality). Landless households and households with less than five *dessyatiny* were at much more of a disadvantage, compared to those with more than five *dessyatiny*. Rates of infant mortality varied from around 215 per 1000 in the poorer categories to 187 for households that had between 5 and 15 *dessyatiny*. At the upper end of the scale of landholding, the rate of infant mortality among households with more than 25 *dessyatiny* fell to 149 (although the source does not specify how many households belonged to this category).[18] Thus, infant mortality would appear to be correlated with the distribution of wealth within peasant society.

The situation is much less straightforward as regards the distribution of literacy. Tsarist statisticians came to the reasonable conclusion that rates of literacy were likely to increase in proportion to the contact peasants had with the market. But it did not follow that rich peasants, because they had a surplus of grain or other products to sell, enjoyed higher rates of literacy than did poor. Poor peasants, who were compelled to seek work 'abroad' (that is, outside the village), also came into close contact with the market. For this reason, the 'middle' peasantry – households with less compulsion to sell surpluses or to sell their labour – were more disadvantaged with respect to literacy than either rich or poor.[19]

The picture of poverty among the Russian population cannot, therefore, be reduced to a single image. Reality was more complex, because of class differences and regional variations. The popular image fails to draw attention to the range of inequality, not just between the small Russian elite and the masses, but also within the category of peasantry. It is an image that approximates to reality in parts of the central black-earth provinces and the mid-Volga region; it is less applicable to the south, the south-east, the north-east and to the non-Russian periphery.

The notion of rural poverty also fails to capture the extent of urban deprivation. Although, as noted earlier, the urban population as a proportion of the total was still modest as late as 1913, the rate of growth of urban centres had led to serious overcrowding in some cities. St Petersburg, in particular, presented an appalling record of squalor during the 1860s and 1870s. Migrant workers congregated in damp and filthy cellars, where they proved most vulnerable to typhus and cholera. Nor had the situation improved here by the early 1900s; the growing numbers of urban poor simply magnified the problem of overcrowding in the garrets and cellars of middle-class apartments. For the privilege of sleeping in the corner of a flooded room, the labourers, shop assistants, cab-drivers and snow-shovellers of St Petersburg paid dearly, in terms of health and money.[20]

Here, too, a more subtle approach is necessary, in order to register the fact that the worst urban living conditions were to be found in those quarters of the city which held recent migrants. This observation applies to Moscow as well as St Petersburg. The labour aristocracy of printers, artisans and skilled factory workers did not experience the depths of misery, in the way that more casual labour did. However, even for these groups, the pressure of people on available living space manifested itself in rapidly rising rents.[21]

Urban poverty also had an ethnic dimension. The visitor to the late nineteenth-century towns in the western provinces would have been struck by the deprivation of their predominantly Jewish inhabitants. The tsarist government restricted the majority of Jews to the so-called Pale of Settlement.[22] The 'May Laws' of 1882 restricted the settlement of Jews in rural areas, even within the Pale. In the towns and cities of Kiev, Bessarabia and elsewhere, Jewish families struggled to make ends meet, as shopkeepers, tavern-keepers or craftsmen. The fact that the majority were poor did not prevent the local peasantry from intermittent attacks on people and property (usually with the blessing or at least the acquiescence of the tsarist authorities). Obviously, not all Jews were poor; Jewish society, like peasant society, was stratified. A handful of Jews were allowed to qualify and to practise in the capital, as doctors, lawyers, bankers or engineers. But their existence, too, was precarious, because of the unpredictability of the regime. Consequently, rich and poor – tailors, pharmacists, musicians and teachers – swelled the ranks of emigrants to Europe and North America. Emigration testified to the twin evils of tsarist oppression and poverty.[23]

To dwell exclusively upon the dimensions of economic backwardness and the incidence of poverty would be to give a truncated portrait of the tsarist economy. Certainly, in comparison with per capita production and income in western Europe, Russia appears relatively backward. In addition, the distribution of income and wealth was such that most Russians experienced poverty, rather than security and a good standard of living. But the tsarist economy *grew*, as the foregoing remarks about urbanization have already implied. The perspective that has been adopted thus has to be broadened still further.

From several vantage points in the later nineteenth and early twentieth centuries, it was not the backwardness of the tsarist economy that struck contemporaries, but its growth and modernity. For instance, German and Austrian generals and cabinet ministers were alarmed at the increase in tsarist military might after 1905. The fact that Russia was getting militarily (and economically) stronger with each passing year encouraged a belief in the desirability of pre-emptive military action against Russia.[24] To take another example, statesmen and entrepreneurs in China, Japan and Persia identified the Russian Empire in 1913 as a major international economic presence, rather than as an economic weakling.

Our understanding of late economic growth has been considerably enhanced by the researches of scholars such as Prokopovich, Kondratiev, Strumilin, Vainshtein, Goldsmith and Gregory.[25] We are now reasonably well informed about the rate of growth of the economy as a whole, and of individual sectoral growth rates. What general observations can therefore be made about the performance of the economy in this period, bearing in mind that the underlying data are much less satisfactory for the early decades?

The two most accessible estimates of tsarist economic growth have been made by two American economists, Raymond Goldsmith and Paul Gregory. In 1961 Goldsmith published an article on Russian economic growth between 1861 and 1913, which concluded that the economy grew by around 2.5 per cent per annum. This estimate took into account the value of output that was generated in industry, agriculture, trade, transport and services.[26] Gregory has also published an estimate of national income in 1861 and 1913 (see Table 2.1), which suggests that the economy grew at roughly the same rate.

Goldsmith and Gregory agree that the tsarist economy grew more slowly between 1861 and 1885 than it did later.[27] However, their estimates of the rate of increase between 1885 and 1913 diverge quite significantly. Goldsmith arrived at an estimate of growth within the range 2.5–3.0 per cent per annum, whereas Gregory suggests that the economy grew by around 3.3 per cent per annum in the years 1885–1913.[28]

Gregory's revision upwards of the rate of tsarist economic growth is attributable to a number of different methods and assumptions.[29] In the first place, Gregory arrives at a higher rate of growth of trade and services. In the case of these sectors, there is no choice but to use data on employment as a proxy for the value of services provided; and Gregory maintains that employment in these sectors grew more rapidly than Goldsmith supposed. The second reason for the higher rate of growth estimated by Gregory is his finding that livestock herds grew more rapidly than Goldsmith argued.[30] Finally, Gregory calculates that cereal production grew by more than 3.0 per cent on average in 1885–1913, compared with the estimate of 2.5 per cent made by Goldsmith. As Gregory indicates, this new finding accounts for as much as half of the difference between his estimate of *total* output growth, and the top end of Goldsmith's range. The reason for this is that grain production was the single most important element of total output, accounting for around one-third of national income in 1913. Gregory constructs his index of cereal production on the basis of a broader geographical coverage than Goldsmith took for his index. More important still, Gregory calculates the growth of *net* cereal production. Since the ratio of net to gross output probably increased by 10 per cent between 1885 and 1913, this is a key explanation for Gregory's finding that the performance of agriculture (and thus the economy as a whole) was better than previous scholars had argued.[31]

The tsarist economy grew at this rate, partly as a result of the addition of new factors of production – that is, labour and capital – and partly through improvements in productivity (greater output per unit of capital and per worker). The growth of capital, the labour force and productivity will be discussed separately in due course. However, some general points may be made here, again drawing upon the findings of Gregory.[32]

At the level of the economy as a whole, inputs of labour and capital both grew rapidly after 1885. As far as labour was concerned, the major reason for the growth of the labour force was the growth in population; however, this needs to be set alongside changes in rural society, which promoted greater differentiation among peasants (see Chapter Three). The total labour force, which cannot be established with any great precision, probably grew by around 1.6 per cent per annum (1885–1913). Total output per worker, therefore, increased by around 1.7 per cent in the same period. If we break this period into two halves, it appears that the rate of growth of labour productivity fell after 1897–1901, compared with the earlier sub-period. This finding largely reflects the increased rate of population growth and the increase in the rate of growth of the total labour force after the turn of the century (see Table 2.4).

Table 2.4

The Growth of National Income, Labour Force and Output per Worker, 1883–1913 (average annual growth rate, per cent)

	National income	Labour force	Output per worker
1883–7 to 1897–1901	3.4	1.4	2.0
1897–1901 to 1909–13	3.1	1.8	1.3
1883–7 to 1909–13	3.3	1.6	1.7

Source: P. Gregory, *Russian National Income, 1885–1913*, C.U.P., 1982, pp. 133–4.

Gregory estimates that total reproducible capital (that is, the stock of equipment in all sectors of the economy, together with livestock) grew by around 3.5 per cent in the years 1885–1913. Therefore, the input of capital increased at approximately the same rate as total output, or slightly in excess of it. Capital inputs can then be weighted with the input of labour to give a general estimate of the total growth of factors of production. Gregory (who assigns weights of 0.7 and 0.3 to labour and capital respectively) arrives at a figure of 2.1 per cent for the growth rate of combined inputs. Subtracting this figure from total output growth, we are left with a residual of 1.1 per cent. In other words, total factor productivity grew by just over one per cent per annum between 1885 and 1913. Put another way, around 70 per cent of total output growth is 'explained' by the growth of inputs of labour and capital, and 30 per cent by increases in productivity. Gregory concludes that Russian economic growth can be described as extensive, rather than intensive, in so far as it depended more upon additions to factors of production than upon increases in their productivity.[33]

No such calculations can ever be regarded as conclusive and unchallengeable. They are only as good as the underlying data and, in particular, as the scholarship that is applied to the raw data. Gregory has argued, plausibly, that the data available on the tsarist economy are in most cases reasonable in quality. The methods he uses and the assumptions that he makes are both presented with admirable care and precision. Accordingly, one may be confident that the above estimates of Russian economic growth are as good as any that are likely to be made in the foreseeable future, and better than some that have been made in the past.

Economic growth creates additional output: to what uses was this increment in output devoted in tsarist Russia? Again, Gregory is an indispensable guide. Gregory has calculated how total product (or income) was allocated as between household consumption, investment and government expenditure. Table 2.5 summarizes the distribution of total product by end-use, for the seven quinquennia between 1885–9 and 1909–13. Several important features of the Russian economy are revealed in this table.

The value of output consumed by households more than doubled (in real terms) over the last thirty years of pre-revolutionary Russia. This increase coincided with a small reduction in the *share* of consumption in total output. This reduction in the proportion of output consumed was not continuous, and was most marked in the periods 1889–93 to 1893–7 and 1905–9 to 1909–13.

In view of the oft-repeated assertion that rural consumption, in particular, was depressed in order to 'pay' for industrialization, it is important to establish the trends in urban and rural consumption respectively. Gregory distinguishes between the two by suggesting that rural housing outlays and the value of farm products retained in the village can together serve as a proxy for rural consumption. Urban consumption – or, more accurately, its proxy – is thus the difference between total consumption and the rural proxy. On this basis, Gregory finds that there was no substantial divergence between the rate of growth of rural and urban consumption. Over the period as a whole, the urban proxy grew slightly faster than the rural. The differential was more marked in the first half of the period, when urban consumption did grow more rapidly; but the differential was reversed in favour of rural consumption in the second half.[34]

The conclusions to be drawn regarding household consumption are, therefore: first, that consumption did not decline in absolute terms during the period 1885–1913; and, second, that rural and urban households alike shared in this improvement. This, of course, says nothing about the experience of individual households. But it does suggest that economic growth was sufficiently rapid for consumption to grow, along with other components.

Table 2.5 also shows that government expenditure and investment grew more rapidly than consumption, which is hardly surprising at a time of rapid economic growth. The share of government expenditure in national income increased from around 8 to just under 10 per cent

Table 2.5

The Growth of National Income and Its Components, 1885–1913
(million rubles, 1913 prices)

	(1) Net national product	(2) Personal consumption	(3) Government expenditure	(4) Total net investment	(5) Net foreign investment*
Annual average					
1885–9	8,478	7,078	690	686	23
1889–93	8,744	7,331	796	602	15
1893–7	11,215	9,200	977	1,220	−182
1897–1901	12,938	10,725	1,111	1,383	−281
1901–5	14,861	12,112	1,453	1,344	− 48
1905–9	14,959	12,203	1,602	1,301	−148
1909–13	18,228	14,502	1,765	2,215	−254
Average annual growth rates 1885–9 to 1909–13	3.25	3.1	4.1	5.0	

* A negative sign indicates a net inflow of foreign savings; thus the sum of columns (4) and (5) gives net domestic savings.
Source: P. Gregory, *Russian National Income, 1885–1913*, C.U.P., 1982, pp. 127–8.

of the total between 1885 and 1913. Net investment increased its share from 8 to just over 12 per cent.

Two comments on government expenditure are in order. In the first place, the proportion of national income that the government accounted for is less than might have been expected, judging from conventional assertions about the role played by the tsarist state in industrial development and about the scale of public ownership.[35] The second comment relates to the character of government spending. As several scholars have pointed out, it is incorrect to assume that a major part of spending by the government had a productive nature or purpose. The priorities of government in Russia lay in defence and in the maintenance of the bureaucracy. The direct role of the state in promoting industrialization should not, therefore, be exaggerated.[36]

The growth in investment derived from domestic and foreign sources. As Table 2.5 shows, foreign investment became important only after 1893. By 1897–1901 it contributed up to one-fifth of total net investment, and a larger proportion still of investment in industry and utilities. To this extent, the picture painted by Gerschenkron about the role of foreign capital is borne out by Gregory's findings. Around half the increase in the rate of investment (in Table 2.5, col. (4) divided by col. (1)) between 1885 and 1913 was thus contributed from abroad. At the same time, it is worth noting that domestic savings contributed a larger proportion of total investment and, almost certainly, of industrial investment. This is not unimportant, in view of the frequent emphasis in the literature upon the obstacles to capital accumulation and investment in tsarist Russia.[37]

To conclude, it is apparent that total output grew sufficiently rapidly to provide for increases in personal consumption, in both rural and urban spheres, and for more substantial increases in investment and government expenditure. The 'pessimistic' interpretation of Russian economic growth, associated in particular with Gerschenkron, thus appears to be untenable. Yet one must emphasize that the revisionist view (which rests largely, though not exclusively, upon the work of Paul Gregory) does not preclude the possibility that some sections of the population experienced no improvement in their living standards. Nor is the revisionist view incompatible with the view that the majority of Russian people were poor. What it establishes is that, on average, households in Russia were less poor in 1913 than they had been a generation earlier.

We are now in a position to refine the characterization of the tsarist economy with which this chapter began. Low levels of income per head of population marked out Russia as a poor country in 1860 and 1913, relative to prevailing European standards of economic development. Low average rates of literacy and high rates of infant mortality typified the poverty of the population of tsarist Russia. Poverty, however, was not confined to the Russian peasantry, which made up the bulk of the population. Nor were all peasants poor. Income, wealth and life expectancy were unequally distributed within the peasantry, as well as between peasants as a whole and the tsarist elite.

At the same time, any characterization of the Russian economy which implies that the population in general was caught in a poverty trap fails to do justice to the record of economic growth, particularly in the period after 1885. Economic growth added to the total wealth of the country, and provided more goods for personal consumption.

he growth in output that was directed to investment and government
urposes did not lead to a reduction in output consumed by
idividuals.

Nevertheless, estimates of national income in a given year and of
he growth of total output can be misleading. Quantitative calcu-
ations, no less than qualitative judgements, can capture only part of
nore complex realities. In particular, the observation that the Russian
conomy grew steadily after 1860 and rapidly between 1885 and
913 does not tell us anything about the way in which the benefits
f growth were distributed within society. Modern studies of less-
eveloped countries draw attention to the fact that the rewards of
conomic growth (which seemed self-evident to a previous generation,
nd which were a central feature of what is here termed the 'liberal'
nterpretation) are unlikely to be distributed equally.

This more critical approach to economic growth is in keeping with
he sentiments expressed by Mikhailovsky, the famous legal populist.
Mikhailovsky had something to say about the liberal preoccupation
vith economic growth, about official government support for indus-
rialization and – by extension – about the marxist emphasis upon
he development of the productive forces. He wrote that 'production
ould grow to a colossal magnitude and tremendous wealth could
ccumulate, while the individual acting within this system received
either the freedom verbally promised him, nor the well-being that
ontinually tempted and eluded him'.[38] Of course, so far as marxist
nalysis is concerned, the lack of 'freedom' (for example, freedom to
ontrol the rhythm of one's work) was a necessary condition of
apitalism. From a marxist viewpoint, therefore, the populist vision
vas a myopic one. But populists and marxists, albeit in different
vays, both drew attention to the fact that there is more to the history
f economic development than the process of economic growth. This
s a salutary reminder.

3 Population Growth, Social Change and the Labour Market

A recurrent theme in contemporary Russian debates about the tsarist economy during the second half of the nineteenth century was the extent and significance of wage labour. Most observers acknowledged that the emancipation of the serfs had wrought major changes in society, in abandoning the principle that peasant serfs were obliged to perform services for feudal lords. But whether the decree of 1861 at the same time created the conditions for the growth of a capitalist labour market was much less a matter of consensus.

Populist observers took the view that emancipation in theory allowed peasant households a new degree of autonomy over their lives, which meant that they could engage in production on the family farm, using unpaid family labour. The implication of this belief was that peasants would not voluntarily enter into agreements to work for a wage, although they might be forced to do so. In fact, for populists, the history of Russian society after 1861 was a lamentable story of government-inspired measures that drove peasants against their will into factories and mines, or into wage work in construction or services. Increased fiscal exactions by government proved to be the main device whereby peasants were driven from their farms. However populists argued that peasants strove to maintain the basic integrity of the household economy by rejecting permanent settlement outside the villages in which they had been born. In other words, the growth of wage labour was an artificial phenomenon that would fail to create a genuine and stable proletariat.

For contemporary marxist observers, the growth of wage labour was neither unnatural nor undesirable. Rather, it reflected the predictable and necessary growth of new social relations in the Russian countryside, which rendered the populist notion of a peasant family farm entirely fanciful. The evidence suggested to marxist scholars that Russian peasant society was becoming increasingly differentiated into a class of capitalist farmers and a class of rural proletarians. The proletariat, formed from the ranks of the 'middle peasantry' who had hitherto supported themselves from the sale of their modest surplus produce, now sold their labour power, either to capitalists in the countryside or to those in the towns. This process was by no means completed in Russia by the end of the nineteenth century, but it was clearly evident. For the bulk of peasant households, accordingly, the future held out the prospect of the progressive expropriation of their means of production and their entry into the capitalist labour market. This new proletariat would unite in a struggle against capitalist exploitation, the result of which would eventually be a socialist society.

Liberal observers did not greet the growth of wage labour with the despair displayed by populists, but neither did they accept that with the development of a proletariat came the prospect of socialism. Liberal opinion regarded the spread of paid employment as a mark of modernity that was long overdue in tsarist Russia. Liberals reached the conclusion that two main tendencies in post-emancipation Russia accounted for the development of wage labour. The first was the rapid growth of rural population on a limited supply of land, creating the potential for the growth of a non-agricultural workforce in sectors of the economy where workers would be used more productively. The second tendency was the increase in demand for labour from employers in a wide range of enterprise, including manufacturing industry and railway construction. However, liberals also pointed out that the labour market did not operate entirely unencumbered by institutional restrictions. In particular, the maintenance of the traditional peasant land commune acted in their view to control the supply of labour from the villages. The result of this control in general terms was that the actual supply of labour fell some way short of the potential labour supply. Consequently, wages were artificially raised and industrialists had to locate their plants with a view to obtaining adequate supplies of labour from nearby village communities.

In the present chapter the material is organized in such a way as to examine the major problems raised by contemporary commentators, as well as to explore the ways in which the problems have subsequently been addressed by historians of the tsarist economy. Three main areas are singled out for attention: first, the growth of Russian population; second, the problem of differentiation in peasant society; and finally the growth of wage labour and the characteristics of the Russian labour market.

2.1 Population Growth

One of the distinctive features of Russian economic development during the second half of the nineteenth century was the rapid growth of population. The total population of the Russian Empire (exclusiv of Finland, Khiva and Bokhara) increased from 74 million in 1860– to 164 million in 1909–13. Between 1883–7 and 1909–13, the popu lation of Russia grew at an average annual rate of 1.6 per cent, a rat exceeded only by Australia, Canada and the United States. But whil each of these countries received substantial net inflows of people fror Europe, in Russia rapid population growth was entirely a functio of natural increase. Indeed, Russia exported part of her growin population, so that in the absence of emigration, total populatio would have been higher still.[1]

What explanations may be offered for the population explosion i tsarist Russia? In theory, population growth may be attributed to fall in the crude death rate, reflecting either a decline in the incidenc and severity of infectious disease or the moderation of subsistenc crises, or some combination of the two. Alternatively, populatio growth might be caused by changes in fertility. A fall in the mea age of marriage among women (for instance, because of increase opportunities to form new and economically viable household units would lead, in the absence of birth control, to an increase in marita fertility. Equally, mortality and fertility changes might act jointly t cause an increase in population. There is no way of telling *a priori* only an examination of the evidence will provide some clues.[2]

The major demographic variables for European Russia ar presented in Table 3.1. The crude birth rate (that is, the number o recorded births per thousand people) remained steady at around fift per thousand until the early twentieth century. The crude death rat was stable until the mid-1880s, after which it fell quite rapidly (th high average for the quinquennium 1891–5 reflects the impact of th famine in 1891). The combination of a high birth rate and fallin death rate produced higher rates of natural increase in Russia toward the end of the century, compared to the situation in earlier decades.

The average birth rate for European Russia was high, even by eas European standards, where rates of around forty per thousand wer common. No west European country had birth rates that came clos to the Russian norm at this time, although rates of around forty pe thousand were recorded in Germany during the 1870s. The declin in the average birth rate in European Russia also set in rather late than elsewhere. This was true with respect not only to western Europe but also to such less developed countries as Spain and Hungary. I would appear, therefore, that sustained economic development wa not a precondition of declining fertility rates; so there could be som other reason for the persistence of high rates in Russia until th beginning of the twentieth century.[4]

The first task must therefore be to account for the persistently higl birth rate in European Russia through to the end of the century. Th

Table 3.1

Crude Rates of Births, Deaths and Marriages in Fifty Provinces of European Russia, 1861–1913

	Average birth rate	Average death rate	Rate of natural increase (per thousand)	Average rate of marriage
1861–5	50.7	36.5	14.2	10.6
1867–70*	49.7	37.4	12.3	10.1
1871–5	51.2	37.1	14.1	10.0
1876–80	49.5	36.7	13.8	9.0
1881–5	50.5	36.4	14.1	9.2
1886–90	50.2	34.5	15.7	8.9
1891–5	48.9	36.2	12.7	9.0
1896–1900	49.5	32.1	17.4	9.0
1901–5	47.7	31.0	16.7	8.3
1906–10	45.8	29.5	16.3	8.6
1911–13	43.9	27.1	16.8	8.0†

* No figures are available for 1866.   † 1911 only.
Source: A. G. Rashin, *Naselenie Rossii za sto let (1811–1913): statisticheskie ocherki*, Gosstatizdat, 1956, pp. 154, 172.

researches of a team of American demographers, headed by A. J. Coale, allow us to distinguish between the two determinants of the birth rate, namely the rate of fertility within marriage and the rate of nuptiality among the female population. Drawing upon evidence provided by the 1897 Census, Coale and his colleagues concluded that the rate of marital fertility in Russia was indeed high. However, it was not noticeably higher than the rate in several other countries, specifically Bulgaria, Norway and Ireland. What distinguished Russia (and Bulgaria) from all other European countries, as well as from the United States, was the fact that Russian women displayed a much higher propensity to be married. Thus, it was the tendency towards universal marriage (the 'non-European marriage pattern', as it has been called), combined with a less uncommonly high fertility rate, that accounted for the large average annual number of births in European Russia.[5]

Any explanation of high fertility in tsarist Russia must pay overriding attention to patterns of peasant behaviour, since peasants comprised the bulk of the population. A high rate of nuptiality among women had been a long-standing feature of Russian peasant society, stretching back at least as far as the sixteenth century. In that period, widespread (and early) marriage reflected the need to encourage the settlement of large tracts of unoccupied land in European Russia. Thereafter, when serfdom became consolidated, each feudal lord promoted marriage between enserfed couples, in order to obtain a fresh supply of labour in due course from their children. The serf-owner could also demand additional obligations at once from a newly married couple, who constituted a taxable unit, or *tyaglo*. A young man and woman who sought to circumvent an injunction to marry one another might register as joint godparents to a child, thereby rendering their marriage illegal in the eyes of the Church. But this strategy, which was probably not widespread, influenced the selection of a partner; it did not undermine the principle of enforced marriage.[6]

Serfdom therefore encouraged a tendency towards high rates of nuptiality among the rural population. After the abolition of serfdom, peasant villages retained a strong commitment to a culture of virtually universal marriage. The language of peasants mocked unmarried adults (according to one proverb, 'A woman without a husband is like an orphaned child') and idealized marriage ('A bird with wings is strong; a woman with a husband is beautiful').[7]

Economic considerations, as well as this cultural inheritance from serfdom, dictated widespread marriage among women in the post-reform village. The inclusion of a young bride in the peasant household added a valuable – and easily exploited – source of labour power. Women were crucial to the household economy, performing virtually all domestic chores and rearing the children. They also helped with the harvest and produced non-agricultural goods for household consumption or, sometimes, for sale. For these reasons, male peasants conceived of women as a valuable asset, not unlike their draught livestock.[8]

High rates of nuptiality were accompanied by high rates of marital fertility. Measured against the fertility schedule of Coale's standard population (the Hutterite Protestant community of North America, where marriage is universal and birth control is prohibited), marital fertility in European Russia in 1879 averaged 76 per cent of the most fertile sample ever recorded. In practice, this meant that a Russian woman gave birth around nine times during her lifetime, although it must be remembered that this is an average for European Russia as a whole.[9]

Figures such as these reflect the early mean age at marriage and the absence of family limitation. Once more, it is the culture and economy of the Russian peasant village that must attract attention. Some explanation for early marriage has already been implied in previous remarks about the impact of serfdom and the recurrent need for labour in the post-reform peasant household. Under serfdom, for example, some lords levied fines on households whose daughters were still unmarried by their twentieth birthday. A commitment to early marriage persisted until the beginning of the twentieth century. In 1900, many villagers still regarded as freaks those women who had not married by the age of twenty. Such women had brought shame on their parents.

The suggestion has been made that there was no economic justification for peasant youths to delay their marriage, as there was in many parts of western and central Europe. Indeed, in Russia it seemed that the prevalent system of land tenure meant that peasants had every reason to marry early. The young couple formed a conjugal unit (*tyaglo*) within the larger household, and this entitled them to a share in the total stock of allotment land at the disposal of the village community, which redistributed the land from time to time. Thus, peasant girls did not have to wait until they and their partners had accumulated sufficient resources of their own, before getting married. Men and, still more, women who remained single much beyond their teens were simply flouting established village norms.[10]

This pattern of early marriage exercised a crucial influence upon marital fertility, since it maximized the reproductive potential of the female population. The tendency for women to bear children with monotonous regularity fully accorded with male peasant sentiment. Peasant men regarded the recurrent pregnancy of their wives as a desirable condition, ordained by God. More to the point, they calculated that the greater the number of offspring, the greater the chances that sufficient children would survive to contribute both to the family labour force and to the eventual maintenance of their parents in old age.[11]

According to one interpretation, the Russian peasant predilection for large families was also directly linked to the traditional communal form of land tenure. The argument is that the commune redistributed allotment land in accordance with the size of the households who were entitled to a share in it. In Pavlovsky's view, 'the *mir* (commune) . . . reliev(ed) the individual peasant of responsibility for the excessive increase of his family. The task of finding room for any new member devolved on the commune, which did it at the expense of the whole village, at the cost of relatively small individual sacrifice'.[12]

The evidence for a close correlation between high fertility rates and communal land redistribution has not been explored systematically. At first sight, it appears to be at its strongest in the Baltic and in the west and south-west, regions where fertility was below the national average and where communal land tenure was either uncommon or absent. However, there were other factors at work in these regions, such as the influence of Protestantism in the Baltic, which probably depressed the rate of marital fertility. In any case, as Dorothy Atkinson has observed, the existence of an association between communal land tenure and high rates of marital fertility does not prove that the former determined the latter. It is equally plausible that the causal influence operated in reverse; in other words, a propensity towards a large family size in the Central Black Earth and in regions to the south and south-east made necessary the periodic repartition of land, and not the other way round.[13]

Some other explanation for high fertility thus appears to be called for. Atkinson points to the correspondence between high marital fertility and infant mortality rates, suggesting that the need to offset the losses of infants led parents in these regions to maintain a constant flow of births. To this suggestion, one might add that high rates of infant mortality could reduce the interval between conceptions, in so far as lactation no longer acted to modify the fecundity of the woman who had just lost her baby. However, this analysis is not supported by Coale, who found no positive correlation between marital fertility and rates of infant mortality. This negative result is also borne out by a less rigorous examination of the evidence. For example, the highest number of recorded births per marriage (in 1910) was found in Tula, Penza and Tambov provinces, but infant mortality there only just exceeded the national average. Furthermore, provinces with the highest recorded rates of infant mortality (Nizhnii-Novgorod, Vyatka, Olonets and Perm) were ranked fourth, seventeenth, twenty-fifth and tenth respectively, in terms of marital fertility.[14]

Doubts have been raised about the role of communal land tenure and high rates of infant mortality as determinants of the high Russian birth rate. A more satisfactory explanation relates the high rate of marital fertility and variations in fertility to the persistence of cultural traditions that formed over several generations and that endured throughout the second half of the nineteenth century. These traditions in their turn may be related to the land : labour ratios that prevailed during the era of serfdom.

In order to appreciate this point, it is worth drawing attention to the different demographic history of the Baltic provinces, the Urals and the west, on the one hand, and that of the Central Black Earth and south-east regions, on the other. In the Baltic provinces, for example, late marriage was the norm during the nineteenth century and a high proportion of spinsters was found in the population. While this pattern doubtless owed something to the existence of impartible inheritance, which deterred early and universal marriage, such tenurial arrangements were themselves the product of a shortage of land, relative to labour. Because labour was relatively abundant, feudal landlords had no incentive to promote early marriage. Nor was the demographic pattern modified by the abolition of serfdom in the Baltic region, between 1816 and 1819. Emancipation created large numbers of landless labourers, who had been deprived of their smallholdings. This further discouraged the conclusion of early marriage. For these reasons, the Baltic was much more typical of the 'European marriage pattern' than any other part of the Russian Empire (see Table 3.2).[15]

Table 3.2

Percentages of Women Married before the Age of 21 (European Russia), 1867–1910

Region	Percentage of total population (in 1897)	Percentage of women married in				
		1867–70	1871–80	1881–90	1891–1900	1901–10
North-West and Central Industrial	18	56	54	51	50	49
Central Black Earth, Mid-Volga and Little Russia	30	66	68	65	64	65
Lower Volga and New Russia	20	63	67	64	62	62
Belorussia and South-West*	21	47	48	48	44	43
North and Urals	9	48	48	49	49	53
Baltic	3	22	21	20	19	20

* Excludes Smolensk province, which is included in the first group.
Source: A. G. Vishnevsky, 'Rannie etapy stanovleniya novogo tipa rozhda-emosti v Rossii', in *Brachnost, rozhdaemost i smertnost v Rossii i v SSSR*, ed. A. G. Vishnevsky, Statistika, 1977, pp. 109, 117.

So far as the Central Industrial Region, Belorussia, the North and Urals were concerned, nuptiality rates were considerably higher than in the Baltic region, but were still well below the rates in other parts of the Empire. By comparison with the Black Earth region, the Mid and Lower Volga, and south Russia, land was in relatively short supply. A relatively high ratio of labour to land was already established prior to the nineteenth century. Furthermore, under serfdom, the feudal landowners had encouraged many male serfs to seek work outside the estate. The fact that a large proportion of the young adult male population rarely visited the estate must have militated against early marriage and certainly depressed the fertility rate in such areas. Such absences from the peasant village continued to be a feature of the economy in the north-west and Central Industrial regions in the aftermath of emancipation. In 1895 the Russian ethnographer D. N. Zhbankov pointed to the prevalence of *otkhod* (literally 'going away') as the reason for the differences in mean completed family size in Russia. In the more industrialized regions, he found that peasant families contained just over five members, whereas in what he termed the more 'settled' regions the average exceeded nine members.[16]

Land was more abundant in the south and south-east, and the peasants who settled there faced no obstacle to their early and universal marriage. In these regions, according to the 1897 Census, nine out of ten women between the age of 20 and 29 were married (fewer than six were married in the north and north-west).[17] As we have seen, feudal landowners promoted the early marriage of serfs, with a view to developing a labour supply on their estates. When serfdom was abolished, the established patterns of nuptiality and fertility were not modified, because additional land could usually be found by peasant communities to support the newly married couples and their offspring.[18]

The Central Black Earth region presents a rather more challenging problem of interpretation. Here the rate of growth of the peasant population eventually resulted in a crisis of 'overpopulation'. Peasant allotments became increasingly fragmented, in order to accommodate the additional numbers. Pavlovsky, as noted earlier, argued that the growth of population continued unchecked, because the repartitional commune could absorb the growing families. But it is doubtful whether the repartitional commune itself was responsible for the increase in numbers. Instead, one may point to the persistence in this region of a peasant culture that had been forged in an earlier generation, when land was relatively abundant and serf-owners encouraged early marriage. The commune itself operated to satisfy an inherited cultural tradition; it was not the original cause of high fertility.

The hypothesis is, then, that nuptiality and fertility patterns were established in rural society long before the abolition of serfdom. Early and nigh-universal marriage persisted among peasants, even when (as in the Central Black Earth region) the original favourable ratio of land to labour had been modified.

The link between the birth rate and the land : labour ratio is also confirmed by the demographic experience of western Siberia. Data on vital rates in Siberia are not available until the late nineteenth century, by which time there had already been a generation of intense settlement in that region. In Tobolsk, Tomsk and Akmolinsk, land was both abundant and of good quality for cereal cultivation. Here the crude birth rate exceeded even the high average for European Russia. In 1911–13, for example, it averaged 48 per thousand in these three provinces, a rate matched only by the Urals and Lower Volga regions. In Tobolsk province, the birth rate reached 58 per thousand, higher than any other part of the Empire.[19]

Land was also relatively abundant in Central Asia.[20] Cultural and religious traditions exerted a still more powerful influence on the predominantly Muslim population, among whom early and universal marriage was the norm. However, there is no doubt that the rate of marital fertility in central Asia was lower than in other parts of the Empire. Perhaps, as one historian has suggested, the high incidence of malaria may have induced an abnormally high rate of sterility or have led to a reduction in sexual activity; perhaps, too, the prevalence of breastfeeding reduced the fecundity of the mother. Furthermore, the mean age of marriage for men was much higher than elsewhere in Russia (a function of their need to accumulate sufficient funds to pay the bride price), and this may have reduced marital fertility.[21]

The crude birth rate in European Russia began to fall before 1900 (see Table 3.1), and this decline now has to be explained. Both components of overall fertility, that is nuptiality and marital fertility, registered a decline from the 1890s through to the Revolution.[22] The reduction in overall fertility is unlikely to have been caused by the spread of contraception and abortion, both of which were practised (so far as one can judge) by only a minority of the population. The explanation lies instead in a tendency towards delayed marriage and a reduced overall rate of marriage.[23]

The fall in the Russian birth rate has been attributed, variously, to the impact of reforms in peasant land tenure; to the reduction in infant mortality; and to the dissemination of a more modern culture among the rural population. Of these explanations, the first is the least convincing. The well-known Soviet demographer B. Ts. Urlanis maintained that the Stolypin land reforms played a significant part in reducing fertility, because they encouraged the formation of individual, enclosed farmsteads after 1905, in areas where the repartitional commune previously dominated. However, the impact of the reforms on land tenure was modest, and in any case the reforms were introduced more than a decade after the fertility decline appears to have commenced.[24]

A reduction in infant mortality (for reasons that are offered presently) may have promoted a reduction in marital fertility, by making it less imperative for parents to reproduce frequently in order to ensure that sufficient children would survive. In addition, parents may have come to realize that their material and emotional resources could best be spread over a smaller number of children, rather than over the large number that the reduction in mortality would otherwise have produced. Although, as noted previously, Coale found no correlation between marital fertility and infant mortality, he and his colleagues do not rule out the possibility that a reduction in the latter may have resulted in a reduction in the former variable.[25]

Most of all, we need to take into account the diffusion of a new culture in late nineteenth-century Russia, a culture that was more conducive to delayed marriage, or even to the outright rejection of marriage itself. It is difficult to be very precise about this; much of the evidence is impressionistic. Contemporary Russian ethnographers drew attention to the emergence of new attitudes that were inimical to early marriage, and they linked these to the growth of market relations, improved communications and the spread of literacy. Literacy, for example, implied the dissemination of more modern attitudes and the confidence to defend them against more traditional authorities.[26]

Such manifestations of a changing culture were not, of course, omnipresent in Russia, even by 1914. They were most likely to have characterized young men and women who had gained experience of work and life in the city: in St Petersburg, Moscow, and the rapidly growing towns of south Russia, such as Kiev, Kharkov and Rostov. These young people imbibed new attitudes towards family life that challenged accepted village norms. When they returned from 'abroad', as the towns were called, it was the village that increasingly had to adjust to these men and women with their new vocabulary and lifestyle, and not the other way round.

Migrant workers were unable for the most part to maintain a family in the towns, because of the high cost of living. In this case, economic conditions may have reinforced the new urban culture with which they came into contact. It does not follow, of course, that peasants who worked in the towns were unmarried. In Moscow, for example, towards the end of the nineteenth century, many such men married no later than did their counterparts who stayed on in the village. However, this seems to have been less true by 1914. Peasant women, on the other hand, who took jobs in the textile mills or as domestic servants were normally unattached. Among those who did marry, the median age of marriage in 1914 was 22.6 years. It is reasonable to conclude that the example of migrant workers must have begun to affect attitudes to marriage in their villages of origin, at least by the turn of the century.[27]

We may deal more briefly with the possible causes of the declining crude death rate in Russia and, more specifically, of the falling rate of infant mortality. To begin with, we can rule out improvements in medical provision as a general factor tending to reduce mortality. Access to reasonable and reliable medical care was restricted for the mass of the rural population, notwithstanding the efforts of the local authorities (*zemstva*), who organized teams of 'assistant doctors' (*feldshery*). On the eve of the First World War, there was on average one such doctor per 20,000 rural inhabitants.[28]

Whether attitudes to childbirth and childcare among the Russian peasantry improved noticeably during the later nineteenth century is a difficult matter to judge. Generalization is impossible; there was no uniform village culture in European Russia. Certainly, in the Central Industrial, Central Black Earth and Urals regions, standards of infant care, even by the turn of the century, were low. Newborn babies were transferred within weeks to a diet of untreated milk and solid food. They were given pieces of bread or rag dipped in beer (*kvass*) or water as comforts to suck. Inappropriate feeding led to recurrent outbreaks of gastro-enteritis. For example, in the central provinces the damp weather during the summer, combined with an inappropriate diet, induced chronic diarrhoea, weight loss and often death. Intermittent outbreaks of typhoid, smallpox and diphtheria also levied a heavy toll. By contrast, standards of infant care were much higher in the western regions; here, too, births were proportionately less concentrated in the summer, when babies were especially vulnerable. In general, however, one cannot be certain that cultural standards became more uniform throughout Russia. Attempts were made to raise them in the more backward regions, but they appear to have met with only limited success.[29]

A more likely cause of reduced mortality in late tsarist Russia was the overall improvement in the quantity and quality of nutrition. Higher levels of food intake will lead to higher consumption of protein and carbohydrates. These will bring benefits to all age groups, but they are particularly important for the health of nursing mothers and infants. They increase the capacity of the newborn to survive infancy and to become healthier and less disease-prone children.

The question of food supply is treated at greater length in Chapter Four. Here, it may be noted that per capita output of grain increased during the period 1885–9 to 1909–13. More to the point, the per capita amount of grain retained within the Russian village also increased. Nor was this increase confined to the years immediately preceding the First World War. According to Paul Gregory, rural consumption grew during the 1890s, no less than in the early twentieth century. In the second place, the overall quality of food intake also improved. This was reflected in the progressive diversification in agricultural production. As a result of these two developments, food consumption in Russia by 1909–13 gave its citizens an average daily intake of calories and protein that was perfectly adequate, by the standards of the modern international community. Russia lagged somewhat only in the proportion of protein that was supplied from animal sources.[30]

Russia continued to experience substantial fluctuations in mortality from year to year. V. Zaitsev, writing in 1927, showed that five years in particular stand out from the period 1871–1913. In those years – 1872, 1882, 1892, 1895 and 1910 – the crude death rate in European Russia was at least seven per cent above the trend line that he had plotted. In 1882 it was 12 per cent above the trend; in 1892, as a result of the great famine in 1891–2, it leaped to 27 per cent. Zaitsev demonstrated that there was no simple correlation between the crude death rate and the harvest in a given year. He even found that, in the Ukraine and Volga regions, the crude death rate *rose* in years when the harvest was above the secular trend over the period 1871–1913 (suggesting, perhaps, that depressed prices had left families there without the means to purchase other foodstuffs; or that the wages of agricultural labourers had been squeezed by employers). The positive correlation between harvest and the crude death rate improved, however, when Zaitsev lagged this variable by one year. That is, he found that a poor harvest tended to inflate mortality in the following year. Younger age groups were especially susceptible to under-nourishment, which rendered them vulnerable to disease.[31]

Major catastrophes, however, were less frequent during the nineteenth century than they had been in earlier centuries (or than they would be in 1921 and 1934). One reason for this was the improvement in inter-regional food supply, occasioned by the construction of the railways from the 1860s onwards. Rail transport ensured that, in principle, grain and other supplies could be moved quickly and easily from areas of surplus to areas of deficit. The famine in 1891, which overwhelmed the tsarist bureaucracy, does not negate this general point. The fact that inter-regional trade did have the broad impact suggested has been confirmed by a recent study, which pointed to the progressive elimination of price differentials in grain.[32]

Apart from the famine of 1891, the other major demographic catastrophe in tsarist Russia was occasioned by war. During the Crimean War (1854–6), losses were put at around half a million, four-fifths of which were attributed to diseases that struck combatants and civilians alike. The Russo-Japanese War (1904–5) involved a much smaller human loss, perhaps of the order of 20,000 men at the most. Not surprisingly, the First World War took a vastly heavier toll. One estimate put total Russian combatant fatalities at around 1.8 million; of this, as much as 1·6 million represented 'excess mortality', that is, the men would not have died in 1914–17 but for the War. Excess mortality among civilians, the result of disease and (in 1917) malnutrition, was of the same order of magnitude. Finally, the disruption of ordinary family life through mobilization and the absence of married men produced a shortfall of births during the War. Taken together with the still more disastrous Civil War in 1918–20, the sustained violence between 1914 and 1920 had far-reaching echoes in post-revolutionary society.[33]

To summarize, rapid population growth in Russia was the product of a sustained high birth rate, which began to fall only after a reduction in the crude death rate had been well established. The high birth rate in the Empire as a whole reflected a high rate of nuptiality and of marital fertility. These in turn have been explained by reference to the availability of land, particularly in the south-east and east, and in Siberia. They were also the product of a culture in peasant society (most marked in the Central Black Earth region) that had been forged under serfdom, and that encouraged early and virtually universal marriage. This pattern obtained much less in the Central Industrial Region and in the western provinces, and was wholly absent in the Baltic region.

The rapid growth in the Russian population between 1850 and 1917 was not curtailed by intermittent shortages of food. Even the famine of 1891 did not interrupt the growth in numbers (though it did have this effect in some of the provinces in the Central Black Earth region). The growth of the population was checked by the First World War; in Central Asia and the north Caucasus, indeed, total numbers actually fell.[34]

What happened to the additional numbers of people? To what extent did population growth lead to the settlement of new regions; to urbanization; and to emigration? These questions are addressed in the following section.

3.2 Migration

(a) General Trends

The population of imperial Russia was constantly on the move. Even under serfdom, which had originally been designed to forestall the spontaneous movement of peasants to lands where serfdom did not prevail, the inhabitants never entirely ceased to be mobile. One reason for this state of flux was that many lords encouraged their serfs to leave the estate and to find work elsewhere, provided of course that the serfs continued to pay their dues. They were also subject to instant recall. Other serfs left the estate without the permission of their owners, and moved eastwards in search of freedom. However, this spontaneous migration proved increasingly risky, because of the extension of imperial administration to far-flung regions.

Territorial conquests during the eighteenth and early nineteenth centuries created extensive opportunities for the colonization of fertile lands to the east and south of the traditional areas of Russian settlement (that is, the area bounded by the upper Volga, the Oka and the upper Dnieper rivers). As a result of territorial expansion, by the end of the Napoleonic Wars the Russian Empire extended south to the Black Sea and to the Caucasus. By the middle of the nineteenth century, the huge territory known as Turkestan had been brought under Russian control. Each of these regions, as yet sparsely settled (and inhabited for the most part by nomadic peoples), attracted increasing numbers of peasants from the Russian heartlands.

The process of colonization began to gather pace during the late eighteenth century and continued through to the First World War. In the period prior to 1800, the main direction of settlement was towards the Lower Volga and the Don regions, with some movement to the Urals as well. During the first half of the century the movement towards the south-east continued, leading migrants into the Caucasus, the population of which almost quadrupled between 1800 and 1860, to three-quarters of a million. After 1850, migration to the southern steppe ('New Russia') began to tail off, but colonization of the Caucasus continued, boosted towards the end of the century by the burgeoning Russian oil industry.[35]

In numerical terms, the most dramatic migration from centre to periphery took place during the last decade of the nineteenth century and the years preceding the First World War. The main points of attraction for settlers proved to be western Siberia and Central Asia. Between 1896 and 1915, an estimated 4.5 million Russians settled permanently in these regions (and in the Far East).[36] As will be seen in the following section, this did not represent migration to regions of rapid industralization. Rather, it reflected a spontaneous movement from the depressed central agricultural provinces by peasants, who sought a more secure existence as farmers.

The general extent of migration in tsarist Russia can be judged best from the results of the census of population that was carried out in 1897. The Census recorded the residence of each individual in the Empire, and also asked each person to state the place of his or her birth. The available published data allow one to assess how many people in 1897 were living in provinces other than those in which they were born. Thus the figures do not capture all migration, because they exclude movement within the same province. Nor do they allow us to conclude that all 'immigrants' had settled permanently in a given locality. This conclusion may be legitimate in the case of the colonization that has been referred to above, but it would not be appropriate so far as many urban in-migrants were concerned.[37]

The Census of 1897 revealed that nearly ten per cent of the population of imperial Russia were living in provinces other than those of their birth (see Table 3.3). What accounts for this propensity to migrate? We have already indicated that the opportunities arose largely as a result of territorial aggrandizement (we can also add that the cost of travel came down with the construction of a railway network); but this does not account for the motivation of millions of men and women to uproot themselves.

Table 3.3

Population migration in Russia, according to the 1897 Census

Region	Number of provinces	Total population	Immigrant population*	Percentage immigrant
		(millions)		
Non-Black Earth	25	37.54	3.34	9
Black Earth	25	55.90	3.98	7
European Russia	50	93.44	7.31	8
Kingdom of Poland	10	9.40	1.20	13
Asiatic Russia	29	22.79	3.36	15
TOTAL	89	125.63	11.87	9

* See text for definition.
Source: B. V. Tikhonov, *Pereseleniya v Rossii vo vtoroi polovine XIX v.*, Nauka, 1978, p. 37.

According to one recent study, a distinction should be drawn between migration to urban areas and migration to the rural periphery. Migration to Russian cities correlated strongly and positively with rates of literacy in the provinces of migrant origin, and it is suggested that potential migrants from areas of greater average literacy were especially likely to be aware of the economic opportunities that cities such as Moscow and St. Petersburg presented. On the other hand, migrants to the sparsely settled parts of the Empire, such as Siberia, were most likely to have been prompted to leave their homes by the threat of agrarian 'overpopulation'.[38]

The implications of this level of internal migration for economic development are reasonably clear. The settlement of new regions allowed agricultural production to expand on fertile lands. It facilitated the development of agrarian capitalism, which in the traditional Russian heartlands had to reckon with the power of semi-feudal landlords. The migration of peasants permitted the growth of manufacturing, mining and construction in cities as far afield as Baku and St. Petersburg. (Urban in-migration, however, was not a necessary precondition for the development of non-agricultural production; many enterprises were located in rural areas.) Migration to cities had a cultural significance as well: 'It increases literacy among the population, heightens their understanding, and gives them civilized habits and requirements'.[39]

But what of the economic impact of migration on the regions from which the migrants had come? In theory, the outflow of peasant families from the central agricultural provinces ought to have raised the level of wages in agriculture. However, such an effect seems not to have materialized. One reason for this negative verdict is that the scale of migration, although substantial, was insufficient to have an impact, because of the rapidity of the growth in population. Besides, the spurt in internal migration commenced only at the end of the nineteenth century, and could hardly have achieved significant results in the central provinces by the time that war broke out in 1914.[40]

A second possible line of enquiry is to ask what migrants contributed directly to the rural areas they left, by repatriating earnings they derived from urban employment or from their new farms. The flow of savings from rural periphery to centre cannot have been great, because the settlers had to invest in the new farm – and to discharge the debts that some incurred in making the journey. Urban in-migrants normally maintained much closer ties with the villages from which they came. Evidence about the repatriation of earnings is scanty and inconclusive. Generally speaking, migrants disposed of only a small pool of savings, due to the low level of urban wages and the high cost of living in the city.[41]

(b) Resettlement in Siberia

Prior to the construction of the Trans-Siberian Railway (which, by 1896, extended from Chelyabinsk to Novonikolaevsk, south of Tomsk), the volume of migration to 'Asiatic Russia' did not assume significant dimensions. The annual flow of migrants beyond Syzran – the small town on the Volga that served as the main crossing point for travellers east – did not exceed 12,000 between 1860 and 1884. Over the next ten years the figure rose only slightly. Furthermore, these estimates apply to gross migration and thus take no account of people who decided to return to European Russia.

The main upsurge in migration took place after 1896, and this turned into a torrent during the five years between 1906 and 1910, as shown in Table 3.4.

Table 3.4

Official estimates of migration to 'Asiatic Russia', 1896–1915 (annual averages)

	(1) Gross migration	(2) Net migration	(3) Percentage returning
1896–1900	146,400	121,000	17
1901–5	68,800	49,200	28
1906–10	433,300	376,700	13
1911–15	180,300	128,900	28
1896–1915	207,200	169,000	18

Source: S. M. Dubrovsky, *Stolypinskaya zemelnaya reforma*, Nauka, 1963, pp. 390–1.

Not all migrants recorded in this Table were destined for Siberia. In some years, according to one source, as many as one-third of them expressed a desire to travel to Central Asia. The figures are also unlikely to capture all migrants to Asiatic Russia; they derive from official records kept (after 1896) at Chelyabinsk. However, since the railway offered the easiest and cheapest route, one may assume that the figures account for the bulk of migration.[42]

Most migrants were peasants from the black-earth provinces of European Russia: the Central Black Earth region and, to an increasing extent, New Russia and the Lower Volga regions provided the majority of those who sought to escape rural impoverishment. Something of the spirit of desperation that motivated such men and women is revealed in the words of a peasant from Poltava province: 'We're told that it's cold in Siberia, but I say that we are colder still here; we're told that you have to feed cattle indoors for six months, but even if you have to feed them for twelve, at least there's something there to give them. Here you can't even feed one cow. Rents are so high that we make a loss on farming, rather than a profit. We end up paying the landlord even for the sweat that we're pouring on to his land.'[43]

A fuller discussion of the background to the plight of such people belongs more properly to the chapter on agriculture. Here, comment will be confined to the intervention of the tsarist administration in resettlement. The government, of course, contributed indirectly to the promotion of internal migration, by undertaking to construct the Trans-Siberian railway. The railway was of the utmost importance in two main respects: first, it reduced the cost of travel to Asiatic Russia (the rail fare from European Russia to Tomsk, a distance of at least 2000 km., came down from 57 rubles in 1890 to only 15 rubles in 1898). Secondly, by helping to develop agricultural exports from Siberia after 1900, the railway induced some degree of confidence in the economic prospects of the region.[44]

The government took a closer interest in the question of Russian settlement in Siberia ten years before the railway was built. The spread of military and commercial interests in the Far East led officials to believe that Russian settlement beyond the Urals was desirable. This belief coincided with a recognition (not, necessarily, in the same corridors of tsarist government) that rural 'overpopulation' in European Russia could to some extent be alleviated by migration. The government was also concerned that continued 'spontaneous' migration could create problems, both in the areas to which migrants went and in those they left.

Accordingly, the Ministry of the Interior introduced laws in 1889 to regulate settlement. Those migrants who were in receipt of a licence would be entitled to a plot of state-owned land, which they could farm in perpetuity, in return for a small rental. The government offered more generous financial aid to such settlers than they had hitherto been able to obtain on their own account. The aim of this scheme was twofold: it would allow the government to determine in which regions the migrants settled, and it would help to ensure that the migrant had discharged any outstanding obligations to the village community which he was leaving. No licence was to be given to people who had not squared things with their communities, presumably because the government had no wish to promote a sense of grievance among the households that remained.[45]

Whether the legislation had much effect on the location of migrant families is doubtful. During the 1890s, most migrants chose to settle in the most fertile parts of Siberia, around Tobolsk and Akmolinsk. By the early twentieth century, complaints were already being made by local officials that these areas had become saturated. Perhaps this is one reason why the rate at which settlers returned to European Russia shot up in the period 1911–15 (see Table 3.4).

Settlement in Siberia, then, was the product of conditions in the agricultural provinces of European Russia, and of favourable economic opportunities – at least until around 1910 – in Siberia itself. The decline in the rate of settlement in the period 1901–5 was probably a unction of the impact of the Russo-Japanese War, which disrupted raffic on the railway, and of the 1905 Revolution. The revolution in he countryside undoubtedly convinced many peasants that they could best resolve their future by taking action against large landowners, rather than leaving their homes. After 1906 the upsurge reflects the boom in the Siberian economy and, perhaps, the repression in the areas where rural violence had been most acute.

c) Urbanization

Between 1867 and 1897 the urban population of European Russia virtually doubled, from an estimated 6.67 million to around 12.49 million. Over the next twenty years the urban population doubled again, to 25.84 million. Thus the urban population almost quadrupled over the half century before the Revolution, while the population of the country as a whole grew by 90 per cent. As a proportion of the total, the urban population increased from around 10 per cent in 1867 to 13 per cent in 1897. By 1916 Russian towns and cities accounted for 21 per cent of the total population.[46]

The rate of urbanization was very impressive. In the case of individual cities it produced spectacular results. The population of St. Petersburg, which in 1867 had an estimated 500,000 inhabitants, rose to 1.26 m. by 1897 and to 2.2 m. in 1914. The influx of refugees and new factory workers during the First World War pushed the total still higher, to around 2.4 m. The growth of Moscow, from 0.35 m. in 1867 to 1.04 m. in 1897, and 1.77 m. in 1914, was hardly less dramatic. In percentage terms, the growth of other major cities was greater still: for instance, the population of Riga, Kiev and Tiflis (the capital of Georgia) – all of them quite different in character and function – doubled between 1897 and 1914.

The growth of urban population in Russia was less a function of natural increase, as of high rates of in-migration. The fact that natural increase explains only a fraction of urban growth can be attributed to high rates of urban mortality. In this respect St. Petersburg stood out among Russian cities. During the 1850s the crude death rate in the capital exceeded 42 per thousand: only Kazan and Tula were distinguished by a higher rate. Officials ascribed this rate to the impact of a notoriously damp climate, to which new in–migrants from the countryside were believed to be especially vulnerable. However, as James Bater has shown, it was the character of the urban environment itself that was to blame. The rapid growth of the city population, as wave upon wave of peasant migrants entered St. Petersburg, led to severe overcrowding and insanitary living conditions. The eastern part of the city (the Vyborg side) experienced recurrent outbreaks of cholera and typhus, which the untreated water supply from the River Neva made inevitable. Nor did the situation improve by the end of the century. Improvements to the supply of fresh water and to sewage disposal failed to keep pace with the growth in demand. Although the crude mortality rate had fallen by 1914, the explanation is not to be found in improvements in age-specific mortality. Rather, the age structure of the city had changed; there were now relatively few infants and young children in the population of the capital, and more able-bodied inhabitants in their twenties and thirties.[47]

St. Petersburg, like most other cities in the Russian Empire, grew as a result of in-migration. The population of the capital city was put at 1.9 million in 1910, but only 17 per cent of the total had been born in the city itself. In the country as a whole, the 1897 Census revealed that more than half the total urban population comprised in-migrants. For the most part, new arrivals had found their way to the city from adjacent provinces (the one major exception was Baku, where Persian labourers made up a large proportion of the workforce in the oil industry). In Moscow, for example, the census of 1902 showed that more than a quarter of in-migrants – who made up three-quarters of the total city population – came from Moscow province, while the remainder came from the seven surrounding provinces. In St. Petersburg the situation was comparable. In 1910 (as, indeed, in 1869), the principal provinces of origin were those near the capital: Tver, Novgorod, Yaroslavl and St. Petersburg itself.[48]

The population of many Russian cities tended to be fluid, rather than settled. It has often been remarked that this transience reflected the propensity of peasants to migrate to the city on a temporary basis, before returning to their villages, either during the summer or after a prolonged absence (see section 3.4). But peasants were not the only transient group. Landed gentry escaped to their country houses during the summer months. The difference was that peasants had to return to their villages, whereas the gentry chose to leave the city when it suited them.[49]

The rapidity of urban growth compelled municipal authorities to assume responsibility for the development of an infrastructure, in the shape of water supply, street lighting, transport, schools, hospitals and so forth. Two factors largely determined the degree of success that the city fathers had in this respect. The first was financial, the second the quality of the urban administrative personnel.

Each municipal authority was empowered to levy taxes on the immovable property of the inhabitants. Some cities were able to obtain additional revenue from other sources. In Odessa, for example, the construction of basic amenities was facilitated by a tax levied on grain exports (which, however, yielded less and less revenue, as grain exports dwindled in the face of competition from rival ports on the Black Sea). Most cities also made a habit of borrowing at home or abroad. Finally, the local authorities sought to make a profit on the operation of municipal utilities, such as water supply and transport. Much of the initial capital cost of urban transport and street lighting was born by foreign enterprises (in particular, Belgian and German firms).[50]

The quality of services, however, frequently left much to be desired, and this failing can be laid at the door of the local officialdom. To be fair, the urban middle classes were perennially uncertain about the intentions of central government, which (in 1890) had eroded much of the autonomy that had been conceded to municipalities in 1870. This may go some way towards explaining the apathy among many officials and the small electorate in the towns. Perhaps, too, middle-class residents were perfectly content, provided that the services to their own property were adequate. So far as the poorer quarters of Russian cities were concerned, the level of amenities remained primitive right through to 1917.[51]

(d) Emigration

No statistics on emigration from tsarist Russia were ever compiled by the authorities, who did not officially recognize the right of an individual to leave the jurisdiction of the Tsar. Historians have to rely instead upon information about the numbers of Russian citizens who crossed at frontier posts each year, in possession of either a passport or short-term permit. The figures that are available, therefore, record the number of temporary travellers (tourists; businessmen; artists; and agricultural labourers who sought work in Prussia), as well as those who intended to settle abroad permanently. The two-way traffic assumed huge dimensions by the beginning of the twentieth century. Between 1909 and 1913, for instance, more than 8.2 million Russians left the country each year on average, while up to 7.9 million returned.[52]

The Russian authority on emigration, V. V. Obolensky (N. Osinsky), having made an adjustment to these figures, concluded that the net outflow from the Russian Empire between 1828 (when figures were first kept) and 1915 amounted to 4.51 million. Of this total, all but a few thousand left after 1860. Around one and a quarter million left between 1860 and 1889; 3.35 million emigrated between 1890 and 1915. As a result, Russia probably contributed about one-tenth of total emigration from Europe between c. 1820 and 1914. However, expressed in terms of the total population, the rate of emigration from Russia was much lower than it was in countries such as Ireland, Italy and Norway.[53]

To relate emigration to total population may convey a misleading impression. Russian emigrants were overwhelmingly concentrated among ethnic and religious minorities. Jews, for example, accounted for around two-fifths of total emigration between 1899 and 1913;

Poles made up a further third; and Lithuanians accounted for one-tenth. The impact of emigration upon the territories they left behind – primarily the Kingdom of Poland, Belorussia, South-West Russia and Lithuania – was far greater than the aggregate picture might suggest.

Sophisticated econometric models of the sort that have been applied to emigration from other countries are hardly needed to account for emigration from Russia (or for its dynamic), which was overwhelmingly in response to official persecution and daily harassment by Russians. The majority of Jews who left Russia were poor, and sought to improve their living standards in America or England. But this was less of a consideration, compared to their search for a more tolerant society. They were 'pushed' into emigration, as witness the increased departures of Jews from Russia in the aftermath of the dreadful pogroms in Kishinev (Bessarabia) in 1903, and throughout the country in 1905 and 1906. For Poles, too, emigration was a response to a generation of 'Russification' that followed the abortive rising of 1863. If poverty alone had been the issue, such people would have followed Russian peasants to Siberia; but, because poverty was so closely tied together with religious oppression, the only escape possible was overseas.[54]

3.3 The Differentiation of the Russian Peasantry

Alternative approaches to peasant society in general, and to its stratification in particular, have been central to debates about Russian economic development. The crucial difference between the liberal and marxist interpretations of rural society, on the one hand, and the populist interpretation on the other, emerged over the question of class formation. Broadly speaking, Russian populists maintained that the village community acted to forestall the expropriation of the Russian peasantry, since the commune ensured that no peasant need be deprived of his land and that no peasant could acquire land at the expense of another household of equivalent size. Liberal opinion regarded the commune with disdain: it tied peasants to their small plots and hindered the formation of private capitalist farms. However, for liberals, the death-knell had begun to sound for the commune by the end of the nineteenth century. Change was being forced upon the peasantry by the growth of rural population and the development of commercial farming. The tsarist government sealed the fate of the commune with the land reforms introduced in the wake of the 1905 Revolution. As a result of the reforms, the enterprising peasant could claim individual title to his allotment, enclose the land and employ wage labour from the ranks of the less enterprising. From a liberal point of view, therefore, the stratification of peasant society indicated social progress and the potential for economic growth. Russian marxists argued that the commune had begun to decompose, well before the land reforms of Stolypin. Indeed, the emphasis upon the commune was entirely misplaced. In Lenin's words, 'the whole process of the differentiation of the agricultural peasantry is one of real life evading these legal bounds'.[55] For marxist observers, rural class formation proceeded irrespective of the commune.

Upon what empirical basis did contemporaries rest their analyses of peasant society? Before 1870, debates about the trends in peasant society (debates that had been stimulated by the emancipation of the serfs) were conducted at the level of anecdote. Most writers simply asserted that the Russian peasantry constituted a broadly homogeneous and egalitarian community. Social and economic differences were thought to be of no significance. However, during the 1870s data became available about the internal organization of peasant households that cast doubt on this verdict.

These data were gathered and published by the *zemstva*, local authorities that the tsarist regime established in most rural areas in 1864. Initially, their efforts at data collection had a fiscal purpose, but they gradually assumed another character, as the *zemstva* statisticians – who were predominantly populist in their political sympathies – sought to uncover the nature of peasant society in post-reform Russia. By 1892 more than 120 districts had been covered, comprising around three million households in all. Dozens of surveys of individual districts were published before 1917.[56]

The results of *zemstva* enquiries were sometimes published in the form of budget studies. The statisticians surveyed in detail those households that they took to constitute a broadly representative sample, and asked questions about the household's access to land, livestock and non-family labour, if any. They itemized the components of peasant income and expenditure, in cash and in kind. Finally, they grouped the households according to a chosen indicator, usually allotment land or the number of horses owned. In this way, the investigators were able to depict the stratification of the peasantry in a given village at a given moment. By 1917 some 11,500 individual budgets had been compiled, from information provided by peasant households in different parts of the Empire.[57]

These budget studies depicted a society that appeared far removed from the conventional populist image of an egalitarian and homogeneous peasantry. One of the most well-known surveys, conducted in Voronezh province in 1887–96 by F. A. Shcherbina, indicated that the gross income of the poorest households (those that sowed no allotment land and those sowing less than five *dessyatiny*) amounted to no more than two-thirds of the per capita income of the wealthiest category. The net income of 'landless' households, again in per capita terms, came to just over one-tenth of the net income of the wealthiest, although the differential was less extreme in the case of those households that sowed up to five *dessyatiny*. Furthermore, the wealthiest households (those with more than 25 *dessyatiny*) were able to set aside a much higher proportion of their income for expenditure on the farm, rather than on the personal needs of family members. At the same time, however, Shcherbina argued that wage labour played little part in the peasant economy of Voronezh: more than eight out of ten households worked their plots with family labour alone. This allowed him to conclude that the general situation among the peasantry was 'probably no different from what it had been twenty, fifty or a hundred years ago'.[58] In other words, there was no reason to expect Russian peasantry to generate class divisions.

Other populist writers had arrived at a similar conclusion. S. M. Stepniak, the radical ethnographer and publicist, wrote in 1888 that inequalities in peasant society simply revealed the regular operation of the traditional commune, and not its imminent demise. The differential allocation of land and of other assets reflected demographic factors; that is, larger households were entitled to a larger share of village resources. According to Stepniak, the poor peasant had every opportunity to improve his status in the village, if and when his family grew in size: 'In the next generation, the chance of birth and death might make him *in his turn* a "rich" man'.[59]

The marxist response was to challenge the assumptions that underlay the presentation of data in the budget studies. In *The Development of Capitalism in Russia*, Lenin pointed out that the data grouped households according to the distribution of allotment land. But allotment land did not constitute the sum total of land at the disposal of the peasantry. Peasants rented or purchased land from private landowners. Lenin showed that a truly scientific method should distinguish between households according to real economic indices, such as total sown area or livestock. Another common pitfall in the *zemstva* data was the tendency to lump together all non-agricultural earnings, without taking into account the completely different forms: a distinction had to be made, for example, between earnings that represented a profit on commercial enterprise, and wages paid to peasant labourers. The populists registered both as income from 'trades' (*promysly*), thereby concealing the real social relations among the peasantry. Summing up, Lenin reminded his readers that any one variable or indicator, such as sown area, had to be related to others: 'To view intelligently the differentiation of the peasantry, one must take the picture as a whole: the renting of land, the purchase of land, machines, outside employments, the growth of commercial agriculture, and wage-labour'.[60]

According to Lenin, the differentiation of the peasantry found expression in the differential access of peasants to the means of production, and in the growth of wage labour. In theory and in practice, the two phenomena were inseparable: the progressive inability of the bulk of the peasantry to support themselves from their allotments drove them to seek paid employment. Lenin emphasized that the process of differentiation was not a straightforward one. However, it was not constrained (as the populists imagined) by the operation of the land commune. Rather, differentiation was hindered by the persistence of semi-feudal relations, which formally attached the smallholding peasantry to their allotments. The two main conditions that allowed this to happen in post-reform Russia were, first, the prevalence of labour-service in agriculture and, second, the widespread recourse by peasants to village moneylenders.

Under serfdom, peasants had been allocated a plot of land by the lord, in return for which they were obliged to perform labour-service (*barshchina*), or to pay a quitrent. The abolition of serfdom, by definition, abolished these feudal obligations. But landlords, especially in the central black-earth provinces (which were the traditional grain-producing region), were eager to retain a supply of labour for their estates. The terms of the emancipation settlement reflected that fact. They afforded landlords the scope to reduce the size of allotment land to which peasants were entitled, by twenty per cent or more in the black-earth region. Furthermore, in practice the emancipation settlement frequently ensured that the lands allocated to the peasantry were awkwardly shaped and positioned. This was deliberately devised by landowners, to encourage peasants to seek access to the privately owned land that was needed in order to make tillage more convenient. Finally, emancipation tended to restrict peasant access to non-arable resources, such as pasture, forests and rivers, resources which they had customarily been entitled to use.[61]

The implication of these measures was that peasants were compelled to seek permission to work this private land, or to obtain access to other resources. Permission was granted, on condition that the peasant supplied his own implements to cultivate the demesne lands. Where peasants 'trespassed' on the demesne, the lord typically fined them, extracting payment in labour-service. In addition, peasants who borrowed from the lord (perhaps to buy grain in order to tide them over the winter and spring) found that they obtained credit, in return for agreeing to provide the lord with labour on the estate during the following summer. The terms, however, were onerous: peasants contracted at winter hiring rates, which were less generous than the summer rates, when demand for labour was greatest. The lords thus extracted a form of *barshchina* from their former serfs. Contemporaries termed the practice *otrabotka*.[62]

The second factor that operated to moderate the process of differentiation was the provision of credit within the village. The majority of peasants were vulnerable to periodic harvest failures, and also needed to borrow in order to pay taxes or to replace livestock and other assets. In these circumstances, peasants had recourse to credit from village moneylenders (or, as noted above, from landlords). In some cases, the rate of interest charged by usurers could be very high, perhaps in excess of 40 per cent. But there are also instances of no money interest being charged on the loan. In whichever case, the object of the moneylender was not so much to recover the principal, at whatever rate was nominally charged, but rather to bind the peasant to the land. By so doing, the moneylender could extract labour-service from the debtor. A default on the debt only served to bind the peasant further to the creditor, and thus to the land.[63]

These semi-feudal relations declined during the later nineteenth century, under the impact of the commercialization of agriculture. So far as usury was concerned, Lenin argued that village moneylenders stood to gain more from transactions in agricultural production than they did from the provision of petty credit. One might add that their monopoly position was also undermined after 1900 by more institutionalized sources of agricultural credit. The incidence of *otrabotka* declined, because landlords preferred to lease land to peasants in exchange for a money rent, or to hire labourers to work on their estates (this was more common in the south and south-east). In addition, where peasants began to lose their land to rich peasants, they no longer needed to submit themselves to labour-service in order to make ends meet. Tied to the land no longer, poor peasants could sell their labour in whichever market offered the most favourable terms.[64]

The growth of commodity production did not proceed at a uniform pace throughout Russia. As will be seen in the next chapter, commercialization was less pronounced in the Central Black Earth, the Mid-Volga and Little Russia, than in the surrounding regions. Even so, the differentiation of the peasantry was unmistakable. In these traditional grain-producing provinces, where generally abject living standards prevailed, rich peasants marketed their grain surpluses under more favourable conditions than their middling neighbours. Whereas the latter had to sell grain immediately after the harvest, in order to meet their tax obligations in cash, the rich were able to draw upon existing reserves of cash and to delay grain sales until the spring, when seasonal prices were at a peak. Here, rich households sought additional land to rent or buy; here, the differentiation of the peasantry with respect to livestock and other complementary assets stood out sharply.[65]

Differentiation was also a characteristic of other regions: the flax-growing province of Smolensk; the dairy-farming provinces in the Baltic and North-West; Vladimir, Moscow and Smolensk, where the wealthier farmers specialized in oats cultivation; and the southern provinces of New Russia, where extensive wheat and barley cultivation prevailed. In each instance, peasant capitalists acquired close control over the means of production: not just land, but horses, cattle, dairy equipment and so forth. The one exception to this process of differentiation appears to have been Siberia, where land was abundant, where fiscal and other pressures on peasants were relatively modest, and where landless migrants could acquire a plot of land. But even here, the situation had begun to change by 1910, with the growth of settlement in Tomsk and Tobolsk and the expansion in commercial agriculture.[66]

The commercialization of Russian peasant agriculture did not imply instant profits and the sudden decimation of the ranks of middle peasant households. Profits for kulak farmers during the 1880s and 1890s were harder to come by than in the preceding and successive decades, because of the slump in cereal prices; as we shall see, this encouraged peasant farmers to diversify. The second phenomenon that has to be taken into account was the pressure on land (especially in the central provinces of European Russia) and the consequential increase in rentals. The increase in the cost of renting land also ate into profits in peasant agriculture, although this was offset to some extent by the growth in the cereal yields.[67]

The tendency for middle peasant households to be squeezed economically was moderated by three developments during the late nineteenth century. In the first place, the increase in rentals encouraged poor peasants to lease their allotment land to middle – not just to rich – households. The poor peasant was thereby freed of his obligation to settle his share of the village community's tax and redemption bills. This strategy allowed him to look for paid employment. But while it further encouraged the creation of a rural proletariat, it also strengthened the position of middle peasant households, as in provinces such as Voronezh and Orel, where villagers termed the new tenants *uprav-shchiki* (stewards). Secondly, even some wealthy peasants, faced with pressure on agricultural profits during the 1880s, leased land to middle peasants. This allowed the rich to go on *otkhod*, in search of more remunerative activity; crucially, it also enabled them to return to the village when farming prospects improved, and to invest their savings in the farm. There is evidence of this in Tula and Voronezh. Finally, middle peasants were able to obtain financial assistance after 1882 from the newly established Peasants' Land Bank. Generally speaking, the rich peasant had less recourse to the Bank, being able to purchase land outright.[68]

Budget studies testify to the existence of income inequalities, corre-

Table 3.5

The incomes of peasant households in Voronezh, 1887–1896

	Horses owned:						
	Nil	1	2	3	4	5 or more	Total
1. Number of households	34	59	47	38	14	38	230
2. Population	148	317	384	441	155	461	1,906
3. Mean household size	4.35	5.37	8.17	11.60	11.07	12.10	8.31
4. Gross income from agriculture (rubles)	60.3	151.6	328.7	604.6	671.5	793.9	386.8
Arable (%)	58	62	71	70	73	63	67
Dairy/poultry (%)	31	35	27	27	26	36	31
Other (inc. rents) (%)	11	3	2	3	1	1	2
5. Other income (rubles)	86.0	57.6	128.4	104.2	156.6	221.6	117.1
6. Total gross income (4 + 5)	146.3	209.2	457.1	708.8	828.1	1,015.5	503.9
7. Percentage received in cash (%)	69	49	46	36	40	46	44
8. Gross income per head (6 ÷ 3) (rubles)	33.6	39.0	55.9	61.0	74.8	86.4	60.6

Source: A. M. Anfimov, *Ekonomicheskoe polozhenie i klassovaya borba krestyan Evropeiskoi Rossii, 1881–1904*, Nauka, 1984, p. 171.

ponding to the inequality in the distribution of assets, such as land and livestock. For example, in Voronezh (where some of the most detailed studies were conducted, by Shcherbina) per capita income from all sources ranged from 34 rubles in the poorest category to over 86 rubles in the top category (see Table 3.5, row 8). A similar differential was observed in a study of 1,300 households in Kaluga province in 1896. These inequalities in income per head are important to note, because many populist observers insisted that economic differences between peasant households were a function solely of differences in family size; if this were true, one would expect per capita differentials in income to be minor or non-existent.

These data also capture the differential monetization of the peasant economy in an important black-earth province. Among all households, just over half the average household income was derived in kind (row 7). But among the poorest households – those without horses – around 70% of gross income comprised cash receipts. This reflected the prevalence of wage labour among the poor peasantry. Middle peasant households (those with two to four horses) derived a greater proportion of their income in kind. The money income of the richest farmers was not significantly greater, as a proportion of total income, than among middle households, but the source of money income did differ. Rich farmers were more likely to diversify into dairy farming, and to obtain income from manufacturing enterprises and trade. Poorer families relied for part of their subsistence upon the modest product of their plots (and upon poultry); their cash receipts derived from leasing land and from *otkhod*.[69]

The budget studies shed light on patterns of peasant household expenditure (Table 3.6). The Voronezh study indicated glaring inequalities in household and in per capita outlays. Among the three bottom categories, food consumption per head (row 1 in Table 3.6, divided by row 3 in Table 3.5) amounted to between 15 and 17 rubles. In the next three categories, food consumption was worth 22–24 rubles. More striking still were inequalities in the consumption of non-foodstuffs. Here, what needs emphasis is the greater proportionate reliance of poor households on the purchase of commodities. The implications of this were far-reaching: it is likely that poor households had to purchase goods, such as sugar, candles and kerosene, that carried high rates of indirect taxation. Rich households, by contrast, probably entered the market as consumers of clothing and other goods, which were not taxed. Middle and rich peasant families were able to substitute for consumer 'necessities' that were liable to tax. The hypothesis is, therefore, that poor peasants were most likely to have borne the brunt of indirect taxation in the countryside.

The final observation that may be made is that rich peasant house-

Table 3.6

Expenditure of peasant households in Voronezh, 1887–1896

		Horses owned:					
Outlay per household (rubles)	Nil	1	2	3	4	5 or more	Total
1. Food	73.7	81.3	127.0	253.0	258.1	291.8	167.0
% cash	55	27	28	16	15	17	21
2. Other personal consumption	44.7	41.8	87.6	128.2	145.2	189.2	96.6
% Cash	89	76	74	65	76	64	70
3. Farm expenditures	30.1	88.2	175.5	319.4	380.6	517.7	224.4
% cash	70	47	47	41	42	50	47
4. Direct taxes and rent	9.4	15.9	26.2	34.0	35.2	44.1	25.9
5. Total outlays	157.9	227.2	448.3	734.6	819.1	1,043.2	513.9
% cash	70	49	46	39	45	46	46

Source: as for Table 3.5.

holds spent proportionately more on the maintenance and expansion of the farm. As with all households, part of this 'farm expenditure' represented the supply of fodder to the livestock. But in the case of wealthy peasants, the outlays also comprised the investment in fixed capital, such as barns and agricultural equipment.[70]

Lenin did not argue that the Russian peasantry were being expropriated in a decisive and unambiguous manner. 'Differentiation' was not synonymous with expropriation. In Lenin's words, 'our literature contains too stereotyped an understanding of the theoretical proposition that capitalism requires the free, landless labourer. This is quite correct as indicating the main trend, but capitalism penetrates into agriculture particularly slowly and in extremely diverse ways.' In other words, peasants did not immediately become wage labourers. They retained, however, only nominal possession of a plot of land, and had no real economic independence. Eventually, they would lose even the nominal access to land. Rich peasants, who hired the labour of their neighbours, became producers of commodities. It is impossible to agree with the currently fashionable view that the peasantry constitutes 'an intrinsically anti-surplus system'. We shall return to commodity production by peasants in the following chapter.[71]

The leninist interpretation of agrarian class formation did not pass unchallenged in the early years of the twentieth century. The critique to which it was subjected has been resurrected more recently, notably by Teodor Shanin. Before concluding this section, we shall explore this so-called 'neo-populist' critique.

During the late nineteenth century, the hypotheses about the stratification in peasant society could be tested only against statistical evidence that was static in character. Each survey produced a snapshot of the distribution among households of land and other variables at a given point in time. The surveys did not provide for the study of socio-economic mobility of all households in a particular village or district over time. Such an approach was open to the charge that it juxtaposed evidence from different areas at different times, and did not permit systematic comparison between households from the same original sample over time. An alternative and arguably superior methodology would analyse the fortunes of all households in a given village.

This approach required a different effort at data collection. During the 1920s these 'dynamic studies', as they were known, became more systematic, but before the Revolution the early attempts were rare and crude. None the less, the basic principle behind dynamic studies was the same. To take a hypothetical case: assume that a survey has been made of the distribution of assets among households in a given district in a given year (t). Several years later, say $(t + 10)$, the picture will have changed. Some of the original households will have disappeared from the sample, either because their members have died or migrated, or because the households have split into new units or merged with others. In each case, these households have lost their original integrity. Russian rural sociologists termed these 'substantive changes' (*organicheskie izmeneniya*).[72] At the same time, a number of the original households will remain intact. Of this group, some may retain their original economic position, defined according to the relevant variable, such as sown area. But others may have experienced either upward or downward mobility.

A concrete example of the dyamics of mobility was provided by P. Rumyantsev in 1906. Rumyantsev obtained data on 13,900 households that existed in Vyazma district of Smolensk province in 1884. Of this original number, only 9,300 could still be identified in 1900. Over 2,000 households had emigrated, 660 had become extinct, and 2,000 could not be traced. Of the residue, that is those households which had undergone no 'substantive change', around half had experienced a change in economic position, as shown in Table 3.7.

Table 3.7

Socio-economic mobility among peasant households in Vyazma district, Smolensk province, 1884–1900

Sown area (dess.)	Number of households*	Percentages of original households which in 1900 sowed:					Percentage which changed stratum
		Nil	<3	3–9 dessyatiny		>9	
Nil	1,329	49.0	26.3	23.6	1.1	100	51
<3	2,249	10.7	39.7	48.3	1.3	100	60
3–9	5,238	4.1	19.6	68.7	7.6	100	31
>9	418	3.2	10.6	65.3	20.9	100	79
Total	9,294						45

* Number of households still intact and traceable in 1900.
Source: P. Rumyantsev, 'K voprosu ob evolyutsii russkogo krestyanstva' cited in T. Shanin, *The Awkward Class*, O.U.P., 1972, p. 75.

Thus, within the 'poor' category in 1884, 50 per cent had undergone upward mobility in terms of land sown. Correspondingly, of the original rich households, 80 per cent had moved downwards in economic terms. The 'middle' peasant category, sowing between three and nine *dessyatiny*, appear to have been more stable in percentage terms.[73]

What explanation could be advanced for this state of affairs, which seems to overturn previous arguments about the *cumulative* differentiation of the Russian peasantry? To begin with, we have to remember that Rumyantsev already discounted households which had undergone substantive change. They, too, must be taken into account in understanding peasant society. Households that disappeared because of the migration of their members tended to be located among the poorer strata. Their lack of resources compelled them to seek work outside the village. Shanin prefers to dwell upon the 'specific' features of peasant society, which influenced young men and women to migrate in search of 'prestige' and 'independence'. This implies that the propensity to migrate was a function of age, rather than of income, and overlooks the possibility that the motivation for migration among rich and poor households would have been quite different.

The other major substantive change occurred when a household fragmented into new units, and became by definition 'poorer' in terms of land sown. This tendency was observed most among the upper stratum, where the needs of the young adult males for 'independence' were accommodated, by allowing them to establish new households of their own. According to Shanin, 'the peculiarities of peasant social structure' again have to be taken into account, because (he says) there were no 'rational' economic grounds on which peasant farmers would agree to the fragmentation of their property. Since Shanin, like other 'neo-populist' observers before him, has already ruled out the notion of peasants as entrepreneurs, this emphasis upon cultural specificity is not surprising; we shall comment on it shortly.[74]

Turning to those households that had not experienced any substantive change (that is, those indicated in Table 3.7), Shanin points out that the observed pattern of 'multi-directional mobility' cannot be accounted for wholly by the operation of the commune. In other words, mobility was not attributable to the recurrent redistribution of communal land among peasant households, in accordance with family size. This is because such mobility also characterized those parts of Russia where the commune was weak (as in Belorussia), as well as those where it was strong. In addition, Shanin argues that the redistribution of peasant household assets extended also to property that did not come under communal control, such as privately owned plots.[75]

Chayanov directed attention to the life-cycle of the peasant household, in order to account for this mobility. He noted that the household unit initially comprised a young couple, but developed a mature form, eventually comprising parents and their young adult offspring. According to his interpretation, the growing household needed to acquire additional resources in order to meet its changing subsistence target. The commune was only one of several devices whereby peasants could relate land holdings to family size: 'In another agrarian regime, less flexible than that of the repartitional commune, the influence of the biological factor of family development on the size of land for use would not stand out so prominently'. But a land market would also serve to adjust allotments to changing family size. Shanin observes that 'the "biological" explanation . . . has remained the only consistent explanation available for the "residual component" to be found emerging from the Russian dynamic studies'.[76]

The 'substantive changes' introduced a statistical levelling effect in Russian peasant society. Poor and wealthy households alike tended to disappear from the village population, thereby automatically raising the profile of the middle stratum. Of the households that remained intact, the rich appeared prone to downward shifts in socio-economic position and the poor appeared to move up the scale, in terms of land held. From these observations, Shanin has drawn controversial conclusions about the 'solidarity', 'internal cohesiveness' and 'loyalty' of peasants. In sum, the marxist emphasis upon the generation of class conflict within peasant society is found to be entirely misplaced.[77]

The 'neo-populist' approach raises serious conceptual and empirical difficulties. For example, the evidence presented in the form of dynamic studies may be interpreted in terms other than the specifically 'peasant' culture and tradition favoured by Chayanov and Shanin. There may have been economic conditions under which it was economically advantageous for wealthy households to partition their holdings. At a time of progressive commercialization in agriculture – as in late-nineteenth-century Russia – rich households might diversify into intensive forms of agriculture and operate on a smaller plot of land. In western Europe, the decline in the size of holdings did not automatically entail a loss of income and wealth, and small-scale units multiplied along with the growth in dairy farming, industrial crops and market gardening. In some parts of Russia, this diversification also occurred.

Dynamic younger elements in peasant households may have sought to take advantage of the new possibilities that opened up. To escape the patriarchal authority that acted as a constraint upon the younger generation, they would demand at least the partial division of the holding. Similarly, in such circumstances, the young adult farmers might wish to escape the obligation to contribute disproportionately to the household budget. If this interpretation is correct, the partitioning process expressed the failure of well-established households to contain the pressure of young entrepreneurial elements, and is consistent with the growth of capitalist relations at the level of the Russian village. The partition of land need not be a manifestation of a deep-seated peasant culture.[78]

Thus a downward shift in terms of land sown – which is essentially what is indicated in Table 3.7 – was not necessarily synonymous with a loss of wealth and status. Furthermore, the 'neo-populist' interpretation affords no insight into the means whereby the poor and, supposedly, upwardly mobile households are able to acquire the complementary assets, such as livestock and implements needed to work the additional land they acquire. It seems much more reasonable to assume that these poor households had nominally acquired more land, but that they leased it to wealthier farmers who had the equipment with which to farm it.[79] Finally, the distinction between households according to sown area overlooks the crucial economic difference in peasant society, between households that hired and those that sold labour. It is significant that the spread of hired labour is systematically ignored in *The Awkward Class*.

The problem with the neo-populist interpretation, as with its populist forerunner, is the failure to observe rural social relations in their entirety. The advantage of the liberal approach is that it recognized at least one obvious context within which the Russian peasantry managed their affairs, namely the growth in population and the fragmentation of holdings. The marxist interpretation also pays close attention to context, in the form of relations between peasants and gentry, and relations between rich, middle and poor peasants. Marxist analysis takes note of the development of commodity production and the corresponding growth of wage labour.

The neo-populist would doubtless retort that these remarks betray a fundamental misreading of the evidence of peasant mentality and economy. In addition, the historical record – of peasant protest in 1905, 1917–18 and 1929–30 – suggests a basic unity and solidarity in peasant society. For Shanin, this unity is underpinned by the multi-directional mobility of peasant households. But this is an untenable position. In the first place, the neo-populist argument cannot account for the growth of wage labour and the expropriation of peasant households. In the second place, the fact that peasants may have been united during the Revolution or in opposition to collectivization would not in itself (even if true) negate the existence of class relations and class division. After all, British society was united in 1939–45 in a struggle against Fascism, but no one seriously suggests that this demonstrates an absence of class division!

3.4 The Labour Market

The development of the labour market in tsarist Russia is not easy to unravel. The main difficulties arise from the variety of occupations and the weakness of the employment statistics. If factory industry alone were at issue, matters would be considerably simplified. However, some account must also be taken of wage labour in non-factory industry, and in mining, transport, construction and services. Nor, finally, can wage labour in agriculture be ignored. In this section, the data on the workforce will be presented first of all; there then follows a more extended elaboration of the issues connected with the tsarist labour market.

There are two basic methods of estimating the dimensions of the pre-revolutionary Russian labour force, neither of which is entirely satisfactory. The first is to rely upon statistics collected by employers or by tsarist officials. Such information was normally limited in coverage, and was never collected routinely until 1900, and even then for part of the manufacturing sector only. More comprehensive evidence about occupational distribution is available in the Census of 1897. The second method is to approach the problem from the point of labour supply, rather than the point of employment. Zemstvo statisticians uncovered a mass of data about non-agricultural employment undertaken by the peasantry. The scale of this off-farm employment is also captured in the statistics of internal passports, issued on behalf of the village communities. The disadvantage with this approach is that such data shed no light upon wage labour performed by people who had no link with the land.

The 1897 Census required all inhabitants to state their primary occupation and other sources of income. The published returns gave a total of just over 9 million for the number of wage-earners in the Empire. Of this total, 3.2 million were engaged in mining, manufacturing, transport, trade and construction. Agricultural labourers numbered some 2.7 million. Domestic servants accounted for 1.6 million, followed by 'day labourers and unskilled', of whom there were 1.1 million. Other 'servants' (*prisluga*), including white-collar workers, numbered half a million.[80]

The Census suffers from a number of deficiencies. In particular the returns underestimated the prevalence of wage labour, because peasants concealed the extent of their non-agricultural earnings. During the 1890s and 1900s, zemstvo studies suggested that, on average, two workers per household contributed a non-agricultural income to the peasant budget. Yet the census returns indicated that only one farm in fifteen generated these 'supplementary' earnings. The fact that the Census took place in January also contributed to a likely underestimate of the workforce in construction and in agriculture.[81]

The most substantial contribution to the statistical study of trends in wage labour has been made by A. G. Rashin. His estimates of the size of the labour force in 1860 and 1913 are reproduced in Table 3.8. Broadly speaking, one can have most confidence in the estimate for transport employment in 1913, because so much of the railway network came under state supervision. In the private sector the data are very variable. Highly differentiated sectors, such as 'industry' (or even 'agriculture'), are more difficult to survey. So far as agricultural employment is concerned, Rashin made an allowance for wage labour in peasant agriculture, as well as for the labour force on large estates. But the figures are no more than informed guesses. The same is true of the estimate for employment in handicrafts and in construction.[82]

Table 3.8

The sectoral distribution of wage labour in the Russian Empire, 1860 and 1913 (millions)

Category	1860	1913
1. Mining and manufacturing	1.60	6.10
(a) Factories, mines	0.80	3.10
(b) Cottage industry and urban crafts	0.80	3.00
2. Construction	0.35	1.50
3. Transport and Communication	0.51	1.41
(a) Railways (incl. clerical staff)	0.01	0.82
(b) Waterways	0.50	0.50
(c) Post, Telegraph, Telephone	–	0.09
4. Other non-agricultural employment	0.80	4.07
(a) Unskilled day labourers	n.a.	1.10
(b) White-collar staff	n.a.	0.55
(c) Trade, Tourism	n.a.	0.87
(d) Domestic servants	n.a.	1.55
5. Agricultural labourers	0.70	4.50
Total	3.96	17.58

Source: A. G. Rashin, *Formirovanie rabochego klassa Rossii*, Sotseklit, 1958, pp. 117, 141, 152, 172.

The situation is less bleak with regard to factory industry. By 1900, regular assessments of industrial employment were being carried out by the factory inspectorate. However, the inspectors were not responsible for all factories: they did not cover state works and enterprises that produced excisable goods (such as spirits, sugar, matches and tobacco). Furthermore, the definition of a factory normally excluded units in which fewer than twenty workers were employed, although this definition was not adhered to systematically. Rashin arrived at a figure of 3.10 million workers in factories and mines in 1913, including 2.28 million in factories subject to the inspectorate and 0.65 million in extractive industry.[83].

Overall, the number of wage-earners more than quadrupled between 1860 and 1913. The workforce in agriculture increased at a faster rate than the numbers engaged in industry, in transport and in construction. This phenomenon reflects the rapid commercialization of agriculture in the post-reform period. Within transport, the number of workers on the railways, not surprisingly, registered the most dramatic increase.

The trends in employment within factory industry and mining can be established reasonably clearly. The number of factory workers and miners grew from 800,000 in 1860 to an average of 950,000 during the 1870s. As industrialization gathered momentum during the 1880s the total rose to just under 1.65 million. In 1900, the workforce stood at around 1.85 million. Over the next ten years, a further half million workers were added to this total. During the pre-war industrial boom as many as 700,000 may have been added. The First World War swelled the workforce by a further half million. By 1917, employment in Russian factories and mines stood at around 3.6 million.[84]

As Table 3.8 indicates, there were already 4 million wage labourers in Russia on the eve of peasant emancipation, the majority of whom were employed outside agriculture. Two main sources of recruitment may be identified. In 1721 Peter the Great sought to overcome a shortage of labour in industry, by attaching groups of peasants to specific enterprises, especially in the Urals metallurgical industry. These 'possessional workers' belonged to the factory, and could not be discharged by the management. Their children became possessional workers in turn.[85]

The second source of non-agricultural labour consisted of serfs who were given permission by their owners to leave the demesne. From the middle of the eighteenth century until the middle of the nineteenth a sustained increase took place in the number of serfs who obtained outside employment. By 1800, these *otkhodniki* (literally, those who 'went away') outnumbered possessional workers in industry. They also predominated in other sectors of the economy, such as transport. Some of these *otkhodniki* eventually became employers, but the majority either worked on their own account or received a wage. Part of their income had to be handed to the lord, who could recall his serfs from their place of work at any time. In practice, the lord probably exercised his powers infrequently, since he derived a regular money income from this source, which he did not wish to jeopardize. But this non-economic power that the lords held over the *otkhodniki* makes it impossible to speak of a capitalist labour market. The enforced attachment of possessional workers to a given enterprise confirms the point.

The tsarist government believed that these arrangements combined the availability of workers for employment in industry or trade with the impossibility of a permanent proletariat in Russia. The possessional workers were given a plot of land on which to support themselves; if work were not available, they could fall back on these allotments. Similarly, the peasant *otkhodniki* would not be thrown on to the streets, to become a potential social threat, but could return to the security of the manor. This was the view put forward by Finance Minister Kankrin in 1844. He went on to say that the servile status of many Russian workers also benefited employers, since 'our factory class does not combine for the purpose of extorting pay rises'.[86]

The emancipation of the serfs called into question the existing arrangements for the supply of labour, since it abolished the right of the nobility to extract feudal obligations from their peasants. But it should not be thought that the decree of 1861 automatically created a modern capitalist labour market, in which workers were mobile and able to sell their labour to the highest bidder. Non-economic compulsion still survived, for at least a generation. In the first place, many former serfs were compelled to perform labour-service on the demesne, either because they had been fined for 'trespass' on the lord's estate or because only in this way could they obtain legal access to much-needed manorial land. This 'labour-rent' (*otrabotka*) was discussed in the previous section. Secondly, possessional workers, although in principle emancipated, were in practice often compelled to stay on. This was the only way in which they could retain their modest allotments, which belonged to the factory. A third source of compulsion in post-reform Russia involved the use of soldiers in construction, agriculture and other activities. In the early nineteenth century, peasants who were conscripted into the tsarist army had to serve for 25 years. By 1874, after the reforms undertaken by War Minister Miliutin, the length of service had been reduced to six years. Tsarist soldiers, like their modern Soviet counterparts, constituted an important labour force in their own right. They worked in order to support themselves, because the army was something of a natural economy; the skills they had acquired in the village were put to use in looking after horses or producing uniforms and footwear. But soldiers also supplemented the available pool of wage labour, by helping to build railways and canals and harvesting crops in the regions where they were billeted.[87]

The main reason why a modern labour market seemed to be delayed in post-reform Russia had to do with the continued attachment that many workers retained to peasant farming. This issue is of the utmost importance. Populists pointed to the retention by factory and other workers of a link with the land, and concluded that a Russian proletariat did not exist. The populist writer N. A. Kablukov encapsulated the issue neatly, when he wrote that 'in the West, work in the factory is the sole means of livelihood for the worker, whereas in our country, with relatively few exceptions, the worker regards work in the factory as a subsidiary occupation; he is more attached to the land'. The sentiments echo those expressed by Kankrin, writing fifty years earlier. The difference was that Kablukov believed that peasants chose to retain a link with agriculture, whereas under serfdom they had been compelled to remain attached to the land.[88]

What was at stake, of course, was not just the existence of a Russian proletariat, but – ultimately – the legitimacy of a Revolution that was carried out in the name of the working class. Liberal observers, no less than populists, found it convenient to emphasize the rural ties of industrial workers, in order to question the basis for the Bolshevik Revolution in 1917. The emphasis is clearly present in the work of most non-Soviet historians who have written about the working class in tsarist Russia. Broadly speaking, a distinction may be made between historians, such as Theodore von Laue, who dwell upon the emotional attachments that workers had to the land, and those, such as Gerschenkron, who stress the institutional obstacles to the formation of a permanent proletariat.[89]

The populist emphasis upon the village as a source of emotional and even economic security to the peasant worker is difficult to sustain. For poor peasants, in particular, driven from their villages by population pressure, lack of alternative employment opportunities locally and the threat of complete destitution, the 'attraction' of the village was hardly very powerful. But populist observers were able to overlook this fact, because they concentrated their attention upon the 'average' peasant, whose motivation and prospects were quite different.

Gerschenkron argued that the mobility of the peasant population was severely constrained by the operation of the land commune. The commune was given the power after 1861 to issue internal passports, which all peasants required if they wished to travel beyond the locality. According to Gerschenkron, the commune issued passports reluctantly, especially for long-term residence 'abroad', because the loss of an adult member of the community represented the loss of a tax-paying 'soul', whose activities outside the village were difficult to monitor. Thus, migrant peasants were eventually reabsorbed into the village, whether they liked it or not.

Gerschenkron's argument should not obscure the dimensions of migration within Russia, which has already been discussed in broad terms. Here, attention will focus upon migration of peasants in search of paid employment. The main source of information is the statistics of passports issued to peasants. The statistics do not reveal accurately the number of individuals who left their villages each year; this is because some peasants may have taken out more than one passport in a given year, and because some families may have travelled on one passport. Nevertheless, the data reveal a large and growing volume of *otkhod* from villages during the period 1860–1913. An average of 1.29m. passports were issued between 1860 and 1870, while in the next decade the figure leaped to 3.69m. The rate of increase slowed down during the 1880s (4.94 m.), but during the 1890s the average number of passports climbed to 6.95 m. Between 1901 and 1910 around 8.87 m. were issued annually. At the beginning of the twentieth century a small cluster of provinces in the Central Industrial Region – Moscow, Tver, Kaluga and Vladimir – contributed disproportionately to the total. Some central black-earth provinces, such as Ryazan, Tula and Tambov, also accounted for a large number of passports. As we shall see, the destination of migrants was not the same in each case.[90]

The evidence in support of the proposition that the Russian proletariat had not severed its connection with peasant agriculture is least ambiguous with regard to the agricultural labour market. Each year, tens of thousands of peasants from the central black-earth provinces and from Kiev and Saratov made the journey to the large gentry estates in the south and south-east. In 1900, according to Maslov, as many as a million men, women and children poured into Kherson, Tauride, Ekaterinoslav, Don and the North Caucasus. Here, as agricultural production expanded rapidly in the half century after 1860, the demand for labour far outstripped local sources of supply. The demand was particularly acute at harvest time, because the dry summers in the southern steppe provinces threatened to scorch the crops on the stalk. Most of the migrant labour returned to their homes after the harvest; only in exceptional circumstances did estate-owners keep workers on.[91]

Migrant agricultural labourers came predominantly from the poor peasantry, driven from the Central Black Earth Region by a shortage of land and lack of alternative employment opportunities. In order to finance their journey, they sold what assets they had, pawned their goods, 'mortgaged' their allotment (if any), or borrowed at exorbitant rates of interest. A third of those who registered at one of the hiring markets in Samara in 1898 and 1899 had come on foot, mostly from adjacent provinces; another third travelled by cart; the remainder came by steamboat, railway or some combination of the two. The average journey time was ten days. Some migrants had spent up to three months on the road.

The evidence that accumulated in the local liberal press testified to the high degree of degradation and exploitation suffered by these migrant workers. In some cases, they had been attracted to agricultural work in south Russia in an unscrupulous manner; estate owners would send agents into nearby provinces, in order to determine which peasants were in debt. The agent would then agree to settle the debt, in return for obtaining the peasant's agreement to work on the distant estate, at a wage well below that offered at the hiring fair. When the labourers arrived, they typically worked up to 16 or 17 hours a day, sleeping with the cattle by night. Disease and industrial injury were both prevalent. These workers can hardly have enjoyed either their journey or their work. When they returned to their place of origin, however, it was necessity, not 'security' or 'comfort' that drove them back.[92]

Conditions did improve somewhat towards the end of the nineteenth century. Landowners complained that they now had to compete for this pool of labour with factory owners in south Russia and in the north. Any improvement in living standards was almost entirely a consequence of these changes in the tsarist labour market, rather than a result of government intervention to improve the lot of agricultural labourers. If anything, the government did its best to perpetuate the misery of migrant labourers. Legislation, introduced in 1886, confirmed that workers could be dismissed for all manner of 'offences', but that the behaviour of the employer did not constitute sufficient grounds for leaving the estate before the contract had expired. The main aim appears to have been to satisfy the wishes of landowners for a stable workforce.[93]

The seasonality of work in non-agricultural sectors of the economy was much less marked. In manufacturing industry, by the end of the nineteenth century, enterprises tended to operate continuously, rather than to cease operations during the summer months. This tendency was established without question in a survey of factory workers, conducted by Dementiev in 1893. Dementiev observed that seven out of ten factory workers remained at work throughout the year. Not surprisingly, the percentage was greatest where entrepreneurs had installed machinery that they could not afford to leave idle during normal trade conditions. Thus, only one in ten workers in the engineering industry returned to the village for field work, and fewer than two out of ten in the textiles industry. In food and drink, however, a majority of workers left for the villages each year: at least six out of ten did so on average. Among workers in the construction industry, few would return to the village during the summer, because this was the height of the building season.[94]

Poor peasants, of course, had no cause to leave their place of work and return to the village at harvest time. After all, it was the lack of adequate arable land that had driven them away from the village in the first instance. Rashin cites two surveys of migrant workers who gained an income from 'trades' (*promysly*): those with little or no land at their disposal remained 'abroad' for twelve months or more. Their dependants did stay behind in the village and, to that extent, poor peasants retained a link with the community. But the family was forced to stay in the village, because the breadwinner could not support them in the expensive urban environment.[95]

Seasonal interruptions to non-agricultural work were reduced by the fact that poor peasants had no incentive to return to their villages at harvest time. Another factor that operated in the same direction was the need on the part of management to ensure that workers did not leave during the summer and disrupt the production schedule. To this end, managers resorted to delays in the payment of wages, to encourage the workforce to stay on for as long as possible. Managers also ensured that workers bought basic necessities on credit from the factory store. The debts that they accumulated served to bind workers to the enterprise. These tactics appear to have been virtually exhausted, at least in factory industry, by the late 1880s. A bitter strike at the Morozov cotton mill (Vladimir province) in 1885 arose over the terms imposed by the owners in the contracts that workers were obliged to sign. In the following year the government introduced legislation, stipulating that managers had to pay wages regularly. The legislation did not apply to enterprises that were outside the purview of the factory inspectorate, but it testifies, nevertheless, to the gradual emergence of a newer dispensation in Russian factory industry.[96]

Management was also concerned to foster the longer-term attachment of workers to factory enterprise. The main aim was to create a more permanent workforce, in order to improve the productivity of labour. The discipline of the factory and the skills that workers acquired had, so far as possible, to be sustained. Entrepreneurs were aided in this task by the fact that many workers had no realistic chance of supporting themselves from communal allotment land, but this still left open the possibility that those men and women could find work other than in the factory, as agricultural labourers, for example. In response to the increasingly competitive nature of the labour market, managers increased industrial wages and provided various facilities for the workforce.

Tugan-Baranovsky estimated that the daily wage rate in industry rose by 20–25 per cent in the Central Industrial Region, between the early 1880s and the late 1890s. In south Russia the increase in wages was still greater: daily rates of pay in metallurgy may even have doubled in the same period, reflecting the magnitude of the industrial boom in the Ukraine and the need to compete with gentry estates for available supplies of labour. Judging from the vociferous complaints registered by landed proprietors during the 1890s, the manufacturing sector looked set to outbid them in the labour market. It is also worth mentioning that the wages paid to industrial workers increased in proportion to length of service. Evidence from the Sormovo engineering factory near Nizhnii Novgorod suggests that this was an incentive to workers to maintain an attachment to the enterprise.[97]

The second means of recruiting labour to industry on a more permanent basis was to devote resources to purpose-built accommodation and ancillary services, such as schools and hospitals. In the metallurgical industry in south Russia, in the oil industry of Baku, as well as in Moscow, management typically built barracks in which to house (and supervise) the workforce. A survey of living conditions among half a million factory workers in 1895 indicated that seven out of ten workers lived in accommodation provided by the management, while the remainder lived at home or in private rooms. The proportion of workers in factory accommodation was greatest in Moscow and lowest in Warsaw and Kiev. St. Petersburg conformed to the national average. Conditions, especially in south Russia, were often depressing and unhealthy: in the Ukraine, miners were expected to pay for water supplies that were inadequate and insanitary. In barracks in Moscow, workers slept in bunks or cots, that were vacated by each successive shift. But since alternative accommodation was either unavailable or poorer still, workers grudgingly tolerated these conditions.[98]

The collective association of workers with a given trade, and even a particular factory, was also strengthened by the organization of recruitment. It was not unusual for managers to send scouts to recruit workers from a specific locality, where there already existed a tradition of craft work. Workers from Tver province, for instance, had a reputation as good carpenters and masons; those from Vladimir and Kaluga were known for their skill in spinning and weaving. The scout would negotiate with the self-appointed spokesman of a group of villagers and advance the sum required for them to travel to the factory. Sometimes, migrant workers organized themselves into a gang or *artel* and made a collective approach directly to the employer. By the turn of the century, these patterns of recruitment were giving way to a system in which the sons and daughters of factory workers followed their parents automatically into the same factory, or at least into the same trade.[99]

There is no doubt that the workforce in manufacturing industry was becoming more stable by the early twentieth century. A survey of 1,400 workers in the Tsindel cotton mill in Moscow (in 1899) showed that each worker had been with the firm for an average of five and a half years. Each worker had spent in all around ten years in manufacturing industry. A larger survey of workers in Vladimir province in 1897 suggested that two-thirds of the workforce had been with the same firm for five years or more; the evidence also revealed that workers with little or no land were more likely to have worked longest in industry. In the metalworking industry in St. Petersburg, two-fifths of all workers in 1908 had been in the industry for at least five years. In state-owned armaments works, the proportion was rather higher. Length of service tended to increase in accordance with skill levels; unskilled labourers were much less likely than skilled craftsmen to have worked in industry without a break.[100]

The average length of service in industry was almost certainly increasing. It was also apparent by 1900 that larger numbers of factory workers came from a working-class background. In some cases, as in the Urals, there was nothing unusual about this; the children of possessional workers before 1861 had always been obliged to follow in the footsteps of their parents, and this tradition persisted through to 1917. But in relatively new and expanding industries, such as metalworking in St. Petersburg, there was also a tendency for a hereditary labour force to emerge. Of those metalworkers who entered the industry before 1905, just over four out of ten were the sons of workers; of those who entered between 1905 and 1913, more than half were second-generation workers.[101]

Many workers, nevertheless, claimed still to have some connection with the land. The evidence from the 1918 Industrial Census, which enquired into workers' rural affiliations in a more comprehensive fashion than any tsarist survey, revealed that 30 per cent of factory workers had access to a family plot of land, and that 20 per cent of the total worked the land with the help of other members of the family. Among workers in metallurgy, 40 per cent had this 'active' connection with the land. In the cotton industry, workers conformed to the average for all industry. But among engineering workers and printers, the proportion of workers who actively cultivated the land with family support fell to 14 and 10 per cent respectively. It should be noted, however, that these figures understate the pre-revolutionary 'link' with the land, because by August 1918 (when the Census was held) many workers had already left their place of work, in order to take part in the redistribution of privately owned estates.[102]

These links with the land must be interpreted with great caution. Some workers retained only a notional affiliation with the village, having 'leased' their modest plot to a rich peasant. Others had been forced to leave their dependants behind – and thus had a very tangible emotional link – but had been compelled to do so, because it was no feasible to support them in the town. The fact that workers' roots in the countryside could be 'more of a hindrance than a help' is captured in the memoirs of P. Timofeev, a skilled metalworker, who wrote o his comrades in 1906 that 'the majority probably feel that the village is nothing but a burden . . . The only exceptions were those with such good land that they did not have to send money home, and those who were the sons of prosperous village artisans and merchants.'[103]

Many workers spent years or even their entire working lives in industry, and then returned to their village of origin. This behaviour appears at first sight to give credence to the notion of significant rural affiliations. But this would be an unjustifiable conclusion. Such retirement, whether premature or not, did not imply that the worker returned to the village in order to take over the family farm or to recover his 'real' identity as a peasant. Rather, most workers who returned to the village were forced out of a job through unemployment, old age or disability. In these circumstances, they had nowhere else to go, but back to the village where they could throw themselves on the mercy of distant – and, probably, none too delighted – kin.[104]

To sum up, the Russian labour market loses some of its rather romanticized aspects under closer scrutiny. The populist emphasis upon a specifically Russian working class, which enjoyed a close and 'organic' connection with the land, and which regarded wage labour as a supplement to the income from a family farm, lacks credibility. Similarly, the liberal emphasis upon the persistence of rural affiliations is overdrawn, in so far as a majority of workers had either severed their rural ties completely or reluctantly retained a tenuous link with the village.

Within the Russian working class there were, of course, important distinctions of occupation, skill, age, gender and ethnicity. Such distinctions were registered in wage rates and earnings. For example, the average industrial wage in the Empire in 1913 was 284 rubles per annum. In the metalworking and machine-building industry, the average wage reached 400 rubles. Printers, too, received well above the average for all occupations in industry. Workers in the food and drink trades tended to be paid well below the average. Regional variations could also be substantial: workers in metalworking and machine-building in St. Petersburg were paid 25 per cent more than the national average in that industry. Skilled workers – generally speaking, mature men – received more than unskilled youths and women. According to one recent study (which, however, is confined to the construction industry in the capital), skilled joiners and locksmiths could expect to be paid twice the rate to which unskilled labourers were entitled. This differential had opened up during the 1880s, and persisted through to the First World War. The War almost certainly reduced the differential between skilled and unskilled workers, as it did in other belligerent countries.[105]

The Russian working class was thus heterogenous in its complexion. This heterogeneity was fostered by the War. In the midst of panic about the war effort, Russian industrialists drafted in thousands of new workers. Some of them, like prisoners-of-war or indentured Chinese labour, were put to the most arduous tasks, such as mining and construction. By the summer of 1915, refugees from the Baltic and western provinces supplemented the workforce in Petrograd. Another major source of labour consisted of army recruits and reservists who, from the employers' point of view, had the advantage of being subject to military discipline and could thus be expected to dampen down labour militancy. The final and most important source of additional industrial labour in wartime comprised women and juveniles. In 1913 30 per cent of workers in all industry were female (the proportion was 55 per cent in textiles); by January 1917 the figure had risen to 40 per cent (67 per cent in textiles). The government assisted this process, by revising the labour code to permit the employment of women and older children on night shifts.[106]

What was the role of the tsarist government in the operation of the labour market? There was no consistent labour policy, because agreement was impossible to reach about the degree to which the government should interfere in industrial relations. In one sense, the regime tipped the scales decisively in favour of management, by proscribing the collective organization of labour. Trade unions were banned, until the government was forced to concede on this issue in March 1906. Strikes, too, were illegal, and the leaders of labour protest normally found themselves imprisoned, or at the very least blacklisted. Even after 1906, trade unions were closely monitored. They had to provide the authorities with copies of their rule books, and they were disbanded for even minor infringements of the rules.

Some sections of the government took the view that official intervention on behalf of workers was desirable, in the interests of social stability. In 1859 the provincial governor of Tver had proposed that 'the liberation of the peasantry ... should naturally be followed by the liberation of the workers from the clutches of the bosses'. The difficulty lay in finding a means of 'protecting' the workers from employers, without introducing the abhorrent principle of collective bargaining. It was in this spirit (and against a background of strikes during the late 1890s and the rise of social-democratic organization and influence), that the Ministry of the Interior devised a system of 'police unions' in 1902. These unions were designed to represent workers and to alleviate their economic position. The events of 1905 exposed the futility of these measures, about which many officials (notably in the Ministry of Finances) themselves had misgivings.[107]

The most significant labour legislation was introduced in 1886. The labour code stipulated that all factory workers should have a written contract of employment or a wage book. The worker was given an assurance that wages could not be cut, while the contract was still valid; nor could the worker claim an increase in wages during that period, or leave his job without permission. But even this law, which also laid down the punishments for participation in strike action, antagonized many entrepreneurs, who resented the intrusion of government in the sphere of industrial relations. Their protest helped to provoke the resignation of Minister of Finances Bunge, who had been responsible for the labour code (as well as for the creation of the factory inspectorate). Subsequent legislation limited the hours of work in factories to a maximum of 11½ (1897) and provided for workers to be compensated for industrial injury (1903). This suggests that the government sought to bring its labour policy more into line with modern capitalist conditions elsewhere. However, as the experiment with police unions suggests, there remained a tension within the tsarist regime, between those who wanted to intervene in day-to-day industrial relations and those who wanted to maintain a more discreet profile.[108]

Many Russian liberals believed that the lack of adequate government protection for workers, combined with the frequently harsh conditions of factory life, created the potential for labour protest. This verdict applied equally to workers in non-factory industry, which was for the most part unaffected by labour legislation. The 'problem' of labour protest, however, was also attributed by liberal opinion to the fact that workers were often newly arrived from the countryside and found it difficult to adjust to the routine and discipline involved, especially, in factory work. Populist observers also believed that labour unrest was linked to the semi-rural character of the workforce. The worker was simply not at home in the environment of the factory; his 'alienation' contributed decisively to intermittent labour unrest in Russia. Finally, Russian marxists acknowledged that the working class in the early twentieth century was in part the product of belated industrialization, and thus, in Trotsky's memorable phrase, 'snatched from the plough and hurled into the factory furnace'. But at the same time, marxist opinion held that a hereditary proletariat had come into being, and comprised 'cadre' workers, who had no connection with the land. Among these workers, labour protest was the product of growing class consciousness. Protest was not, as liberal opinion maintained, the straightforward outcome of deprivation; nor was it, as populists believed, a response to the traumatic (if temporary) expulsion of peasants from the rural womb.[109]

Conclusion

Tsarist Russia was a country of people on the move. The spatial mobility of the population was not confined to the period after 1861. As we have seen, many serfs were encouraged by their masters to migrate in search of employment, provided that they paid the quitrent. However, migration undoubtedly increased in scale and incidence during the second half of the nineteenth century, as feudal ties were progressively loosened. This mobility derived in part from the rapidity of population growth, but population growth ought not to be divorced from the changes taking place in rural society. The differentiation of the peasantry was a further pre-condition of the inter-regional movement of people.

Migration to new territory, especially in western Siberia, was a consequence of declining living standards among peasant farmers in the areas of traditional and (by the 1880s and 1890s) dense settlement. But many peasants were not attracted by the prospect of pioneer farming. Instead, the lack of resources among the poor peasantry drove them to seek work as wage labourers, in factories, transport, services and on agricultural estates. These men and women had little or no meaningful affiliation with the villages in which they were born. By the early twentieth century the labour force was being replenished by the next generation of rural emigrants, and by the children of wage labourers.

One can detect little direct institutional influence on the formation and operation of the Russian labour market. The tsarist government was not the decisive agent of migration, nor did the commune exercise a significant control over the flow of people in and out of the village. Instead, wage labour developed in accordance with the transformation of rural social relations and with the growing demand for labour on the part of capitalist employers.

4 The Agricultural Sector

The agricultural sector assumes crucial significance in the liberal approach to economic development. Agriculture is seen as a source of labour upon which other sectors can draw, and as a source of savings that can be transferred to non-agricultural sectors either voluntarily or compulsorily. This scenario is justified by the assumption that the marginal returns to labour and capital are higher in non-agricultural sectors. In addition, the function of agriculture is to supply food (both to sustain the growing urban population and to obtain export earnings) and raw materials for industry. In short, agriculture is called upon to perform a range of functions that are crucial to economic development. Much depends, as we saw in the first chapter, on the degree of technical change in agriculture. However, the liberal view of Russian agriculture is that technical change was modest, at least until the beginning of the twentieth century. The main explanation for this stagnation was the prevalence of peasant farming in agriculture.

In the marxist interpretation, attention focuses upon the social relations within agriculture. These relations determine the scope for the growth of output and productivity. Under serfdom, power in rural society resides with a class of feudal landlords, who extract service from their peasant serfs. The stranglehold they have over their work force is backed up by the power of the state, which compels peasants to serve the lords. The landowner is primarily concerned with the recurrent payment of services, rather than with the means of increasing the productivity of the land or of labour. Under capitalism this 'extra-economic' compulsion no longer applies; the capitalist obtains a supply of labour, in return for the payment of a money wage. Unlike the feudal landlord, however, the capitalist is interested in increasing the productivity of his inputs, in order to obtain profit and to compete with other farmers. So far as Russia was concerned

he marxist view is that capitalist relations did penetrate rural society
y the end of the nineteenth century, but that this process was uneven.

Both the liberal and marxist interpretations assume that progress
1ay be measured in terms of the development of a market economy.
1 other words, economic development is seen in terms of growth of
pecialization, the expansion of inter-regional trade, the adjustment
f the product mix to changes in the cost of inputs and the price of
roducts. These assumptions are not present in populist economics.
nstead, populists emphasize the importance of household production
nd consumption in peasant agriculture. In this interpretation, only
artificial' measures, such as government fiscal policy, will induce
easants to enter the market in significant numbers. Left to them-
elves, peasants are reluctant to provide a surplus. This is not because
hey are 'backward', but because their values are *sui generis*.

The present chapter begins by considering broad changes in agricul-
ural output. This section is followed by two extended sections,
evoted to the question of landholding and to the problem of agricul-
ural productivity. The interaction of supply and demand in agricul-
ure is brought together in a discussion of price changes. The chapter
oncludes with a brief overall assessment of the performance of the
gricultural sector.

.1 General Trends in Output and Investment

he most complete and careful estimates of the growth of total agri-
ultural production have been made by Raymond Goldsmith (1961)
nd Paul Gregory (1982). Before looking at these estimates, we should
onsider the raw data underlying them. Reasonably reliable figures
n crop harvests (cereals, potatoes and industrial crops) only became
vailable after 1883, when the Central Statistical Committee (TsSK),
nder the Ministry of the Interior, published annual returns, based
pon information supplied by local correspondents, about the area
nder cultivation and the average yield for each crop. Before 1883,
ata on sown area and yields are more fragmentary, although the
oviet historian A. S. Nifontov has compiled a series on grain output
vhich derives from records of provincial governors. In each case, the
gures relate only to the 50 provinces of European Russia and thus
xclude Siberia, the Caucasus and Central Asia. As far as livestock
erds are concerned, the picture is still more blurred. The government
equired village police officers to conduct a regular count of herds in
ach district, but it is easy to imagine the misrepresentation and error
hat must have crept in. The same consideration applies to the periodic
rmy horse censuses. As in the case of grain production data, this
nformation did not (prior to 1900) take into account livestock herds

99

beyond European Russia. Thus, to obtain an idea of growth in total output in the Russian Empire an allowance must be made for the Russian 'periphery'.

Goldsmith constructed an index of output for the major grains and industrial crops and incorporated an estimate for the growth in livestock, which he reckoned grew at one per cent per annum between 1860 and 1913. Total crop production was estimated to have grown by two per cent per annum in the same period, with the highest rates of growth in wheat and barley and the lowest in rye. Overall Goldsmith suggested that between 1860 and 1913 agricultural output in European Russia grew by between 1.5 and 1.9 per cent annually. Gregory's estimate is rather different. He confines himself to the period from 1883–7 to 1909–13. Gregory has a more positive assessment than Goldsmith of the growth of livestock herds, which according to Gregory, grew by 1.5 per cent per annum. In addition, Gregory maintains that grain output increased by 3.1 per cent per annum, whereas Goldsmith had put this at around 2.3 per cent for the same period. The difference is explained in two ways. First, Gregory takes into account the growth of grain production in the faster-growing parts of the Empire (such as Siberia), and not just European Russia. Second, he derives an estimate for grain output on a net basis (gross production, less harvest losses and allowances for seed). Since the ratio of net to gross crop production increased during this period, the growth rate will be higher than if gross output data were used.[1]

Grain production dominated aggregate agricultural output throughout the nineteenth century. In 1913, major cereals accounted for two-fifths of gross agricultural production, and one may surmise that the proportion was between two-fifths and one-half in 1850. The significance of grain production for domestic food consumption, animal feed and exports cannot be doubted, and this must be reflected in any analysis of Russian agriculture.

Increases in grain production are a function of changes in the sown area and in yields, so it is necessary to establish the broad trends in these variables. They are summarized in Table 4.1. Nifontov's data for the period 1850–1900 (European Russia only) suggest that about one-quarter of the increase in output represented an expansion of the area under crops. Higher yields accounted for three-quarters of the increase. There is some indication that sowings increased more noticeably during the late 1860s to early 1870s and again during the late 1890s. After stagnating for a decade and a half, average cereal yields grew steadily, with some interruption in the early 1870s.

In order to assess general developments beyond 1900, when Nifontov's data terminate, Table 4.1 incorporates material from the TsSK series, covering the period 1883–1914. This has been converted to a

Table 4.1

Indices of grain production, sown area and yields, 1851–1914, in 50 provinces of European Russia

(1886–90 = 100)

1. All grains	Production	Sown area	Yields
1851–5	68	92	75
1856–60	70	94	75
1861–5	71	94	75
1866–70	75	90	84
1871–5	81	98	83
1876–80	84	98	86
1881–5	93	100	94
1886–90	100	100	100
1891–5	109	99	110
1896–1900	120	105	114
1901–5	141	114	124
1906–10	142	117	122
1911–14	158	120	131

2. Rye	Production	Sown area	Yields	3. Oats	Production	Sown area	Yields
1871–5	85	96	89		78	87	90
1876–80	82	97	85		88	88	100
1881–5	93	99	94		92	96	95
1886–90	100	100	100		100	100	100
1891–5	103	98	105		101	97	104
1896–1900	111	98	113		115	103	117
1901–5	121	100	121		128	108	119
1906–10	109	98	113		131	109	121
1911–14	127	99	127		138	109	127

4. Wheat	Production	Sown area	Yields	5. Barley	Production	Sown area	Yields
1871–5	75	103	73		66	94	71
1876–80	76	102	74		72	94	77

Table 4.1—Continued

4. Wheat (Cont.)	Production	Sown area	Yields	5. Barley (Cont.)	Production	Sown area	Yields
1881–5	99	99	100		87	100	88
1886–90	100	100	100		100	100	100
1891–5	129	107	120		145	116	125
1896–1900	140	125	112		152	137	111
1901–5	207	142	150		186	150	124
1906–10	207	163	126		221	167	132
1911–14	227	173	132		250	181	134

Sources: A. S. Nifontov, *Zernovoe proizvodstvo Rossii vo vtoroi polovine XIX veka*, Nauka, 1974, tables 34, 39 (for 1851–1900); V. M. Obukhov, 'Dvizhenie urozhaev zernovykh khlebov v Evropeiskoi Rossii, 1883–1915gg.', in V. G. Groman, ed., *Vliyanie neurozhaev na narodnoe khozyaistvo Rossii*, Priboi, 1927, vol. 1, pp. 2–5. I have spliced the series together by adopting the quinquennium 1886–90 as a common base. 'All grains' comprises the four major cereals, together with buckwheat, millet, maize, peas and spelt (*polba*).

similar base (1886–90) in order to make the two series compatible. The material suggests a significant increase in the sown area during the early twentieth century, especially by comparison with the preceding decades. Yields continued to improve, but suffered a setback in the quinquennium 1906–10. If allowance were made for Siberia and the north Caucasus, this expansion in the area under cereal cultivation would be still more marked. S. G. Wheatcroft has calculated that the growth in cereal yields in the Russian Empire as a whole accounted for only two-fifths of the increase in output between 1895 and 1914, compared to nine-tenths in the period 1883–95.[3] In other words, the increase in the cultivation of new land accounted for a greater proportion of output growth than it had in the 1880s and early 1890s. It should also be borne in mind that yields were highly favourable on this virgin soil.

This aggregate picture conceals significant differences in the behaviour of the variables for individual crops. The crops that grew most rapidly during the last quarter of the nineteenth century and the beginning of the twentieth were wheat and barley. These were pre-eminently export crops. The production of oats (consumed for the most part domestically, by horses) increased more rapidly than rye (the typical domestic food grain), especially after 1900. In the case of rye and oats, much of the increased output reflected higher yields: the area sown to rye remained roughly the same, taking European Russia as a whole. The area sown to wheat and barley did not increase very fast until the 1890s. Again, the underlying data exclude western Siberia and the Caucasus, and the inclusion of these regions would reinforce still further the trend towards expansion of the area sown to the main export crops.

Overall, the area sown to grains in European Russia increased by just over ten per cent over the second half of the nineteenth century. This conceals wide regional variations. At a still highly aggregated level, a broad distinction can be drawn between the non-black earth region, where the sown area fell by some eight per cent between 1850 and 1890, before recovering at the end of the century, and the black-earth region, where the sown area increased by more than fifteen per cent. At a less aggregated level, a striking contraction in the area under cereals took place in the Central Industrial Region where, apart from a brief interruption during the 1880s, sowings declined by more than 25 per cent. As a result, this densely settled region saw its share of the total sown area decline from 17 per cent in the 1850s to only 11 per cent in the 1890s. On the other hand, the area under cereals actually increased in the Urals provinces, increased substantially in the Baltic and, after the 1880s, in the North.[4].

As far as the black-earth region was concerned, the most dramatic expansion in cereal sowings occurred in New Russia: initially in the southern steppe provinces (Kherson, Tauride, Ekaterinoslav) and, after 1880, in the Don and north Caucasus. In the 1850s these regions were sparsely settled and offered considerable scope for cultivation under the stimulus of rising domestic and foreign demand. Within the region as a whole, however, several provinces experienced a cutback in the sown area, in particular in the Central Black Earth and, after 1880, the Lower Volga.

Grain could be sown extensively in sparsely settled regions where land was fertile, such as the south and south-east and – after 1890 – western Siberia. Most of the increase in the sowings here reflected a preference for the higher-value crops, wheat and barley. In other parts of Russia, the scope for sowing grain became more and more limited as the ratio of people to land increased. Numerous contemporary commentators towards the end of the nineteenth century pointed to the increased cultivation of potatoes, and argued that peasant farmers substituted them for cereals as a basic source of nutrition. At a very general level, this was true of the Central Industrial Region and the Central Black Earth, where an 'Irish solution' to rural overpopulation emerged. However, increased sowings of potatoes also reflected a transition to improved four-course rotations, such as in Yaroslavl and Tula after 1900. In addition, the increase in cultivation of potatoes was not confined to peasant allotments, but was also characteristic of privately held land, suggesting a growing commercial interest in the potato as an input for distilling.[5]

The extension of arable was not exclusively a function of the colonization of new territory. Indeed, part of the 'agrarian problem', so far as contemporary opinion was concerned, had to do with the fact that peasant farmers had been compelled by population growth to plough up pasture land in regions of traditional settlement (in particular, the central black-earth provinces). As a result, the rural economy appeared to be unbalanced and over-reliant upon grain towards the end of the century. In a pre-mechanized agriculture, of course, the role of the draught animals hardly requires emphasis, and so any decline in pasture entailed serious repercussions. At the same time, it is also striking just how large an area suitable for cultivation was not regularly cropped. Given the persistence of traditional three-field cropping arrangements, one-third of cultivable land lay fallow at any given time, and not just on peasant allotment land. Nor was this the only reserve. Land was also used to demarcate the boundaries between allotments. Furthermore, the 1887 Land Survey revealed that in many areas of European Russia at least five per cent of suitable agricultural land (that is, non-waste) neither formed part of a regular rotation nor sustained other activity. In the South-West the proportion reached ten per cent; in the Central Black Earth, where population pressure was most acute, it fell to three per cent.[6]

Although cereals dominated agricultural production, other crops were growing in importance. Gentry landowners in the Ukraine were already turning land over to sugar beet well before 1860. Industrial crops, such as flax, also formed a traditional part of peasant agriculture, especially in parts of the Central Industrial Region. Towards the end of the century, tobacco and cotton cultivation had spread to Central Asia, and tobacco was grown in such diverse provinces as Chernigov, Poltava, Ryazan and Tambov. The extent to which regional specialization took place in agricultural production is treated at greater length below.[7]

Brief mention has already been made of the rate of growth of livestock herds. In this connection, attention may be drawn to their composition and geographical distribution. The composition of the livestock population as a whole reflected the lack of mechanization and the need for a large stock of draught animals. This need did not diminish with the growth of new forms of transport. The army continued to absorb millions of horses; peasants continued to take produce by cart to the town or railhead. Indeed, the horse population expanded rapidly during the second half of the nineteenth century, in response to the settlement of new land to the south and south-east and, later, in Central Asia and Siberia. By 1914, these latter regions accounted for a much larger proportion of the total horse population, reflecting a decline in pasture in the older black-earth provinces and in the south. Also noteworthy was the progress of intensive dairy farming in parts of the non-black earth region – the Baltic, North, Belorussia – where advanced crop rotations enabled cattle to be supported more easily.[8]

Draught animals constituted a significant element in the agricultural capital stock. What were the main trends in capital investment in agriculture? The aggregate picture has been drawn most convincingly by Gregory. Gregory concludes that the total stock of capital in agriculture increased at a rate well in excess of the growth of population, between 1895 and 1913. Measured in constant prices, livestock grew just fast enough to keep pace with the growth of population (around 1.8 per cent per annum). Investment in rural structures, that is farm dwellings and buildings, increased by 3.5 per cent on average. These figures derive from the valuations of their property that peasants were required to make for insurance purposes. Gregory assumes that the value of non-peasant structures increased at the same rate, which is a reasonable assumption. Finally, according to Gregory, investment in agricultural machinery and rural transport grew by an average annual rate of 9.0 per cent. The estimate reflects the low starting-point and the spurt in the installation of equipment (ploughs, dairy equipment, etc.) in the early twentieth century.[9]

Gregory does not dwell on regional differences, but it may be assumed that this growth in the agricultural capital stock did not take place uniformly. The expansion probably occurred most noticeably in the north and west, and in western Siberia; to a lesser extent, in the Central Industrial Region and in New Russia. Almost certainly, it was least apparent in the Central Black Earth and Lower Volga regions.

4.2 Land Ownership and the Land Market

In most pre-industrial societies, land is the key asset that generates wealth and status. Accordingly, the way in which land is distributed between social groups, and the mechanisms by which it may be transferred, tell the historian a great deal about the nature of such societies. Access to land does not in itself indicate complete command over the means of production in agriculture, nor does it necessarily imply that those who own land will have complete control over the agricultural product. Nevertheless, there is a close correlation between landholding and economic power in pre-industrial societies. These observations would have to be modified with respect to Russia in the period prior to 1861, and in two senses. First, status in pre-reform

Russia traditionally hinged upon the performance of services to the state by the nobility, in return for which the Tsar granted them the right to own estates. Second, to those estates were attached serfs, without whom the land could not realistically have been worked (a 'free' peasantry would have sought an independent livelihood on unsettled land further south or east). Serfdom was given legal recognition in 1649, and during the eighteenth century the Tsar confirmed the exclusive right of gentry to own serfs.

By long-established practice, the Tsar exercised wide-ranging control over the disposition of land. The royal family itself owned huge estates, while the state (on whose behalf the Tsar acted as custodian) owned arable, forest and mineral-bearing land, which by 1850 amounted to nearly half the territory of European Russia alone. In Siberia, the proportion of state-owned land was greater still.[10] In addition, the Tsar rewarded distinguished servants or favourites with grants of land and serfs. Most important of all, the Tsar extracted from the nobility as a whole an undertaking, not only to serve the state, but also to supply money and military recruits, in return for the right to hold land and pass it on to their successors. In the course of the eighteenth century, the nobility established a monopoly among social groups of the right to own land and serfs. The relationship between these noble privileges and state services was abandoned by Catherine II, who confirmed that the nobility had hereditary titles to their estates (that is, their property rights were no longer conditional upon state service).

In these circumstances, the development of an active land market could hardly be said to have begun prior to 1861. The Russian nobility had limited scope for transferring inherited land beyond the confines of the family. In 1801 Alexander I ended the monopoly of land ownership enjoyed by noblemen, but the extent to which merchants and others availed themselves of the opportunity to buy land was quite modest, because the land had to be free of serfs. Serfs themselves engaged in land transactions, but only with the permission of the lord and in his name. Serfs had no secure property rights. State peasants, too, had no property rights. All such peasants could be relocated at the behest of gentry or government respectively.[11]

The corollary of serfdom was that the enserfed peasantry occupied an allotment at the discretion of the lord. Allotments were supposed to maintain the peasant family, so that its members could work productively on the estate or in some other capacity. Peasants organized themselves into communities in order to assign available allotment land to productive units, in accordance with obligations to the manor and to the Treasury, and corresponding to the capacity of each household to till the land. Enserfed peasants thus had a degree of autonomy in determining the access of families to allotment land.

By the early nineteenth century their interests, and those of the lord and state, led to a situation in which allotment land in many regions was periodically redistributed to take account of changing demographic circumstances. On land owned by the state, on which there were 27.4 million peasants in 1858, village communities also practised redistribution.[12]

Thus land was not a mobile factor of production in pre-reform Russia. Access to land reflected the organization of society into distinct estates. In some respects, reality may have belied this rigid principle, but it remained true that only noblemen had a consciousness of property in land, recognized by the state. Peasants had property rights neither in law nor in practice, although the recurrent protest mounted against the regime indicated profound unease at the inequality of landholding and at serfdom itself. In practice, peasants had some scope for decision-making – extending sometimes beyond the allocation of allotment land, to decisions about cropping methods and patterns – but this was no substitute for the absence of either private or collective title to landed property.[13]

The emancipation of the serfs in 1861 and of state peasants in 1866 transformed landholding in European Russia, because for the first time peasants could legally engage in transactions without being bound by the claims and wishes of their social superiors. The government sought to protect noble interests by confirming their title to the demesne, but landowners formally lost the servile labour force that had hitherto been attached to it. Land was to be earmarked for peasant use from the manorial property. The freed peasantry were obliged to accept these allotments as a condition of emancipation, that is, they were not free to move. The allotments were to be held by the village community as a whole and could not be alienated. The principle of individual peasant proprietorship thus found no place in the 1861 settlement.

At the same time, peasants (like all other social groups, with the exception of most Jews) could rent or purchase land outside the allotment reserve. As time passed, these transactions were swelled in number by the increasing demand for land from the growing rural population and by the willingness of gentry proprietors to offer land for rent or purchase. During the 1880s the government acknowledged this trend and established financial institutions specifically to provide credit for land transfers. Even so, this financial help was designed to encourage the acquisition of land by village communities, rather than by individual peasants. Only after 1905, when the value of the peasant community as a force for social and political stability proved questionable, did the regime change course. A new situation developed in the land market. By this time, large tracts of former gentry-owned land had already been transferred to other social groups.

The government embarked on the emancipation of the serfs in the face of noble resentment, but resentment did not spill over into outright opposition. This reflected in part the traditional subservience of the nobility to the state in Russia, but it was also apparent that the government would not trample on the property rights of the landowning elite. Besides, many *pomeshchiki* had only a weak commitment to serfdom as an economic system, even if they regarded it as a basic privilege. Any firm resolve on the part of government to abolish it was likely to prompt them to seek the most favourable terms possible in the circumstances. Why the government came to believe in the necessity of abolition had to do with a sense of unease following the Crimean War (1854–6); the unease was heightened by a fear of peasant rebellion. The fact that emancipation formed part of a series of reform measures also indicated a general willingness to devise new arrangements in society.[14]

The tsarist bureaucracy were lukewarm about the privileges traditionally enjoyed by the nobility and sought to avoid excessive noble influence in determining the outcome of the settlement, which Alexander II had already insisted upon in broad terms at a private gathering of Moscow noblemen in March 1856 and again during other exchanges with Russian nobility during 1857. One result of this 'bureaucratic' approach was the insistence that peasants should receive a plot of land upon emancipation, whatever the feelings of landowners. In 1858 the gentry set up provincial committees to discuss abolition, but the government informed them that their views were sought on the best way to implement a landed settlement; they were not to question the principle itself. The aim was to 'guarantee the existence of the peasantry and (to enable them to) meet their obligations to the government and to the proprietors'.[15] The land would be taken from the demesne and would in due course become the property of the former serfs as a whole.

A handful of the provincial noble committees suggested that the new holdings should be equivalent to the current allotments worked by the serf population, but the majority proposed some reduction in allotments with a view to ensuring that families had to spend some time working on the demesne land in order to support themselves. The final decree set out arrangements for four broad areas: the South-West; Lithuania and part of Belorussia (Minsk, together with part of Vitebsk); Little Russia; and the rest of European Russia. Abolition had already been implemented in the Baltic provinces in 1816–19, giving the peasants no ploughland at all and compelling them to work as estate labourers. In each of these four areas a maximum and minimum norm was defined for the amount of land that might be allotted to each male 'soul'. In addition, safeguards allowed landowners to retain at least half their original estate (in Little Russian provinces) or one-third (in the case of other parts of European Russia). Where the proposed allotments, worked out in detail at a local level, exceeded the maximum norms laid down for each region, the gentry were entitled to 'cut off' the surplus and incoporate it within the demesne once more.[16]

When the decree was published, serfs in most provinces found that for two years they remained formally bound to the lord in the customary manner, during which time preparations were to be set in motion for surveying allotment land. Thereupon they remained 'temporarily obligated', a status under which the lord retained full ownership of the allotment land and the right to demand service from the former serfs; this condition persisted until such time as the peasantry entered into an agreement to redeem the land. Redemption was the concept built in to the emancipation settlement in order to recognize that the gentry's property rights had been violated and that some sort of compensation had to be devised for the loss of land and especially feudal services. In offering the gentry a financial inducement to renounce serfdom, the tsarist government probably took the decisive step towards extracting their consent.[17] From the peasants' point of view, it was incomprehensible that payment should be made for land that they recognized as rightfully theirs.

The lord and his serfs, with the help of government-appointed arbitrators (*mirovyie posredniki*) were expected to reach an agreement about the precise terms of the land settlement and of compensation, which would be entered in a special charter (*ustavnaya gramota*). The proposed arrangements involved a determination of the 'value' of the allotment, by capitalizing at six per cent the annual rent paid during the period of 'temporary obligation'. Since these rents had been inflated in the first instance and exceeded the old quitrent (*obrok*), the scheme tended to overvalue the land by comparison with the situation before 1861. The agreement was supposed to be voluntary between the two parties, but redemption could be enforced by the gentry (not by the peasantry), in which case the gentry forfeited 20 per cent of the redemption sum.[18]

The emancipation of the serfs not only saddled them with an inescapable obligation to compensate their former owners for the land they had been granted, but left them with less allotment land on average than they had worked before 1861. This situation emerged as a result of the scope given to landowners to 'cut off' allotment land, either because the allocation of land left the lord with less than one-third of the non-waste area of the original demesne (one-half in Little Russia), or because the potential allotment exceeded the maximum norm that had been stipulated. Emancipation also frequently ensured that the allotments were fragmented and misshapen. Peasants were also deprived of their customary access to non-arable resources. All these devices served to ensure that land-owners could, where appropriate, make the manorial lands available to peasants in return for money or 'labour' rent.[19]

In the South-West, the settlement was more generous to peasants. This region, which had been annexed from Poland in the eighteenth century, was dominated by Polish noblemen, who actively opposed tsarist rule. The government now took its revenge, by allowing the emancipated serfs the right to retain their allotments in full. State peasants (freed in 1866) also secured more favourable treatment than their fellow serfs in the other parts of European Russia. State peasants usually obtained title to allotment land that corresponded in size to the land they had worked before. Where the government imposed a maximum holding, it varied between eight and fifteen *dessyatiny*, compared to a maximum norm of between three and eight for the serf population. As a result, former state peasants farmed on average as much land as they had prior to 1866 and paid less per acre for the privilege of calling it their own.[20]

Estimates of the quantity of allotment land worked by former serfs suggest that on average they were deprived of around four per cent of their traditional holdings. But this average figure conceals crucial variations from region to region. In the South-West and in Belorussia and Lithuania, where the emancipation was more generous, the area available to peasant households increased quite substantially: by around 18 and 24 per cent respectively. On the other hand, in Little Russia and the Mid- and Lower Volga provinces the reduction amounted to close on 25 per cent. As Gerschenkron put it, such a manoeuvre helped considerably in reconciling the gentry in the fertile black-earth provinces to peasant emancipation.[21]

The simplest way of summarizing the position in which all peasants (former serfs and state peasants) found themselves as a result of the 1860s reforms is to consider the evidence gathered in the 1877 Land Census. The census material allows us to gauge the distribution of allotment land according to the male peasant population in each province. For the thirty provinces of European Russia (exclusive of those in Little Russia and New Russia) the distribution took the form shown in Table 4.2.

Bearing in mind that the original emancipation decree had sought to enable the peasantry to subsist and pay taxes; that the government had thought in terms of allotments of up to eight (or, in areas of abundant land, fifteen) *dessyatiny*; and that Kiselev, in discussing the reform of state peasants' economic conditions during the 1840s, assessed the minimum allotment for subsistence at five *dessyatiny* – bearing these considerations in mind, the position must be judged unsatisfactory, even by official standards.

Table 4.2

Percentage distribution of male peasant 'souls' according to size of allotment, 1877

(30 Provinces of European Russia)

Region	<1	1–2	2–3	3–4	4–5	5–10	>10	
			(*dessyatiny* per 'soul')					
Central Industrial (including Smolensk)	0.8	4.3	13.9	39.2	23.5	17.4	0.9	100
Central Black Earth (including Penza)	4.4	7.7	30.8	21.7	14.4	20.8	0.1	100
North-West	0.4	1.2	3.1	11.8	26.5	52.9	4.0	100
Mid-Volga	4.8	8.3	9.6	26.8	20.8	28.2	1.5	100
Urals (including Orenburg and Ufa)	5.6	5.3	6.1	9.7	11.2	45.2	16.8	100
Lower Volga (Samara and Astrakhan)	1.7	3.4	1.1	2.6	6.5	48.6	36.1	100
North	4.1	9.7	10.4	9.9	15.2	36.1	14.6	100
TOTAL	3.5	6.1	15.8	22.5	17.4	28.9	5.7	100
Absolute number of 'souls' (m.)	0.49	0.86	2.24	3.18	2.45	4.09	0.81	14.13

Source: N. M. Druzhinin, *Russkaya derevnya na perelome, 1861–1880gg.*, Nauka, 1978, p. 120.

The response by government to accumulating evidence of a 'land shortage' among the peasantry might take one or other of the following forms. First, measures could be taken to promote the transfer of land, either temporarily (through rent agreements) or permanently to peasant farmers. In principle, a permanent transfer could be either voluntary or compulsory, involving a forced redistribution of land from gentry to peasantry. Second, the rural labour 'surplus' could be moved from areas of dense settlement to areas of abundant land or to urban centres, where they might be able to engage permanently in non-agricultural employment and thus renounce traditional ties to allotment land. Thirdly, official assistance could be offered to agricultural producers in areas of 'land shortage' to improve the yields on existing allotments, or to engage in more intensive exploitation of the land, thereby improving the productivity of the allotment and raising the income of peasant producers.

Clearly, the government was not the only potential agent of transformation. Peasants could take it upon themselves to improve methods of cultivation. They could, and did, engage in transactions with private landowners to buy or rent land. They could, and did, move to towns or to new land, with or without permission. Not least, they could (and did) seize land when they met with official resistance to their legitimate demands for land redistribution.

In the central and southern black-earth provinces, peasants had to extend their access to arable and other resources by renting demesne land in exchange for a share of the crop. In these circumstances, land that formally belonged to the gentry was cultivated by peasants who used their own implements. Those landowners who had little working capital found this an appropriate arrangement, since it obviated the need to acquire or modernize their inventory and cushioned them against the fall in cereal prices during the 1880s and 1890s. Peasants also paid rents in cash, but this was more common in the South-West.

It is difficult to gauge the relative importance of money and 'labour' rent (*otrabotka*), compared to the cultivation of privately owned estates by landed proprietors themselves, at least until the second half of the 1880s. By this time, information provided to the new Noble Land Bank (founded in 1885) gives some idea of the general means whereby land was cultivated:

Table 4.3

Forms of cultivation of gentry estates, 1886–1900

	Percentage cultivated by proprietors		Percentage leased		Percentage with mixed arrangements	
	BE	NBE	BE	NBE	BE	NBE
1886–90	33	31	32	30	35	39
1891–5	31	27	32	35	37	38
1896–1900	22	20	44	54	34	26

BE = Black Earth provinces; NBE = non-Black Earth provinces.
Source: A. M. Anfimov, *Zemelnaya arenda v Rossii*, Nauka, 1961, p. 21.

However, these figures derive from a sample of estates of more

han 500 *dessyatiny* in size. A different series, taking account of all
properties mortgaged with the Bank, gives a higher proportion of
arms cultivated by the owners, suggesting that smaller estates were
more likely to farm on capitalist lines. Capitalist relations on privately
held land did not appear to increase in proportion to the size of the
arm. The sources all testify to the willingness of private landowners
to lease their land at a time of agricultural depression.[22]

How important was the renting of land to peasant farmers themselves? Answers to this question have differed sharply, partly because
of the problem of allowing for transactions that went unrecorded.
One insight into the scale of leasehold derives from zemstvo budget
studies, first explored by Karyshev in the early 1890s. Karyshev
concluded that peasants may have leased as much as 54.5 m. hectares,
which represented the equivalent of around two-fifths of available
allotment land. The Soviet historian Anfimov, who has made a special
study of rents, gave a figure of 40.3 m. hectares for all privately
owned land leased to peasants in 1905. The volume of rented land
declined as peasants began to acquire land on a larger scale and some
landlords took to commercial farming on their own account.[23]

According to the Land Census of 1877, over one-third of all land
in European Russia was held by peasants as allotment, one-quarter
was privately owned, and two-fifths (mostly forest) belonged to the
state. In 1861 only a small amount of land was owned privately by
peasants, who had acquired this with the permission of their masters.
If we assume that the area under private peasant ownership in 1861
did not exceed 5 m. hectares, then the land owned by the gentry
amounted to around 95 m. hectares. By 1877 it had fallen to below
80 m., and the process did not end there. In 1905, when the next
major survey of landownership was conducted, the area ascribed to
gentry owners (on comparable territory) was put at no more than 57
m. hectares.

Table 4.4 presents a summary of available data on the sale of land
by gentry in European Russia between the abolition of serfdom and
the outbreak of the First World War. The information also takes
account of purchases of land by members of the gentry. The scale of
land purchase raises serious doubts about the imminent 'decline of
the nobility'.[24]

Between 1863 and 1904 gentry proprietors disposed of around 39
m. hectares in 45 provinces. Other sources suggest that the rate of
disposal was somewhat higher in the non-black earth provinces, and
particularly in the Central Industrial Region. Landholding in the Urals
and Baltic provinces proved much more stable. In the black-earth
provinces, land was sold at a faster rate in New Russia, but gentry
landholding hardly fell at all in the South-West.[25]

Those gentry landowners who owned properties of between one

Table 4.4

Land sales and purchases by gentry, 45 provinces of European Russia, 1863–1914

(million hectares)

	Total sales	Total purchases	Net loss
1863–72	17.60	10.56	7.04
1873–82	25.59	15.22	10.37
1883–92	19.66	10.58	9.08
1893–1902	22.95	11.99	10.96
1903–4	3.13	1.69	1.44
1905–14*	n.a.	n.a.	10.78

* Data refer to 47 provinces.

Sources: A. P. Korelin, *Dvoryanstvo v poreformennoi Rossii, 1861–1904*, Nauka, 1979, p. 57; 1905–14 figure from A. M. Anfimov and I. F. Makarov, 'Novyie dannyie o zemlevladenii Evropeiskoi Rossii', *Istoriya SSSR*, no. 1, 1974, pp. 82–97.

and five thousand *dessyatiny* exhibited the greatest readiness to sell land between 1877 and 1905. The tendency was less marked at the upper end of the scale and still less at the very bottom (estates below 100 *dessyatiny* in size). The huge properties in the Urals, the South-West and in the Don territory were destined to remain more or less intact. The medium-sized properties in central Russia proved more vulnerable, their fate immortalized in Chekhov's *The Cherry Orchard*. Similarly, after 1905, it was not so much the large as the medium-sized estates that came under the hammer. Soviet historians emphasize that these properties were least capable of modernization along capitalist lines: the small estates had diversified, while the very largest had become big granaries. Much of the transfer of gentry property within this class also represented acquisitions by the biggest owners, confirming the picture of stability and even consolidation of large landholding.[26]

Between 1877 and 1905 the amount of land available to peasants as allotment increased from around 122 m. hectares to 134 m.[27] This hardly did more than re-establish the situation that existed prior to emancipation, and during those three decades the peasant population had increased much faster than the allotment reserve. However, the amount of land held privately by peasants increased at a much faster rate, from about 7.2 m. hectares in 1877 to 25.7 m. in 1905. Those living in the black-earth provinces held a slightly larger proportion of private peasant property.

This process of peasant land acquisition was fostered (though not initiated) by the Peasants' Land Bank, which the government established in 1883. In the early years of its operation, only one-fifth of peasant purchases reflected assistance from the Bank. This owed much to the conservative provisions of the statutes, which did not allow the Bank to purchase land on its own account. The Bank's main function was to assist peasant associations (*tovarishchestva*) and village communities. Only after the turn of the century did the acquisition of land by individuals assume greater importance. The results of this new emphasis, in the case of individual provinces, could be quite dramatic:

Table 4.5

Land purchased by peasants in Kursk Province, with assistance from Peasants' Land Bank, 1884–1915

	1884–95		1896–1906		1907–15	
	Number of loans	Total area (hectares)	Number of loans	Total area	Number of loans	Total area
Village communities	80	20,921	54	19,188	54	13,892
Associations	142	17,444	989	100,072	673	66,285
Individuals	18	94	419	3,997	1347	48,064

Source: R. M. Ivanova, 'K izucheniyu materialov Krestyanskogo pozemelnogo banka', in *Problemy istorii SSSR*, Nauka, 1973, p. 274.

An analysis of the status of applicants to the Peasants' Land Bank suggests that most of them were 'middle peasants'. Presumably, the wealthiest could either buy land outright or borrow from other sources. Poor peasants, of course, had neither the financial resources to acquire private land nor the draught animals.[28]

None of this activity in the land market affected the basic grievance of peasants, namely that they felt cheated of land that rightfully belonged to them and were forced to pay for allotments which could not support growing numbers. This profound disquiet surfaced in periodic outbreaks of protest, most seriously in Little Russia (in 1902) and again, in a devastating show of opposition to landlords and their agents, during the spring and summer of 1905 and 1906. 'Trespass' on private estates was commonplace, accompanied by the destruction of agricultural fixed capital (farm buildings, machinery), attacks on manor houses and the seizure of crops, hay, timber and land itself. The seizure of fodder and pasture and the illicit cutting of timber were widespread in European Russia, indicating how the original emancipation settlement had overlooked the importance of non-arable resources. In the Central Black Earth and New Russia, arson attacks affected the majority of districts. On large estates in the Baltic, Little Russia and the South-West, agricultural workers went on strike, demanding better treatment and higher wages.[29]

The provincial landed gentry, who bore the brunt of these attacks, responded in different ways. Some hurried to the cities to escape the rural 'illuminations'; others attempted to negotiate; others met force with force, with government assistance. Some gentry urged upon the government the need to accede to peasant demands by means of a land reform, even if this meant losing part of their property.[30]

Most of the business of the new parliament (Duma), established by tsarist decree in response to the 1905 revolution of workers and soldiers, was taken up with the question of land reform. Left-wing deputies insisted upon the complete expropriation of private estates and the redistribution of land to peasants without compensation. The Socialist-Revolutionaries (SRs), who enjoyed widespread support among the peasantry, argued that all land should be 'socialized' and exploited by all households able and willing to work it on their own account. Lenin, on behalf of the new Bolshevik Party, outlined a programme for the abolition of private property in land and the creation of a free market that would further accelerate the development of capitalism. Menshevik policy similarly favoured the abolition of large estates, but urged that the land thus released be administered on behalf of peasants by new municipal authorities, elected by peasants. Representatives of the liberal Constitutional Democratic Party (Kadets), who made up the largest fraction in the new Duma, also brought forward a project for expropriation; this involved only partial alienation and stipulated that peasants should compensate the former landlords, albeit at terms that reflected a 'fair' valuation of the land rather than the market price, which had been inflated by population pressure. Whether the land would then be farmed communally or individually proved more difficult to decide, but mainstream opinion in the party favoured individual tenure, on the grounds that this would inspire technical change in backward agriculture.[31]

Hand in hand, the tsarist government and the resurgent provincial gentry defeated the proposals for land redistribution, and formulated instead a very different 'agrarian reform'. In June 1906, with the backing of the Ministry of Internal Affairs (MVD), the government brought forward a project for the conversion of communal to hereditary individual land tenure. This change of official policy had to do in part with a growing belief in the economic irrationality of the commune. But there was more to it than that. Underlying the new policy was the assumption that peasants who had private property of their own would be less likely to attack the private property of landlords: 'It is enough (said A. V. Krivoshein in 1906) to make the peasant an owner for him to recognize the full monstrosity of the expropriation of property'.[32] When the Duma showed no sign of capitulating on the central question of land redistribution, it was dissolved, and Nicholas II issued an imperial decree in November 1906 which allowed the head of a peasant household to declare the allotment land he held of the commune to be his individual property. Furthermore, he could ask for his strips of land to be consolidated, if two-thirds of the commune's membership agreed. These were the famous 'Stolypin reforms'.[33]

As the information on land sales in Table 4.4 indicates, the land reforms had little impact on the transfer of land from gentry to other social groups. Net sales of gentry land in the decade 1905–14 amounted to nearly 12 m. hectares, equivalent to the volume of sales in the previous decade; only now, the stimulus of falling cereal prices was no longer felt. In so far as most of this land was purchased by individuals (with or without the aid of the Land Bank), it may be thought that the government policy of encouraging a shift away from communal tenure had borne fruit. However, the reforms failed to tackle the basic injustice felt by Russian peasants, which they tackled themselves during the summer months of 1917. In short, the reforms neither ended gentry land sales nor crushed the revolutionary potential of the peasantry.[34]

In one respect, nevertheless, expropriation did become official policy. During the mid-nineteenth century tsarist forces had extended Russian control over the area north-east of the Caspian Sea, subjugating first the Kazakh nomads and (by 1876) the Uzbeck khanates of Kokand, Bokhara and Khiva. By 1881 the entire area of Kazakhstan and Turkestan – down to the borders with Persia, Afghanistan and China – had come under Russian domination. In 1884 a government commission drew attention to the scope for Russian settlement, both as a 'buffer' against the Chinese and as a means of alleviating pressure on land in European Russia. In Kazakhstan, the government seized Kazakh land and declared it state property, henceforth available to be granted to Russian colonists. Early peasant settlers came from western Siberia and from Samara and Saratov. During the 1890s around a quarter of a million people settled in Kazakhstan; between

1906 and 1915 this figure shot up to one million. There was plenty of land to spare: around 20 m. hectares (as of 1895), and more still, if one assumed that the indigenous nomads could be 'persuaded' to switch to cereal farming. In Turkestan, settlers were encouraged to buy land from native farmers, but intermittent revolts against Russian rule allowed the government to confiscate property. Most Russian peasants settled in the eastern region (Semirechye), where once more the government made grants of land and, from 1910 helped out with cash as well.[35]

In Siberia, by the middle of the nineteenth century, indigenous nomads had either been driven further east or been compelled to adopt a more settled way of life. When, during the 1890s, the Russian government turned its attention to the colonization of Siberia on a large scale, it again adopted the principle that the land was under its control and could be granted to Russian settlers. At least until 1910 there was little concern about the availability of land for the migrants who had flooded into Siberia. An official survey of Siberian land-holding, in 1911–12, estimated that farmers who had already settled in Siberia for ten years or more had an average holding of more than 18 hectares. As one historian says, this characterized 'the generally higher economic level of peasant life in Siberia'.[36]

Land was a precious asset in pre-revolutionary Russia. It was also the clearest manifestation of division in tsarist society: between gentry and peasant, between kulak and poor peasant, between Russian and non-Russian. Over time, Russian farmers gained more than non-Russian from the transfers that took place. Rich peasants consolidated their socio-economic position at the expense of poorer peasants. The transfer of land from gentry to peasantry was striking, but it suggests not so much a wholesale 'crisis' as a weeding-out of less dynamic elements and a strengthening of the economic position of entrepreneurial landowners, specializing in cereals, dairy products or industrial crops. All the same, there was no escaping the overall drift away from gentry landholding and the fact that more land was being worked by peasants, either as communal (and, later, individual) proprietors or as leaseholders. As we have emphasized, this hardly satisfied peasant aspirations to lay claim to all land on behalf of toiling people; but it had other implications as well. The liberal view was that land was being transferred to the class of people least able to farm it efficiently, and that the consequences for agricultural productivity and the food market could be dire. Accordingly, it is to the question of productivity that we now turn.

4.3 Productivity in Russian Agriculture

Information on agricultural productivity in tsarist Russia comes in two main guises: data on the productivity of land, and estimates of agricultural labour productivity. Attention has already been drawn to trends in crop yields, and some explanations for the level and growth of yields will be considered presently. So far as labour productivity is concerned, there are enormous problems in arriving at firm conclusions.

The tsarist authorities compiled no data on the size of the agricultural labour force. In the absence of such data, historians have been driven to assume that the agricultural labour force (and the total number of man-hours worked in agriculture) increased at the same rate as the total rural population. This assumption is valid, provided of course that no change occurred over time in the participation rate of the rural population in non-agricultural production. On this basis, according to calculations made by Paul Gregory, output per worker in Russian agriculture increased by around 1.4 per cent between 1883/7 and 1909/13. This rate is equivalent to about three-quarters of the estimated growth rate of labour productivity in Russian industry. As Gregory points out, the performance of agriculture appears in a more favourable light than is suggested in the work of Gerschenkron and other pessimists.[37]

The concept of 'agriculture' is a highly aggregated one, and trends in agricultural labour productivity and in the productivity of land may not have been uniform throughout the sector as a whole. In this section, attention will concentrate upon the respective performances of the 'gentry' economy and the 'peasant' economy.

Historians have sometimes assumed that the level of productivity on gentry estates was low, because proprietors had been brought up in a climate of serfdom, which left them incapable of adjusting to modern economic conditions after 1861. Such bald generalizations leave much to be desired. The transfer of land, as suggested above, could itself be taken to imply a displacement of gentry who were ill equipped to cope with commercial farming. There is also abundant evidence of gentry entrepreneurship in diverse sectors of agriculture (wheat, sugar, livestock breeding).

Nevertheless, conditions did not always encourage gentry to farm estates in a productive manner. The desperate search by peasants for additional arable led many private landowners to lease land, so that the eminent economist A. I. Chuprov concluded in 1906 that 'civilized gentry estates, well-endowed with capital and know-how, are isolated outposts, concealed among a mass of mediocre and neglected properties, based simply upon the leasing of land to the peasantry and the extortion of rent'.[38]

Peasants obtained access to gentry land in return for the payment of labour-rent (or *otrabotka*), or for cash. By the end of the nineteenth century, money rent had grown in importance. In each case, however, the implications for the productive use of land tended to be the same. Peasants were offered only short-term leases, for one or two seasons only. Most land leased to peasants was cultivated according to the three-field system, which left one-third of the land fallow at any given time. Peasants applied to the rented land the same modest inventory they used on their allotments. Peasants had no incentive to improve farming methods or to improve yields. They were not compensated for any improvements, and landlords were likely to find other applicants for leases when the term expired. Thus, according to one contemporary source, yields on rented land tended to be no higher – and were frequently lower – than yields on peasant allotments.[39]

In this respect, little had changed in the post-reform agrarian economy, compared with the situation before 1861. The researches of Confino have established that demesne land was often in effect cultivated by peasants according to their own semi-autonomous decisions and routines, which dictated that the three-field system prevailed on the estate. Gentry proprietors themselves conspired to perpetuate traditional farming techniques, because they could not bear to disrupt established patterns and to assume the costs of resettling peasants who would be forced off the land as a result of the enclosure of open fields. It was less trouble to continue as of old, in the knowledge that any increased output, designed to satisfy growing demand, could be obtained by extending the area under crops (ploughing up waste and commons).[40]

In another respect, too, gentry proprietors have been accused of failing to adopt advanced methods on their lands. It has been argued that they exploited the fertile lands in New Russia by cropping the soil continuously, until it became exhausted and required several years' rest. The main evidence for this derives from the reports submitted to the Valuev Commission in the early 1870s. The criticism is not entirely fair: this 'long fallow' was rational, where land was so abundant. Later on, landlords in the south tended to diversify into other products, but this was not because land was no longer fertile. Rather, other items (grapes, tobacco, sheep farming) gave a better return.[41]

The situation was not uniformly dismal. In the South-West, landowners cultivated sugar beet, the waste from which was fed to cattle and thus increased the level of manure. In the non-black earth, landed gentry did not universally renounce productive agriculture and rent or sell land. In the Baltic and North-West, and in parts of Belorussia landlords abandoned the old rotation and sowed grasses on fallow. One classic instance of such improvements was described by A. N

Engelhardt in a series of articles entitled 'From the Village'. Engelhardt showed that in just fifteen years he had doubled rye yields on his Smolensk estate. He had extended the arable acreage by reclaiming waste and forest. On this land he had applied organic fertilizer, supplied by the large livestock herds which he maintained on meadows leased from his neighbours. Engelhardt also experimented with new rotations and was a passionate advocate of artificial fertilizer. Perhaps he was the exception to the general rule, one of Chuprov's 'isolated outposts' (he was, interestingly, an exile from the capital, confined to his estate for criticizing the regime). In any event, he showed what might be done with some entrepreneurial imagination.[42]

The evidence from the 1916 Agricultural Census suggests that the general level of gentry farming improved markedly during the half century after 1861. The most likely explanation for this process is that the weakest gentry farmers had been eliminated from the scene, having taken advantage of good land prices to sell up. This left a still significant number who increasingly came to specialize in cereals, dairy or other products; who responded to shifts in relative prices for agricultural commodities (see below); and who acquired a more modern inventory. Among the more important innovations were steam ploughs in the Ukraine, mechanical threshers and ploughs in New Russia and the Lower and Mid-Volga provinces.[43]

The trend in crop yields on gentry estates cannot be precisely quantified. Official statistics distinguished simply between 'private' and 'allotment' land. While peasants exclusively cultivated the latter, private land belonged to gentry, peasants and others. Besides, as we have stressed, much nominally gentry land was in fact cultivated by peasants. Kondratiev, the famous Russian economist, followed the official convention and drew up a table of trends in cereal yields (see Table 4.6), but this does not allow any conclusions to be drawn about the relative performance of gentry as distinct from peasant producers. It is presented only to give a broad indication of trends in yields of allotment and non-allotment land.

A more accurate guide to the differential in cereal yields between gentry and peasant cultivators was published in the results of the 1916 Agricultural Census. According to this source, the gap between the two categories was of the order of 17 per cent, but to what extent the differential had declined over time is difficult to tell. Pavlovsky argued that it was as high as 50 per cent at the turn of the century, but this is hard to accept.[44] If the differential were this large, the consequences for aggregate productivity in Russian cereal agriculture would have been very serious, given the transfer of land to the peasantry. In so far as some peasants became owners of this land, we may

Table 4.6

Cereal yields on private and allotment land, 1861–1910

(tsentners per hectare)

	1 Privately owned land		2 Allotment land		3 Percentage difference (1 − 2 ÷ 2)
1861–70	5.90	(100)	5.18	(100)	14
1871–80	6.61	(112)	5.54	(107)	19
1881–90	7.51	(127)	6.09	(117)	23
1891–1900	8.40	(142)	6.97	(134)	21
1901–10	9.65	(163)	7.69	(148)	25

Source: N. D. Kondratev, *Rynok khlebov i ego regulirovanie vo vremya voiny i revolyutsii*, 1922, p. 6.

assume that the yields were better than they would have been, had they continued to rent land on a short-term basis.

The evidence on crop yields in Table 4.6 suggests that over the fifty years from 1860 to 1910 they improved by something like 50 per cent on peasant allotment land. Although this appears to have been too slow a rate of increase to reduce the differential between allotment and privately owned land, it is nevertheless sufficiently striking to cast some doubt on the more colourful denunciations of Russian peasant farming. Nor does the trend suggest that the greatest gains took place in the period after 1900. But before examining the origins of productivity growth, it is necessary to outline some of the conventional arguments for the stagnation of peasant farming in tsarist Russia.

A common explanation for the low level and slow growth of productivity in peasant agriculture takes the following form. Most peasants organized themselves in communities which sought to equalize the distribution of land of varying quality, by dividing it into strips. These strips were then allocated to households according to their ability to work the land, or according to the mouths they had to feed. Because the relationship between land and household size changed over time, land had to be reallocated periodically. The division of land into small parcels, accentuated still further by population growth, made it difficult for an individual farmer to innovate, because the efficacy of most improvements depended upon mutual action. Instead, communal tradition and peasant inertia perpetuated a rigid three-field system of crop rotation, whereby one in three of the open fields were sown in successive years with a winter crop, a spring crop, then left fallow (leaving one in three fallow in any given year). The reallocation of land also hindered the introduction of improved methods of cultivation, because the individual farmer had no guarantee of reciprocal improvements on the land he was due to receive on giving up his current allotment.[45]

There are a number of problems with this interpretation. In the first place, the argument about the deleterious effects of land redistribution carries less weight, the more it is considered. There is no reason why the commune membership should not have devised some mechanism for rewarding those peasants who proved most capable of improving the strips they farmed, as a means of raising the general standard of cultivation: at least, no reason integral to the community itself. In fact, Soviet historians have shown that land which had been improved in some way (drained or properly fertilized) was *excluded* from communal partition, at least during the 1870s. Even the government which, in the 1890s, sought to protect the commune against zealous individualists, insisted that peasant 'improvers' should be compensated for land they subsequently lost during any redivision.[46]

Secondly, it is worth asking why peasants adhered to a system of open-field farming, when the apparent benefits of enclosure in terms of higher output per hectare were so substantial. Medieval English peasants did not, according to Donald McCloskey, adhere to scattered strips in order to equalize tax burdens. In his view, tax obligations could have been adjusted to take account of differences in land quality or accessibility. He suggests that the real reason, in medieval England at least, had to do with the household's need to insure itself against the risk of partial crop failure, excessive flooding of particular lands and so forth. Given that Russian peasants adhered to open-field agriculture when the tax burden diminished, it is reasonable to ascribe their behaviour also to the need to equalize access to land of variable quality.[47]

Open-field farming was no more a universal phenomenon among Russian peasants than was the practice of land redistribution. Many historians have pointed out that the redistributional commune was hardly known in southern Russia, and only predominated in central Russia. Open fields were not found in the western region – Belorussia, the South-West and in Kherson province. Why was this? Pavlovsky argued that the absence of the commune and of open-field agriculture reflected an adjustment by peasant farmers to the demands of commercial agriculture. Where the market was underdeveloped, peasants sought to guarantee their own subsistence, as there was no imperative to do otherwise. The intermingling of strips and redistribution of land made sense in this context, as a means of collective survival. In those regions where market demand was strong (close to central Europe, to export outlets on the Black Sea, to urban markets in the Baltic), peasant commercial farmers either abandoned open-field systems or, where land was newly settled, at once established enclosed farms.[48]

Faced with rural revolution in 1905, the government decided to increase the political weight of a yeoman class within the village. These farmers would, it was hoped, set up enclosed farms. A decree issued in November 1906 provided that each householder had the right to declare his allotment to be his private property, and to demand that the village offer him a consolidated plot in exchange for his scattered strips. Legislation passed in March 1906 provided that new 'Land Settlement Commissions' were to be established in each province and district. They were to help with the consolidation of scattered strips, since it was also the intention that a two-thirds majority of heads of households in each commune could decide upon the enclosure of scattered plots. In a further development, the government decreed in 1910 that all communal land that had not been subject to a general redistribution since 1887 was henceforth to be regarded as hereditary property.[49]

The interpretation of official statistics on land reorganization is fraught with difficulty, but some general conclusions may be drawn. By 1917, most peasant holdings which had traditionally been worked as scattered strips continued to be farmed on the same basis. Estimates of the number of households which had become 'individualized' by 1917 vary considerably; calculations by Dorothy Atkinson suggest that the number of households that had petitioned the authorities by 1917 to become 'individualized' represented 22 per cent of the total number in existence in 1905. In terms of land held, some 16 per cent of peasant allotment land had been 'consolidated' by 1917, but this represented no more than 10 per cent of total peasant holdings. Some of this consolidated land was still farmed on a communal basis. Land that was by then hereditary property remained scattered on the eve of the Revolution, the financial and technical difficulties of 'reorganization' proving arduous in the extreme, even for the teams of enthusiastic, not to say demonic specialists in the land settlement commissions.[50]

We should beware of falling into the trap, as did so many pre-revolutionary enthusiasts for the Stolypin land reforms, of attributing all signs of improvement in the post-1906 rural economy to government intervention. The reforms coincided with a recovery in agricultural prices, so gains that might be attributed to the reforms could have taken place in any event. But more important than this, some signs of productivity growth were apparent well before the reforms, and the characteristic measures taken to promote land enclosure had also been taken voluntarily by some farmers before 1906.[51]

Many economists and agrarian reformers argued that the real problem of peasant agriculture was that peasants suffered not from a shortage of land, but from a shortage of technical knowledge and a lack of acumen. In Antsiferov's words, 'No actual shortage of land over existed. The feeling of congestion was purely the result of technical inferiority'.[52] While most people ascribed those deficiencies to the commune, it was not necessary to introduce the commune into the argument. Pavlovsky, for example, distinguished between the commune and the open-field system, finding in the persistence of the latter the main obstacle to innovation within peasant farming. Vorontsov denied even the relevance of open-field organization and argued that neither this nor the commune constituted a brake on the performance of peasant agriculture. The agrarian history of parts of France suggests that the abolition of the open fields was not a necessary precondition for improvements in agricultural productivity.[53]

The specific technical changes that contemporaries had in mind were the changes that had gradually been introduced in western Europe, which improved the fertility of the soil without leaving the land fallow for one or more years. Farmers planted clover or grass (timothy), legumes (peas, beans, vetch) and root crops (turnips), but these new rotations did far more than just fix nitrogen in the soil and thus prepare it for future cereal cultivation. They increased the fodder supply and thus allowed farmers to keep more (and healthier) livestock, which in turn generated a larger supply of manure. Over several generations, these innovations had paid dividends in terms of higher yields.[54]

We have already seen that these methods were known to Russian farmers, and that some individuals adopted them during the 1860s and 1870s on large estates. Pavlovsky argued that the use of grasses as part of improved rotations spread only slowly among peasant farmers, while by 1916 large farms were much more active in this respect: grass represented less than two per cent of all crops sown on peasant land, whereas the proportion was over eight per cent on large farms. In both cases, the most advanced rotations were found in the North-West and Central Industrial Region. On peasant farms in the central black-earth and central industrial provinces, where pasture had been converted to arable as a result of population growth, the increased use of fodder crops had the important effect of compensating for the loss of hay and of sustaining the livestock and therefore the fertilizer supply.[55]

There does not appear to have been a close correlation between the adoption of new rotations and the absence or abolition of the communal, open-field system. Chuprov pointed out that peasant communities in the Central Industrial Region and North-West switched to grasses in place of fallow. The increased use of potatoes in conjunction with grass as part of new rotations had a favourable effect on yields, as in those regions and in Belorussia. These new rotations were less marked in New Russia, although the cultivation of sugar beet did have a positive effect, in so far as the waste could be fed to cattle.[56]

We can see these broad changes reflected in the changing cultivation of land at the level of the individual village. A survey of enclosed and unenclosed peasant farms in Tver province revealed that the proportion of sown area devoted to cereals fell from around 85 per cent in 1883 to between 42 and 60 per cent by 1913–16. Grass and clover, which had been unknown in 1883, now formed between 15 and 26 per cent of all sowings. Flax cultivation also expanded, but in some instances this appeared to threaten soil fertility (that is, where it was not properly integrated with ley grasses). Observers in Tver and in Tula found that peasants sought to change the traditional three-field rotations as little as possible. Ideally, peasants should have adopted six- or even nine-field rotations, allowing the soil to recover properly through the greater use of clover and grass. The author of a recent study of this subject concludes that modern rotations may have played a less important role in raising crop yields compared to other, less visible improvements, such as the use of better varieties of seed and the more effective use of fertilizer (areas in which zemstvo agronomists often figured prominently).[57]

New rotations improved the supply of organic fertilizer in the long term. Contemporary agronomists ascribed many of the problems of peasant agriculture to the relative dearth of livestock, in particular, because of the consequences for the supply of manure. Lokhtin suggested that the optimum number of cattle in European Russia – based upon livestock : land ratios in the west – was 115 million, but in fact the actual number did not exceed 25 million. In New Russia, the problem did not arise, because there was fertile land in abundance and plenty of scope for grazing livestock. Here, manure constituted a fuel source, not a fertilizer. The situation was more serious in the Central Industrial Region and in Little Russia, where conversion to arable had been rapid and where (in the former) the quality of the podzolic soil made good fertilizer supply a precondition of higher yields. The number and density of cattle did increase significantly in the central industrial provinces, and in Belorussia and the North-West, suggesting both an increase in the supply of fertilizer and a switch to more intensive dairy farming. It is worth noting that the supply of artificial fertilizer was very modest (mostly imported), and its application largely confined to cotton-growing in Central Asia.[58]

Other technical changes in farming can have an important impact on productivity, for example by improving methods of breaking up the soil and preparing it for cultivation. Improved techniques of harvesting and threshing can also boost productivity, by reducing waste. In regions of especially extensive cultivation of cereals, where it may be important to harvest the crop quickly before it scorches (south-eastern steppe), efforts to mechanize the production process will be important as well. Generally speaking, however, mechanization played little part in Russian agriculture (gentry or peasant) before 1900 and, as elsewhere in Europe, modifications to hand tools proved more decisive.[59]

In peasant farming, the traditional plough (*sokha*) prevailed throughout central European Russia and the Mid-Volga, at least till the early twentieth century. In New Russia and the Urals, the more modern plough (*plug*) had already been adopted by the 1880s. Anfimov detects a shift to the use of the iron plough in the central Russian provinces after 1900, and suggests that this process was encouraged by a decline in the price of the new plough, relative to the price of agricultural products. The dissemination of these cheaper ploughs was also promoted by the *zemstva*, and by cooperatives, and by firms such as International Harvester. But we should not overlook the importance of modifications to the traditional wooden plough; the use of an iron tip allowed the plough to cut deeper, but it was less heavy to work than the very modern equipment, which also required more draught power.[60] Peasants – and agricultural labourers on large estates – harvested crops by hand. In the central provinces they used the sickle, because this allowed them to cut close to the ground. But where the ears of corn were higher up and the land tended to be less uneven, they used the scythe. Threshing, too, was for the most part a manual task, with some evidence of mechanization by the 1890s. In general, therefore, Russian agriculture was characterized by modifications to traditional hand tools, and the use of mechanized equipment, at least before 1900, was limited. Studies of agriculture in the 1920s also confirm that the technological level of peasant farming remained relatively backward, but this is not to deny that modest gains were made in peasant farming.[61]

We must now ask under what conditions peasant farmers, in particular, decided whether to innovate or not. In the first place, there could be 'internal' pressures, at the level of the village community, such as increasing density of peasant population. This could lead farmers to reduce the fallow, cultivate land more intensively and boost yields through an increase in fertilizer inputs. An increase in livestock herds (and weight) would also improve food supply per capita. This response to population pressure has been outlined by Ester Boserup, and on the face of it appears to have some applicability to the situation in the Central Black-Earth Region and elsewhere. It is supported, for example, by a study of peasant farming in Kazan, undertaken by Fortunatov during the 1880s. Fortunatov pointed out that the yield of rye on peasant farms increased by sixteen per cent between 1870–4 and 1883–7, and he also detected a close association between the density of population in each district and the size of yields per hectare.[62]

A second possibility is that improvements will reflect changes in 'external' conditions. Pavlovsky, for example, maintained that the crucial element in the modernization of peasant farming was the stimulus provided by the market. The growth of market demand encouraged peasants to produce a surplus, and this required the more intensive use of land (and labour) on peasant farms in central European Russia, and an extension in the area under crops in south Russia. Until the market expanded, became more unified and less prone to annual fluctuations in price (through transport innovations), producers had no incentive to innovate. If the market was weak, peasants would secure their own subsistence and have no regard for long-term gains in productivity or in profitability. When they did orientate themselves to these goals, this was because the risks of innovation seemed less acute and the rewards more evident.[63]

This approach has the merit of drawing out the relationship between productivity and commodity production. Accordingly, the next section looks at the development of the market in agricultural output.

4.4 Commodity Production in Russian Agriculture

The development of commercial agriculture, defined simply as an increase in the proportion of agricultural output that entered the market, can be dated back to the sixteenth century. However, the process of commercialization gathered pace towards the end of the eighteenth century. Peter Struve, the author of a classic work on the manorial economy (published in 1913) argued that the 'emancipation' of the Russian nobility in 1762 gave a significant boost to the production of grain for the market, in so far as gentry producers could henceforth concentrate on agricultural enterprise instead of service in the bureaucracy or army. However, this would not in itself explain why the level of surplus production expanded. Struve himself pointed to the growth in demand for grain from the expanding urban population, and for industrial raw materials (sugar and flax) from new factories. Latterly, scholars have suggested that an important additional stimulus derived from the gentry's desire for additional income, in order to satisfy their growing consumption requirements.[64]

The American historian Jerome Blum suggests that commodity production was not sustained during the first half of the nineteenth century. He argues that gentry found it easier to satisfy their demand for money income by extracting a quitrent (*obrok*) from serfs, rather than corvée (*barshchina*).[65] But this assessment conceals important changes within the half-century. For instance, grain prices were buoyant during the period before 1820, and it is likely that gentry in the Central Black Earth expanded the cultivation of the demesne (and thus intensified *barshchina*) in order to exploit the opportunities. After 1820, however, grain prices fell and remained low for at least two decades. It now behoved landowners to intensify the burden of *obrok* which might be obtained from serfs who were engaged on non-agricultural work. When prices rose once more, *barshchina* reasserted itself.

However, when gentry producers sought to expand still further the area under crops they found that the margin of cultivation in the Central Black Earth had already been reached. In the 1840s and 1850s grain production per head of population had fallen by ten and twenty per cent respectively over the 1802/11 level.[66] For the first time, traditional grain-producing regions encountered competition from new, fertile lands to the south and south-east. In New Russia, estates expanded the production of grain for the market; even when prices fell, the costs of production were sufficiently low to enable gentry farmers to survive without difficulty. When prices recovered after 1840, landowners took on more hired labour to supplement the services of their serfs. At the same time, farmers here turned to the production of sugar beet, to distilling and stock-breeding. This diversification may have begun as a response to changing relative prices of grain and other products.[67]

It should not be thought that serfs (or state peasants) had a uniform lack of access to the market for agricultural products. In fact the contribution made by peasants to the total grain surplus was quite substantial. At one time, historians believed that only ten per cent of marketed grain derived from peasant allotments prior to emancipation, but this figure is now questioned. One modern estimate puts the contribution of peasant producers to the volume of marketed grain as high as 45 per cent.[68] Even if this figure is inflated, as it may be, it still remains the case that peasants gained something from the increase in cereal prices between 1840 and 1860. At least, this applies to the stratum of wealthier households that was already identified in the Russian village before 1861. Some of this additional income was probably creamed off by landowners in the form of higher *obrok* payments, so the net gain was probably modest. As for poor peasants, the increase in grain prices acted to their disadvantage, because they entered the market as net consumers.

Changes in demand and supply schedules reveal themselves in the behaviour of prices. In general, agricultural prices continued to be buoyant up to 1880. The growth in world population and income per capita, especially in the western hemisphere, stimulated demand both for cereals and foodstuffs with a higher income elasticity of demand. On the supply side, changes in the availability of land and methods of cultivation, notably in North America, enabled global agriculture to produce a larger volume of food. The dramatic outflow of grain from the north American continent did not begin until after 1875, when steamships reduced transatlantic shipping costs, and so Russian grain producers were well placed during the 1860s and 1870s to take advantage of the increase in European as well as domestic demand.

The spread of rail transport after 1860 allowed Russian producers to ship grain from the main producing areas (Tambov, Ryazan, Saratov, Penza and Simbirsk), first of all to Moscow and the northern ports of Riga and St. Petersburg. During the 1870s the rail system was extended to connect the grain surplus provinces with Odessa and Rostov. Rail had the advantage over water and carting that it was faster and more reliable. The railways increased the potential surplus from the major grain-producing provinces, because those that had hitherto had to retain stocks as a buffer against periodic shortages in their area could now release them, on the assumption that railways could move stocks into the province during an emergency. In the past a good harvest had often meant that grain surpluses had to be distilled or even left to spoil in barns; now the surplus could be sold at home or abroad. Between 1865/7 and 1875, total grain shipments doubled in volume; whereas in the first period only 15 per cent of grain had been shipped by rail, the figure exceeded 55 per cent in 1875. Exports of grain increased fourfold in volume between 1860/4 and 1875/9 and rose from 6 per cent of the total net harvest to nearly 20 per cent between those dates.[69]

As the rural and urban population grew, particularly in the Central Industrial Region and the North-West, the production of grain in these regions did not keep pace. Furthermore, during the 1860s and to a lesser extent during the 1870s, the production of grain in the Ukraine failed to satisfy regional consumption requirements. Thus the role of the Central Black Earth provinces was especially significant as a source of supply to the internal market. S. G. Wheatcroft has estimated the volume of grain that was surplus to regional consumption (or, correspondingly, the grain that was needed in order to offset a deficit). He expresses the surplus (or deficit) as a percentage of production, as in Table 4.7.

As these estimates suggest, the central industrial and northern provinces remained in need of grain supplies from surplus-producing prov-

Table 4.7

Regional grain surpluses, 1850–1900

(Grain surplus or deficit, after allowing for regional consumption, expressed as percentage of regional production)

Region	1850–9	1860–9	1870–9	1880–9	1890–9
Northern consumer	− 9.6	− 6.5	−10.9	− 9.9	− 5.7
Southern producer	2.9	−15.3	− 0.1	12.1	26.7
Central producer	15.5	20.5	23.5	22.0	23.4
Eastern producer	23.7	5.3	17.1	16.2	39.9

Northern Consumer = Central Industrial, North, North-West, Belorussia
Southern Producer = South-West, Little Russia, New Russia
Central Producer = Central Black Earth, Mid-Volga, Lower Volga
Eastern Producer = Urals, Western Siberia
Source: S. G. Wheatcroft, 'Grain production and utilization in Russia and the USSR before collectivization', unpublished PhD thesis, University of Birmingham, 1980, p. 271.

prices. Prior to 1880 the main areas of surplus were the Central Black Earth and Mid-Volga; thereafter, the eastern region (Lower Volga) increasingly functioned as a source of supply. These regions provided the surplus available for export as well. The most dramatic turnaround took place in New Russia, which in the 1860s produced insufficient grain on balance to satisfy the regional consumption, but which in the 1880s and 1890s produced huge surpluses.

These trends indicated a progressive widening of the market, affording regions the opportunity to begin to specialize in agricultural commodities and engage in interregional trade. Grain producers in the south and east found an outlet for their products in the markets of the north and centre, and in exports. Where, prior to 1860, a *chetvert* of wheat had sold on average for five or six rubles, by the early 1870s producers obtained eight rubles. Oats fetched between 1.7 and 2.0 rubles, compared to 0.7 before 1860. The price increases had been most dramatic at the point of production, such as in Saratov and Tambov (Morshansk and Kozlov), where the rail network had revolutionized the scope for marketing grain.[70]

How did Russian farmers respond to changes in the market for agricultural commodities during the late nineteenth century? After 1880 the secular trend in cereal prices was downwards, reflecting the fact that the world supply schedule in cereals shifted quite sharply to the right. European food producers now confronted cheap wheat. from America and elsewhere. The competitive position of American producers was revolutionized by the combined effect of the prairie railways and the steamship. The price of Russian cereals on foreign markets began to fall from the end of the 1870s, but alarm about the scale of the decline surfaced most prominently in the early 1880s. Cereal prices on the Russian market started a prolonged decline then. which lasted until 1900 and which was interrupted only by the harvest failures of 1883 and 1891. The movement in the price of the major grains is outlined in Figure 3.[71]

Winter wheat prices held up better than those for other crops, and it was rye that most of all depressed the general index of cereal prices. An official enquiry into the effects of the depression, in 1888, concluded that the cultivation of wheat remained profitable, at least on the private estates to which the survey was confined.[72] This applied especially to the main wheat-growing belt in the south and south-east, where other crops too yielded profits. In this region, the scope for extensive cultivation of fertile land was still large. Compared to cereal cultivation in other regions, output here was higher for given inputs of labour and land. With lower transport costs as well, these provinces came to enjoy a cost differential over the Central Black Earth provinces, where producers now sought protection from the 'periphery'. The advent of grain supplies from western Siberia from the 1890s onwards only served to intensify the threat.

In theory, a positive response from agricultural producers to the secular fall in cereal prices would involve a progressive conversion to those products in which they might enjoy a comparative advantage over the new grain surplus-producing provinces. Farmers in central European Russia would do better to convert from rye and other cereals to dairy products, livestock and industrial crops, where urban markets were more accessible in which they could take advantage of cheaper feed. Critics of 'traditional' agriculture have suggested that peasants did not respond positively to changing market conditions: that peasants continued to plant rye while prices were depressed and converted pasture to arable, in order to feed the expanding rural population. Kaufman ascribed this behaviour to 'ignorance and inertia' on the part of the Russian peasantry, and this was a commonly held view.[73] But there is no reason to suppose that Russian peasants were any less rational or intelligent than farmers anywhere else. The risks and uncertainty that substitution of one product for another entail need to be recognized. In a society in which periodic harvest failures were common, peasants were naturally acutely conscious of the risks in farming, and it was by no means clear that these would be diminished by switching to (say) non-cereal cultivation.[74]

A more refined verdict is that the market for non-cereal products

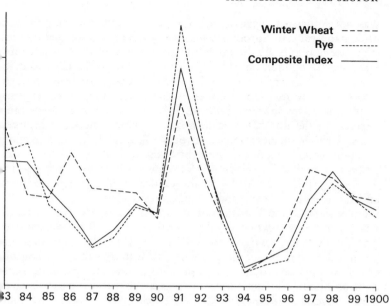

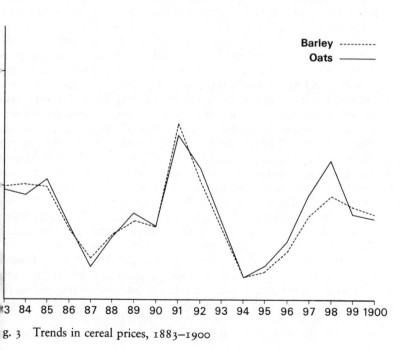

g. 3   Trends in cereal prices, 1883–1900

133

was not sufficiently developed before 1900. Pavlovsky saw the lack of demand for dairy products, market gardening produce and industrial raw materials as the key obstacle in the path of diversification. He correctly pointed out that this applied more to the Central Black Earth than it did to the Central Industrial Region or Belorussia. He also pointed to the opportunities in those areas for non-agricultural employment. Lyashchenko, writing in 1908, also acknowledged that 'farmers in the non-black earth provinces have long since begun to transfer either to more intensive forms of agriculture or to entirely different forms of application of their labour'.[75] A comparison of the pattern of regional sowings in 1880 and 1900 shows that peasants were substituting flax for rye in the Central Industrial Region, Baltic and North-West; dairy produce and livestock for rye in Belorussia, the North-West and Yaroslavl; and oats for rye in Moscow province where the *izvoshchiki* or cab-drivers purchased oats for their horses. This did not mean that rye disappeared from peasant crop rotations, but it did disappear from many of the fields that were sown to spring crops, as opposed to winter crops. The traditional 'peasant crops' such as buckwheat and millet, gave way to export crops, such as barley. Again, however, the Central Black Earth largely missed out on the dynamic substitution process.[76] Nor should it be forgotten that the gains of diversification were unequally distributed between peasant households. The poorer farms stuck to rye, buckwheat and potatoes. The rich diversified.

Generally speaking, livestock and dairy farming developed more rapidly in the north than elsewhere. Between 1850 and 1900 the pasture acreage in the south fell sharply, as farmers began to specialize in wheat and barley: in Kherson province, grazing lands fell from 52 per cent to 30 per cent of the total farm acreage; in Bessarabia, from 60 to 30 per cent. This affected sheep farming more than anything else. In New Russia, the number of sheep fell by one-third between 1880 and 1900. On the other hand, in Belorussia, the North-West and Baltic region, and in parts of the Central Industrial Region, farmers switched from arable to dairy farming, albeit on a less dramatic scale. Livestock herds per capita remained static between 1880 and 1900 for European Russia as a whole, but in the north they rose.[77]

The price of dairy products and livestock was undoubtedly higher at the end of the nineteenth century, relative to the price of cereals. The differential was definitely noticeable in the early twentieth century, and this further encouraged the process of diversification within Russian agriculture (see Table 4.8). Cereal prices recovered after 1900, not least because of a strong upward movement in the price of barley. Contemporaries drew attention to the improvement in the general fortunes of agricultural producers, and all the signs were that this reflected a recovery in prices, rather than the direct

Table 4.8

Agricultural product prices, 1900–1913

(1890–9 = 100)

	Rye	Wheat	Barley	All grains	Livestock and dairy products
1900–9	115.6	115.3	128.5	119.9	131.4
1910–13	126.7	133.2	152.6	130.1	155.2

Note: all prices are expressed as the average domestic price at local markets, except for barley, which is the price quoted at south Russian ports.
Source: *Planovoe khozyaistvo*, no. 7, 1927, p. 72.

effects of agrarian reform. The domestic market was buoyant, because the urban population had grown rapidly during the 1890s; the industrial sector continued to generate a demand for raw materials (sugar, flax, cotton); and Russian producers found new outlets in western Europe for products other than wheat and barley.

Another clear indication of progress can be found in the development of agriculture in western Siberia. Here, there were huge tracts of virgin steppe in the region bounded by Tobolsk and Chelyabinsk to the north-west and south-west, and by Tomsk and Semipalatinsk to the north-east and south-east. With the construction of the Trans-Siberian railway during the late 1890s, the potential Siberian grain surplus could now be sent westwards. The railway turned into a nightmare for Russian landowners in the central provinces of European Russia. Competition was exacerbated by the fact that grain was carried at cheap rates by railway companies anxious to attract additional traffic from Siberia. The government initially encouraged the adoption of a differential tariff that reduced the costs of transporting products over long distances, the main aim being to promote grain exports from whatever source. But a commission of enquiry in 1888, under V. K. Plehve, pointed out that central Russian producers already faced ruin from the Siberian grain trade. Eventually, in 1893, the government acceded to this pressure from its traditional gentry supporters, and grain shipments became subject to a duty that was calculated separately on freight up to Chelyabinsk, and on the journey west of this 'break'. Even before the rail link with western Siberia had been completed, European Russian producers had won a significant political victory. Not willing to ruin the Siberian grain trade entirely, the government built a rail link from Perm to Kotlas on the North

Dvina river, whence grain could be transported by steamship to Archangel. The arrangement was not entirely satisfactory: the river was
frozen for much of the year and grain had to be stored over the
winter and early spring, imposing additional costs. All the same, these
obstacles did not decisively hinder the expansion of grain shipments
from Siberia, which rose nearly fourfold in volume between
1896–1900 and 1909–13.[78]

The development of commercial farming in western Siberia owed
everything to the initiative of peasant farmers, who had settled there
in increasing numbers after 1890. The sown area in the three main
regions increased as shown in Table 4.9

Table 4.9

Cereal agriculture in western Siberia, 1901–1915

	Sown area (m. hectares)		Gross output (m. tons)	
	1901–5	1911–15	1901–5	1911–15
Akmolinsk	0.29	1.03	0.17	0.61
Tobolsk	1.27	1.62	0.89	0.95
Tomsk	1.59	3.65	1.03	2.41
Total	3.15	6.30	2.10	3.97

Source: L. M. Goryushkin, *Sibirskoe krestyanstvo na rubezhe dvukh epokh*
Nauka, Novosibirsk, 1967, p. 139.

The most important cereal crops were wheat and oats, and in a good
year farmers marketed as much as one-third of the net harvest, mostly
outside Siberia. The potential for further expansion remained
considerable, since the belt of fertile soil that stretched eastwards had
only begun to be exploited by 1913. This applied less to Tobolsk
which was densely settled by Siberian standards, and where a provincial grain surplus was less easy to obtain after 1910. Farmers had cultivated the land for five or six years in succession, before leaving it
to recover, and there were signs that yields were declining as a result
In other words, Siberian grain production in future would depend at
least as much on the improvement of farming methods in the western
provinces, as on the extension of the sown area further east.[79]

Faced with obstacles put in the way of grain marketing by the
Russian government, and encouraged by the growth in demand for

dairy products, Siberian farmers mounted one of the most effective campaigns of diversification in pre-revolutionary agriculture. Butter production expanded dramatically, helped by investment in creameries and refrigerated wagons, first by Danish firms and then by Siberian cooperatives. Butter exports rose from under 800 tons in 1897 to 93,000 tons in 1913. Along with eggs, the value of these products as a proportion of total export values rose from six per cent in 1900 (grain accounted for 43 per cent) to eleven per cent in 1913 (grain fell to below 40 per cent). If, as seems likely, the costs of producing grain were rising in parts of western Siberia, and the costs of dairy production fell because of technical and organizational improvements, then this diversification along the line of the railway made good sense.[80]

The discussion has concentrated so far on the growth of agricultural production and upon the development of the food market. The question remains as to whether agricultural production grew sufficiently rapidly to feed the growing population and to provide an export surplus. The question is important, in view of the assertions by contemporary populist writers (and the echo of those assertions by Alexander Gerschenkron), to the effect that agriculture had been squeezed in order to boost Russian export earnings. After all, had not the Minister of Finances himself, in the shape of Vyshnegradsky, given voice to the government's intention, by his appeal: 'Let us starve, but let us export'?

Research by Gregory does not corroborate the 'pessimistic' interpretation of the impact of grain marketings on rural households. Gregory has estimated the volume of marketed grain from transportation statistics. He then deducts this figure from his estimate of net harvest output, to arrive at a figure of grain retained within the village. His estimates include grain movements and output in non-European Russia as well as the fifty central provinces. Gregory concludes that the volume of retained cereal crops *increased*, both in absolute terms and as a proportion of net output, between 1885–9 and 1897–1901. In this, the key period of rapid industrialization, village consumption of grain increased at the same rate as Net National Product (NNP: see Table 4.10), although total retail sales in town and country grew faster still. By the early twentieth century the growth of retained cereals exceeded the growth rate, both for Net National Product and retail sales. This suggests that peasant households devoted part of the extra grain to their own consumption, and part to feeding livestock (thus improving both the potential marketing of meat and dairy products, and the capacity of draught animals). One ought not to jump to conclusions about the implications of this research for the hypothesis about rural living standards – it says nothing about the distribution of food within the village, or about the consumption of other

Table 4.10

Growth rates of grain retained in the village and of other indicators, 1885–1913

	Percentage annual average annual growth rates of:			
	Retained food grains	Total retail sales	NNP	Population
1885–89 to 1897–1901	3.5	4.8	3.6	1.5
1897–1901 to 1909–13	3.7	2.0	2.9	1.6

Source: P. Gregory, 'Grain marketings and peasant consumption in Russia, 1885–1913', *E.E.H.*, no. 17, 1980, p. 148.

items – but it is sufficiently impressive to make one pause before accepting at face value the pessimistic verdict about peasant impoverishment during the late nineteenth century. Peasants may have been poor, some of them desperately so, but it is not certain that they became poorer during the 1890s, still less that this happened because of government fiscal policy.[81]

The grain market, and indeed the food market in general, was convulsed during the First World War. The seriousness of the food shortages in Russian cities during 1917 is well known. What is less often appreciated is that there existed no aggregate grain shortage in Russia, even in 1917. Enough grain was available to satisfy all domestic needs. Production on large gentry estates had, of course, been adversely affected by the mobilization of agricultural labourers, and this could not but affect the volume of grain marketings. At the same time, however, the claims on Russian grain output had been reduced during the First World War by the cessation of exports, which in 1913 accounted for around 15 per cent of net output. The critical problem was not one of production so much as of distribution. Regional grain surpluses existed in western Siberia and in the Lower Volga, but transport suffered the strains of wartime military requirements. As a result, railways were unable to move grain to the centres of urban population.

This problem was exacerbated by the disruption in the market mechanism. Put bluntly, grain producers were deprived of access to manufactured goods that they normally purchased in exchange for grain. Instead, they were being asked to hold paper rubles that depreciated sharply between 1915 and 1917. By 1917, Russian peasants had turned away from the food market, a response that the government encouraged, by fixing grain prices in an attempt to control inflation. Within three short years, all that had been achieved over the past two generations to develop the agricultural commodity market had been undone.[82]

Conclusion

The modernization of Russian agriculture was reflected in the growth of the capital stock, in the expansion of commodity production and in product specialization. Agriculture proved capable of supplying food to the growing non-agricultural population, whilst satisfying the claims of rural producers. To this extent, the overall performance of the agricultural sector emerges in a favourable light.

The popular image of agricultural stagnation in tsarist Russia was never very compelling. It derives what validity it has from an emphasis upon the traditional food-producing region, the Central Black Earth. Here, it is hard to find evidence of significant technical or other progress. But when attention switches to the North-West, the Baltic, the South-West, New Russia and Siberia, a more dynamic picture is evident. In these regions, farmers responded well to the new market opportunities that presented themselves. The advantage of accessible and expanding markets for producers in south Russia and Siberia was compounded by the abundance of fertile soil. To sum up: in the centre, progress was peripheral, but on the periphery there was progress.

Another major feature of agriculture in post-reform Russia was the progressive extension of cultivation and marketing by peasant farmers. In general terms, on the eve of the First World War, peasants contributed around 86 per cent to total cereal production (no estimate is available for aggregate agricultural production), and accounted for 75 per cent of grain marketings. On the eve of the Crimean War, the peasant share of marketings did not exceed 45 per cent.[83] Again, regional differences in landholding and marketings are important. Gentry farming predominated in the Baltic and in the Ukraine: but peasant farming was no less predominant in other major commercial regions, such as Siberia, the North-West and South-West.

Lest the impression may have been given that everything fell into place in Russian agriculture, it is worth drawing attention to one source of recurrent difficulty. Russian agriculture remained prone to annual fluctuations in production, especially of cereals. These fluctuations could play havoc with domestic food supply, as well as exports. One positive sign was that annual fluctuations in yields were becoming less violent in south Russia. But they remained intense in the Central

Black Earth, and in the Mid-Volga. In the last 25 years of tsarism, the harvest failed on five occasions: 1891, 1897, 1901, 1906 and 1911. Poor precipitation as germination occurred, and once again when the first flowers appeared, could have devastating consequences. Quite marginal changes in rainfall and temperature could have a profound impact on yields.[84] Only the increased importance of the Ukraine and, subsequently, of Siberia, prevented harvest failures in the Centre from becoming national disasters. Interestingly, the 1891 crop failure was the last in pre-revolutionary Russia to be thought of as a 'famine'.

Any temptation to attribute to the tsarist government the major responsibility for agricultural progress should be firmly resisted. From one point of view, the government definitely played a part in agricultural production: the regime laid down the terms of peasant emancipation, and thus shaped the context for agricultural production. But the government did not directly stimulate the growth of agricultural output. Emancipation – and, for that matter, railway construction – was a necessary, but not a sufficient condition for the development of commodity production and agricultural productivity. Nor did that famous rural institution, the commune, play the crucial role that some historians have attributed to it, as an obstacle to change. Change occurred when the risks became less intolerable to peasant farmers and the rewards most apparent to the capitalists who emerged from their ranks. The New Economic Policy during the 1920s was perhaps an acknowledgment of that fact.

5 The Manufacturing Sector

A central question in late nineteenth-century debates about the tsarist economy concerned the preconditions for sustained industrialization. Discussion concentrated upon the size of the potential market for manufactured goods. Broadly speaking, the liberal interpretation assumed that the stimulus for industrial development could derive from one of two sources. The growth of agricultural productivity and of rural incomes, and thus consumer demand, was one such prerequisite. Alternatively, demand for manufactured goods could expand by means of technical change in industry, which reduced unit costs and relative prices. This second strategy was the one identified by Witte in his famous Memorandum of 1899, and it served as the main justification for his policy of attracting foreign capital into Russian industry.[1]

The populist view was that the market for manufactured goods was already satisfied by cottage industry, which enjoyed a close and 'organic' connection with agricultural producers. The growth of market demand was ruled out, because of the poverty of the mass of the Russian peasantry, who were being exploited by the state and by landlords. However, populists had to give some explanation for the observed increase in the rate of industrial development during the late nineteenth century. They attributed it to the 'artificial' measures adopted by the tsarist government, which fostered and supported factory industry, at the expense of cottage industry. In the populist view, this strategy would ultimately founder on the lack of market demand at home and abroad.

The marxist interpretation denied the populist assertion about the lack of a home market for manufactured goods. Marxists pointed to the differentiation of the Russian peasantry, who had to enter the market as consumers of industrial products. This process reflected the autonomous development of capitalism, and not (as populists maintained) the nefarious policies of the tsarist government. Furthermore, capitalist competition required that capitalists continuously invest in new capital equipment; this created an additional market for industry, and was something that populists overlooked. For marxists, this continuous accumulation would culminate in an overproduction crisis. In these circumstances, capitalists would take appropriate action, such as organizing monopolies in order to reduce competition.

These issues have been echoed in the historiography. Gerschenkron gave an ingenious twist to the liberal argument, by suggesting that the domestic market could not grow sufficiently rapidly to sustain an industrial revolution. The low level and slow growth of productivity in agriculture ruled this out. In his view, industrialization required that the government substitute for missing demand, for example by constructing railways. The regime's fiscal policies during the 1890s depressed consumer purchasing power still further; only after 1905 were the policies relaxed, and the market became broadly based. Gerschenkron thus attributed a progressive role to the government in the long run (this distinguishes his from populist views), and detected the emergence of a 'westernized' market in Russia by 1914.[2]

Kahan took a somewhat different line on the question of demand for manufactured goods, arguing that the tsarist government obstructed gains in agricultural productivity and (through its fiscal policy) hampered the long-term accumulation of savings in agriculture. The possibility that a sustained increase in rural income would generate a demand for manufactured goods – with an increase in the former registering as a disproportionately greater increase in the latter – was never allowed to emerge. Olga Crisp is less persuaded than Gerschenkron that the home market was weak. She points out that there were several dynamic consumer goods industries (even before 1861), such as cotton textiles and sugar, which had less difficulty in realizing their output than is implied in Gerschenkron's analysis. Even during the 1890s, rural consumption was more buoyant than is usually realized. However, there was still plenty of scope for improved productivity in the manufacturing sector and for reductions in costs. The problem was that the market was too fragmented to permit significant economies of scale and cost reductions.

Soviet scholars have paid more attention to the organization of industry and to labour supply than to the specific question of demand. They have charted the significance of government purchases as a stimulus to industrial production, but have followed Lenin in stressing the existence of a mass market, created by the differentiation of the Russian peasantry. Gindin has been more unorthodox in suggesting that the market was weak and that the government had to take a more direct role.[3]

5.1 General Trends in Industrial Production

Information on industrial production in tsarist Russia derives from contemporary assessments of the value of gross factory output, and from data on physical output. Available estimates of industrial production are not reliable for the period prior to 1885. But from the mid-1880s onwards the new factory inspectorate was charged with the responsibility for keeping a record of factory production. By definition, this information takes no account of cottage or urban handicraft production. The government also arranged for periodic censuses to be held, on four occasions: 1887, 1900, 1908 and 1912. Both types of data pose statistical problems. In the first place, figures of gross output incorporate an element of double-counting. From the point of view of estimating growth rates this does not matter, but only so long as the ratio between 'gross' and unduplicated output remained constant. Secondly, definitions of which enterprise constituted a 'factory' and which did not were prone to change. This makes it difficult to compare the data from one census to the next. Finally, the value of output in current prices has to be adjusted by an appropriate index of wholesale prices, in order to eliminate inflation.[4]

Alternatively, one may approach the measurement of industrial production from the direction of physical output. An appropriate basket of commodities can be selected, and assumed to be representative of industrial production as a whole. Each item can be weighted to construct a composite index of output. This was the method adopted by the famous Russian economist N. D. Kondratiev, upon whose original index most subsequent researchers have drawn.

Goldsmith, who recomputed the index first compiled by Kondratiev, came to the conclusion that gross factory output increased in real terms by between 5.0 and 5.5 per cent per annum between 1883 and 1913. The difference depends upon the price weights that are adopted. This estimate makes no allowance for non-factory output. In the absence of appropriate data, Goldsmith suggests that handicraft production grew at two-thirds the rate of factory production. After allowing for this, he estimated that *total* industrial production grew by between 4.5 and 5.0 per cent annually. Within this period (1883–1913), growth was most marked during the late 1880s and 1890s, when the average annual rate rose to between seven and eight per cent. Between 1900 and 1906, industrial growth was imperceptible, but a second industrial upsurge took place in the years immediately preceding the First World War.[5]

Turning to estimates of labour productivity in industry, it must be stressed that these can only be treated with some uncertainty. Accurate figures on the industrial workforce and on total hours worked do not exist. Gregory has attempted what he terms a 'rough and questionable' calculation, which suggests that output per person in industry – together with construction, transport and communications – grew by around 1.8 per cent annually, between 1883–7 and 1909–13. He detects a more rapid rate of growth during the first half of this period.[6]

The growth of industrial capital has been computed by Kahan, whose estimates derive from the value of assets that was reported to insurance companies. According to Kahan, total industrial capital (buildings, equipment and inventories) virtually quadrupled between 1890 and 1913, rising from 1,140 m. to 4,100 m. rubles (in constant prices). His estimates suggest that the value of capital per worker in industry increased by around 55 per cent during the same period.[7]

To sum up, total industrial production during the last quarter century of tsarist Russia grew by around five per cent. The stock of industrial capital grew somewhat in excess of this figure: Kahan's estimates suggest that the rate was around 5.7 per cent per annum. The labour force increased by around three per cent on average, according to Gregory. Thus the rate of growth of total industrial output cannot be attributed solely to increases in 'factor' inputs. Some increase in labour productivity can be observed, taking Russian industry as a whole.

One final noteworthy aspect of industrial production was the composition of total output. It was not the basic industries, such as mining and metallurgy, that dominated industrial production, so much as consumer goods. As late as 1913, after three decades of rapid industrialization, the two broad categories of textiles and foodstuffs together accounted for around one-half of gross industrial production. This was twice as much as mining, metallurgy and engineering combined. In terms of energy consumption, food and textiles more than held their own, consuming 38 per cent of total industrial horse-power, compared with 39 per cent used by metallurgy and engineering. If an allowance were made for small-scale units, the proportion of total industrial production that 'light' industry contributed would be greater still. To put it bluntly, the history of industrialization in Russia was not synonymous with the growth of heavy industry.[8]

5.2 Aspects of Industrial Development before 1860

Industrial development in the century before 1860 offered an example of fitful activity by the state, especially by comparison with the measures taken by Peter the Great. Private enterprise was less rudimentary and inadequate than is sometimes supposed. Private entrepreneurs did not simply call upon the government to purchase their products; this dependence upon the state held good in respect of the early eighteenth century only, when even factories that produced glass, orcelain and paper worked largely for government commission. From the middle of the eighteenth century onwards, one is struck by he growing attempt by entrepreneurs to provide manufactures for he private market.

Such a market undoubtedly existed in the remainder of the eighteenth and early nineteenth centuries. In the first place, the total population grew rapidly in the eighteenth century, with a faster rate of growth of urban population. In the second place, as Arcadius Kahan pointed out, gentry landowners developed a new range of consumer tastes as part of a conscious desire to emulate the west European aristocracy. Finding new ways to increase their revenues, the Russian gentry were able to satisfy the 'costs of westernization' and to consume a greater quantity of dress, luxury furnishings and foodstuffs, paper and the like. Only part of this increased demand was satisfied by imports. Thirdly, the territorial expansion of the Russian empire during the latter part of the eighteenth and early nineteenth centuries created an additional potential for the export of manufactured goods to the Crimea (after 1783), Georgia (1801) and the Caucasus (1790s onwards). Finally, Russian industry satisfied the growing demand from western Europe for iron: around half the iron output of Urals industry was exported during the second half of the eighteenth century, with three-quarters directed to Britain. Given the high degree of exploitation of forced labour, and the abundant supply of timber for charcoal-smelting, Russian iron enjoyed an advantage in such markets, notwithstanding the high transport costs. It also satisfied the foreign demand for high-quality iron.[9]

The Urals iron industry lost this advantage within the space of two generations, and by the 1850s the export of iron did not exceed eight per cent of total output. Neither coke-smelting, nor puddling of iron, nor the rolling-mill were adopted. Why not? As far as coke-smelting is concerned, the reserves of charcoal in the Urals were sufficiently large and the costs of obtaining it so low that it hardly seemed rational to abandon its use, the more so as coke-smelting produced a weaker, albeit lighter pig iron. With the puddling process, metallurgists were concerned that there was still too much waste in the process to justify its adoption (this problem was not solved in England before the late 1830s). The rolling mill made sense as a labour-saving device and in circumstances of large-scale production, but in the Urals 'possessional' labour was still cheap (at least until the 1850s) and ironworks were for the most part small-scale enterprises. A rolling-mill was beyond the reach of the owner and was also not justified by the scale of activity at most plants. Some modest innovation did take place in the industry prior to the emergence of the Ukraine as the main centre of advance after 1880, but the abundance of labour and (to a lesser extent) charcoal operated in favour of traditional technique. It might be argued that this backwardness was dictated, not by factor costs, but by the narrowness of the domestic market, prior to the construction of the railways. However, when railways did generate a huge demand for iron, the Urals iron industry failed to respond: it lost its cheap labour after 1861, and the costs of fuelling the furnaces rose further. But the fragmentation and dispersal of iron works forestalled the innovation that was now imperative.[10]

The most organized branch of textiles before 1800 was the manufacture of woollens, in which manorial enterprises were commonplace and serf labour predominated. Gentry industrialists set up or acquired woollen mills in order to exploit the demand for cloth generated by the Russian army. The army increased in size from 290,000 in 1762 to 450,000 in 1797 and reached 1,120,000 by the middle of the nineteenth century. Uniform costs were put at 16 rubles per soldier per annum, so military purchases were substantial, bearing in mind that Tengoborsky valued total output of woollens at 46m. rubles in 1855.[11] We should not exaggerate the significance of official purchases, however, even of woollen cloth. The population grew more rapidly than the armed forces in the second half of the eighteenth century (though the army increased three times as fast as the population in the next half century). It is in the growth of civilian population, with its more diverse taste, its demand for cheap and comfortable fabrics and its elasticity of demand (making it responsive to a fall in the cost of the product), that stimulated Russian textiles.

While older gentry enterprises continued to use serf labour in order to produce the coarse cloth required by the army, 'free' labour was increasingly employed in the production of finer fabrics, linen, worsteds and cotton goods. Not that the bulk of workers were employed in factories and workshops. This was true of cotton-spinning, which developed rapidly after 1840, and bleaching, dyeing and printing. But weaving cotton or woollen cloth, and processing flax and hemp, was characteristically performed by the peasant household or by weavers whose looms were grouped in village huts (*svetelki*), like the weaving sheds in England around Leeds. Production was therefore dispersed, except where new technology made it desirable to centralize production and possible to reap economies of scale. Cotton-spinning and printing were the most obvious examples.[12]

Official estimates of the total volume of textile output in the pre-reform period covered only the tip of a large iceberg. One means of gauging its approximate size is to work out how many looms would be required to weave the yarn consumed, given that we know the volume of imported yarn and the average capacity of each loom. A Soviet scholar estimates that the total number of looms in the early 1850s cotton industry must have been closer to 250,000 than the official figure of 175,000. Finance Minister Kankrin admitted the magnitude of non-factory output, arguing (in 1832) that the true figure for cloth output was around 107 m. metres, rather than the official figure of 60 m. metres.[13]

The factory exercised a key role in rural industry, as it came to supply the peasant with yarn produced by Russian cotton-spinning factories in larger quantities, from the second quarter of the nineteenth century onwards. In Russia, as in Britain, the factory and domestic organization of labour developed in parallel rather than in opposition. By the 1850s, for instance, 58 cotton textile factories in Vladimir accounted for 900 looms and 5,800 workers on the actual premises, but more than 45,000 looms and 65,000 workers were associated with them in the surrounding villages. The same was true of Moscow province. In such circumstances, it hardly made sense to speak of 'peasant industry' as if it were divorced from the realities of capitalism. The perceptive writer of an article on industry in an official handbook recognized as much in the 1860s: 'Of course, the possession of land still preserves the character of the peasant as landholder ... but his subordination to capital is hardly weaker than any homeless (dispossessed) factory worker ... Many pure *kustari*, for all their apparent independence in production, are completely dependent upon a buyer-up (*perekupshchik*), who is in fact an industrialist (*fabrikant-zakazchik*), only without a firm.' To talk, as did Tengoborsky, of weavers who worked 'without quitting their own fireside', was to romanticize reality.[14]

The Russian cotton industry began to challenge the linen industry during the first half of the nineteenth century. Although by the 1850s the total workforce in cotton (factory and domestic workers) barely exceeded one-twentieth of the workforce in linen and hemp, the value of its output was already one-half. The progressive substitution of cotton for linen derived from a mixture of new technology, organizational changes (which shifted part of the burden of competition on to the domestic weaver), tariff protection and favourable market conditions (growing population, urbanization). The revolution in spinning techniques in Britain during the 1780s first gave Russia access to cheaper yarn, and then allowed her to acquire the technology herself. Even before Britain removed the barrier to the export of textile machinery, in 1842, Russia had made progress in this field, with the state-owned Alexandrovsk works in St. Petersburg taking the lead. The tariff on yarn in 1822 was introduced at a time when domestic firms were far from being able to supply the needs of weaving and finishing businesses and served largely to swell import receipts, but the tariff of 1841 did boost domestic production of yarn. It reinforced the market conditions that already existed in Russia, since it offered greatest protection to the cheaper calicoes and fabrics (the tariff was levied by weight). Higher counts of yarn were thus less well protected, but the market for these products was less extensive and the cotton industry less geared to the technical requirements of production.[15]

By the end of the pre-reform period the cotton industry was firmly established. Total spindleage reached 1.5 m. by 1860, compared with 0.3 m. in 1843. This was not a development that found universal approval. Gentry industrialists and wealthy merchants bemoaned the tendency for a new generation of 'serf-entrepreneurs' to organize the production of linen, then cotton. As Roger Portal has demonstrated, it was from the cotton industry that the emergent Russian bourgeoisie derived and challenged the older, semi-feudal enterprises. As a 'factory' industry, cotton textiles enraged populists as well. Tengoborsky wrote in 1855 that 'instead of struggling to produce articles of luxury and great fineness, requiring highly complex machinery and skilled operatives, (producers should) confine their attention to the improvement of those branches which are more appropriate to the ensemble of our material and intellectual resources'. But the cotton industry was doing just that, providing a cheaper and better quality product.[16]

The growth in the market for manufactured goods before 1861 derived largely from the growth in rural and urban population and from the spread of regional specialization and thus of interregional trade. Some indication of this is provided by the growth in trade turnover at local and national fairs, such as the major fairs at Nizhnii Novgorod and Irbit. Some of the transactions here involved foodstuffs and raw materials (leather and fur), and some goods were brought from abroad. But the bulk of the trade comprised iron goods, cottons and linen. Between 1815 and 1860 the volume of trade at Nizhnii Novgorod here expanded more than fourfold. At Irbit, total sales rose from 10 m. rubles in the early 1840s to 45 m. in the early 1860s.[17]

The increase in trade in manufactured goods also reflected the favourable terms of trade for the agricultural sector. During the years between the end of the Napoleonic Wars and Emancipation agricultural prices moved steadily upwards, while the prices of manufactured goods fell rapidly between 1815 and 1825, stabilized over the next twenty years and then fell sharply once more. Part of the secular fall in industrial prices (wholesale) is to be explained by the gains in productivity associated with technological change, mostly in new capitalist industries such as cotton. In semi-feudal industries – iron, woollens, sugar – industrialists kept costs down through the more intense exploitation of servile labour.[18]

A brief examination of the import composition of Russian foreign trade will indicate the extent to which substitution was taking place by the mid-nineteenth century. A large share of Russian imports in the early nineteenth century comprised luxury items such as tea, sugar, tobacco, wine and fruits, but imports of cotton yarn alone accounted for one-fifth of the total in 1820. The gradual industrialization of Russia was reflected in the changing composition of imports. Imports of yarn gave way by the 1840s to imports of raw cotton from the United States. Little import substitution took place in dyestuffs and chemicals. But in the production of sugar there was a marked tendency for domestic production to replace imports by the 1840s, imports falling in absolute terms as well as proportionately. Finally, industrialization was also registered in the growth of imports of machinery of all kinds. While the value of Russian imports doubled between 1820 and 1860, the share of machinery rose from two to eight per cent. Domestic machine-building firms had begun to produce textile machinery and other equipment, but progress was slow before 1850. Within a decade, however, Russian firms accounted for 55 per cent of total machinery consumption.[19]

How was this pattern affected by tariff policy? The tariff of 1822 marked a break with the post-Napoleonic reductions in duty, and imposed a high degree of protection which lasted in general until 1850. A duty of 600 per cent was levied on pig iron, so the Urals iron industry retained its position in the Russian market. Refined sugar (but not sugar cane) was also prohibited, so Ukrainian producers could take advantage of the protection. The duty levied on cotton yarn (1841) served to protect the nascent Russian cotton-spinning industry, but at the expense of the weaving and finishing branches. It was from such sectors that pressure was put on the tsarist government to reduce duties. Quite how significant the tariff had been in accelerating the development of this sector is difficult to say; any positive effect it did have was a by-product of the government's policy, which was mainly designed to increase revenue, even though the first move to protection in 1822 took place against a background of industrial depression. The tariff of 1831 was also directed at Polish industry; in the aftermath of the revolt of 1830, duties were raised on the import of manufactured goods from Poland.[20]

Contemporaries associated the tariff with the argument for and against the creation of an industrial base, whatever the intentions of the Russian government. The Minister of Finance (F. P. Vronchenko) argued in 1845 that industry 'increased the sales of agricultural products and the prices of these products inside the country, because of the growth in the number of consumers', and defended the tariff on these grounds. Opponents pointed to the artificially high prices paid by the consumer. During the 1850s the landed interest won the day by pointing up the advantages of increasing grain exports in the context of free trade. Furthermore, the beginning of sustained railway construction required that duties on iron also be reduced.[21] Accordingly, tariffs came down in 1850 and 1857.

This survey of industrial development prior to 1860 suggests that marked progress took place in consumer goods sectors of industry. The market for these products was large and growing, and the government offered indirect support to private enterprise, by no means all of which comprised large-scale units. After 1860, the most dramatic changes were to be registered in heavy manufacturing industry. In this respect, the railways exercised a crucial influence.

5.3 Railway Construction and Industrialization

The first major railway building boom in Russia lasted from 1868 to 1878; during that time the total track increased from 6,800 to 22,400 km. (see Fig. 4). Most of these lines were built and run by private companies, but this obscures the real contribution made by the government. Domestic production of iron in the quinquennium 1867–71 amounted to an annual average of 330,000 tons, and barely exceeded iron imports. Half the imported iron comprised rails, but only ten per cent of domestic production was destined for rail track. In 1870 only two factories in the Urals were capable of producing rails, and these suffered from technical and supply problems. Accordingly, the government relaxed the import restrictions on iron to allow duty-free imports of rails from 1868. In addition, the Ministry of Finances subsidized several rail producers, such as Putilov, who manu

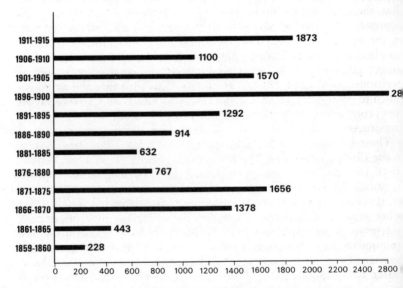

Fig. 4   Annual average additions to railway track, 1859–1913

actured rails by processing imported scrap and pig iron. Whereas at he beginning of the boom imports accounted for more than three-quarters of rail consumption, by the late 1870s this proportion had declined by half. None the less, this situation had not been achieved by means of any transformation of the Russian metallurgical industry.[22]

While rail-producing factories continued to have access to cheap foreign scrap, the government imposed higher tariffs in 1877 on locomotives and wagons and restricted the import of rails. Rails were ordered from selected firms, such as the new Hughes firm in south Russia, at prices that were much higher than imported rails. In rolling-stock factories, the government injected nearly 70 m. rubles between 1868 and 1878, representing orders for 900 locomotives and 32,000 freight wagons. Whilst the government resolved to reduce its dependence on foreign suppliers – both to protect the trade surplus and to insure the country against potential interruptions at times of tension – the private engineering industry received a massive injection of working capital. In this way (and by contrast with Spain and Italy), Russia substituted for imports.[23]

The early railway mania in Russia differed little from comparable booms in Britain or Germany. During the years 1870–73, 53 m. rubles was invested annually in railway companies, representing nearly half the total industrial and commercial corporate investment. The boom coincided with a general upswing in the economy, affecting cotton, sugar and leather, as well as coal, iron and machine-building. What is particularly striking, especially in view of the oft-repeated assertion that the end of the railway-building boom set off an industrial depression, is that the slump in light industries was already evident by the autumn of 1872, following a financial panic. This squeeze had no effect on railway-building for two or three more years, given the longer gestation of investment in this sector. Coal, iron and steel performed well until 1875. The slump in 1875 and 1876 owed as much to poor harvests and their effects on exports and foreign investors' confidence, as to the completion of the first phase of railway construction.[24]

These features were magnified still more during the second boom in the 1890s. Between 1890 and 1901 the track increased from 30,600 to 56,500 km. The trend in railway investment (excluding investment in railway equipment) is presented in the accompanying graph (Fig.). Railway investment generally followed the trends in investment in other areas, but it is the magnitude of the investment that stands out, especially during the early and late 1890s. Indeed, during the quinquennium 1896–1900, railway investment represented one-quarter of total net investment; this proportion would certainly creep closer to 30 per cent if investment in transport equipment were included in the total for railway investment. In other words, such

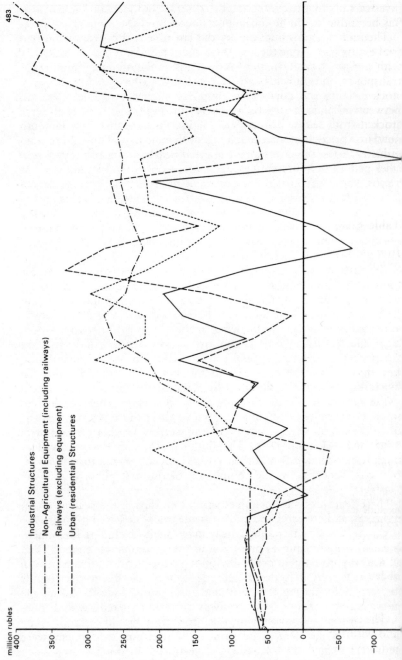

Fig. 5 Trends in net investment (industry, housing, railways), 1885–1913

investment certainly exceeded the 25 per cent of total investment that has been claimed to be crucial for German industrialization.[25]

The railways did not alone create the conditions for Russian industrial expansion during the 1890s. They have to be seen in conjunction with a broadly based process of capital formation in industry and transport.[26] Nevertheless, annual additions to the railway capital stock usually exceeded additions to the industrial capital stock between 1890 and 1905, and it was the investment in rails and rolling-stock that generated demand on a scale broad enough to sustain the new iron and steel industry in south Russia and the engineering industry in St. Petersburg. Table 5.1 indicates the volume of iron and steel production directed towards the railway industry in the late 1890s.

Table 5.1

Iron and steel supplied to Russian railways, 1895–1899 (net of imports)

('ooo tons)

	1 New lines	2 Additions to lines	3 Rolling-stock	4 Repairs to lines stock	5 Total consumed	6 Domestic output	7 Percentage supplied to railways
1895	267	125	94	259	745	1,299	57
1896	347	137	118	277	879	1,495	59
1897	424	157	111	285	977	1,694	58
1898	569	89	124	308	1,090	2,051	53
1899	882	162	132	354	1,530	2,383	64

Note: the quantities given in the source have been adjusted, in order to exclude imports (cols. 1, 2 and 4 have been deflated by 1 per cent; col. 3 by 20 per cent).

Source: A. M. Soloveva, *Zheleznodorozhnyi transport Rossii vo vtoroi polovine XIX veka*, Nauka, 1975, pp. 276–7; domestic output is taken from P. A. Khromov, *Ekonomicheskoe razvitie Rossii v XIX–XX vekakh*, Gospoli-tizdat, 1950, p. 457.

The bulk of Russian rail output came from factories in south Russia, and within this region a small handful of enterprises dominated the industry: Hughes's New Russian Works, the South Russian Dniepr

Factory, the Bryansk Ironworks, the Donets Steel Company at Druzh-kovka and the Russo-Belgian Metallurgical Company. At the last two factories, around 80 per cent of output was directed towards the railways; elsewhere, the proportion was around 50 per cent. These factories owned coal mines and formed integrated enterprises, combining pig iron and steel rolling-mills, and allowing them to cut the cost of supply of these inputs. The volume of the orders enabled them to achieve the economies of scale in iron and steel production. Throughout the 1890s the import of rails did not exceed 1 per cent. Imports of rolling-stock also dwindled, to less than a fifth of total consumption; here, the bulk of Russian locomotives was supplied by three giant engineering works, the Kolomensk, Bryansk and Putilov factories.[27]

In principle, the 'backward linkages' described (that is, the demand for iron and steel generated by railways) might have been available from other sources. The capital absorbed in railways (amounting to 4,800 m. rubles by 1900) might have been invested more productively elsewhere; for instance, in other forms of transport. But the situation in Russia was the same as in Germany a generation or so earlier: there was no comparable source of demand for iron and steel. As to other forms of transport, roads and, in particular, waterways were improved during the 1890s, and beyond.

The advantages for Russian industry of the railway system need to be set in the context of the performance of Russian industry as a whole. By 1900 Russian capitalists were in a position to exploit the improved access to material supplies, and to market their goods more easily.[28] But to what extent did the manufacturing sector reduce its unit costs? This question is addressed in Section 5.5.

5.4 Cottage Industry (Kustar)

The development of factory industry appeared to offer little comfort to people who were engaged in small-scale industrial production. It gave even less to populist writers, who believed that cottage industry constituted the authentic and appropriate form of industrial organiz-ation for Russia. Populists began to point out as early as the 1870s that the factory was challenging and supplanting the rural craftsman. To what extent was this perceived threat to *kustar* markets a real one?

Meaningful information on the size of the non-factory manufac-turing sector, and on numbers of urban and rural craftsmen, is difficult to obtain. The leading Soviet specialist on the subject quotes estimates for the number of rural craftsmen in 1880, which range from 4 to 15 million individuals. The main reason for this discrepancy is that the term *kustar* had a variety of meanings. It comprised the peasant who devoted part of his or her time to craft production for household use, and it usually included the peasant producer who took his finished wares to a local market or tramped with them from place to place. But the term could also include peasants who worked for a middleman (who put out the material and collected the product), as well as peasants who worked on direct commission from a local factory.[29]

Kustar producers thus worked for different sorts of customer. This is also evident from a brief summary of the range of goods they produced. Products included goods used in construction and packaging, such as prepared timber, tar, rope, brick and nails; furnishings and utensils for the peasant market; items, such as silks, lace and enamelware, destined for prosperous consumers; and goods, such as cotton cloth, that entered into later stages of production in the factory. Some *kustari* accordingly dealt with factory consumers, while others worked for rural households and others for the luxury end of the market. Such variety in the scope of *kustar* activity suggests that populist generalizations about the 'organic' connection of cottage industry with agriculture were wide of the mark.

The conventional and tidy notion of conflict between the factory and *kustar* is, of course, oversimplified. The two forms of industrial organization proved complementary in several respects. As Lenin said, the cottage was an 'appendage' to the factory. In the first place, *kustari* frequently relied upon the supply of materials from factory sources, and the development of large-scale production created the conditions for increased supplies of iron, cotton and leather. The situation was not so very different from that elsewhere in Europe at an equivalent stage of industrialization. This was one form of coexistence. In the second place, rural craftsmen supplied factories with semi-finished products. Again, textiles provides the most obvious example, in which *kustari* worked up cotton yarn into cloth, passing it on to factories to be dyed and printed. Other examples include the supply of rope or sacking to factory industry, for use in packaging and carriage. To give some idea of the importance of this association between the two forms of production, Tugan-Baranovsky concluded that around six out of ten rural craftsmen in Moscow province (*c.* 1875) were engaged in trades that had a direct link with factory production. This type of association is also confirmed by the parallel trends in industrial activity which the factory and the *kustar* underwent. For instance, the boom in the level of industrial production during the early 1870s affected both sectors; and both experienced the slackening in activity in the later 1870s.[30]

Advanced forms of industrial organization could, therefore, confer benefits on the small-scale producer, providing him with materials and – in some instances – a ready market for his output. Furthermore, as Tugan-Baranovsky pointed out, the factory also disseminated skills throughout the handicraft sector, because former factory metal-workers or weavers could set up on their own, exploiting the training they had received in modern techniques of production (although it is difficult to say to what extent this was more important than the skills that were passed on from one generation of *kustar* producers to the next). However, none of these conditions appears to have held good beyond 1880 or 1890, either because mechanization spread to hith-erto unmechanized crafts or because costs of production were rising in the *kustar* economy. Tugan-Baranovsky drew attention to the mechanization of cotton and woollen cloth weaving, flax-spinning, nail-making and the manufacture of felt boots, all within the space of a few years around 1880. Production costs were increasing during the 1870s and 1880s, especially in trades connected with the production of metal goods: the main explanation for this was that fuel (charcoal) costs at the forge were putting pressure on producers of nails, harness, cutlery and hardware. It is also very likely that the costs of fuel, and of iron itself, rose again during the early years of the twentieth century, not least because of the formation of syndicates in coal and metallurgy. Attempts to assist *kustar* producers – by the *zemstva*, and by some central government officials – did not alleviate these pressures.[31]

The result of such changes, according to Tugan-Baranovsky, was to induce a fall in the number of small workshops after 1880 (an assessment that was based on impressionistic evidence). His main point, however, was to demonstrate that the corresponding increase in numbers of individual craftsmen did not signify a progressive inde-pendence of *kustari* from capitalist control. Rather, it reflected a desperate attempt to stay in business by reducing costs wherever possible, and in particular by taking smaller margins from production. The fact that *kustar* flax weavers survived at all in 1890 owed every-thing to 'the extremely small earnings with which they content them-selves'. The advantages – of low overheads and local monopolies of production and distribution – that craft producers hitherto enjoyed over factory enterprise had largely disappeared by 1900. Where indi-vidual craftsmen and 'gangs' of tradesmen continued to operate, it was normally as appendages of the factory or the vassals of a capitalist middleman. In each case, the lack of legislative protection facilitated this exploitation of cottage industry.[32]

Whatever the problems facing the *kustari*, it would be mistaken to overlook the continued existence – and indeed proliferation – of small-scale enterprise. Lyashchenko made a special study of the flour-milling industry, and revealed the persistence of petty village mills and the relative lack of development of large power-driven mills. He attributed this to the vulnerability of large mills, with expensive capital equipment, to the Russian harvest fluctuations. Only along the Volga, in Nizhnii Novgorod, Saratov and Samara were large mills to be found, which were geared to the grain trade with north Russian centres of consumption. The implications of his study are important, because they suggest that even after a generation of rail transport, problems of access still conferred an advantage on small-scale flour mills, whose opportunity to exploit peasant producers of grain (there were no formal weights and measures; the miller levied a hefty charge for his services) was encouraged by their monopoly position.[33]

Small-scale enterprise was also evident in the structure of pre-revolutionary wholesale and retail trade. Itinerant merchants dominated the retail trade for at least a generation after 1850. Larger and permanent outlets did not emerge outside the major cities of the Empire until the railway network had been extended. But, even then, the railway seems to have encouraged thousands of petty tradesmen to enter the market, with only modest capital resources. They, too, moved from village to village, making a small percentage on each item sold, but maintaining a large turnover of goods. By the turn of the century a sizeable network of shops and stores existed throughout the Empire – well over half a million by 1900, excluding retail stalls and market booths; and another quarter of a million shops were added before the War. But they were heavily concentrated in Moscow, St. Petersburg and the Baltic provinces. Elsewhere, the system left only about 50 or 60 fixed retail establishments for every 10,000 inhabitants. Clearly, where the rural market is concerned, more formal institutions had not supplanted traditional devices for distribution.[34]

5.5 Manufacturing Costs

Reductions in manufacturing costs derive from a number of sources. A reduction in unit costs could result from the growth of labour productivity, consequent in part upon technical change. Historically, technological change has been accompanied by less obtrusive, but equally significant changes. For instance, changes have been made to the organization of work within the enterprise, facilitating greater managerial control over the labour process ('scientific management'). Manufacturing costs can also be reduced by capitalists' attempts to cut down on the wage rate.

This section addresses itself largely to factors that influenced labour productivity in industry. It also considers the efforts made by employers to control the wage rate in industry. It begins with a few observations about the problem of construction and installation costs.

The building industry developed a capitalist form only gradually.

At the end of the century, Lenin described an industry dominated by artisans or gangs who worked according to individual commissions. In some instances, a large contractor organized a workforce on a more permanent basis, and several firms began to specialize, for instance in brick-making. But it would be wrong to exaggerate the trend: even during the 1920s, small workshops remained in the ascendancy and 'in the first stages of the industrialization programme, building costs and efficiency proved particularly difficult to control'.[35] What struck pre-revolutionary contemporaries was the additional costs imposed by the tariff on iron and other building materials. One observer argued that this factor alone explained fifty per cent of the differential in construction costs between Russia and Germany. Of course, the reduction in iron costs during the 1890s must have prevented the difference from growing, but by how much it is difficult to say. Correspondingly, the inflation in domestic iron prices in the immediate pre-war years served to increase construction costs. Where firms did experience difficulties in financing the cost of factory construction, they could in some cases take over existing buildings, as International Harvester did in 1910.[36]

Installation of plant presents a similar picture, of much larger outlays on equipment in Russia relative to other industrial economies. In textiles, it cost a potential Russian mill-owner twice as much as a British businessman in 1900 to set up spindleage. More than a decade later, Savin calculated that total initial costs − of factory construction and installation − were on average 75−100 per cent higher in Russia than they were in western Europe. He used these figures to attack prevailing tariff rates.[37]

What of technical change in industry? As we have seen, change was not entirely absent in the Urals iron industry before 1861, but the industry was slow to respond to advances being made elsewhere. Even as late as 1890, only one enterprise (with French participation) had adopted the hot-blast method of smelting pig iron and introduced modern rolling mills. Other firms must have needed to economize on charcoal for smelting, as the hot-blast method allowed, because timber reserves were being depleted and fuel costs therefore rising. But they did not innovate. In the Ukraine, the organization and technology of the industry presented a sharp contrast. Innovations introduced by foreign capitalists increased the capacity of blast furnaces, improved the use of by-products and modernized iron and steel rolling. The average capacity of the blast furnace was less than in Belgium or Germany, but the difference was offset by the higher-quality iron ore used in the Ukraine, which yielded more pig per ton of ore. Between 1890 and 1913 the average size of furnace grew from between 120 and 180 tons to around 250 tons. Modern integrated plant used both the Bessemer and Martins method according to the requirements of he market (the former for bulk production of basic steel, the latter or special orders). Bessemer production in Russia was no less sophis- icated than western methods, though the Martins process continued o use scrap metal, a practice being abandoned elsewhere by 1913. The capacity of the hearth doubled between 1895 and 1913, from .o to 40/50 tons, approaching the contemporary German norm. Rolling-mills were also fully in accord with western practice, though hey used steam at a time when the most modern German and Belgian irms were switching to electricity.[38]

None of this progress would have been possible without the partici- pation of foreign capital (or, of course, the rail link between the Donets coal basin and the Krivoi Rog ore deposits – Donets ore being ow in iron content). McKay notes that advanced methods were being adapted to Russian conditions by the early twentieth century, rather han being implanted without regard for appropriate local need. In heory, Russian entrepreneurs could have installed advanced western echnology under licence, but this option was not available in practice: oreign firms were too keen to exploit the protected Russian market hemselves.

In oil exploration and extraction, the significance of foreign partici- pation in Russia was if anything even greater, but the gains in productivity were not sustained. The main fields lay in the Caucasus, at Baku and Grozny, where output increased at an average annual ate of 20 per cent (1860–72) and 17 per cent (1873–1916). Nobel and other foreign consortiums supplied advanced drilling equipment; Nobel was also intrumental in revolutionizing the transport of oil across Europe (though oil exports never exceeded in value terms the export of timber or of flax). In the early period, production costs were as much as 50 per cent below the prevailing costs in the U.S.A. However, this reflected not just technical advance, but also the abun- dance of easily extracted oil deposits. Marginal and average costs rose subsequently, because of the need to drill deeper. The cost advantage over America disappeared. Technical change was unable to keep up with the problems of accessibility of oil deposits: it is estimated that t took eleven hours to extract a ton of oil in 1913, where it took only nine in 1903 and six in 1889. When world prices for oil fell, as hey did rapidly after the turn of the century, Russian firms reduced their capacity. Without the prospect of future profitability, investment in new technology lagged. The new oil monopoly was more concerned with staving off further price reductions, than in instituting techno- logical change and seeking cost reductions.[39]

Technological change in coal mining could hardly have been more limited. As in oil extraction, the initial gains in productivity derived from the fact that deposits were easily accessible, and output per person increased sharply between 1885 and 1900. This increase was not sustained. Where mechanization took place in coal mining, it was confined to bringing coal to the surface; coal was hewn from the face and carried to the shaft manually. As in oil, the industry responded by seeking to protect its position through market control: the syndicate *Produgol* was formed in 1902. Increased costs were passed on to consumers. In short, manufacturing industry, which during the 1880s and 1890s had obtained cheap energy, now faced higher energy prices as a result of the failure of suppliers to tackle productivity constraints more positively.[40]

In cotton textiles, the most significant technological change took place during the last decade of the nineteenth century, with the progressive substitution of rings for mules in cotton spinning. Whereas in 1890 there were fewer than 30 ring frames in use for every 100 mules, by 1899 the figure had risen to nearly 70. By 1910 rings outnumbered mules. During this time, output per spindle increased by 20 per cent. The ring frame was more suitable to spinning lower counts of yarn, where demand showed most signs of expansion. No less important was the fact that it was more suited to a relatively unskilled workforce. Manufacturers tended to run their equipment more intensively by 1900, in order to offset the statutory reduction in hours, and the rings produced more yarn with fewer risks of breakage. In cotton weaving, the 1890s witnessed the final triumph of factory over domestic looms. Mechanical looms were similarly worked at a faster pace. The results, in terms of costs and profits, were dramatic. Yarn prices were falling, and the cost of cheaper calicoes fell by a third in this decade. Since prices fell much less rapidly (by about ten per cent), this was a time of excellent profits for the industry.[41]

Information is harder to come by on technical change in other branches of consumer goods. Varzar, drawing upon the 1908 industrial census, pointed to the importance of hand labour in the food trades, such as confectionery. In some other branches, such as flour milling, steam power was already well established. Lenin suggested that the number of steam-powered flour mills had quadrupled between 1879 and 1892 (although productivity of each mill remained static). The production of paper was mechanized, but printing retained its traditional 'craft' character. In a number of other trades, for example leather, pottery and jewellery, the growth in output was the result of additional manual labour (or changes in workshop organization) rather than increased use of mechanized power.[42]

In engineering and metalworking, Russia resembled Germany or Britain in the preceding generation, that is, the technologically modern plants in some branches of engineering (such as locomotives) coexisted with plant where manual skill and power continued to dominate. Varzar indicated the widespread use of hand technology in metalworking, in the manufacture of cutlery, locks and nails, and in the repair of rolling-stock. It was in the giant machine-building works in St. Petersburg, and in some of the shipyards on the Black Sea and the engineering works in Ekaterinoslav, that steam power was concentrated. Even here, however, many of the auxiliary operations were performed manually.[43]

Summarizing the trends in mechanical power, Varzar pointed to the increase both in the number of engines installed in manufacturing industry between 1887 and 1908, and in their capacity (Table 5.2).

Table 5.2

Mechanical motive power in Russian industry, 1887–1908

	1887	1900	1908
Total engines	6,400	16,700	21,000
Total H.P. ('000)	166	854	1,230
Average H.P. per engine	24.4	51.1	53.3

Source: V. Varzar, 'Factories and Workshops', in A. Raffalovich, ed., *Russia: Its Trade and Commerce*, P. S. King, 1918, p. 128.

In the period to 1908, both the number and capacity of internal combustion engines, and of electrical equipment, expanded more rapidly than other forms of power. By 1908, water power accounted for just five per cent of industrial power consumption, compared to 87 per cent for steam and six per cent for gas and naphtha engines.

The general level of labour productivity was affected by education and by training in industrial skills. The industrial labour force became increasingly literate by the end of the nineteenth century, reflecting in part the impact of educational reforms introduced during the 1860s. We can gauge something of the later dynamics by comparing literacy indices among workers at the time of the first national census in 1897, with those derived from the industrial census of 1918 (Table 5.3).

The differential between heavy and light industry appeared to be narrowing. In the case of textiles, this owed much to gains in literacy among women workers. On the reasonable assumption that there is a strong correlation between literacy and the quality of the workforce, the data suggest a source of substantial improvements in labour productivity. Some Russian entrepreneurs recognized the potential, and made formal provision for the education of workers and their

Table 5.3

Literacy rates among Russian factory workers, 1897–1918

	1897			1918		
	Male	Female	Average	Male	Female	Average
Mining	33.5	12.2	31.8	} 74.0	42.6	70.0
Metallurgy	39.3	12.5	38.2			
Metalworking	66.8	32.1	66.2	81.4	50.0	76.5
Textiles	53.9	12.2	38.9	–	–	–
Cottons	–	–	–	76.4	37.9	52.2
Woollens	–	–	–	68.2	37.1	52.2
Linen	–	–	–	78.3	40.3	55.5
Food and drink	52.6	28.9	49.7	75.0	48.3	66.0

Source: O. Crisp, 'Labour and industrialization in Russia', in P. Mathias and M. M. Postan, eds., *Cambridge Economic History of Europe*, Volume 7, Part 2, C.U.P., 1978, p. 392.

children. Many workers took their own initiative for self-improvement.[44]

Formal technical education was much less satisfactory. By 1913 the Ministry of Trade and Industry had responsibility for 650 middle and lower technical schools, providing instruction for around 100,000 students. These facilities were still only at an early stage of development. Neither the *zemstva* nor factory managers filled the gap. Some workers, of course, obtained on-the-job training from foremen, for instance in firms where foreigners had been engaged. But communication cannot have been easy, and only modest substitution of Russian for foreign foremen took place before 1913.[45]

Where literacy and skills were acquired, it was important that they should not be dissipated. In order to reduce the rapidity of turnover among the workforce, employers resorted to various devices, ranging from the offer of bonuses and higher wages as incentives to long-established employees, to delays in wage payment and even withholding workers' passports. Where a worker was valued, he or she might be offered a long-term contract; to break this was a criminal offence. As we saw in Chapter Three, there was a growing tendency for workers in industry to work all year round, rather than to leave for field work in the summer. Nevertheless, employers complained hat the number of days worked on average in Russian industry was ower than the number in western Europe and the United States. The igure was close to 270 in the early twentieth century, compared to around 300 in West European industry. According to Grinevetsky, his reflected the continuation of 'pre-industrial' habits, such as extra nolidays, excessive drinking bouts and village work.[46]

In order to cope with the generally low levels of skill among the growing industrial labour force, and to discourage such manifestations of 'indiscipline', management tended to recruit a larger proportion of supervisory staff, certainly by comparison with the ituation in more advanced industrial economies (the 1918 Census gave a ratio of one employee for every 14 workers). This partly explains the larger average size of Russian factories. Supervisors were employed to monitor the use and performance of industrial equipment, to check the flow of work and to minimize wastage. In general, hey acted to control and discipline the workforce, not always with great success: shopfloor workers frequently complained about their behaviour.[47]

The high level of workers per unit of output also reflected the use of unskilled labour to perform auxiliary tasks in and around the factory, such as carrying materials from one shop to another. In cotton textiles, Mendeleev calculated that the ratio of workers to spindles was of the order of 17 per thousand, compared to three per thousand in the largest English factories. Even the largest and most modern Russian works (the Krenholm factory on the river Narva near St. Petersburg) employed six per thousand, and advanced factories in central Russia had a norm of 10 or 12. In weaving factories in Vladimir, one worker serviced only 0.8 looms, while in England the average was one worker for three or four. The conclusion reached by Mendeleev and others was that the costs of employing Russian labour on this scale (together with the smaller capacity of Russian machinery and the higher degree of wastage) tended to cancel out the low wages paid to Russian workers. In short, unit costs were higher in Russia than in European or American industry.[48]

Contemporary technical specialists and some Russian managers maintained that a significant contribution to improved productivity could be realized through a simplification of the work process, in order to take account of the lower average level of skill among the labour force. But efforts to introduce the implied mass-production techniques hardly amounted to much. In general, Russian manufacturing industry oriented itself towards a custom-based or commission type of trade, where the emphasis was on production of individual products for a particular client. Neither in machine-tools, agricultural machinery nor transport equipment can we find evidence of standardization. One firm in Tula produced nearly 30 different types of plough (in 1918 the new management reduced this to three!); even the Ministry of Transport succeeded in confusing its suppliers by changing the specification of rolling-stock on a regular basis. Thus, even the existence of recurrent demand for specific items did not lead to mass-production methods. As one expert later put it, 'the elements of machinery have until now had a size and form that is frequently fortuitous, depending almost entirely on the customs, traditions and routines of the factories concerned'. The factory only followed the pattern of demand from its customers. A factory that produced ploughs also sought orders for electrical equipment and rolling-stock. Only in a few instances did full specialization emerge, and these were enterprises which had long-term orders for transport equipment or armaments. One example of successful mass production of a standard item demonstrates the greater entrepreneurial imagination of foreign firms (or, perhaps, the availability of reserves needed to undertake the risk). Singer produced for a mass market that its executives felt sure existed for sewing machines: the firm had only to locate in Russia and to penetrate the tariff barrier. This suggests that greater efforts at standardization might have been made in other spheres, with corresponding effects on costs. But neither the government (as a mass customer) nor the syndicates in existence by 1913 had engineered such changes.[49]

What scope, finally, did capitalists have for keeping down the wage rate in industry? An answer to this question must begin by making distinctions between different periods. In the aftermath of Emancipation, as Tugan-Baranovsky noted, the general wage rate increased, because compulsion no longer sufficed to retain the labour force. The gains did not last long: in the Central Industrial Region, for example, rural labour turned to factory employment in greater numbers, and this depressed wages. During the late 1880s and 1890s wages rose (in nominal and in real terms), because of the industrial boom and the demand for labour it generated. The slump at the turn of the century ushered in a quinquennium of low wages, but they recovered after 1905. In this respect, two factors were significant: first, during the revolutionary situation in 1905, capitalists granted concessions over wages to striking workers. The gains were not equally distributed – workers in printing, leather, flax and other textiles benefited most, with metalworkers some way behind. The second influence on the wage rate was the renewed industrial growth from 1907 onwards.[50]

Generally speaking, the wage rate was kept low, prior to the 1890s, by a combination of government repression, entrepreneurial tactics and the link that peasants retained with the land. Tugan-Baranovsky placed special emphasis on the last condition, arguing that the existence of a family plot represented a form of subsidy to the capitalist employer. The role of government should not be minimized: until

906 the regime proscribed trade unions and even after 1906 ubjected them to restrictions. Capitalists themselves had a whole rmoury of powers at their disposal in order to exploit the labour orce. These ranged from fines for 'lateness', 'rudeness' and poor vork, to the exploitation of workers by means of the truck system f payment. The government intervened to try and stop some of the vorst abuses, by providing (in 1886) that factory owners should pecify the misdemeanours for which workers were liable to be fined, nd at what rate. However, the ratio of inspectors to factories was niserably low, and the legislation did not affect small workshops.[51]

A similar consideration applies to the question of hours of work. During the 1880s the average length of the working day in industry vas 12 to 13 hours (exclusive of mealtimes and of the time taken to ravel to and from work). By 1913 the average had fallen to around o. The reduction reflected partly the impact of factory legislation (in 885 an eight-hour maximum was stipulated for children between 12 nd 15 years old, and in 1897 the government decreed that the naximum number of hours for adults was to be 11½). It reflected in art the reductions conceded by employers in 1905. Finally, employers hemselves began to recognize that a reduction in hours did not imply loss of output. A judicious use of shift systems might actually ncrease output per man-hour.[52]

As indicated, the context within which employers operated did hange in 1905. The reduction in hours and increases in wages – nore marked in factories than in small enterprises – led capitalists to ntensify the pace of work, by running machinery more quickly and y supervising production more closely. Examples of this can be ound in the metalworking industry of St. Petersburg, and in cotton-pinning and weaving. Employers also demanded additional overtime, vhich workers accepted in order to boost their pay during the pre-var inflation. In these circumstances, it was hardly surprising that the question of hours of work figured so largely in the demands made by vorkers in March 1917.[53]

Before leaving the subject of industrial costs, we need to ask vhether government subsidies and the tariff cushioned enterprises rom competition, stifled innovation and maintained high-cost firms n business. Further, how significant was the tariff in maintaining upward pressure on the cost of finished products, by compelling nanufacturers to pay more for imports than under a system of free rade?

Tsarist finance ministers paid lip-service to the ideal of non-inter-erence in commercial operations in industry. Bunge, in particular, oiced his concern about the support given in the past to speculative entures, which ought (he said) to stand on their own feet, or not at ll. Like his predecessors and successors, however, who sought to curb government spending where possible, Bunge continued to extend support to private enterprise, not least in the metallurgical and engineering industries. The Soviet historian I. F. Gindin argued that subsidies to Urals firms helped to perpetuate inefficient industry, while elsewhere they discouraged cost-cutting among engineering firms (transport equipment, ship-building, armaments). The evidence for this comes from a comparison of prices paid by government agencies for locomotives and other items, and those obtained on the open market. However, the commercially inept firms frequently collapsed even with this state support, only to be rescued, reorganized, and often sold to private owners.[54]

One cannot assume that government tariff policy was solely designed to stimulate industrial development. A plausible case can be made for the view that the primary aim of the regime was to secure additional revenue. Kahan and Crisp, echoing the views of several pre-revolutionary economists, argue that high duties were levied, not just on manufactured goods, but on foodstuffs and raw materials – for fiscal motives. A more rational policy, from the perspective of manufacturing industry, might have been to provide cheap inputs to the producers of finished goods. For instance, an enterprise producing agricultural machinery in Russia operated in a market which protected the production of simple items, but faced high prices for inputs of iron because the tariff also protected producers of semi-finished metal. However, from the point of view of industrialization on a broad front, the government's tariff policies were not wholly irrational.[55]

Table 5.4 indicates the relative incidence of the tariff on three broad categories of imports, and suggests that as a proportion of import values the tariff fell most heavily on foodstuffs and (in 1903) on raw materials and semi-finished items, rather than on manufactured goods as a whole.

Between 1868 and 1891 the duties on pig iron had increased between five- and tenfold (depending on whether imports were admitted by land or sea). This level of protection affected the rolling-mills and engineering firms in the north-west and in Poland that relied on imported pig iron (and coal, which also carried duty). The region that stood to gain was the metallurgical region in south Russia, where firms were integrated and produced rolled iron and steel: in other words, they set their own input prices, and obtained coke and pig iron at cost. A similar advantage wa conferred on contemporary integrated steel firms in Germany at this time.[56]

Tugan-Baranovsky argued that these duties on raw materials and semi-manufactures remained in force, long after the relevant Russian industries had established themselves. Industrial consumers of cotton and iron still paid heavy duties on inputs in order to boost government revenues. From their point of view, tariff policy was inflexible and

Table 5.4

Imports, customs duties and their incidence, 1869–1903

	Foodstuffs			Raw materials and semi-manufactures			Manufactured goods			All items
	1	2	3	1	2	3	1	2	3	
1869	87.6	27.6	31%	189.5	9.4	5%	161.9	14.2	9%	12%
1879	89.8	36.6	41%	275.3	28.2	10%	127.4	18.7	15%	17%
1889	53.9	38.2	71%	238.0	44.8	19%	72.6	20.5	28%	28%
1899	70.8	54.2	77%	289.9	88.0	30%	200.7	52.9	26%	33%
1903	84.4	75.3	89%	330.3	100.6	30%	149.0	39.4	26%	38%

Note: col. 1 gives official value of imports (million rubles, current prices); col. 2 the recorded duties on imports; and col. 3 expresses duties as a percentage of import values.
Source: V. P. Litvinov-Falinsky, *Nashe ekonomicheskoe polozhenie i zadachi budushchego*, St. Petersburg, 1908, p. 75.

incoherent. Three comments are in order in this context. First, the government was certainly aware of the problem, and indeed took occasional steps to cancel duties, in order to alleviate the difficulties faced by firms in the engineering industry. Secondly, the tariff protection afforded to German steel producers did not necessarily stand in the way of technical change and improved efficiency, because it reduced the risks faced by entrepreneurs who had to take major investment decisions: perhaps a similar case could be made for the Russian industry. Finally, input prices were determined by a range of factors, rather than the tariff exclusively; other factors included the cartelization of domestic industry.[57]

5.6 Crisis and Growth, 1900–1917

(a) Industrial 'crisis': an assessment

The rapid increase in industrial activity came to a halt at the turn of the century. Opponents of government economic policy took this industrial 'crisis' to be a vindication of their views, either about the burden that fiscal policies had placed on household consumption or about the 'artificiality' of Russian industrialization in general. Opposition to government policy surfaced within the government itself. There is nothing surprising about this, because the tsarist government comprised men of different and even irreconcilable views, whose only common bond was that they had each been selected by the Tsar. Witte was exposed to attack from the Ministry of the Interior in particular, whose dislike of industrialization stemmed from its long-standing fear of potential public disorder. Lobko, the State Comptroller, also orchestrated a campaign against Witte and put forward the proposition that 'the demand of our domestic market cannot keep up with the excessive growth of our industry. The equilibrium between industry and the domestic market has been destroyed, and with it the basis of a successful economic development'. According to such critics, the current crisis was more than just a manifestation of periodic fluctuations in economic activity. It was an indication that 'over-production' would become a permanent feature of Russian life.[58]

Outside government, Vorontsov responded to the slump by arguing that the government had sacrificed the needs of households at the altar of railway-building mania. Construction had become an 'end in itself', the extent of which was made possible only by the availability of subsidies. No thought had been given to the future utilization of manufacturing capacity; although the building boom had forged backward linkages with heavy industry and had expanded aggregate purchasing power, these were transitory developments. The market was simply too poor to support further expansion, even of consumer goods industry. P. P. Migulin, Professor of Economics at Kiev University (and by no means a populist in his outlook) also maintained that industry had developed far in excess of the absorptive capacity of the market. Migulin believed that purchasing power had actually fallen, not least because of harvest failures (1897) which came on top of a prolonged squeeze on peasant incomes. If indirect taxes were reduced, then peasant households would be able to afford to buy a larger volume of manufactured goods. However, since Migulin also proposed that tariffs be reduced, this additional purchasing power might simply swell the import bill.[59]

Such views found their way into a broader public arena, not least because of new channels of communication opened up by Witte himself. In 1902, in a move designed to head off criticism, he established a 'Special Conference on the Needs of Agriculture', which in turn spawned more than six hundred local committees. Here, gentry and professional hostility to tariff and tax policy reached a climax, amidst the general chorus of complaint that 'industry' had been favoured at the expense of 'agriculture'. This critique was a cynical device to extract greater concessions from Witte, such as price support for cereals, lower tariffs on agricultural equipment, and cheap credit. In the rural handicraft producer and the archetypal *muzhik* were found convenient symbols of tradition and a means of concealing gentry self-interest.[60]

Witte rejected the view that the 'crisis' reflected the inability of the market to absorb industrial output, in a situation where the government had cut back on orders for railway products (see below). He retaliated by arguing that the crisis was merely the culmination of a speculative boom in company formation during the mid-1890s and, as such, served to weed out the less competent and well-organized firms. Investors would soon recover their confidence in the stock market, and share prices would settle down at a level that reflected the real value and prospects of companies. The 'crisis' certainly did not reveal any permanent structural weakness in the economy, induced by a lack of purchasing power.[61]

Contemporaries first detected a 'crisis' in the sudden rise in interest rates in western Europe and Russia, which B. F. Brandt attributed to the growth of European investment overseas and, more specifically, to the demands created by unproductive expenditures in southern Africa and the Far East. The discount rate of the State Bank, which set the level of interest rates throughout the economy, rose from 4.5 per cent in May 1899 (this had been the average for the past four years) to 6 per cent by the end of the year. The commercial banks followed suit and restricted credit. The implication for the stock market was bound to be serious, in so far as the banks had previously greatly enlarged their lending to individual investors and to industrial clients. As the banks called in commercial loans, their clients unloaded more shares on to a jittery market in order to try and obtain funds to meet their liabilities. This simply reinforced the decline in share prices, some indication of which is given in Table 5.5.[62]

The fall in share prices continued during 1900 and 1901, and prompted the government to take action to prevent a complete collapse. In the first place, the State Bank suspended interest paid on private accounts, in an effort to persuade investors to transfer funds to the commercial banks. Secondly, the Bank stepped in to make medium-term loans to banks and industrial firms: such outstanding loans to industry amounted to 6.3 m. rubles on 1 January 1899, but by 1 January 1902 reached 33.1 m. The real figure may, according to Gindin, have been much higher. The State Bank also extended more short-term credit, especially to the commercial banks. Discounting operations were worth 275 m. rubles on 1 January 1899; three years later they had risen to 560 m. This helped to keep interest rates lower than they would otherwise have been, and by 1902 they began to come down. Finally, the State Bank organized a 'Red Cross' of the stock exchange, which involved the banks in the coordinated purchase of industrial securities, in order to forestall a further fall in share prices.[63]

Table 5.5

Trends in share prices, 1899–1901

	Bryansk Company (mechanical engineering)		Donets-Yurevsk Company (metallurgy)	
	H	L	H	L
1899	523 (May)	443 (Sept.)	680½	470
1900	502 (March)	223	530	190
1901	295 (May)	136	93½ (July)	40 (July)

	St. Petersburg International Bank		St. Petersburg Loan and Discount Bank	
	H	L	H	L
1899	597	434	809	635
1900	430	320	665	460 (July)
1901	328 (Sept.)	256 (July)	473 (May)	325 (Nov.)

H = highest monthly average quoted on stock exchange in St. Petersburg (January, unless otherwise stated)

L = lowest monthly average quoted on stock exchange (December, unless otherwise stated).

Source: B. F. Brandt, *Torgovo-promyshlennyi krizis*, St. Petersburg, Volume 2, p. 98.

Generally speaking, the prices of raw materials and manufactured goods held firm during 1899, but the trend was not sustained beyond 1900 (see Table 5.6A). As the cost of credit rose, so the volume of wholesale trade declined. In the metallurgical industry, the situation was aggravated by the evident cutback in government orders for the transport sector: whereas unsold stocks of pig iron in south Russia amounted to one-tenth of output in 1900, by 1903 this proportion reached one-quarter.

Production and consumption figures reflect the same trend (see Table 5.6B), with the peaks being reached in general a year later than the peak in prices. For example, output of pig iron reached a peak in 1900; coal and oil in 1901. The most dramatic decline in physical output took place in iron and, to a lesser extent, in oil. Production of rails also fell quite considerably after 1900. Consumption of textiles stagnated between 1899 and 1901, although cotton was more adversely affected than other branches of the industry. The production and consumption of sugar increased throughout the period of industrial crisis (although, given the fall in prices, the value of sugar production increased less markedly). Food and drink as a whole

Table 5.6

Industrial prices and industrial production 1896–1904

A. *Wholesale prices of selected commodities*

	Pig iron		Donets coal	Baku crude	Refined sugar	Cotton yarn (38/40 weft)
	Urals	South				
		(kopecks/*pud*)			(rubles/*pud*)	
1897	91.3	96.0	22.0	7.7	5.24	15.65
1898	93.0	96.5	22.5	9.8	5.19	16.04
1899	100.0	112.0	23.3	14.0	4.97	17.58
1900	95.3	89.8	25.0	15.7	4.91	16.58
1901	85.1	76.3	22.8	8.2	4.99	16.31
1902	72.3	68.0	19.8	6.7	4.85	15.72
1903	71.6	65.9	19.0	8.2	4.65	18.09
1904	71.9	71.6	19.0	13.3	4.77	20.98

Note: pig iron prices are those quoted in St. Petersburg; coal, those in Moscow; oil, in Baku; sugar and cotton in Moscow.

B. *Main trends in output of selected commodities*

	Pig iron	Coal	Oil	Wagons	Rails	Cotton*	Sugar†
	(million tons)			(units)		('000 tons)	
1898	2.24	12.31	8.25	744	460	233	534
1899	2.71	13.98	9.02	875	450	264	557
1900	2.93	16.16	10.34	1005	500	262	590
1901	2.87	16.69	11.57	1225	480	264	678
1902	2.60	16.53	10.98	1160	419	285	829
1903	2.49	17.91	10.32	922	337	295	808

* Consumption of domestic and imported raw cotton.

Table 5.6—Continued

C. *Index of aggregate industrial production* (1896 = 100)

	Group A (capital goods)	Group B (consumer goods)	Total
1896	100	100	100
1897	113.2	108.9	109.7
1898	129.2	110.2	116.5
1899	140.2	112.3	121.6
1900	153.2	114.3	127.2
1901	148.7	123.7	132.0
1902	137.5	129.6	132.2
1903	144.5	138.9	140.8
1904	162.5	146.5	151.8

Sources: A. F. Yakovlev, *Ekonomicheskie krizisy v Rossii*, Gospolitizdat, 1955, pp. 259–82; V. I. Bovykin, 'Dinamika promyshlennogo proizvodstva v 1896–1910', *Istoriya SSSR*, no. 3, 1983, pp. 20–52.

maintained a steady progress throughout, with a slight interruption in the case of flour-milling in 1899–1900.[64]

No estimate of the value of aggregate industrial production was available to contemporaries, and only in 1930 were such estimates fully worked out (see Table 5.6C). Aggregate data reveal that there was no overall decline in the value of production, notwithstanding the fall in commodity prices. Only in the capital goods sectors (Group A) did output fall between 1900 and 1903. The consumer goods industries held up well.

Populists insisted that there was a *general* industrial crisis at the turn of the century, but this verdict is not borne out by the evidence. The main sectors to suffer were in energy supply: in coal, and in oil extraction and refining. The 'crisis' thus seems to have been manufactured by sections of the Russian gentry – smarting from the recent failure to prevent the adoption of the Gold Standard, by industrialists, pained at the fall in prices and rising interest charges – and by the populist intelligentsia. The mass market was capable of absorbing manufactured goods, and had not been 'exhausted' by government fiscal policy. In any event, as one authority wrote in 1909, 'the view that Russian industry is supported only by state orders cannot get way from the fact that in a country with 150 million inhabitants here must be a huge market for industrial goods'.[65]

The reduction in government expenditure was bound all the same o have a deleterious effect, at least in the short run, on the engineering and metallurgical sectors. This reduction was only evident after 1902, where expenditure on the railway-building programme was concerned see Table 5.7). Why did this retrenchment take place? Witte argued before the Tsar in 1899 that his Ministry had difficulty in negotiating a loan abroad to cover the overall budget deficit which, he privately acknowledged, did exist. Witte maintained that spending had to be brought under control where possible, the more so because Russia had assumed imperial ambitions in the Far East and in Persia. In the short term, railway construction was an obvious target for retrenchment. The pressure was relieved slightly in 1899, when Witte floated a loan inside Russia, and in 1901, when he negotiated a loan in France, but these were stopgap measures. The difficulty of expanding tax receipts in the immediate future, together with new commitments abroad, served to explain the lower level of spending on the railway-building programme, which persisted until 1912.[66]

Since the prospects for railway construction were less favourable after the turn of the century than they had been in the second half of the 1890s, industrialists had to consider other alternatives in order to maintain the viability of their enterprises. This problem was clearly more acute for heavy industry than for light, and prompted businessmen to adopt both 'offensive' and 'defensive' measures. The former included attempts to penetrate foreign markets; the latter comprised the formation of syndicates. These will be considered in turn.

(b) Export markets for manufactured goods

Soon after he became Minister of Finances, Witte called upon Russian consular officials to assist the efforts of businessmen in exploring and exploiting overseas markets for Russian manufactured goods. The Far East was one potential market; the Near East another (Persia and Turkey in particular). Prior to the end of the nineteenth century most trade with these regions comprised goods with a high ratio of value to bulk. But without more adequate communications trade was unlikely to grow substantially, still less assume the role of engine of growth in the Russian manufacturing sector.[67]

When the government embarked on the appropriate revolution in transport, strategic considerations were uppermost. The construction of the Transcaspian railway during the second half of the 1880s was designed to extend Russian territorial control in Central Asia. The control of trade along the border with northern Persia was a secondary consequence. The proposed Trans-Siberian railway had

Table 5.7

Expenditure on railway construction, 1893–1914

(million rubles, current prices)

	Construction of new lines	Improvement of existing track	Chinese Far Eastern railway	Total state outlays	Private sector outlays
1893	45	10	–	55	n.a.
1894	50	10	–	60	104
1895	96	13	–	109	117
1896	132	21	–	153	6
1897	130	26	–	156	121
1898	114	41	25	180	53
1899	102	44	60	206	9
1900	103	46	86	235	n.a.*
1901	37	84	82	203	–
1902	156	100	102	358	–
1903	166	99	n.a.†	265	–
1904	99	90	–	189	–
1905	73	82	–	155	–
1906	41	71	–	112	–
1907	49	75	–	125	–
1908	60	74	–	134	–
1909	60	71	–	131	–
1910	63	65	–	128	–
1911	96	68	–	164	–
1912	111	66	–	177	–
1913	133	87	–	220	–
1914	93	95	–	188	–

* No data are available for private sector outlays after 1900; some private spending is implied in the 'subsidies to private railway companies', which amounted to 51 m. rubles in 1904.

† There is no indication of outlays on this item after 1902.

Sources: A. M. Soloveva, *Zheleznodorozhnyi transport Rossii vo vtoroi polovine XIX veka*, Nauka, 1975, p. 289 (for 1893–1902); P. A. Khromov, *Ekonomicheskoe razvitie Rossii v XIX–XX vekakh*, Gospolitizdat, 1950, pp. 523–9; private sector outlays derived from B. F. Brandt, *Torgovo-promyshlennyi krizis*, St. Petersburg, 1904, Volume 2, p. 62.

been under consideration for ten years before work on it began in 1891. The Tsar's rescript in 1891, which gave the project the final seal of approval, spoke of a railway 'capable of uniting the abundant gifts of Siberian nature' with the existing network in European Russia, but an important consideration was the need to transfer troops more rapidly from west to east in the event of hostilities. In the event, of course, the 'peaceful economic penetration' of this region by Russia was to encourage rather than lessen the chances of such hostility, if not with China then with Japan.[68]

The new railway lines did encourage the growth of trade, especially when the government provided further inducements to merchants and industrialists. For instance, the extension of sugar and cotton goods exports into Persia was helped by the decision to close off the Caucasus to non-Russian trade (there was hitherto an active transit trade to Persia) and, above all, to subsidize exports of these products. In the Far East the government closed the free ports on the Siberian seaboard, so that Russian merchants could take advantage of the new rail link to sell their goods (again, largely cotton) in the border region. Finally, the government played a major role in the formation of new financial institutions which helped to provide credit to merchants in both regions: the Russo-Chinese Bank began to function in 1896, the Persian Loan and Discount Bank two years earlier. The former, although effectively controlled by French capital, assumed responsibility for the tea trade with China and the pursuit of new concessions in Manchuria. The Persian bank not only provided credit at favourable rates of interest to Russian merchants (provided they dealt in Russian goods), but also, like the Russo-Chinese, bought Russian goods on its own account.[69]

The volume of trade continued to grow during the 1890s and through to the First World War. As the Trans-Siberian neared completion, total Russian exports to China rose from two million rubles in 1891 to nearly ten million in 1901. By 1914 they stood at more than thirty million, half of this being made up of cotton goods (China took one-third of her cotton goods imports from Russia). The Russian penetration of the Chinese market would have been still greater, had not the port of Dalny been declared open to all trade in 1905, thereby allowing merchants to move their goods along the railway to northern Manchuria, to compete with Russian goods. Russia remained in deficit with China, given the sustained growth in tea imports, but exporters remained confident about the potential in this market.

The Foreign Minister Lamsdorff had spoken privately in 1904 of the need to persist in a policy that would make Persia 'obedient and useful', particularly in view of the rivalry between Britain and Russia in that region. He pointed to trade as the main means of perpetuating

Russia's presence in Persia. The tsarist government encouraged trade through subsidies and forced upon Persia a revised tariff treaty in 1903 (significantly, this followed two loans to Persia in 1900 and 1902), which raised the duties on British cottons. Against this background, by the early twentieth century Persia took close on half of her imports from Russia (mostly sugar and cotton goods). Whenever other competitors threatened to break the Russian stranglehold, the government promptly raised the export bounties to Moscow cotton industrialists and Kiev sugar magnates.[70]

The evidence of increased trade with China and Persia suggests that the potential for 'peaceful economic penetration' was most easily realized in sectors which were not affected by the industrial 'crisis' of 1900–3. It is difficult to say whether Witte had expected anything else when he acknowledged in 1903 that 'many branches now require export outlets'. Heavy industry gained nothing from the construction of the Chinese Far Eastern Railway (linking the Trans-Siberian more directly with the port of Vladivostok by cutting across northern Manchuria). Most of the orders for rails and rolling-stock went to non-Russian suppliers. The expectation must have been that the benefits to Russian capital goods industry would take decades to be realized, and that there would be little immediate and direct demand from the Far Eastern markets. Similar considerations applied to the Near East.[71]

The Russian Minister of War, Kuropatkin, warned the government in 1900 of the risks of an active foreign policy in the Far East: 'If Russia, feverishly developing the growth of her industry along with other powers, also reaches the stage of over-production of various items then, in order to find a market, she will be drawn into a terrible struggle for outlets'. The particular point he was making was that Russian ministers ought not to become embroiled in the affairs of Russian capitalists. (In fact, by 1902, Kuropatkin would himself be convinced of the need to keep Russian troops in Manchuria against hostile attacks on the Chinese railway). Between 1885 and 1914 the government's policy of penetration had brought about a considerable improvement in trade with the Far East. Even the disastrous war against Japan in 1904–5 had no serious consequence for Russian trade: the settlement with Japan and with Britain (1907) proved beneficial to Russian exporters.

If such countries as China and Persia might, as Lenin argued in 1917, be regarded as semi-colonies of tsarist Russia, they nevertheless functioned as markets for Russian textiles and (to a lesser extent) capital, not as markets for capital goods. As Lenin himself was aware, it would take years for the political and economic subordination of these countries to translate itself into a demand for the products of Russian heavy industry. Figures on the composition of Russian xports to all destinations suggest that the changes between the 1890s nd the outbreak of war did not amount to much: the average share f all manufactured goods in 1894–8 was 3.5 per cent; in 1909–13 t had risen to just 4.5 per cent (total exports had increased by 115 er cent over that period). If Russian industry were to improve on his performance, then the government would have to subsidize xports of goods other than sugar; industry would have to become nuch more competitive; new 'protected' foreign markets would have o be sought; or – not entirely fancifully – Russia's main continental ival, Germany, would have to be reduced in international economic ignificance. Is it any wonder that Russia's industrial bourgeoisie nthusiastically supported the war effort against Germany in 914–17?[72]

c) Corporate industrial policy

ndustrialists responded in two other ways to the stagnation in the evel of business activity, first by forming syndicates to allocate market hares among member firms and thereby to curtail opportunities for lomestic competitors in the Russian market. To this tactic, largely onfined to the basic extractive and metallurgical industries, the Russian government had an ambivalent attitude. The second response vas a demand from industrialists that they receive renewed support rom government through contracts for finished goods, whether for he state-owned railway system or the armed forces. Russian industri- lists formed pressure groups – along the lines of their German ounterparts – in order to make their case known to the government oureaucracy.

The attitude adopted by the metallurgical and engineering industries vas that the mass market for manufactured goods remained limited n the early years of the twentieth century: 'to dream of consolidating our metallurgical industry on the basis of horseshoes, axles, wheels, oloughs and roofs for the peasantry . . . is not something in which oractical men can indulge'. Entrepreneurs judged the rural market lemand to be *unstable*, rather than inherently inadequate in aggregate erms. It was thought that rural household consumption and invest- nent fluctuated from year to year in accordance with the harvest. Heavy industry, with so much capital tied up in plant and overheads, iad to have a more secure foundation. During the late 1880s and the 890s, railway building had provided that foundation. If it could no onger do so, then industrialists sought other forms of public expendi- ure to provide them with guaranteed orders. Accordingly, one indus- rialist called upon the government to act as a 'regulator' of demand; ven if the Treasury were not the main initiator of demand, it should it least insure against the failure of household demand. Such appeals, of course, were subject to the same qualifications that had attached to the railway-building programme. That is to say, the economic stimulus of government was conditional upon the capacity of the Treasury to raise the necessary revenue through borrowing or taxation, or by printing money. Thus, industry would almost certainly again be confronted by periodic fluctuations in demand. Continued reliance upon government orders was not without risks to industry. Some initiative had to be taken by industry itself.[73]

Just as the main impact of the industrial depression at the turn of the century was felt by heavy industry, so too the tendency towards monopoly control over the market was most clearly revealed in the iron and steel and coal industries. Towards the end of 1901 the major metallurgical firms in south Russia, following the lead given by French banking interests earlier in the year, embarked upon a series of discussions, which culminated early in 1902 in the formation of 'Prodameta' (the Society for the Sale of Metallurgical Products of Russian Industry). Twelve firms concluded an agreement, which limited the amount of iron and steel each could market in a given year. The initial agreement covered only a small number of specific items, such as sheet iron, girders, and axles and tyres. Only in 1909 did Prodameta subject the production of rails and rolled iron (*sortovoe zhelezo*) to an agreement on market shares. By then, around thirty firms had joined the syndicate, though not all were involved in quotas for each product.[74]

Most of the firms involved in Prodameta had close links with French capital, through the Société Générale or Banque de l'Union Parisienne, but it was the joint considerations of the Russian metallurgical industry, the Ministry of Finances and foreign capital that contributed to its emergence. French capital hoped to safeguard the position of those firms in the metallurgical industry in which it had an interest; Witte supported the move in order to give an assurance to foreign investors that the government had their interests at heart; and industrial firms hoped to secure their future market position. Stabilization of prices was not the sole consideration. Firms also sought to create a more unified sales system, which would reduce the leverage of the merchant houses (*torgovyie doma*) and enable them to improve the conditions under which they were obliged to grant credit. When they sold in small quantities to such intermediaries and to other clients, they had to accept long waits between supply and recovery of payment; now they could dictate terms and reduce their commercial costs.[75]

The contribution of government to monopoly power in the market for iron and steel extended to more direct intervention. For example, in 1902, shortly after the formation of a syndicate of locomotive producers, the government agreed to allocate the bulk of its reduced orders for rails and rolling-stock to a handful of major metallurgical and engineering firms. In the case of rails, eight firms in south Russia received orders for rails which were priced at the 1899 level, when demand for rails was at a peak. This explains the delay in arranging the inclusion of rails in the quotas drawn up under the aegis of Prodameta. After this agreement was reached in 1909, members turned their minds to firms which did not belong to Prodameta. These included firms in the Urals, which had a competitive edge over southern factories in the Mid-Volga, on account of lower transport costs. Prodameta dumped iron and steel on these markets, while maintaining the monopoly price in other markets. As a result, Urals metallurgical companies had a struggle to retain their market share even in the production of roofing iron, where they were traditionally strong. Furthermore, at a time when diversification was rendered difficult by the activities of Prodameta, prices for roofing iron fell between 1908 and 1912.[76]

The formation of syndicates such as Prodameta testifies to the growth of corporate control over the market for industrial raw materials and semi-finished goods; characteristically, it was in the market for coal, oil, iron and steel and non-ferrous metal that syndicates enjoyed greatest success. By 1911, for instance, Prodameta controlled 90 per cent of the sales of assorted and sheet iron, 96 per cent of girders and channels, and 74 per cent of pig iron production (pig iron was not controlled by quota, but it normally entered into further finishing processes, where items were subject to quota restrictions). The organization of industry did not, however, reach the stage where the entire range of decisions about production and pricing came under the control of a single trust. The most famous attempt to form a trust, in the metallurgical industry in 1908, came to nothing, partly because of political hostility to the project, but more particularly because the rivalries within the proposed grouping made a formal agreement impossible to implement. The lack of 'trustification' of production should nevertheless not be taken to signify the absence of monopoly control. Throughout the period immediately before the First World War (and during the War itself), Russian heavy industry became highly integrated. Typically, metallurgical plants would be united with coal and iron ore mines under the same corporate control. These industries were also associated formally or informally (through the medium of the major banks) with finishing industries, such as engineering firms producing industrial equipment, agricultural machinery, construction material, shipbuilding and defence goods.[77]

The profits from metallurgical companies' monopoly position in the iron and steel market (and, especially, financial support from the banks) allowed them to finance the acquisition of ore and coal deposits. In 1910, nine of the leading south Russian metallurgical firms owned or rented iron ore mines; by 1913 the number had risen

to twelve, and they controlled 80 per cent of iron ore supplies in the
Ukraine. Furthermore, they produced more than 2.1 m. tons of coal
surplus to their requirements. As a consequence, such firms were able
to take further advantage of the rise in ore and coal prices after
1910.[78]

The pre-war surge in metal and fuel prices came to be associated
in the minds of many contemporaries with the activities of the syndicates. The evidence suggests that it was less the existence of Prodameta
or Produgol as such that produced the so-called 'famine', as the
tendency towards vertical integration, combined with the rapid
growth in demand before 1914. The 'famine' was not the result of a
reduction in output of iron and steel, but a reduction in the rate of
increase at which it was supplied to customers. Members of Prodameta held back a larger proportion of their output, instead of
supplying the growing needs of metal-working, engineering and other
industrial consumers. Metallurgical firms retained iron and steel for
the expansion of their own plant, and − more important still −
processed more metal in order to produce finished goods on their own
account. Some of these firms integrated further forwards, producing
munitions, although this became widespread only after 1914. The
main losers in this process were smaller engineering factories which
produced agricultural machinery or rolling stock, and they provided
most of the ammunition for agitation about the 'famine'. For their
part, the metallurgical giants took advantage of the fact that semi-
finished iron and steel used in 'internal' consumption was not subject
to quota restrictions, and were able to increase their leverage at the
expense of smaller finishing metal-working enterprises.[79]

Before 1908, Russian heavy industry could hardly have been happy
with its efforts to shake off the effects of the slump at the turn of the
century. In 1907 only just over one-quarter of all rolling-stock
capacity was being exploited; even in less vulnerable areas the situation was unsatisfactory, with merchant iron capacity utilized to the
extent of only 62 per cent, and roofing iron 70 per cent. Against this
background, demand for state support reached new heights. Industrialists' associations, in particular the Association of Trade and Industry
and the southern Russian industrialists' federation, called for a greatly
accelerated programme of railway construction and for other state
initiatives, such as armaments, dockyards and so forth. They coupled
this with the demand for orders to be passed to private rather than
state producers.

The Russian government was caught in an interesting dilemma by
such demands. There was every reason to suppose that tsarist officials
would reject these calls, on the grounds that the government was not
just a milch-cow for private enterprise. A further consideration was
that state finances were too strained to permit any expansion of

state demand (something that both the Ministries of Finance and of Transport were at pains to point out). Pressure also came from industrial consumers, the *zemstva* and politicians to reduce tariffs in order to force down the price of iron and steel. The government listened sympathetically, but took no decisive or systematic countervailing action. Its one plan to increase imports (in 1913–14), was mooted only on the assumption that domestic prices were unaffected.

The government had to accede to the demand for a greater level of support for industry, not because it wanted to oblige industrialists, but because the need for rearmament was urgent after the defeat in the war against Japan. Great power considerations were now at stake, and tsarist Russia was necessarily drawn into the general European rearmament after 1905. Taken together, the loss of military capability after 1904–5 and the need to retain international status in Europe represented powerful forces which led to the satisfaction of industrial pressure groups. In defence production they found considerable recompense for the decline in government railway orders.[80]

The government paid the rising costs of weapon procurement, on the grounds that this contained a necessary element of subsidy to private firms which had been asked to convert to a different and technologically more advanced form of production. The firms involved, like the government, could absorb the increased cost of raw materials without too much difficulty. As already suggested, the loudest complaints came from other quarters: state and private railway companies, smaller-scale industrial consumers, and the *zemstva*. The latter represented the interests of landowners and were at the forefront of demands for cheaper agricultural machinery, which could only be obtained if tariffs on iron and steel (and the machinery itself) were cut. Railway companies (which accounted for one-quarter of all Prodameta sales) complained that their suppliers first delayed the completion of their orders, and then promptly demanded higher prices for iron and steel than were originally agreed. They too called for imports to be stepped up. The results for heavy industry – metallurgical and engineering firms alike – were highly favourable in the period 1908–13: rising prices for output, higher profits, enabling them to finance further integration, and thus market control. They were in a strong position to challenge still further the role of the pre-existing state sector during the First World War. As we have seen, industry forged pressure groups to press its case, and had informal contacts with members of the government bureaucracy. But it was the imperatives of the tsarist state in its search for great power status, requiring a concomitant military support, that ultimately secured the position of big business.[81]

The structure of consumer goods industries tended to be highly concentrated only in the case of cotton textiles. In Moscow province, in 1895, just under ten per cent of cotton textiles firms had more than 1,000 workers, and accounted for more than two-thirds of gross output. This was a greater degree of concentration than in metalworking, where such firms (a smaller proportion of the total) only accounted for 38 per cent of output. At the bottom end of the scale, 56 registered enterprises (out of a total of 178), employing fewer than thirty workers, contributed just one per cent of total production. The largest firms in Moscow cotton textiles (those with more than 1,000 workers) used around 83 per cent of steam engine capacity in this industry. Although size was not necessarily an indication of advanced development, it was here that technical change was most likely to be found.[82]

The high degree of concentration in cotton textiles did not lead to successful efforts to enforce corporate control over the market for finished goods or spun yarn. Despite various attempts to demonstrate otherwise, the organization of the textile industry was not in the hands of cartels or syndicates during the early twentieth century. As far as cotton-spinning is concerned, Lyashchenko mentions the Moscow cotton syndicate (1907), combining 47 firms with a total of 3.7 million spindles. However, total spindleage was two and a half times greater, and he acknowledges that outsiders kept up pressure on the syndicate. The average price of yarn did rise in 1907, but this was not sustained. From time to time, cloth producers assembled to complain – in 1900, 1908, 1911 and 1913 – about the low prices prevailing for cloth, and problems in realizing their output. But these were always meetings of businessmen from either Moscow or Ivanovo, the main centres of cotton cloth production, and competition between the two prevented any systematic or comprehensive control over the market. Attempts to increase the price of calico prints by Moscow firms led Ivanovo firms to dump excess output on the market and keep prices down. Even within the region, firms frequently refused to cooperate. The similarities of culture and outlook, so often mentioned by historians of the Moscow bourgeoisie, did not lead these family firms to carve up the market between themselves.[83]

The general situation for the Russian cotton textiles industry after 1900 must be regarded as satisfactory. There were problems: demand continued to fluctuate from year to year, as it had done throughout the previous century. Sometimes the government stepped in to offer assistance, as happened during the 1900–1903 crisis; although Witte refused to reduce the tariff on imported cotton, whose price had fallen less rapidly than the price of finished goods, he agreed to reduce freight rates on cotton goods sent from the central producing region to south Russian markets, and to subsidize the export of cotton goods. But the overall trend in the price of cotton textiles was favourable: between 1900–1904 and 1909–13 the price of calicoes rose by more than 20 per cent. Although the cost of yarn increased more rapidly (30 per cent) in the same period, improved efficiency in weaving and finishing firms helped to stabilize total costs, and those firms which faced difficulties with rising costs of materials could shift the burden on to the wage labour force. In this competitive industry, no firm could easily pass on higher costs to the consumer.[84]

The reason for the steady upward drift in the price of finished goods is not to be found in the operation of syndicates which, as already established, had little impact in textiles, but in the growth in the rural and urban population and in the rising real incomes of households. The high level of demand between 1905 and 1914 helps to explain why the general rate of profit in textiles – and, for that matter, in food and drink as well – was so high. Profits in consumer goods industries regularly exceeded the average profits in heavy industry, even during the boom periods of the 1890s and 1910–13.

From what has already been said about the cost of raw materials, which accounted for more than two-thirds of the total production costs of cotton textiles firms, it is clear that these enterprises had a close interest in establishing firmer control over the market for raw cotton. This became easier to achieve once the production of domestically produced cotton expanded in the last decade of the nineteenth century. As production in Turkestan increased and the railway system was extended in Central Asia, cotton-spinning firms engaged more closely in the trade, setting up agencies to deal directly with peasant suppliers. They also moved into the business of cleaning and ginning the raw cotton. By 1908, for instance, although locally owned ginning factories outnumbered Russian firms by two to one, the bulk of the trade was in the hands of metropolitan capital. Increasingly, however, cotton textiles producers themselves surrendered the trade in cotton to the agents of Moscow banks and the big commercial firms such as Wogau and Vtorov, whose interests extended also to trade in crops such as tobacco and tea. This suggests that the traditional independence of cotton textiles factories declined. They could only assume control over local cotton-ginning factories through the financial support of the banks, while the transactions with the original producers were also handled by institutional intermediaries. As far as the final product is concerned, Moscow textile firms began to exercise control over retail distribution. Traditionally, cloth had been taken to large markets such as Nizhnii Novgorod, but towards the end of the nineteenth century this had been supplanted to a large extent by sales to wholesalers in the major cities. After 1900, however, some of the large firms in Moscow, such as Emil Tsindel, set up retail outlets themselves, thereby reducing the distribution and handling costs previously levied by intermediaries.[85]

In the case of the sugar industry, the tsarist government itself took a hand in supervising production and distribution. The decision to establish a quota for each factory was taken in 1895, in order to protect producers from the rapid decline in sugar prices on the domestic and foreign markets. Since the firms were owned by gentry industrialists, such intervention by government had political as well as economic significance. The industrialists, of whom there were about 250 in 1895, now operated under closer regulation than they had achieved by themselves. Firms in fact frequently exceeded the quotas that had been established. There were a number of reasons why this happened. In the first place, firms deliberately sought to underestimate norms of consumption from which the quotas were derived. As output was absorbed by the domestic market, the excess could be sold at a higher price. Although the production of excess sugar attracted a penalty in the form of an excise, this duty could be tolerated without difficulty. For example, technical change in the industry had brought the cost of one *pud* of sugar down to 1.45 rubles by 1900. The excise amounted to 1.75 rubles, but with an average selling price of 4.10–4.20 producers were still left with good returns. Besides, any excess output could be exported, without attracting any excise from the government. In effect, the so-called *normirovka* also amounted to an export subsidy, since producers could always sell their sugar in Russia at inflated prices, while dumping the residue on foreign markets. Although the Brussels sugar convention in 1902 sought to prevent subsidies on sugar, Russia refused to sign. The fact that west European markets were then closed to Russian sugar was not serious (in any case they were reopened in 1907), because the home market was buoyant and exports to Finland and Persia began to soar.[86]

The production of lump sugar (*rafinad*) was more highly concentrated than the production of crude. A handful of Ukrainian landowners, including Tereshchenko (later a minister in the Provisional Government), Brodsky, Kharitonenko, Bobrinsky and Yaroshinsky, monopolized production accounting for around two-thirds of output. Their factories took four-fifths of the output of granulated sugar, so their leverage was extensive. When they formed a Union of Refiners in 1902, in an attempt to wrest from government greater control over sugar quotas and to force up the price of lump sugar relative to crude, other producers were alarmed at the implications. However, the government assured them that the *normirovka* would be maintained. Since this guaranteed each producer a quota, it was difficult for any individual entrepreneur to secure an increased share of output at the expense of the others. At the same time, the price support enabled even the small firms to make profits. The government thus forestalled greater concentration in the sugar industry as a whole. It thereby satisfied its gentry supporters, while also obtaining a revenue from the excise (140 million rubles by 1913).[87]

(d) The First World War

The First World War was a godsend for Russian heavy industry. From early 1915 it became apparent that neither the state arsenals nor the existing armaments firms in the private sector were capable of meeting the insatiable appetite of the military. Accordingly, and in response to generous contracts and prices from the procurement authorities, large and small engineering firms alike converted to the production of armaments. The giant metallurgical firms that belonged to Prodameta switched to the production of high-explosive shell. As in all belligerent countries, the output of shell and other ammunition was revolutionized by the new techniques of mass production. From a managerial point of view, the use of continuous flow methods helped to boost the productivity of the abundant unskilled labour that flooded into the Russian factories. The War created a large and unified market for industry, and showed what results could be achieved where demand for a homogeneous product was buoyant.

By 1916 industrial production was already some 20 per cent higher than it had been in the last full year of peace, and in real terms. However, the aggregate growth conceals the shift in the composition of industrial output that had taken place. Defence requirements were paramount, and were satisfied ultimately by diverting resources away from consumption and investment. No amount of productivity growth in defence industries could provide for the needs of the army. One estimate of the distribution of total industrial output is that close on 30 per cent of output by 1916 was destined for the war effort, compared to 5 per cent in 1913. In the case of machine-building, the proportion in 1916 reached 66 per cent. Household consumption took 60 per cent of the total, compared to 80 per cent in 1913. The production of investment goods was also curtailed; nor did imports compensate for the decline in output.[88]

The government contributed to the reallocation of resources by establishing a series of 'Special Councils', for defence, fuel supply, transport and food supply. The government also intervened in the allocation of iron and steel, fixing prices for the delivery of materials to defence contractors and, in 1916, controlling the disposition of all iron and steel output. In pinning its hopes on a massive expansion of armaments output, the tsarist regime hoped to win the war as quickly as possible, but it was not to be: the war dragged on, and non-defence industry (and thus civilians) went to the back of the queue for available resources. The result, by late 1916, was a chronic shortage of consumer goods; in addition, the need to replace worn and damaged capital equipment in industry and transport had to be given attention. As things turned out, this problem could not begin to be addressed until the end of the Civil War in 1921.[89]

Conclusion

The evidence presented in this chapter suggests that it is of limited value to generalize about the manufacturing sector as a whole. Two important distinctions need to be made: between factory and cottage industry, and between 'heavy' industry and 'light'.

Cottage industry did not sink without trace during the first industrial upsurge of the 1870s, nor even during the boom in the 1890s. Tugan-Baranovsky argued that 'young capitalism grows at the expense of other economic forms which it displaces'. But this displacement was far from complete by 1900. At the same time, the character of *kustar* changed. Even when *kustari* continued to operate, on an apparently independent basis, they did so within the ambit of the factory and under the dictates of the capitalist market.

The progressive transformation of industry did not necessarily imply rapid technological progress, or that factories reaped substantial economies of scale. Many factories embodied a blend of old and new techniques of production; many retained a diversified product mix, especially in the case of capital goods industries. The reason for this had to do with the fragmentation of the market, and the fact that the market was still relatively small for capital equipment. Indeed, the *kustar* producers frequently revealed themselves to be more specialised in their output than were the factories.

The allusion to the market brings us to the second major distinction, between capital goods industry (iron and steel, engineering) and consumer goods (textiles, food and drink). The market for capital goods did indeed depend largely upon the state. Before 1914, the private sector demand for capital equipment in industry – and in other sectors – was becoming more significant, but it could not substitute for state demand. This suggests that Gerschenkron exaggerated the transformation in the pattern of industrial development after 1905. But the verdict is no more favourable to the populist case: populists were guilty of generalizing from these basic industries to the manufacturing sector as a whole.

The market for consumer goods was buoyant, and reflected the growth in consumer purchasing power in town and country. This can be attributed to the monetization of the peasant economy and the differentiation of the peasantry; and to the growth of agricultural productivity that was discussed in Chapter Four. In addition, manufacturers in light industry appear to have been more successful than others in keeping down costs: partly because of technical change, and partly through the exploitation of the workforce.

The contrast with capital goods (and, by extension, with the energy supply industries) is a marked one. In these sectors, investment in new plant had grown during the 1890s. But entrepreneurs faced a slump in their fortunes at the turn of the century. The 1905 Revolution exacerbated the effects of the slump, by forcing up wages and thus unit costs. One response to the slump was to establish greater corporate control over the market. Industrialists also looked to government to get them out of their difficulties. Export markets seemed to offer little prospect as an outlet for Russian capital goods in the short term. Attempts to boost labour productivity did not have dramatic results: Witte's much-vaunted hope of achieving substantial cost reductions was hardly fulfilled before 1914. The First World War relieved capitalists of these dilemmas, but it hardly offered a long-term solution to the 'market question'.

6 Capital and Credit

The standard liberal interpretation of the tsarist economy maintains that the autonomous accumulation of capital was hindered by the lack of productivity growth in agriculture. Since agriculture comprised the main economic activity for the majority of the Russian population, this was a serious problem. The potential for capital accumulation was further constrained by the rapid growth of rural population. As a result of the growth in numbers, more output had to be consumed, leaving less available for savings. The tsarist government compounded the problem of savings, by levying oppressive taxes on peasant farmers. Thus private accumulation by rural entrepreneurs was frustrated by the low level and slow growth of agricultural productivity, by population growth and by government fiscal policies.

According to this approach, the main difficulties were experienced by peasant producers. Their problems were not eased by the provision of rural credit, which might have encouraged them to invest. The supply of credit was inadequate to the demands of peasant agriculturists. Credit was more readily available to gentry landlords, by virtue of their power and influence in tsarist society. However, the Russian gentry did not make use of the money market for the purpose of productive investment. Instead, they obtained credit to finance the debts that they had incurred over several generations of conspicuous consumption.

Finally, the liberal view is that the tsarist government devoted the bulk of the resources it extracted from the peasant masses to unproductive purposes. Public investment – for example, in railways – played only a modest part in official calculations of government priorities. Government revenue was directed largely into unproductive channels: defence, administration and payments on the national debt. To the extent that the government was also obliged to borrow from foreign or domestic creditors, it exacerbated the difficulties faced by private entrepreneurs. The latter had to compete for funds with a government whose appetite for credit seemed insatiable.[1]

There are, of course, differences of emphasis within the liberal interpretation. Gerschenkron, for example, did not regard the problem of agricultural productivity as an insuperable obstacle to capital accumulation. He argued that in the first instance the government had to substitute for the lack of domestic savings by private individuals. In his view, public investment and indirect government support for private entrepreneurs were crucial to Russian industrialization. The tsarist regime also created the conditions for the inflow of foreign capital. Gerschenkron's argument is in sharp contrast to other, more negative assessments of the role of government.[2]

Another area of debate concerns the extent to which fiscal policy placed an intolerable burden upon peasant households. Some scholars have expressed reservations about the pressure to which peasants were subjected. The main issue arises in the context of the increased rates of indirect taxation that were introduced during the late 1880s and 1890s. However, the implications of this debate for investment by peasant households are not clear. Any growth in peasants' disposable income may have resulted in increased consumption or in the purchase of additional land, and not in capital investment. As we saw in Chapter Four, most scholars have doubted that peasants had any incentive to invest, given the existence of communal land tenure and land redivision.

The populist interpretation may be summarized more briefly. Like many liberals, the populists believed that the peasant economy was being squeezed by the government's fiscal policies. The pressures on peasant savings were intensified by the upward movement in money rents, which transferred income from peasants to rapacious landlords and which did nothing for capital accumulation. The government, for its part, did not invest in agriculture. Instead, resources flowed largely into unproductive channels. As government commitments increased, so Russia became more and more subordinated to foreign bondholders: foreign credit was a millstone around the neck of the people.

The populist critique of the money market dwelt in addition on its bias towards the needs of factory industry. This bias diverted credit away from agriculture and cottage industry, and allowed village money-lenders, landlords and merchants to exploit the peasantry, by charging extortionate rates of interest. The alternative, which populists espoused by the turn of the century, was cooperative credit, which was designed to strengthen the traditional rural community and to afford a degree of autonomy to peasant households.[3]

The main differences between contemporary Russian liberals and populists can be summarized as follows. Liberals welcomed the growth of capital investment in industry, but wanted to see evidence of further progress in private investment in all spheres of the economy. To this extent, the government had a duty to simplify the procedures for the formation of corporate enterprise and to facilitate the access of private entrepreneurs to the money market. Populists attacked the concentration of investment in sectors other than peasant agriculture and criticized the 'dependence' of Russia on foreign credit.

The marxist interpretation paid particular attention to the 'original' accumulation of capital, which both preceded and facilitated the development of the fully fledged capitalist economy. Marx traced this process in England, through an examination of foreign trade, colonial plunder and the expropriation of the producers from the means of production. On the face of it, conditions seemed far less propitious in mid-nineteenth-century Russia. Russia had itself been ravaged by invaders and impoverished by the wars against Sweden during the early eighteenth century. Russian foreign trade was modest by European standards. Serfdom tied the producer to the means of production. Nevertheless, Russian marxists argued that the first signs of original accumulation could be detected in Russia before 1861. Hired labour was encouraged by those lords who sought a money income; this labour in turn allowed factory owners – gentry, merchants and even serfs – to accumulate profits. Merchants also profited from the sale of grain and spirits, the latter under government licence.

As the capitalist system developed after Emancipation, so the main source of accumulation became the profits generated in capitalist enterprise, including the profits made by kulaks in agriculture. The conventional assumption has been that profits were greatest in heavy industry, which boomed during the 1880s and 1890s. But there is some question in modern Soviet historiography as to the validity of this assumption. Orthodox historians have emphasized the role of syndicates in pre-war Russia, suggesting that they boosted the rate of profit in heavy industry. But Gindin has disputed the profitability of this sector and has suggested that the profit rate was higher in textiles, foodstuffs and trade.

Finally, marxist scholars have drawn attention to the revolution in the supply of credit in late tsarist Russia. In this respect, the most important phenomenon was the growth of monopoly power in financial institutions. Russian banks and big business collaborated with the representatives of foreign capital, to increase their collective influence in industry and trade. The joint-stock banks no longer confined their operations to the supply of working capital to commercial enterprises, but engaged in company promotion and reorganization, where they made enormous profits. By 1913, a handful of financial institutions dominated the Russian money market; this concentration of power represented, for Lenin, the final stage of capitalism. The creation of a 'financial oligarchy' in Russia was not just the result of the activities of Russian and foreign capitalists: it was encouraged by the tsarist bureaucracy, which had a stake in the new industrial and financial monopolies.[4]

A number of questions arise from this summary of the main propositions that have been advanced within each tradition. We may begin by drawing attention to the question of investment. The first issue concerns the main trends in capital investment. The next concerns the means by which private investment was financed: by recourse to credit at home or abroad, or by means of retained business profits? In this respect, it is worth recalling Gerschenkron's hypothesis, that the initial impulse for industrial development had to come from government, rather than through retained profits. However, he maintained that, after 1900, the banks were able to provide credit and to replace the government as a source of support for industry. A third issue concerns public investment. How did the government finance its investment programmes: by taxation, by credit or by printing money?

These considerations prompt other questions in turn. Some indication is needed as to the extent to which the private sector was able or unable to generate profits. This applies to agriculture, no less than to industry, and to gentry and peasant farmers alike. In so far as the issue concerns the peasantry, it is necessary to ask to what extent the government absorbed their savings and left them nothing for potential capital investment. In so far as the issue concerns private entrepreneurs in industry, did the government 'crowd out' private borrowers, through its own demand for credit? This could happen in several ways: for example, the government could obstruct the operation of new financial institutions that sought to provide credit to industry. The government might push up the cost of credit, by virtue of its own demands on the money market. The final question relates to the other commitments undertaken by the government. To what extent did government expenditure prove difficult to control, and lead to new demands for credit, whether at home or abroad?

The first section addresses itself to general trends in capital investment and to the pattern of investment. The following sections consider the financial position of the peasantry, the gentry, the private sector in industry, and the tsarist government. Attention focuses upon the different claims on income, and in particular upon the scope for investment. The recourse that these groups had to credit will also be examined. The chapter concludes with a section devoted specifically to the supply of foreign credit.

6.1 Capital Investment

Evidence has been presented in earlier chapters to indicate the growth of capital investment. An overview will now be provided. According to Paul Gregory, total net investment in Russia grew by around five per cent (in real terms) between 1885–9 and 1909–13. Within this period, growth was most marked in the years 1889–93 to 1893–7, and 1905–9 to 1909–13. In absolute terms, the real value of investment more than trebled; in per capita terms, it more than doubled (see Table 6.1).

Table 6.1

The distribution of total net investment, 1885–9 and 1909–13

(per cent)

	1885–9	1909–13
Government capital expenditures*	7.6	6.8
Agriculture	31.0	26.3
Livestock	14.7	4.4
Equipment	1.0	3.1
Structures	15.3	18.8
Industry	23.9	29.0
Equipment†	7.6	11.9
Structures	12.1	9.7
Inventories	4.2	7.4
Trade inventories	13.7	10.6
Transport and communications‡	13.1	10.1
Residential (urban)	10.1	17.1
	100	100
Total (1913 prices million rubles)	686	2,218
Population (million)	113	164
Net investment per head (rubles)	6.07	13.52

* Excludes defence.
† Includes all non-agricultural equipment.
‡ Excludes railway equipment.
Source: P. Gregory, *Russian National Income, 1885–1913*, C.U.P., 1982, pp. 56–7.

Table 6.1 indicates how this investment was allocated among different sectors of the economy. The data suggest that progress took place on a broad front. Not surprisingly, the percentage share of investment devoted to agriculture declined. But the decline took place wholly in livestock, where the real value of investment stagnated over the period as a whole. To some extent, this stagnation was offset by the growth in capital investment in agricultural equipment, which expanded rapidly in the pre-war years. These observations suggest that the more colourful descriptions of agricultural crisis are in need of modification.

A separate series of capital formation in agriculture, compiled by Arcadius Kahan, also indicates significant real growth in the value of the stock of capital, especially in farm machinery and other equipment. However, Kahan estimated that the value of the productive capital (that is, farm buildings other than dwellings, and livestock, transport equipment and farm equipment) increased in real terms by only 22 per cent. Since the rural population grew by something like 35 per cent in 1890–1913, the amount of capital per person in agriculture was less in 1913 than in 1890. This is not incompatible with the evidence presented in Table 6.1.[5]

As one might expect, the percentage share of industrial investment increased, from around 24 per cent to 30 per cent of the total. Surprisingly, the share of investment devoted to industrial buildings was lower in 1909–13 than it had been in 1885–9, while the share of inventories was higher. Kahan offered one possible explanation, in terms of the dispersed character of the Russian market and the distances and journey-times involved. These factors made it incumbent on industrialists to hold stocks of materials and work in progress. In the particular instance of International Harvester, the value of its inventories in 1914 was eight times the value of its Russian factory and its warehouses. Kahan also suggested that 'credit was more abundant for short-term investment in inventories, rather than for long-term investment in fixed assets'. Be that as it may, Table 6.1 also suggests that an increased share of investment was devoted to non-agricultural equipment, including railway equipment.[6]

Another striking characteristic of the pattern of capital investment is the increase in the share devoted to urban housing, which increased from 10 per cent to 17 per cent of the total. The figures suggest that the housing stock grew at around the same rate as the urban population. Kahan observed that the capital market demonstrated a 'generally favourable response to the demand for housing construction'. While this may be true for the country as a whole, however, the sharp rise in urban rents in St. Petersburg in the pre-war decade suggests that the assessment does not apply to the Russian capital.[7]

The evidence indicates that only a small proportion of total net investment represented investment by government in the public sphere. The proportion would be somewhat higher, if an allowance were made for investment in defence enterprises. It may also be doubted whether the proportion of government investment would have declined, in these circumstances, because of the likely impact of pre-war rearmament. Nevertheless, public investment remains unimpressive – and virtually stationary – when set against other investment.[8]

Finally, attention may be drawn to net investment in the railways. Kahan observed that the railways did not absorb an overwhelming proportion of capital investment. Over the period 1890 – 1913, the growth of the railway capital stock was no greater than the increase in the real value of the industrial capital stock. He concluded that the growth of industrial capital outstripped the growth of railway capital after 1900. Again, this tends to confirm the point about the broad spread of investment in late tsarist Russia.

6.2 Trends in Peasant Savings and Investment

One of the key assumptions in the liberal analysis of the tsarist economy is that the scope for peasant farmers to generate savings was constrained by the low level of productivity in agriculture and by the lack of productivity growth in the nineteenth century. This assumption has already been examined and found to be questionable, when applied to Russian agriculture as a whole. In this section, attention will focus on another basic assumption, common to populist and marxist observers as well, namely that the Russian peasantry were unable to generate savings voluntarily, because of the pressure of fiscal and other demands on their incomes.

Before 1861, serfs and state peasants were required to pay a poll tax to the state. The tax had been introduced in 1724, and was not abolished until 1886. The government fixed a sum to be levied each year, which was apportioned between the estimated number of male 'souls'. The poll tax does not appear to have been a heavy burden on the pre-reform peasantry, when its value is expressed in real terms. Indeed, Jerome Blum has estimated that the burden fell quite considerably between the 1760s and the 1840s, when the tax is measured in terms of rye.[9]

Serfs were also liable to pay labour service or a quitrent (*obrok*) to the lord, in accordance with his requirements and at a rate determined by him. Normally, he arrived at an aggregate figure – number of labour-days, or quitrent in money and kind – and left the peasant community to apportion the total among its members. The nineteenth-century historian of serfdom, V. I. Semevsky, estimated that the real burden of *obrok* declined during the late eighteenth century. Other estimates suggest that *obrok* remained static during the first half of the nineteenth. But the question of the burden cannot be resolved with any certainty. What can be said is that there is abundant evidence of arrears in the payment of *obrok*. Arrears in the payment of the poll tax were also commonplace; so much so, that successive Tsars customarily cancelled outstanding debts.[10]

Under these circumstances (and assuming that arrears reflected peasants' inability to pay, rather than an unwillingness to pay), one may conclude that the scope for peasant savings was limited. This is likely to have been especially true of serfs in areas where the opportunity for earnings from non-agricultural work was limited. So far as investment is concerned, it is reasonable to suggest that the incentives did not exist, even if the resources did. Contemporary descriptions of peasant homes and inventory (such as in the short stories of Turgenev) testify to the poverty of serfs' capital stock.

The Emancipation of the serfs in 1861 did not immediately do away with feudal obligations. Until 1863 serfs were required to perform labour-service or *obrok* as before. Furthermore, until the peasant and lord came to some agreement about the date on which redemption would commence, the peasant remained 'temporarily obligated'. Where *barshchina* prevailed, as in much of the black-earth region, legislation in June 1862 provided for its conversion into a quitrent. In this interim period, many lords took the opportunity to increase the level of *obrok*, for reasons that will become clear.

Once peasants entered into a formal agreement to recompense the lord for the loss of feudal dues, they had to pay 20 per cent of the redemption value to their former owners. The landlord forfeited this sum only if he enforced an arrangement on the serfs against their will. The total redemption sum (*vykup*) was calculated by capitalizing the prevailing *obrok* at six per cent: that is, where *obrok* amounted to 6 rubles per annum, the redemption sum was fixed at 100 rubles. This explains why lords tried to inflate the *obrok* after 1861. The remaining 80 per cent of the redemption was paid over to the lords by the government, in the form of interest-bearing certificates that yielded a fixed rate of interest (6 per cent) on the total sum. For their part, the former serfs were required to repay the government over a period of 49 years, at a rate of 6.5 per cent, designed to allow the government to recoup administrative costs.[11]

These arrangements had the effect of overvaluing the allotments actually assigned to the ex-serfs, and of creating a recurrent claim on peasant income, in the form of redemption payments (*vykupnyie platezhi*). The redemption sum did not bear any relationship to the current value of the land. Local arbitrators determined the *obrok* rate that corresponded to the maximum allotment; they reduced the rate for smaller allotments, but less than proportionately, so a peasant household with the minimum allotment might pay twice as much per hectare as was required from the nominal maximum allotment. A. E. Lositsky, the author of the authoritative study of redemption, estimated that the average price of each allotment in the black-earth provinces was some 12.5 rubles in excess of the average sale price of land at the time. In the non-black earth provinces, the figure was higher still, reflecting the success of landowners in obtaining greater cash compensation for the loss of feudal services. These figures suggest that allotments were valued by the redemption procedure at two or even three times their market value.[12]

How great a burden were the redemption payments on the former serfs? In cases where the lords enforced redemption upon the peasantry, the latter were relieved of the need to find 20 per cent of the total sum. If they came to a mutual agreement, peasants had to find this sum themselves. For this reason, peasants were reluctant to enter into such agreements, especially where opportunities of obtaining cash incomes were limited (as in the central black-earth provinces). Sometimes the lords waived this 20 per cent portion of the redemption sum; normally, they loaned peasants the cash, and extracted labour-service from the peasantry in lieu of interest payments.[13]

The main problem, however, was that peasants paid redemption according to an inflated *obrok*. Almost at once, they fell behind in their payments to the Treasury. The magnitude of arrears is indicated in Table 6.2.

The arrears were least serious in provinces where there was a high concentration of state peasants and relatively few former serfs (Vyatka, Perm, Astrakhan). But there does not appear to be a close correlation between the level of arrears and the availability of non-agricultural earnings. Arrears were modest in Yaroslavl – a province with abundant handicraft activity – but were huge in 'industrial' provinces such as St. Petersburg and Moscow.[14]

The Treasury took the view that peasants should be compelled to improve their agricultural practices in order to escape growing indebtedness. Failing this, local tax inspectors were urged to take a tough line with defaulters. Other officials recognized the futility of this last approach, pointing out that to seize peasant assets would deprive tax-payers of the opportunity to make ends meet and settle their debts in due course. In this spirit, the government eventually embarked upon a significant reduction in the redemption dues in 1881, equivalent to around ten per cent of the outstanding sum and 27 per cent of average annual payments.[15]

Some observers believed that the difference between the new redemption payments and the old *obrok* did not amount to much in real terms. This ignores the fact that the *obrok* had frequently been

Table 6.2

Arrears in redemption payments by former serfs (1866–1881), 29 provinces

(Expressed as percentage of annual assessment for the given year)

Province	1866	1871	1876	1881
Moscow	31	39	55	158
Vladimir	29	21	11	16
Yaroslavl	14	5	2	5
Kostroma	21	17	26	49
Tver	19	28	18	29
Kaluga	42	22	25	22
Smolensk	79	160	173	249
Ryazan	48	21	52	45
Tula	18	5	13	5
Orel	46	18	62	59
Kursk	40	15	12	7
Voronezh	10	7	18	25
Penza	45	49	33	13
Tambov	19	10	24	20
St. Petersburg	35	130	83	113
Novgorod	98	151	148	189
Pskov	42	75	79	131
Nizhegorod	29	34	34	46
Kazan	47	5	1	79
Simbirsk	33	22	18	40
Saratov	57	19	24	79
Vyatka	35	7	3	10
Perm	37	3	7	12
Orenburg	56	14	56	146
Ufa	109	56	96	174
Samara	16	10	81	242
Astrakhan	5	1	4	15
Olonets	37	112	117	183
Vologda	13	6	1	1

Source: 'Otchet Gosudarstvennogo Banka po vykupnoi operatsii', 1893, cited by N. M. Druzhinin, *Russkaya derevnya na perelome, 1861–1880gg.*, Nauka, 1978, pp. 76–7.

inflated in advance of redemption agreements. In addition, peasants experienced difficulties in meeting payments, because they now incurred additional obligations to meet out of their income. These included taxes levied by the new *zemstva* after 1864, and rents. Yanson, in a study published in 1877, put total direct taxes payable by the peasantry at 195 m. rubles (in 1872), compared to 13 m. paid by the gentry. Of this total, 42 m. rubles represented the poll tax, 95 m. the land taxes (including redemption payments) and 60m. comprised other obligations. Nor did the estimate take into account dues that were paid in kind.[16]

The effects of the emancipation settlement were not the same for all peasants. Wealthier peasants sometimes took it upon themselves to pay the redemption dues of poorer households, in return for the use of their allotments. Another crucial difference concerns serfs and state peasants, who were freed in 1866. In the case of state peasants, there was no private pressure to force up the value of the land they received. An official source suggested that, in 1879, former state peasants paid just over 9 rubles per male 'soul' in taxation, whereas former serfs paid around 12.5 rubles. Finally, it should be remembered that the peasants who had belonged to Polish lords in the western provinces did considerably better from the emancipation settlement than other peasants.[17]

The contraction in the average size of allotments, noted by all shades of opinion during the 1860s and 1870s, suggests that the ability of peasants to pay their dues was seriously curtailed. Evidence presented in Chapter Four (see Table 4.1 page 101) suggests that the decline in holdings was not offset by any improvement in yields of rye during the 1870s. Against this background, the Valuev Commission of 1872 and a tax commission in 1879 both concluded that peasants were hard put to satisfy their own subsistence, let alone produce a marketable surplus. The situation was bleakest in parts of the black-earth by the early 1880s. In some provinces – Ufa, Tambov, Samara and parts of Perm, Voronezh and Saratov – peasants seemed to be reasonably well provided with land, but this reflected the fact that many other households had accepted so-called 'beggars'' allotments after 1861, as a means of avoiding redemption charges altogether. Statistically, therefore, these households vanished from the scene as they became landless labourers. In the non-black earth, the situation was somewhat better. Opportunities for diversification within agriculture and for non-agricultural work were more widespread, and this enabled former serfs to finance their obligations. None the less, as we shall see, the general situation in the early 1880s was sufficiently serious for the tsarist government to contemplate some changes in its fiscal system.[18]

Next, we shall consider the potential for savings by Russian peasants during the last two decades of the nineteenth century. The hypothesis to be examined is that savings were constrained by three main factors: first, the pressure exerted on peasant incomes by increases in rental charges; secondly, the impact of higher rates of indirect taxation on peasant necessities; and, lastly, the impact of the decline in agricultural product prices after 1880.

Rental payments increased during the 1880s and 1890s, as a result of the upsurge in peasant demand for land. The peasantry sought to offset the losses they incurred after Emancipation, and to adjust to the deterioration in the land:labour ratio brought about by population growth. In European Russia as a whole, money rents increased by around 38 per cent between the late 1880s and late 1890s. The increase was greater still in the Mid-Volga and Central Black-Earth regions. But how much of a burden did this increase represent? One way of answering this question is by examining household budget studies: a survey of 3,700 households in Smolensk province in 1899 suggested that rents accounted for a significantly larger proportion of peasant cash outlays than did direct taxation: on average, taxes accounted for 15 per cent of peasant expenditure, compared with 20 per cent for rents. Another approach is to relate the rent charges to the gross value of output per hectare. Anfimov has calculated that the average rents in non-black earth provinces in European Russia represented around 26 per cent of gross production per hectare during the late 1880s. By the end of the century the proportion had risen slightly, to 28 per cent. In the black-earth region, the proportion remained stable, but at a much higher level: some 47 per cent of the gross value of the product per hectare was absorbed in rents. These figures conceal regional variations, of course: in the mid-Volga and central black-earth provinces, where pressure on available land was most intense, the burden was still heavier.[19]

The burden remained heavy, because the value of the agricultural output was falling during the late nineteenth century. The fact that the burden did not increase, generally speaking, surely reflects the fact that yields did improve significantly at the same time.

The decline in cereal prices has already been referred to in an earlier chapter. Here we shall confine ourselves to some remarks about its impact on peasant incomes. Given the fact that the wealthiest households typically marketed a larger proportion of their output than did middle peasant households, it might be thought that the former felt the impact of the agricultural depression most sharply. Doubtless this happened in the Central Black-Earth region. Elsewhere, however, it is likely that wealthy peasants were able to respond to the fall in cereal prices by diversification. Rich households, with labour and cash reserves at their disposal, were probably well placed to allocate resources in a flexible fashion. Certainly, evidence from two non-black earth provinces, Vladimir and Smolensk, suggests that rich farmers were able to switch to non-agricultural activities, such as handicrafts and carting (*izvos*). To the extent that such kulaks may have got into debt in order to finance the diversification of their economy, they were also best placed to finance the interest charges out of income.[20]

Turning to the impact of fiscal policy upon peasant incomes, we enter a hornets' nest of controversy. According to many historians, and to contemporary critics of the government, the level of taxation by the end of the century was intolerable. The main charge against the regime – and, in particular, against Witte – is that the peasantry had been 'exhausted', as a result of the increased rates of duty applied to basic peasant necessities. Recently, this view has been challenged by James Simms, who has argued that peasant purchasing power was not curtailed by indirect taxation. Simms points out that the increase in receipts from indirect taxes increased faster than the rate of duty applied to consumer goods. In other words, part of the increase in revenue reflected a real growth in rural consumption. By extension – although this is not part of Simms's argument – it might be suggested that peasants also had some scope for investment, as well as for increased consumption.[21]

It will help to clarify matters if we offer some rather simple observations. To begin with, there is no doubt that the tsarist government was intent on raising a larger proportion of its revenue through indirect taxation, and accordingly raised the duties on a number of consumer goods. But where did the incidence of taxation have its greatest effect? The answer to this question is surely that the main consumers of taxable items – alcohol, sugar, matches, tea and sugar – were poor peasants and urban inhabitants. It was among these groups that the consumption of commercially produced items was greatest. Middle and rich peasant households found perfectly adequate domestic substitutes for the taxable goods: candles and peat for kerosene, *makhorka* for tobacco, home-brew (*samogon*) for vodka, and honey or jam for sugar. These peasants purchased those goods, such as clothing and footwear, that carried no duty. The rich households, furthermore, purchased capital goods as well. We shall return to this point presently.[22]

The Soviet historian A. M. Anfimov has recently attempted an overall assessment of the combined impact of taxation and rental payments on the peasantry of European Russia. He concludes that direct and indirect taxation absorbed around 18 per cent of peasants' gross income from agriculture in 1901 (this proportion would be lower, if allowance were made for income from non-agricultural activities as well). Rents, together with interest payable to the Peas-

ants' Land Bank, accounted for another 11 per cent. A fuller breakdown is given in Table 6.3.

Table 6.3

*Estimated payment of taxes and rents by peasants in European
Russia, 1901*

(million rubles)

Direct taxes	166.2
central government	91.0
zemstva	29.3
commune	45.9
Insurance and other payments	21.5
Indirect taxes	194.8
alcohol	143.9
tobacco	13.2
sugar	26.9
kerosene	8.4
matches	2.3
Customs duties and miscellaneous excises	103.0
Total	488.5
Rents and interest due to Peasants' Land Bank	279.3
Grand total	764.8
Rural population (50 provinces)	87.8 millions
Taxes and rents per capita	8.7 rubles
Peasant income from agriculture	2,660.0 m. rubles
Income per head, net of taxes and rents	21.6 rubles

Source: A. M. Anfimov, *Ekonomicheskoe polozhenie i klassovaya borba
krestyan Evropeiskoi Rossii, 1881–1904*, Nauka, 1984, p. 110.

A comparison with the situation on the eve of the First World War
reveals a considerable change in the fortunes of Russian peasants,
and suggests that peasant incomes, net of tax and rents, were much
greater. Vainshtein calculated that taxation, insurance charges and

rents in 1912 did not exceed ten per cent of the gross income of peasants.[23] What had happened in the intervening decade? First, there was a rural revolution in 1905 and 1906, which forced the tsarist government to cancel outstanding redemption payments, with effect from 1 January 1907. Secondly, the incomes of peasants had increased as a result of the upturn in cereal prices and the growth in demand for other agricultural produce after 1900. Finally, the peasant demand for rented property diminished after 1900, largely because wealthier households gained more freehold access to land.

The increment in peasant incomes resulted in the growth of deposits in state savings banks, whose numbers grew rapidly during the 1890s. By 1 January 1912 savings banks contained deposits to the value of 1,630 m. rubles, of which more than one-quarter comprised deposits made by peasants. Two years later deposits had increased to 1,830 m. rubles, and peasants accounted for a slightly larger proportion of the total. Deposits attracted interest at the rate of 3.6 per cent.[24]

Wealthy peasants could draw upon their savings in order to purchase land or to acquire complementary assets, such as livestock or equipment. Kahan pointed out that the main priority of Russian peasants in the late nineteenth and early twentieth centuries was to acquire land. There is doubtless a large element of truth in this; the process was encouraged by the government, which had set up the Peasants' Land Bank to that end. In addition, the government approved the formation of credit cooperatives in 1895, which were modelled on the continental Raiffeisen banks. These, too, helped peasants to finance the purchase of land.[25]

All the same, it may be doubted that this strategy precluded the possibility of peasant investment in other assets, especially by a minority of rich households. Capital investment in agriculture was not the preserve of gentry landowners. Indeed, the Agricultural Census in 1917 revealed that peasants owned nine out of every ten farm implements in Russia. Nor was this simply a reflection of the ownership of simple items, such as ploughs. Peasants also owned the same proportion of mechanical reapers; here, their purchase of the Russian *lobogreika* was actively promoted by the energetic salesmen of International Harvester and other companies, who provided peasants with the credit to finance their purchase.[26]

The growth of the peasants' capital stock also reflected the growth of agricultural production on the periphery: in the south-east, during the 1870s and 1880s, and in Siberia during the 1890s and 1900s. After 1900, the diversification of peasant agriculture stimulated a demand for new equipment: for dairy farming in the north-west and in western Siberia. Here, too, it is reasonable to assume that peasants financed their investment in part through savings. They also received assistance from the credit cooperatives, which by 1914 were lending their eight million members loans that averaged 60 rubles. The older 'loan-savings associations', formed in the 1860s, advanced on average more than 150 rubles. Loans helped to finance the purchase of land; but were also made to peasants who purchased livestock or who built grain elevators, as they did in south Russia.[27]

Many peasants were poorly endowed with land and other assets. This feature of Russian peasant agriculture was neatly captured in the words of a peasant from Novgorod, speaking in 1900: 'We have been living for almost half a century at the same level, and if this same standard applied to the army, then soldiers would still be carrying flintlocks and the navy would still be using sailing ships, equipped with iron cannon'. These sentiments are typical of the lament about the 'crisis' in peasant agriculture at the turn of the century. But they should not blind us to the fact that generalizations about the inventory of the 'average' peasant will be misleading. The value of the capital equipment owned by the rich peasant might be five times as great as that owned by the peasant who worked a small allotment. To continue the image created by the peasant from Novgorod: if the majority of peasants were foot-soldiers, there was a corresponding officer class of peasants – and they were wealthier still by 1914.[28]

6.3 The Financial Position of the Russian Gentry

The gentry economy, before and after the emancipation of the serfs, does not emerge in a very positive light. According to the conventional assessment, gentry landowners did not display entrepreneurial attributes before 1861, being concerned only with the regular receipt of service from their serfs. Before 1861, and still more thereafter, gentry were living beyond their means and accumulating large debts. They failed to modernize their estates. However, this failure could not be attributed to any lack of finance. The capital market extended credit to gentry proprietors, but they used it to discharge old debts, rather than to invest. Having made no attempt to become efficient farmers, the gentry felt the full force of the agricultural depression in the late nineteenth century, and this accelerated the sale of land that had commenced after 1861. By the end of the tsarist period, the majority of Russian gentry were impoverished. Against this background of economic self-destruction, the 1917 Revolution gave the final push to the tottering edifice of the gentry economy. This section is designed to test some of these observations about gentry finances.[29]

Serfdom was a near-perfect system for the transfer of resources from peasants to gentry landowners. The landlord obtained revenue from the sale of the product from the demesne, which was cultivated by serf labour; he derived a revenue from peasants who were employed away from the estate, and who rendered him a quitrent; and he received goods in kind from his workforce. On some estates proprietors operated a mixed system, whereby part of the workforce rendered labour-service and other serfs paid a quitrent; elsewhere, one or other type of obligation prevailed. In all cases the object was the same – to satisfy the consumption requirements of the landowner and his family.

In these circumstances, capital investment assumed only modest dimensions. Michael Confino has demonstrated that many estates were farmed in the same manner as peasant allotments, namely according to the three-field system of crop rotation. There was little investment in land improvement. The inventory consisted simply of the rudimentary implements owned by peasants, who had no incentive to increase the rate of net investment. For their part, the feudal lords regarded the concept of investment with bewilderment.[30]

Gentry incomes did increase during the later eighteenth century, but this did not raise the level of investment in manorial agriculture. Instead, the gentry spent the increment on luxury consumer goods, such as dress, foodstuffs and furnishings, and on foreign travel. The growth in money income derived from making further demands on the peasantry, for higher rates of *obrok* or additional labour service. Gentry landowners could also increase their revenue by selling grain or vodka to their serfs at higher prices.

Nevertheless, there were large numbers of landed gentry who could hardly be considered wealthy in the pre-reform era. The census of peasant 'souls' in 1858 revealed that the distribution of serfs was highly unequal: two in five serfowners owned only three per cent of all male serfs. The more impoverished members of the gentry estate found it especially difficult to obtain credit from the banks, because loans were secured against serfs. Thus the provincial noble land banks that had been set up in 1785, 'in order that each proprietor should be able to retain his land, improve it and establish for all time the necessary income for his household', did not benefit all gentry equally.[31]

This negative assessment of the manorial economy before 1861 is in need of modification. Some proprietors revealed an entrepreneurial instinct, as is evident from the growth in the number of manorial factories in the late eighteenth and early nineteenth centuries. Typically, gentry factories were found in woollens, ironworking and paper, products that were procured by the Russian government. However, factories that produced sugar and spirits were oriented towards the mass market. It is impossible to gauge the overall level of profits in such enterprises, although it is clear that wages were miserably low and some serfs received only a small subsistence allowance. The government encouraged potential reinvestment, by levying only modest taxes on gentry enterprise. There is evidence of capital investment in new buildings and equipment, such as in the mechanization of distilleries and beet-sugar processing. To this extent, there were some signs of dynamism in the gentry economy before 1861.[32]

In principle, the potential for the growth of gentry savings and investment received a substantial boost as a result of the provisions of the emancipation settlement. One of the main aims of the reform had been to give gentry landlords a regular fixed income from the redemption certificates. However, so great was the need of many landlords for liquid funds that they cashed in the certificates without delay. This enabled them to discharge their obligations to the noble land banks and to private creditors. One authority estimated that debts to the former stood at 426 m. rubles in 1859. By 1881, two-fifths of the redemption payments that peasants had made – some 300 m. rubles – went to pay off debts. Of the remainder, some was obviously consumed at home or abroad. But part of the windfall that gentry received after 1861 found an outlet in investment in new securities, such as railway bonds. In other words, it would not be true to say that the cash from redemption was entirely squandered.[33]

No sooner had gentry proprietors adjusted to the abolition of serfdom than they faced a fall in cereal prices after 1880. The price of wheat, which was typically produced on gentry estates in the black-earth, fell less rapidly than rye, but a greater proportion of the wheat crop entered the market and was therefore exposed to the depression. In these circumstances, gentry sought to maintain their income by leasing land to peasants and by obtaining financial assistance from the government.

The agricultural depression did not curtail the demand by peasants for land. Landlords raised the level of rent or, in the case of sharecropping arrangements, extracted a higher proportion of the crop from peasants. In 1895, according to Kaufman, peasant sharecroppers were required to pay more than one-half of the crop in seven out of ten instances; by 1900, this applied to nine out of ten agreements. The economic advantages to the landlords of the prevailing level of rent should not be exaggerated – Kaufman maintained that some landlords lost interest in offering land for rent because of peasant inability to pay, and the accumulation of arrears lends some support to this last point – but income was nevertheless being transferred to gentry. One or two instances of the significance of rentals to gentry landowners will illustrate the point. In 1880 a Tambov landowner drew an income of 9,000 rubles from the cultivation of his estate, but a further 8,500 came from sharecropping agreements and 2,300 from rentals. On the estates of the Orlov-Davydov family (one of the wealthiest in the Empire, and not typical of all gentry), net income from rentals in

1899–1900 represented 67 per cent of total net income (560,000 rubles).[34]

Faced with falling cereal prices, landowners obtained support from the tsarist government. In 1893 the government adopted railway freight rates that offered producers in European Russia protection from grain produced in the North Caucasus and western Siberia. In addition, the government intervened in the grain market by purchasing stores for the army or acquiring 'reserves', as a deliberate means of price support.

Some of the difficulties confronting gentry landlords were alleviated by the extension of credit. Prior to 1885, gentry obtained long-term credit from the joint-stock land banks (of which there were eleven in 1880), from mutual credit societies that were founded by landowners themselves, and from the Kherson Zemskii Bank. Normally, these institutions made loans of between 1,000 and 30,000 rubles, although isolated instances are recorded of loans in excess of 500,000 rubles. In 1885 these banks were joined by the Nobles' Land Bank, which offered credit to the gentry at 4½ per cent, below the prevailing commercial rate of interest. Loans were secured against the landed estate. At the end of the nineteenth century, these banks recorded outstanding debts amounting to 1,500 m. rubles, two-fifths of which was owed to the Nobles' Land Bank.[35]

According to Pavlovsky, 'the land banks, as a rule, were not very particular about the uses to which the money was put', and he suggests that the growth of credit to the Russian gentry largely subsidized spendthrifts. The difficulty in assessing the validity of this view is that most of the available evidence about gentry finances relates to the upper echelons, who were not representative of the class as a whole.

Without doubt, some landowners used the credit they obtained in order to diversify into non-agricultural enterprise during the later nineteenth and early twentieth centuries. By 1903, according to one authority, 1,900 gentry owned just over two thousand industrial enterprises, mostly in mineral processing, timber and foodstuffs. More than half of these businesses had been founded during the 1880s and 1890s. Like other industrial enterprises, they received intermittent government support. Gentry also invested in banking, railway companies, mining and urban property. By 1913 the famous nobleman A. D. Sheremetev earned nearly one million rubles from his investments, twice as much as from his own estates.[36]

Short-term credit probably posed more of a problem for landowners. The commercial banks paid little attention to their needs; indeed, before 1898 they were not allowed to discount notes presented by landed proprietors. Some efforts were made by the land banks and the State Bank, which in 1884 opened accounts on behalf of landowners and accepted their promissory notes, secured by the estate.

However, this facility appears to have been extended infrequently. Perhaps the financial institutions believed that more liberal credit arrangements would be used to finance unproductive expenditure by the gentry; but 'improving' landowners do not seem to have complained about a shortage of credit.

The most reasonable conclusion is that the Russian gentry had the opportunity to avoid the worst consequences of the agricultural depression, by a recourse to credit. In 1881 the reactionary publicist M. N. Katkov complained that, whilst 'not stinting with huge annual subsidies to half-foreign railway companies . . . we are refusing to lend similar support to the landed nobility'. By 1900 such complaints could no longer be justified, notwithstanding gentry attacks on Witte for ignoring the 'needs of agriculture'.[37]

Like the Russian peasantry, landlords gained from the upturn in cereal prices after 1900. The pre-war years also witnessed a growth in the volume of net investment by landowners. The value of the agricultural capital stock on the Orlov-Davydov estates increased by 60 per cent between 1900 and 1911, to 1.2 m. rubles. This growth was financed out of profits from agriculture, which yielded enough to allow the family to acquire a large portfolio of securities, issued by banks and industrial enterprises. Far from this being a period of progressive immiseration for the Russian gentry, the pre-war years were a golden age. The prosperity owed something to the supply of credit to landowners, but most to the improved prospects for commercial farming and diversification. By 1914 the agrarian crisis – like the peasant revolution – seemed like a bad dream.[38]

6.4 Credit and Capital Accumulation in Industry

The literature on the tsarist economy habitually emphasizes the difficulties that Russian industrialists experienced in obtaining credit, especially prior to 1890. The difficulties arose, so it is argued, because potential Russian lenders were relatively few in number, and were unwilling to risk their funds in industry. Instead, they preferred to place their money in securities that carried a fixed and guaranteed return. This tendency was accentuated by the policies pursued by the tsarist government, which put obstacles in the way of joint-stock company formation and thereby hindered the formation of a market in shares. The problem of industrial finance also arose, because industrialists made only modest profits; although profits could, of course, be reinvested, they were hardly sufficient for the expansion of industry. Long-term investment in the private sector only became possible when foreign lenders took an interest in Russian industry, in the aftermath of the stabilization of the exchange rate and the introduction of the tariff.

This summary suggests that the conventional view emphasizes the shortage of long-term credit, relative to industrialists' demand; and that industry could not generate the resources required for self-financed growth. It is with these arguments that this section is mainly concerned.

Limited opportunities for profit and for ploughing back profits in industry did exist in pre-reform Russia. In this regard, a distinction should be drawn between different types of industrial enterprise. Profits were probably lowest in the so-called 'possessional' factories. The wage-rate here was abysmal, but so too was labour productivity. In addition, the drain on factory receipts was bigger than in other forms of enterprise, because factory owners had a statutory obligation to support the workforce, even during a slump in trade. In a period of rising food prices, such as the late 1850s, this obligation severely restricted the scope for investment out of profits, as metallurgical factories in the Urals discovered.[39]

The tsarist state did not make life easy for another category of entrepreneurs, the merchantry or *kupechestvo*. Merchants were compelled to perform time-consuming administrative duties. Bureaucratic regulations also hampered entrepreneurial initiative. The *kupechestvo* comprised three guilds, each of which had different rights and obligations. If a merchant failed to pay the annual sum that entitled him to the corresponding guild certificate, he forfeited his right to trade as before. In effect, this required him to begin the process of accumulation over again, and explains why there was considerable downward social mobility among the merchantry.

Part of the profits from mercantile enterprise did find its way back into the business. But there were plenty of other claims on merchant income. Among the close-knit families of Moscow merchants, it was incumbent upon the head of the business to pass on a sizeable fortune to his children; in this way, firms' assets might be dissipated. Each family also sought to maintain a high standard of living, to patronize the arts, to found and support charities or to subscribe to memorials to the Tsar. All these voluntary efforts reduced the scope for reinvestment. The most abstemious among them, such as the Old Believers, eschewed such ostentation and tended to invest more readily in the family firm. But, in general, the merchantry followed the gentry in consuming any profits.[40]

Among serf industrialists, there were a handful of remarkable men who created substantial businesses. Many of the cotton mills in Ivanovo ('Russian Manchester') were founded by serfs, such as Morozov, Ganelin and Grachev. Profits from the distribution of craft products, and later from the control of textile production, were typically reinvested in the business. Cotton printing was especially profitable. Serfs faced the possibility that the lord could deprive them of their commercial freedom of manoeuvre, but this did not happen often, because the gentry gained a regular income from this source. Of course, the wealth might be dissipated, if and when these serfs were freed: the average sum demanded in Ivanovo before 1861 was around 20,000 rubles, equivalent to the total annual sales of an average textile mill. Not surprisingly, serfs reportedly concealed their assets, in order to keep down the price of freedom.[41]

The pre-reform capital market was hardly geared to supply credit to such businessmen. Financial institutions existed largely to satisfy the needs of gentry and government. The State Commercial Bank, founded in 1817, did discount commercial paper and lend funds to merchants and industrialists against the security of their inventories. Yet the loan and discount operations amounted to just 10 m. rubles in 1825, and had only reached 25 m. by 1859. These are not impressive figures, when set against the deposits that the Bank attracted: 28 m. rubles in 1825, and 200 m. in 1859. The explanation, surely, is that Russian industrialists made only modest demands on the commercial banking system. They probably relied more on informal credit arrangements for working capital. Thus, any suggestion of a credit shortage in pre-reform Russia misses the point.[42]

In the post-reform period, some tsarist officials began to voice concern that the Russian capital market did not satisfy entrepreneurial claims for credit, for long-term investment. M. Kh. Reutern, Finance Minister between 1862 and 1878, maintained that 'the dimensions of state loans, which are repeated every year on such a large scale, divert all the free capital away from private enterprise and industry, and give rise to entrepreneurial complaints about a shortage of credit'. As we shall see, he coupled this with a call for a reduction in the level of government spending, as a precondition for the freeing of funds for private borrowers.[43]

This was not the only step the government contemplated in order to respond to the perceived problem of long-term finance for industry. The Finance Minister also encouraged the contemplation of a reform in financial legislation, to make it easier for businessmen to establish joint-stock companies. However, the commercial crisis in 1873 put paid to these proposals, and by the end of Reutern's career he was making the traditional noises about stock-jobbers and speculators. One of his successors, N. Kh. Bunge, also pleaded initially for a more liberal legal framework, arguing that 'the industrial development of Russia has been held back by the absence of modern company law'. But little was achieved in the tsarist period to simplify the labyrinthine procedure for company registration. Each new company had to be approved by officials in the Ministry of Finances.[44]

Nevertheless, it would be wrong to place too much emphasis upon the official suspicion of the stock market. Industrialists in Britain and Germany managed well enough, prior to the full legalization of limited liability, in 1862 and 1870 respectively. More to the point, perhaps, the issue is not that the tsarist government hindered the flotation of industrial companies, or competed for funds. Rather, the private businessmen made no great demand upon the capital market for long-term investment funds, at least until the 1890s.

Industrialists – especially in textiles and food processing – typically borrowed money from relatives (or went into partnership with acquaintances), and ploughed back the profits into the business. By these means investment in light industry was financed, up to the First World War. Profits were high in textiles, foodstuffs and distribution, sectors where fixed costs did not loom as large as they did in iron and steel or engineering. In the textiles industry, for example, costs were minimized by using the labour of peasants in their own homes. Gindin demonstrated that profits were substantial in the post-reform trade in cotton goods, tea and sugar. Textile producers in Moscow frequently assumed direct responsibility for the distribution of their output. Sometimes they took with them the products of other enterprises, receiving a percentage commission on the sales.

The profit rate in light industry was persistently higher than in other branches of industry throughout the later nineteenth and early twentieth centuries. In 1900–10, the average annual profits in the Moscow textile industry exceeded 43 m. rubles, which was more than twice as high as the average profits in the Baku oil industry, five times higher than in south Russian metallurgy and fourteen times higher than in the Donets coalfields. In fact, the profits were even greater than the published figures indicate, because firms concealed them under the guise of amortization charges. Such profits allowed the predominantly family firms in textiles and foodstuffs to plough back receipts and to maintain a large degree of independence from the commercial banks.[45]

This strategy could not be pursued in heavy industry, which had to finance large initial capital outlays, and which never achieved the same level of profitability. Capital outlays, as indicated in the preceding chapter, involved more than the construction of plant and the installation of equipment. In many cases, entrepreneurs had to build schools, hospitals and workers' accommodation – in the Baku oil industry and in the Ukraine iron and steel industry, for instance. Varzar estimated that these outlays were equivalent to five or six per cent of the total wages bill in Russian industry.[46]

Low levels of industrial labour productivity, along with the need (in new regions) to pay for housing and other facilities, depressed the overall level of industrial profitability. There were, of course, tendencies that worked in the opposite direction: the prohibition on labour organizations until 1906; the tariff, which enabled entrepreneurs to pass on to the Russian consumer some of the additional costs; and the development of corporate control over the market. However, the formation of syndicates may reflect a failure of firms to obtain profits.

The publicity given to the profitability of ventures in mining, metallurgy and petroleum gives a misleading impression of the general level of profits. Russian banks and industrialists tempted foreign investors, by painting a rosy picture of current and prospective profits. The profits obtained by a handful of such firms during the mid and late 1890s were indeed outstanding. The South Russian Dniepr Metallurgical Company paid its shareholders 40 per cent on their investment each year between 1895 and 1900. But this overlooks the poorer performance of many other firms. In 1897 the average dividend in the south Russian steel industry barely exceeded six per cent. Many ventures were shaky and unprofitable. Even well-organized and well-equipped firms found after 1900 that the situation was disappointing, and managed only modest profits or none at all. Profits had to be paid out to investors in the form of attractive dividends, in order to maintain their interest and confidence; even this was often impossible. By the time that firms had also paid depreciation charges on their capital stock, the potential for plough-back was limited. After 1900, only those firms with government contracts, for rails or armaments, were well placed to maintain profitability.[47]

Cumulative investment in commercial enterprise – industry, banking and trade – amounted to 900 m. rubles in 1893. It climbed to 2,000 m. in 1900, and reached 4,300 m. rubles by 1914. This increase is in itself an indication that private enterprise in Russia enjoyed considerable success in attracting funds from foreign and domestic sources. We shall see presently how the tsarist government stimulated this process, and how great a contribution was made by foreign capital. Here we shall concentrate upon the role of financial institutions in Russia.

By 1900 there were more than forty commercial banks in Russia. Those in St. Petersburg offered shares in particular companies to prospective customers, who were invited to open special accounts for their acquisition. The accounts were secured by the commercial securities themselves. These 'on call' accounts were worth 120 m. rubles in 1895, and 150 m. in 1900. During the slump operations were curtailed, but the value of the accounts reached 800 m. rubles by 1914. The banks thus acted as intermediaries between investors and industry, assuming risks on behalf of lenders who might otherwise have preferred to maintain more traditional portfolios of fixed-interest stock. It is, however, worth noting that businessmen recognized the need to accommodate such lenders, by issuing bonded stock ('obligation capital') that attracted higher rates of return than government bonds and that had a prior claim on corporate profits: new firms in mining and metallurgy raised between 30 and 50 per cent of their total capital requirements in this manner.

The fact that joint-stock banks were able to extend these facilities was in turn a function of the willingness of the Russian public to deposit cash with them. Since the rate of turnover in current accounts was modest, the banks could hold assets in a relatively illiquid form. In addition, the State Bank was no longer a rival for the deposits of the public, as it had been before 1890; this was a deliberate move by Witte to promote the commercial banking sector. Finally, the banks drew upon the deposits placed with them by the Treasury, which by 1914 accounted for more than a fifth of the total funds in the commercial system.[48]

The joint-stock banks exercised considerable influence over company activity, particularly in heavy industry, by floating shares and by opening special accounts to industrial clients, that were secured by shares. As the banking system became increasingly concentrated, a handful of banks occupied a position of pre-eminence. In 1900 the six leading commercial banks accounted for 47 per cent of total bank liabilities, a proportion that had increased to 55 per cent by 1913. Each bank was surrounded by affiliated companies, whose shares it marketed, whose bills it discounted and upon whose boards its directors had seats. A. I. Putilov, chairman of the Russo-Asiatic Bank (founded in 1910), was also chairman of the engineering company that bore his name, a director of at least three oil companies, the Nikolaev Shipbuilding Co., the Lena Goldfields Co., and the Moscow-Kazan Railway. The Russo-Asiatic Bank had interests in at least 46 industrial companies, and specialized in armaments, oil and tobacco. The International Bank (formed in 1869) had a similar number of affiliates, especially in shipbuilding, transport and engineering. The Azov-Don Bank (formed in 1871 in Taganrog, and based in St. Petersburg after 1903) sought out firms in coal, sugar, cement and steel.[49]

Behind some of these leading banks stood French and German capital, although their participation varied from bank to bank. It was highest in the Russo-Asiatic, 80 per cent of whose shares were subscribed by the French, and the International, to which German banks subscribed 40 per cent. But this does not mean that foreign banks effectively controlled Russian industry. In the first place, as implied above, banks exercised less leverage over light industry. In the second place, many banks displayed only small foreign participation. What may be suggested, instead, is a manifestation of the coalescence of finance capital – Russian and foreign – and Russian heavy industry. This phenomenon was acknowledged by socialists (such as Hildferding, Lenin and Bukharin), and by Russian industrialists themselves.[50]

According to Lenin, the growth of finance capital was no less marked in tsarist Russia than in Germany or the United States. The era of the autonomous industrialist had, by 1914, long since passed. Instead, enormous financial and industrial control was concentrated in the hands of a few international businessmen. As they competed with each other to subject new areas of the globe to their control, so imperialist rivalries intensified, culminating in the World War. However, Lenin was confident that the concentration of credit and corporate power would make the tasks of the Russian proletariat much easier, when they seized power. Whatever the merit of this last point, there can be little doubt about the pre-war and wartime concentration of finance.[51]

Financial support to private enterprise derived from the tsarist government, as well as from the commercial banking system. The main source of credit was the State Bank, which had been founded in 1860, with the partial aim of stimulating investment in fixed capital. The resources at the disposal of the State Bank, like those of the joint-stock banks, were swelled by Treasury deposits. However, the Bank only became a significant creditor of private enterprise after 1880, by which time it had settled accounts with those who had held deposits with the old pre-reform institutions. Directly, the State Bank made loans and subsidies to private firms, although these were normally kept secret. Gindin has shown how these 'non-statutory loans' became an accepted practice early on. State support was especially important during industrial slumps, such as in 1873–5 and 1900–1902, but it was not confined to counter-cyclical operations. Many firms in engineering had cause to be grateful to the Bank for subsidies that enabled them to expand. The Bank also participated in share issues, such as in the Baltic Ironworks. This policy was justified on the grounds that such firms had 'state significance'; even the laisser-faire Bunge accepted this argument. Yet the Bank also sustained textiles and sugar firms, suggesting a very generous interpretation of the principle of supporting enterprises that mattered to the state.[52]

The capital market also operated to provide working capital to industry, and it was here that the main demands of industry as a whole were to be found. The entire system of inter-regional trade was built upon the need for abundant short-term credit. Distances were enormous and goods might be months in transit, not least because of the vagaries of the climate. The firm that produced cotton goods might wait a long time for payment from merchants, whose customers were far-flung and who themselves sought credit. Such a firm required credit from the supplier of cotton yarn and dyestuffs in turn. Where financial mediation was absent, transactions depended upon mutual assurances between producers and customers. The use of cash was limited. If mutual confidence was lacking, then trade could obviously suffer.[53]

Commercial banks discounted bills on behalf of their clients. This took up the bulk of the activity of Moscow banks, such as the Merchants' Bank (1874) and the Moscow Discount Bank, both of which helped to finance trade in textiles, tea, tobacco and sugar. These banks were cautious about granting credit, extending it only to customers whose reputation was founded upon the integrity of the owner. Common bonds of religion or marriage undoubtedly smoothed the arrangements. This insularity may have retarded the development of short-term credit in some parts of the Empire, such as Siberia and the Far East. But by the early twentieth century the problems had been alleviated. The joint-stock banks in St. Petersburg were willing to discount commercial bills on a large scale, without the need for the more elaborate face-to-face transactions required by their Moscow counterparts.[54]

The supply of credit was, of course, subject to fluctuations. Restrictions on its availability were particularly pronounced after 1899, and did not ease until after 1906. At such times of depression the tsarist government intervened, as we saw in the previous chapter. More important, however, firms that were experiencing difficulty in obtaining fresh credit, and which had depleted their reserves, were reorganized by the commercial banks. The original capital was reduced and new shares were issued. This procedure enabled bankers to extend the control they had over enterprises.[55]

To sum up, the supply of long- and short-term credit to Russian industrial enterprise developed along institutional lines after 1861. Heavy industry had recourse to the foreign and domestic stock market for its long-term requirements, which became substantial only after 1890. The government also lent assistance to industry by means of loans and subsidies. By contrast, light industry made only modest demands for long-term investment finance, and satisfied its requirements by ploughing back profits. Where heavy industry had a predominantly corporate character, light industry typically comprised the family firm. The provision of working capital also became more organized towards the late nineteenth century. As a result of these developments Russian industrial operations – and especially industrial investment – were not stifled by a shortage of credit.

6.5 Fiscal Policy and Government Demand for Credit

The other main source of claims upon available credit was the tsarist government. We have already quoted the remarks made by Reutern, to the effect that the government competed for funds with the private sector. His remarks have been echoed by Arcadius Kahan in a celebrated article on government economic policy.[56] This is one of the themes that will be taken up in the present section. The other issue concerns the growth and incidence of government revenue from taxation. Both questions will be set in the context of the growth of government spending.

During the 1850s around two-fifths of total central government expenditure was devoted to defence. The other main outlays comprised debt charges and administrative costs, including the costs of tax collection. Ordinary revenue, that is direct and indirect taxation and customs duties, was not sufficient to cover these expenditures. The government had either to reduce the growth in its commitments, or to seek ways of increasing its recurrent income. Faced with a growing deficit, however, the government sank deeper into debt.

It was in these terms that a Ministry of Finances spokesman, Yu. A. Hagemeister, wrote a blistering indictment of government finances in 1860. Hagemeister pointed to the persistent recourse of the government to foreign loans, which were concluded on unfavourable terms. The Crimean War (1854–6) had made this problem acute. The War had also compelled Russia to print paper currency, that undermined the stabilization of the ruble achieved by Finance Minister Kankrin before 1854. Hagemeister pointed out that the instability of the currency did not encourage confidence on the part of potential lenders. In 1854 Russia abandoned the silver standard that had been adopted a decade earlier, and the paper ruble was worth between 91 and 93 kopecks during the late 1850s. In the following decade the rate fell still further, to between 80 and 85 kopecks. After the war against Turkey (1877), the rate fell to 67 gold kopecks. The extension of tsarist international commitments thus seemed to emphasize the vulnerable and unstable financial health of the country.[57]

In these circumstances, Hagemeister wondered whether the government could withstand the strain of financing peasant emancipation and railway construction. He believed that the railway-building programme could eventually be financed through profits from freight and passenger traffic, but this did not solve the immediate problem of construction. The compensation of thousands of gentry serfowners, numbering 104,000 in 1858, was also likely to prove costly, especially if emancipation took place at once. In fact, as we have already seen, the decree of 1861 did not provide for immediate compensation to be paid, nor did redemption become compulsory until 1881. This still left the problem of financing railway construction.

Reutern exempted railway construction from his strictures about excessive government expenditure. He hoped that the state would play a supporting role, however, by underwriting the flotation of shares by private railway companies. In fact, the sale of railway shares to the public proceeded somewhat hesitantly, to begin with. According to one source, the value of shares held by the public – on which the government paid a guaranteed five per cent – did not exceed 440 m. rubles, while the assets of the companies were put at 1,600 m. rubles. The bulk of the shares were purchased by the State Bank.[58]

Many railway companies experienced difficulties, arising from the high costs of construction and large operating expenses. As a result, they were compelled to borrow more and more to stay in business. The government again provided the main source of assistance, and by 1880 the private railway companies were in debt to the government to the tune of around 1,100 m. rubles.

The government responded by allocating this debt to the so-called extraordinary account, supposedly representing non-recurrent items of expenditure. While this created an appearance of budgetary respectability (Reutern was even able to claim a budget surplus in 1871–5), it none the less imposed on the government the inescapable need to borrow still more, in order to finance the new obligations it had incurred. The leading historian of the tsarist debt, P. P. Migulin, calculated that the debt grew by 2,200 m. rubles during Reutern's period of office. Of this increase, 50 per cent represented new state loans, 20 per cent the assumption of the debt of private railway companies, and 23 per cent the issue of redemption bonds. The residue largely comprised the debts of the old pre-reform financial institutions, which the State Bank took over in 1860. New state loans were incurred to cover the costs of interest payments on old debt (including payments to foreigners) and the cost of the war against Turkey. By the early 1880s railway construction had tailed off, and much of the new expenditure involved the construction of ancillary lines, depots for rolling-stock and warehouses. Between 1880 and 1890 the government regularized what had already become a fait accompli, and took over direct responsibility for the development of the railway network. The government also continued to purchase the hopelessly indebted private lines.[59]

In accordance with the needs of the government, the Russian capital market dealt for the most part in fixed-interest securities: state bonds, mortgage paper, railway debentures and redemption certificates. Until the 1880s, all but a fraction of the stock issued in Russia consisted of such paper. As Table 6.4 indicates, the market in unguaranteed securities only developed rapidly after 1881. Even during the period of rapid industrialization, the bulk of stock held by Russian investors took the form of gilts and other fixed-interest paper.

What interpretation should be placed on these figures? Kahan argued that the tsarist government was in direct competition for funds with private industry. According to this view, the slackening rate

Table 6.4

The growth of the Russian stock market, 1861–1914

(million rubles)

A.

	(1) Government bonds and other guaranteed stock*		(2) Share capital		(3) Bonded debt of corporations†		(4) Total
1861	1,558	(96%)	72	(4%)	Nil		1,630
1881	5,781	(94%)	355	(6%)	20	(–)	6,156
1893	7,332	(88%)	899	(11%)	78	(1%)	8,309
1900	9,730	(82%)	1,962	(17%)	216	(3%)	11,908
1908	13,555	(82%)	2,603	(16%)	356	(2%)	16,514
1914	16,450	(78%)	4,310	(20%)	398	(2%)	21,158

* Includes railway company bonds, mortgage bonds and municipal stock.
† 'Obligation capital' in Russian terminology.

B. Percentage share of the increase in each category attributable to domestic subscriptions:

	(1)	(2)	(3)	(4)
1861–81	52	71	70	53
1881–93	71	80	51	72
1893–1900	60	58	39	59
1900–08	65	53	49	63
1908–14	87	56	–	74

Source: I. F. Gindin, *Russkie kommercheskie banki*, Gosfinizdat, 1948, pp. 444–5.

of growth of government demand for savings 'enabled the Russian industrial entrepreneurs to borrow more freely'. Whether one accepts this interpretation depends upon the assumptions one holds about industrialists' demand for credit. Whilst it is true that the Russian government had a large appetite for credit, and that lenders probably had a preference for government bonds, it does not follow that the government 'crowded out' the private borrower. The market may simply have responded to the lack of demand for credit from the private sector.[60]

The government certainly did help to create a climate for more speculative investment by the Russian public, when industrial demand for credit expanded. For example, the government decision to purchase privately owned railway companies indirectly stimulated interest in more speculative securities, because the old bonds were replaced by government paper that carried a lower rate of interest (four, instead of five per cent). The conversion of public debt that Witte carried out in the early 1890s also encouraged a switch from gilt-edged securities, especially among foreign investors. Investors now looked to industrial and commercial securities, where the average dividend during the 1890s was around six per cent and where the rewards could be four or five times greater.[61]

The increase in government borrowing after 1861 must be placed against a background of budgetary difficulties. On the face of it, the budget gave no grounds for alarm during the 1860s and 1870s; expenditure increased by 47 per cent between 1861–65 and 1876–80, while recurrent revenue increased by nearly 62 per cent. However, government officials doubted that fiscal policy could remain unchanged. According to an independent observer, Yanson, the government relied too heavily upon direct taxation, to which the peasantry made a disproportionate contribution. This view found favour with Bunge, who reduced redemption payments, abolished the poll tax, and engineered a shift towards indirect taxation.[62]

The main trends in recurrent budget revenue are set out in Table 6.5. Receipts from customs duties and indirect taxes rose threefold between 1890 and 1913, and together accounted for nearly 90 per cent of total tax revenue. Direct taxes, which represented one-quarter of tax revenues in 1890, contributed just over a tenth in 1913. Revenue from government property, and in particular from the state-owned railways, increased more rapidly than revenue from other sources, and by 1913 accounted for around one-third of total ordinary revenue.

The burden of direct taxation fell more heavily upon urban property and business after 1890, compared to the preceding era. In 1891 the government raised the rate of taxation on company profits. In 1898 Witte introduced a tax on businesses, according to the capital employed, and this yielded additional revenue as the number of registered companies increased. In 1895 the government began to tax bank deposits; earlier, it had introduced a tax on share dividends. According to one authority, the proportion of direct taxes 'in any way connected with the commercial and industrial life of the country'

Table 6.5

Ordinary revenue of the central government, 1890–1910

(million rubles)

	Direct taxes*	Customs duties	Indirect taxes†	Royalties and income from state property‡	Miscell- aneous receipts	Total
1890	181.6	60.1	475.2	145.3	96.9	959.1
1891	159.3	62.1	440.5	152.0	86.2	900.1
1892	168.4	66.5	474.9	181.8	88.0	979.6
1893	199.5	68.8	511.9	183.4	95.3	1,058.9
1894	194.8	72.6	581.4	222.1	95.4	1,166.3
1895	207.2	72.1	597.2	300.1	99.5	1,276.1
1896	196.5	74.7	610.4	416.7	129.7	1,428.0
1897	190.0	75.2	648.9	433.1	82.3	1,429.5
1898	190.0	86.3	737.0	497.7	75.1	1,586.1
1899	216.8	96.0	769.8	508.0	80.7	1,671.3
1900	228.1	88.3	776.1	553.0	138.6	1,784.1
1901	220.9	94.6	850.0	554.5	114.8	1,834.8
1902	222.8	101.1	913.1	585.9	102.2	1,925.1
1903	224.0	107.3	982.5	635.5	108.0	2,057.3
1904	216.5	104.2	962.1	643.4	106.2	2,032.4
1905	182.3	100.0	1,018.0	630.1	113.2	2,043.6
1906	198.2	113.3	1,191.8	682.8	102.8	2,288.9
1907	183.9	122.6	1,217.0	720.4	128.2	2,372.1
1908	194.9	137.4	1,235.5	733.8	141.1	2,442.7
1909	199.5	151.7	1,248.7	804.8	137.5	2,542.2
1910	217.0	170.4	1,359.8	896.7	154.1	2,798.0

* Includes redemption payments until 1906.
† Includes gross revenue from sale of alcohol.
‡ Includes gross receipts from state railway network.
Source: A. Babkov, 'National finances and the economic evolution of Russia', *Russian Review*, no. 3, 1912, p. 175.

rose from under 30 per cent in 1890 to 80 per cent in 1910. Similarly, increased receipts from railway freight owed most to an increase in the carriage of industrial raw materials and manufactured goods. By 1900–1910, iron and coal were more important than grain as a source of railway freight receipts.[63]

Indirect revenue derived to a great extent from excise duties levied upon the sale of kerosene, matches, sugar and (above all) vodka. Receipts from indirect taxation on the consumption of such items increased by 63 per cent between 1890 and 1900, and by a further 75 per cent between 1900 and 1910. Why did the receipts increase? Witte's critics attributed the increase to the decision to raise the rate at which such items were taxed; in his defence, it was argued that the growth in revenue reflected the growth in population and in consumption per head. The whole question, as noted earlier, was – and is – bound up with the question of rural living standards. But this may be something of a red herring.

Generalization about indirect taxation can be misleading, because the duties on the consumption of different items were raised at different times and by different amounts. For instance, duties on kerosene rose by between 50 and 67 per cent in 1892, but the duty on matches rose by 100 per cent; the duty on sugar rose by 75 per cent, but in 1894; and so on. Thus, any simple juxtaposition of receipts from indirect sources in, say, 1890 and 1913, together with 'average' rates of duty, will conceal more than it will reveal. It is necessary to disaggregate the sources of indirect revenue.

The growth in receipts from the sale of vodka reflects the extension of the vodka monopoly to new parts of the Russian Empire. Per capita consumption of spirits did not increase in the country as a whole, between 1892 and 1901. By contrast, the increase in receipts from the sale of sugar and kerosene did reflect an increase in per capita consumption. Consumption of sugar increased by nearly 40 per cent (from 3.6 to 5.0 kg. per head), and kerosene consumption increased by 28 per cent between 1892 and 1901.[64]

The bulk of these commercially produced items was purchased by urban inhabitants, who had no domestic substitute, unlike many peasants. Per capita consumption of these 'necessities' was indeed higher in the towns than in the villages. On average, a Russian who lived in town consumed three or four times as much vodka as his rural counterpart. Urban consumption of kerosene exceeded rural consumption by a factor of twenty. It thus makes sense to ascribe the increase in receipts from indirect taxation to the growth in the urban population and, perhaps, to a real growth in per capita urban consumption. Of course, this does not mean that peasants were exempt from the payment of indirect taxes; but it implies that peasants paid indirect taxes, not as villagers, but as migrants to the towns. In so far as the urban population became more settled, the tax burden fell increasingly upon the urban working class.[65]

The change in fiscal policy and the increase in government borrowing were designed to satisfy the growth in government commitments. Total outlays doubled between 1861–5 and 1886–90, and doubled again between 1886–90 and 1901–1905. Foremost among government expenditure during the late nineteenth century were outlays on administration, defence and payments on the state debt. But by the end of the 1890s, expenditure on government enterprises, notably the state-owned railway network, had become the heaviest claim on total budget expenditure, as shown in Table 6.6.

Table 6.6

The growth and distribution of central government expenditure, 1885–1913

	Total	Percentage devoted to:					
	(m. rubles, current prices)	Admin-istration	Health and Educa-tion	Defence	Debt charges	Govern-ment enterprise*	Subsidies and transfers†
1885	866	22	3	28	36	6	6
1891	983	25	3	30	26	10	6
1896	1,361	22	2	25	20	27	4
1903	2,072	19	2	21	14	39	5
1910	2,592	21	4	22	16	35	3
1913	3,383	17	5	29	13	31	6

* State-owned railways and the vodka monopoly.
† Subsidies to private railway lines included.
Source: P. Gregory, *Russian National Income, 1885–1913*, C.U.P., 1982, p. 252.

Many scholars have made the point that the money spent on the railways included a sizeable element of unproductive spending on the administration of the system. The outlays on government administration, defence and the state debt also suggest that it would be idle to maintain that tsarist budget expenditure had a productive purpose. The amounts spent on subsidies to the private sector, and on investment in public health and education, were trifling by comparison with other claims on the public purse. Given the nature of the political system and the values espoused by the tsarist bureaucracy, one could hardly expect a different profile to the budget.[66]

6.6 The Inflow of Foreign Capital

Arguably, the Russian government played an important role in industrial development, but in more indirect ways. Among the possible forms of indirect assistance, the promotion of foreign capital investment looms largest, and it is to this aspect of the tsarist economy that attention now turns. Here, an attempt will be made to give an overview of the volume and trends in foreign lending, and an assessment of the costs and benefits to the Russian economy.

The inflow of foreign capital may take a number of forms, ranging from foreign investment in commercial enterprise to the purchase of fixed-interest bonds, issued by the host government. Typically, most foreign investment in the nineteenth and early twentieth centuries was in government securities and in railway stock that gave a guaranteed return. More than half of German foreign investment before 1914 assumed this character. The corresponding proportion of French and British overseas investment was 75 and 70 per cent respectively.

The explosion in foreign lending after 1850 reflected the increase in the incomes of the European bourgeoisie, and the plough-back of profits into overseas lending. By 1874 cumulative overseas investment amounted to $6,500 m., and by 1914 this sum had swelled to $44,000 m. There was a close correspondence between the need of middle-class savers for a stable rate of return and the requirements of overseas countries that needed to finance an expanding infrastructure or new military commitments. The geographical distribution of foreign investment suggests that Britain favoured India, Latin America and, later, the Dominions (Australia and Canada), while France retained a close interest in Europe. By 1914 France and Germany had each allocated half their cumulative foreign investments to Europe, including Russia.[67]

Russia was in the market for funds, along with other customers, and we need to ask why she was so successful in attracting funds on the scale she did. According to P. V. Ol foreigners held around 50 per cent of Russian government debt, and the same proportion of share capital. Political considerations obviously had an importance that cannot be overlooked. For example, Bismarck promoted the flow of German capital to Russia during the late 1870s and early 1880s, in order to cement the Dreikaiserbund (1879). He did this, even though he harboured doubts about the credit-worthiness of the tsarist regime. A decade later, the French government sought to replace Berlin as the main market for Russian government borrowing, in order to cultivate Russian support for an alliance against Germany, which was concluded in 1894.

Political considerations alone do not explain the dimension and trends of foreign investment in Russia. Some French investors ignored the blandishments of the financial press and the Quai d'Orsay, because they had no wish to lend to a despotic and anti-semitic regime. Similarly, the failure of the Dreikaiserbund did not prevent Germany from lending to Russia, albeit on a reduced scale. The willingness of foreign investors to seek out Russian securities was also a function of the higher relative rate of return that was offered, at least until 1900. Too much should not be read into this, because the differential reflected the greater risks inherent in investment in Russia – in particular, the fluctuation in the value of the ruble on the foreign exchanges. The differential between French and Russian government bonds narrowed by 1900, after Russia had joined the Gold Standard, which fixed the ruble in relation to other major gold-backed currencies. Rates of return on investment in Russian commercial enterprises were still higher than dividends available from French firms, and this helps to account for the attractiveness of Russian equities.[68]

The tsarist government, as already mentioned, assumed additional commitments between the 1850s and 1870s, in connection with the Crimean War, railway construction and, to a lesser extent, Emancipation. The war against Turkey saddled the Treasury with further obligations: according to Migulin, the public debt rose by 25 per cent between 1877 and 1881, to more than 6,000 m. rubles, more than half of which was held abroad. Berlin and Paris stepped in to supply the necessary credit. But Russian finances were in disarray after 1878, and some attempt had to be made to restore monetary and budgetary stability.[69]

In 1880 Russia had reached a position in which the income she received from transactions with foreigners was insufficient to cover outgoings. In other words, there was a deficit on her balance of payments current account. The situation is revealed in Table 6.7. Although the trading account showed a surplus of receipts from exports over import payments (row 1), the obligation to pay interest on the debt held by foreigners – together with other items, such as net tourist expenditures, which alone almost cancelled out the trade surplus – created an overall deficit. To cover the shortfall, the Ministry of Finances needed to attract additional foreign funds, or accept the flow of gold out of the country. This latter prospect was not tolerable, because the Russian government had in mind the accumulation of gold reserves, both as a cushion against future emergencies (such as war), and as the basis for the eventual adoption of a gold-backed ruble.

The government did not have much room for manoeuvre. Bunge, who held office from 1881 to 1886, strove to reduce the budget deficit in order to avoid the need for new borrowing, but this was difficult to reconcile with his attempt to reduce the burden of taxation. In any case, an additional inflow of funds was made necessary by the appearance of the deficit on the balance of payments. One reason for this was the decline in the value of grain exports, as a consequence of the international decline in cereal prices. Accordingly, Russia built up more liabilities with foreigners. Bunge's successor, I. A. Vyshnegradsky (Finance Minister from 1886 to 1892), was able to eliminate the deficit in 1886–90, first by building up a massive trade surplus (helped by bumper harvests in 1887 and 1888), and secondly by rescheduling Russian debts. This allowed the government to reduce the burden of interest; the policy was facilitated by the rapprochement with France, which offered more favourable terms than Germany. However, the balance of payments surplus did not persist. Although the potential trade surplus was encouraged by the adoption of high rates of tariff protection in 1891, the effect of this was moderated by the increased rate of investment in industry and transport, which created a greater demand for imports of equipment and semi-finished goods. This situation continued during the last quinquennium of the nineteenth century.[70]

Finance Minister Witte, who held office between 1892 and 1903, also recognized that the financial position of Russia necessitated the continued inflow of foreign funds. Witte believed that it was most desirable to attract foreign investment directly into Russian industry and utilities. He argued that foreign investment would bring with it a package of benefits, including entrepreneurship, skills and advanced technology. Witte maintained that this package would eventually generate the resources to pay creditors and to invest in the autonomous development of Russia. The conditions for such an inflow included, on the supply side, an abundance of funds in western Europe. But Witte had to stimulate renewed confidence in Russia by means of budgetary and monetary stability. The first of these followed in part from the adoption of higher rates of taxation on the sale of consumer goods (see above), and in part from the manipulation of the budget. For example, items of government expenditure were transferred to the 'extraordinary' account, so that the increase in net losses from the operation of state railways was not allowed to affect the picture of budgetary health.[71]

The stabilization of the ruble had already been commenced during Vyshnegradsky's period of office. Vyshnegradsky built up the gold reserves and smoothed out fluctuations on the foreign exchanges.

Table 6.7

The balance of payments of tsarist Russia, 1881–1913

(million rubles, current prices)

	1881–5	1886–90	1891–5	1896–1900	1901–5	1906–10	1911–13	Total
Visible balance	272	1260	788	303	1535	1423	873	6454
Invisible balance*	−172	−192	−313	−453	−605	−877	−804	−3416
Net property income from abroad to:								
Government	−562	−697	−714	−756	−829	−1057	−668	−5283
Companies	−48	−70	−99	−216	−258	−356	−403	−1450
Non-incorporated enterprises and municipal authorities	−24	−36	−48	−60	−54	−85	−91	−398
Total	−634	−803	−861	−1032	−1141	−1498	−1162	−7131
Net foreign investment†	−534	265	−386	−1182	−211	−952	−1093	−4093
Net foreign investment: net property income from abroad	0.84	−0.33	0.45	1.15	0.18	0.64	0.94	0.57

* Mainly net tourist expenditures.
† Net foreign investment = visible balance + invisible balance + net property income from abroad. On this definition it includes the net export of bullion.
Source: P. R. Gregory, *Russian National Income, 1885–1913*, C.U.P., 1982, pp. 97–8.

Witte had initially been against the adoption of a gold standard, bu by 1894 he had decided to bring Russia into line with othe developing countries and their creditors. Between 1894 and 1897 h supervised a monetary reform that involved the convertibility of th paper ruble to gold, and other gold-backed currencies, at a fixed rat of exchange. The arrangement did not provide for gold and pape rubles to be exchanged at parity, because the paper or 'credit' rubl had fallen to just two-thirds of the value of the gold. To fix convert ibility at par would have meant a revaluation of the ruble whicl would have inflicted an intolerable burden on Russian exporters. Th reform was unpopular enough already with gentry farmers, becaus the depreciation in the credit ruble had moderated their debt burden These men saw the introduction of a gold standard as a cross whicl they were forced to bear in the interests of foreign investors.[72]

The new measures imposed a restriction on note issue. The Stat Bank could only issue notes up to a total of 600 m. rubles, beyon which each note had to be fully covered by gold reserves. Critics o government monetary policy at the time argued that this was a unnecessarily restrictive policy, and the debate has been resurrecte in the *Journal of Economic History*. Barkai argued that the deman for money between 1861 and 1903 increased by four per cent pe annum, while the estimated supply grew by no more than three pe cent. The gap between supply and demand was still wider during th 1890s. However, it has been shown that Barkai took a very narrow view of money supply, overlooking the fact that the State Bank hel deposits on behalf of the public and the government. His estimat rested only upon currency and deposits held by the joint-stock banks On the broader definition of money supply adopted by Drummond total money supply was more than adequate to meet demand. Besides as we have seen, there is little evidence that demand was not bein satisfied. The banking system was becoming more flexible, anc borrowers could normally turn to foreign sources of credit. It may b true that the government immobilized its gold reserves at the begin ning of the century, instead of using them to counteract the slump i industry, but the criticism is hardly fair, given the orthodox prevailing at the time.[73]

How much of a burden did the acquisition of foreign debt represen for tsarist Russia? Contemporary critics of Witte believed that th burden was heavy, and was borne by peasants and other farmers who were required to release grain for export and to pay the cost o the tariff, in order that Russia could generate a large trade surplus.[7] However, the trade surplus does not appear to have been achieved a the expense of rural household consumption, and so this particula criticism is untenable.

The trade surplus, as is evident from Table 6.7, was not sufficien o cover the growth in Russian obligations to foreigners. Net tourist expenditures were a large and growing component of the overall balance, and payments to foreign investors and bondholders showed no sign of abating. Foreign debt increased in 1904–6, as a result of the need to finance the war against Japan. These commitments tailed off only slightly in 1911–13. In general, it remained necessary for Russia to finance the payments deficit by continued foreign borrowing.

Foreign investment has to be judged also against the additional output that it generated. Boris Brandt, the author of the first serious study of foreign capital in Russia, pointed out that foreign direct investment was indispensable to the growth in industrial production during the 1890s. He also argued that foreign investment did not simply create enclaves (the one exception was British investment in the oil industry), and so the injection of foreign capital created additional jobs and output in other sectors of the economy. Finally, Brandt maintained that foreign investment generated income that remained in the host country; that is, the royalties, profits and salaries were ploughed back into Russia.[75]

Profits were, of course, reinvested, as is evident also from the researches that have been undertaken by John McKay. But by no means all the money earned by foreigners in Russia found its way back into the Russian economy. Table 6.7 indicates that only in 1896–1900 did net foreign investment exceed the total net income from investments in government and in private enterprise. Over the period 1885–1913, only 60 per cent of foreigners' property incomes was reinvested.

Tsarist Russia was not, however, a semi-colony of western Europe. To begin with, the Russian government did not automatically follow the dictates of its creditors, nor did it become over-reliant on any one source of credit. In the heyday of the Franco-Russian alliance in the 1890s, more than half the tsarist debt floated abroad was taken up in countries other than France. French attempts to influence the tsarist government either came to nothing (in 1909 France planned to lend on the understanding that Russia placed military orders with French contractors, but the condition was not met); or simply coincided with the wishes of the Russian government (in 1901 Delcassé, the French Foreign Minister, insisted that French aid be used to construct a rail link between central Russia and Poland, and in this he was enthusiastically supported by the Russian military). The fact was that foreign investors were at least as dependent upon Russia as Russia was upon foreign credit. Any failure to satisfy tsarist demand for credit carried the risk of Russian default.[76]

Trends in foreign investment in industry and banking are indicated in broad terms in Table 6.8. But the figures have to be treated with

Table 6.8

Foreign capital in Russian industry and banking, 1880–1915

	Cumulative foreign capital (million rubles)	As percentage of joint-stock capital		Foreign capital as percentage of total new investment in industry
1880	97.7		1880–9	41
1890	214.7	25	1890–2	33
1895	280.1	26	1893–9	55
1900	911.0	37	1900–1902	47
1905	1,037.4	35	1903–5	81
1910	1,358.1	38	1906–8	37
1915	2,205.9	38	1909–13	50

Source: J. P. McKay, *Pioneers for Profit: Foreign Entrepreneurship and Russian Industrialization, 1885–1913*, University of Chicago Press, 1970, pp. 26–8.

some caution. Ol, who compiled the most commonly cited data, assumed that all companies that were registered abroad were entirely foreign-owned, which was a gratuitous assumption. He made it, because he was anxious to demonstrate the magnitude of the foreign 'yoke' in Russia.

The other reason why these figures only serve as a general indication of foreign investment is that they measure the nominal value of corporate shares. As Carstensen has observed, it is not true that the incorporation of an enterprise – and each share issue – corresponded to real investment. He makes the point that Ol's figures probably distorted both the magnitude and the timing of foreign investment. Finally, Carstensen indicates that the frequent emphasis upon the foreign contribution to fixed capital formation overlooks the provision of working capital from foreign sources.[77]

Conclusion

Tsarist Russia was a relatively poor country, by nineteenth-century European standards. The society was characterized by the highly unequal distribution of wealth, concentrated in the hands of the upper nobility. In these circumstances, the fact that tsarist Russia invested around 12 per cent of national income by 1909–13 (see Table 2.5) was a notable achievement. Of this total, one-fifth comprised net foreign investment. As the figures in Table 6.8 imply, the contribution of foreigners to investment in industry and banking was certainly higher than this. But this should not detract from the domestic contribution to capital formation.

The material presented in this chapter confirms that investment in agriculture became attractive to Russian farmers, especially after 1900. The contribution of some gentry entrepreneurs and most kulaks was, inevitably, of greater significance than that of the peasantry at large. Investment in agriculture was almost certainly financed more from profits than from credit, although some note should be taken of cooperative credit at the end of the period. There are indications that the informal and unorganized pattern of rural credit was being undermined by 1914, especially on the periphery.

Investment in industry was stimulated by government incentives to Russian and foreign lenders. The growth of investment in heavy industry (which included investment in factory accommodation, as well as in industrial structures, equipment and stocks) depended particularly upon the provision of credit from foreign and domestic sources. In light industry, whether small- or large-scale enterprise, expansion was financed largely through the plough-back of profits.

The tsarist government has been charged with failure to make funds available to private entrepreneurs, especially in industry, prior to 1890. However, there appears to have been little manifestation of a credit shortage in the private sector. Entrepreneurs made relatively little demand on the formal capital market until the late 1880s. When demand for long-term credit did expand, foreign and Russian banks adapted to the new situation, in the expectation of good profits from promotions and commissions. By 1914 the banks' influence over industrial clients, notably in heavy industry, was considerable. The First World War strengthened these ties still further. In the provision of credit for operating needs, the commercial banking system also acquired a more prominent profile.

The government was, nevertheless, a major presence in the capital market, being unable to finance its growing domestic and foreign commitments out of recurrent income. Income from taxation (especially indirect taxation) did increase, but not sufficiently fast to finance expenditures. The regime had recourse to the bond market in

order to finance the deficit. The international ambitions of tsarism –
evident in 1854, 1877, 1904 and 1914 – imposed additional debt
that had to be funded. Only the Bolshevik repudiation of tsarist debts
solved the problem of future repayment.

Conclusion

The temptation to describe pre-revolutionary Russia as a backward economy is powerful, but it is a temptation that should be resisted. The truth is that the tsarist economy grew rapidly between 1850 and 1917, and that many of the characteristic features of economic backwardness – mass illiteracy, high rates of infant mortality, subsistence crises – had been substantially moderated by the beginning of the twentieth century. So far as particular sectors of the economy are concerned, it would be incorrect to argue that pre-revolutionary agriculture was uniformly backward, while Russian industry was dynamic and progressive throughout. The material presented in this book suggests that progress did take place in particular regions and branches of agricultural production. The primitive organization and technology employed by peasants and gentry in much of the Central Black Earth Region bore no resemblance to the advanced farming methods that characterized agriculture in the Baltic, parts of the Central Industrial Region and western Siberia. Within the industrial sector, generalization is similarly hazardous. The assumption that technological change, productivity gains and profitability were most marked in capital goods industries, and that consumer goods industries lagged behind, cannot be sustained. Even at the level of the individual enterprise, let alone the individual sector of industry, traditional and modern techniques coexisted. Finally, a more nuanced assessment is also required in respect of the capital market, where informal devices for the supply of credit continued to exist alongside financial institutions.

The foregoing remarks also suggest the need to qualify any description of the tsarist economy as a capitalist economy, especially prior to 1900. As Lenin observed in 1899, 'the process of transformation must, by the very nature of capitalism, take place in the midst of much that is uneven and disproportionate'.[1] Highly developed forms of capitalist organization in industry and agriculture were clearly evident, in the shape of conglomerates and farms with a high degree of division of labour. At the same time, pre-capitalist forms of organization survived, as in the persistence of semi-bonded labour in agriculture (winter hiring, *otrabotka*), especially in the Central Black Earth, and in parts of industry (the Urals iron industry). The tendency, nevertheless, was for capitalist forms to grow and supplant pre-capitalist forms. The persistence of small-scale units of production in agriculture and industry cannot be taken to indicate the absence of capitalist relations in late tsarist Russia.

One of the underlying themes of this book is that the role of political institutions in Russian economic development has been overstated. The progressive, if uneven, transformation of the tsarist economy cannot be attributed wholly or even predominantly to the state. Yet the notion of an all-embracing and interventionist state has enjoyed enormous currency in liberal, populist and marxist discourse. It is not difficult to see why this has been the case: each tradition sought to confront and eventually to supplant the tsarist state. Naturally, the adherents of each tradition tended to emphasize the economic power of the state, as well as its political power. However, the evidence presented in this book suggests that government policy was but one of a series of influences that shaped economic development. Much more allowance than is customary has to be made for the expression and influence of autonomous social forces, notably capitalist entrepreneurs in agriculture and industry. The other familiar institution in the history of the Russian economy is the land commune. The impact of the commune on the level and rate of change of agricultural productivity, and on the development and operation of the labour market, has been overstated. The history of peasant agriculture in tsarist Russia was one of 'real life evading legal bounds'.[2] The longstanding emphasis upon the commune reflects the political importance attached to it by populists, and the liberal belief that it frustrated the emergence of a class of yeoman farmers, who would be a political and economic mainstay of a liberal democracy in Russia. But the emphasis upon the commune obscures the all-important relations between peasants and gentry and within the peasantry itself.

What of the implications of economic change for the political system? The material presented here poses a challenge to one influential version of events, namely that the collapse of the tsarist regime in February 1917 was a product of the declining living standards of the bulk of the population. As has been stressed more than once, the living standards of the Russian peasantry were rising, especially after 1900. Even during the 1890s, the evidence is weak for the proposition that peasant living standards were depressed as a result of government fiscal policies. If economic deterioration did not occur, then what alternative explanations may be offered for the collapse of tsarism?

Gerschenkron, it will be recalled, attributed its demise to the traumatic impact of the First World War. Undoubtedly, the War imposed enormous demands upon the tsarist economy, as upon the economy of every belligerent. But the War cannot satisfactorily account for the end of the tsarist regime. To say that it does is to overlook the evidence of powerful and unresolved conflicts within Russian society before 1914, which the War intensified. In particular, the recurrent antagonisms between workers and employers, and between peasants and gentry, were not stifled, even after the suppression of the 1905 Revolution. For example, the Stolypin land reforms did not attack the root cause of peasant revolution, namely the continued preponderance of gentry landholding (the much-vaunted 'decline of the Russian nobility' completely misses the point about the intensity of peasant feeling). By 1917, it may be argued, peasants and workers had an acute sense, not only of their immediate economic grievances (wages, hours of work, rents and so forth), but also of the fact that their circumstances were inextricably linked to the behaviour of the tsarist state. Workers identified the daily oppression to which they were subject with a regime that upheld the rights of capital and curtailed the freedom of labour. The peasantry recognized that the state maintained the sanctity of gentry landownership. Mass protest against employers and landowners was quickly and unavoidably translated into protest against the state. Arguably, workers and peasants had learned from the experience of 1905 how closely related economics and politics were in tsarist Russia. If this interpretation is correct, then the First World War was less the exogenous shock to a stabilizing society that Gerschenkron imagined than an opportunity for well-entrenched class conflict to reassert itself and be transformed into a revolutionary movement.

What were the prospects for the Russian economy in the aftermath of tsarism? The legacy of the old regime to the new could hardly have been less propitious, thanks to the immediate impact of three years of war and of the bitter civil war that quickly followed the victory of the Bolsheviks. The destruction of physical capital (machinery, rolling-stock, buildings and bridges) accompanied the loss of human life.[3] In the longer term, the Bolshevik leaders found that they had inherited an economy with plenty of potential for economic growth.[4] However, the context in which growth took place had changed in several key respects. First, the international climate was hostile to the new government, and this imposed upon it the need to finance new investment almost entirely from domestic sources. Secondly, most large-scale, non-agricultural assets (and financial institutions) had been taken under state control; decisions about the organization of production, investment and pricing could, in the last resort, now be determined by the state. Thirdly, the rural economy had been transformed by the abolition of large estates and the redistribution of land. In this respect one 'problem' had been resolved, only for another to emerge. The confirmation of peasant smallholdings suggested to the new government that savings would be difficult to extract from agriculture. To the extent that savings were accumulated, this would indicate the likely accumulation of economic power by kulaks, and thus by a class enemy of the proletariat. Little more than a decade after the Revolution, Stalin's 'revolution from above' would destroy the kulaks and with them the last vestiges of the tsarist economy.

Notes

Introduction (pp. xii–xvi)

1 This summary draws upon the following: A. Gerschenkron, *Economic Backwardness in Historical Perspective*, Harvard U.P., 1962; idem, *Continuity in History*, Harvard U.P., 1968; idem, *Europe in the Russian Mirror*, C.U.P., 1970. For further comment, see S. L. Barsby, 'Economic backwardness and the characteristics of development', *J.Ec.H.*, no. 29, 1969, pp. 449–72; L. G. Sandberg, 'Ignorance, poverty and economic backwardness in the early stages of European industrialization: variations on Alexander Gerschenkron's grand theme', *J.E.E.H.*, no. 11, 1982, pp. 675–97; and the work of Crisp and Gregory, cited below. A discussion of Gerschenkron's work from a Soviet viewpoint will be found in I. N. Olegina, *Industrializatsiya SSSR v angliiskoi i amerikanskoi istoriografii*, Izdatelstvo Leningradskogo universiteta, 1971, pp. 86–92.

2 P. R. Gregory, *Russian National Income, 1885–1913*, C.U.P., 1982. For the less favourable verdict on the rate of growth of agricultural production see R. Goldsmith, 'The economic growth of tsarist Russia, 1860–1913', *Economic Development and Cultural Change*, no. 9, 1961, pp. 441–75.

3 Strictly speaking, the former serfs reimbursed the tsarist government, which had compensated the feudal landowners on their behalf. See Chapter Four.

4 P. R. Gregory, 'Grain marketings and peasant consumption, Russia 1885–1913', *E.E.H.*, no. 17, 1980, pp. 135–64; J. Y. Simms, 'The crisis in Russian agriculture at the end of the ninettenth century: a different view', *S.R.*, no. 36, 1977, pp. 377–98. But see also E. Müller, 'Der Beitrag der Bauern zur Industrialisierung Russlands, 1885–1930', *Jahrbücher für Geschichte Osteuropas*, no. 27, 1979, pp. 197–219; and the exchange between Simms and J. T. Sanders in *S.R.*, no. 43, 1984, pp. 657–71.

5 O. Crisp, *Studies in the Russian Economy before 1914*, Macmillan, 1976; A. Kahan, 'Government policies and the industrialization of Russia', *J.Ec.H.*, no. 27, 1967, pp. 460–77; idem, 'Capital formation during the period of early industrialization in Russia, 1890–1913', in P. Mathias and M. M. Postan, eds., *Cambridge Economic History of Europe*, vol. 7, part 2, C.U.P., 1978, pp. 265–307. See Chapter Six.

6 L. Haimson, 'The problem of social stability in urban Russia,

1905–1917', *S.R.*, no. 23, 1964, pp. 619–42, and *S.R.*, no. 24, 1965, pp. 1–23; V. E. Bonnell, *Roots of Rebellion: Workers' Politics and Organization in St. Petersburg and Moscow, 1900–1914*, University of California Press, 1983. See also R. T. Manning, *The Crisis of the Old Order in Russia: Gentry and Government*, Princeton U.P., 1982.

7 Gerschenkron, *Europe in the Russian Mirror*, pp. 79, 86.

8 T. H. von Laue, *Sergei Witte and the Industrialization of Russia*, Columbia U.P., 1963; idem, 'The high cost and the gamble of the Witte system: a chapter in the industrialization of Russia', *J.Ec.H.*, no. 13, 1953, pp. 425–48; idem, 'The state and the economy', in C. E. Black, ed., *The Transformation of Russian Society*, Harvard U.P., 1960, pp. 209–25; idem, 'Problems of industrialization', in T. Stavrou, ed., *Russia Under the Last Tsar*, University of Minnesota Press, 1969, pp. 117–53.

9 P. Anderson, *Lineages of the Absolutist State*, Verso, 1979, esp. pp. 353–60; P. I. Lyashchenko, *History of the National Economy of Russia to the 1917 Revolution*, Macmillan, New York 1949; A. L. Sidorov, *Istoricheskie predposylki Velikoi Oktyabrskoi sotsialisticheskoi revolyutsii*, Nauka, 1970.

10 The Fundamental Laws of 1906, promulgated in the aftermath of the 1905 Revolution and the October 1905 Manifesto, did not satisfy those liberals who desired a more democratic franchise and a more powerful parliament. See the discussion in H. Rogger, *Russia in the Age of Modernization and Revolution, 1881–1917*, Longman, 1983, pp. 213–20. The views of Miliukov and Vinogradoff are outlined in P. Miliukov, *Russia and Its Crisis*, New York, 1905, and P. Vinogradoff, *The Russian Problem*, London and New York, 1914.

11 I would also locate the following scholars in this tradition: Robinson, Pavlovsky, Crisp, Kahan, Falkus and Gregory (see Bibliography).

12 The following are valuable introductions to populism: I. Berlin, 'Russian populism', in his *Russian Thinkers*, Pelican Books, 1979, pp. 210–37; F. Venturi, *Roots of Revolution: A History of the Populist and Socialist Movements in Nineteenth-Century Russia*, Weidenfeld, 1960, reissued by University of Chicago Press, 1983. See also Rogger, op. cit., pp. 135–42.

13 A. P. Mendel, *Dilemmas of Progress in Tsarist Russia: Legal Populism and Legal Marxism*, Harvard U.P., 1961; A. Walicki, *The Controversy Over Capitalism: Studies in the Social Philosophy of the Russian Populists*, O.U.P., 1969; M. Perrie, *The Agrarian Policy of the Russian Socialist-Revolutionary Party from its Origins through the Revolution of 1917*, C.U.P., 1976.

14 T. Shanin, *The Awkward Class: Political Sociology of Peasantry in a Developing Society, Russia 1910–1925*, O.U.P., 1972; see also P. Worsley, *The Three Worlds: Culture and World Development*, Weidenfeld, 1984. There is also a semi-populist tone about G. L. Yaney, *The Urge to Mobilize: Agrarian Reform in Russia, 1861–1930*, University of Illinois Press, 1982, notwithstanding his disclaimer on pp. 8–9. For general discussion see G. Kitching, *Development and Underdevelopment in Historical Perspective: Populism, Nationalism and Industrialization*, Methuen, 1982.

15 G. V. Plekhanov, *Selected Philosophical Works*, vol. 1, Lawrence and Wishart, 1961; V. I. Lenin, *The Development of Capitalism in Russia*,

1899; (second edition, 1907; Progress Publishers, 1977); N. Harding, *Lenin's Political Thought*, 2 vols. in one, Macmillan, 1983; L. D. Trotsky, *1905*, Pelican Books, 1971; idem, *Results and Prospects*, Pathfinder Press, 1978.

16 Lyashchenko, op. cit.; V. K. Yatsunsky, 'The industrial revolution in Russia', in W. L. Blackwell, ed., *Russian Economic Development from Peter the Great to Stalin*, New Viewpoints, 1974, pp. 111–35; A. Hussain and K. Tribe, *Marxism and the Agrarian Question*, Macmillan, 1983, chapter 7.

Chapter One (pp. 1–28)

1 W. A. Lewis, 'Economic development with unlimited supplies of labour', in A. N. Agarwala and S. P. Singh, eds., *The Economics of Underdevelopment*, O.U.P., 1963, pp. 400–49. This essay first appeared in 1954.

2 Unless, of course, one relaxes the assumption of a 'closed' economy and introduces into the picture other coexisting economies, which themselves have 'unlimited' supplies of labour.

3 See the discussion in Lewis, op. cit., pp. 431–3, and in A. P. Thirlwall, *Growth and Development: With Special Reference to Developing Economies*, 2nd edition, Macmillan, 1978, p. 96.

4 R. Pipes, *Russia Under the Old Regime*, Penguin, 1974, p. 167.

5 S. M. Dubrovsky, *Selskoe khozyaistvo i krestyanstvo Rossii v period imperializma*, Nauka, 1975, p. 147.

6 G. T. Robinson, *Rural Russia Under the Old Regime*, 1932, reprinted Univ. of California Press, 1973, pp. 109–11. One estimate put the labour 'surplus' at 25 m. in 1906 (that is, 7 m. workers for whom there was 'not enough work to go round', and 17.5 m. dependants). See V. P. Litvinov-Falinsky, *Nashe ekonomicheskoe polozhenie i zadachi budushchego*, St. Petersburg, 1908, p. 55. There is a useful general discussion of various other contemporary estimates of the 'surplus' in P. P. Maslov, *Perenaselenie russkoi derevni*, Gosizdat, 1930.

7 The standard liberal accounts of emancipation are to be found in Robinson, op. cit., chapter 5, and in A. Gerschenkron, 'Agrarian policies and industrialization, Russia, 1861–1917', in M. M. Postan and H. J. Habakkuk, eds., *Cambridge Economic History of Europe*, vol. 6, part 2, C.U.P., 1965, pp. 728–30.

8 Robinson, op. cit., p. 99. The other classic English-language source for this interpretation of peasant farming is G. A. Pavlovsky, *Agricultural Russia Before the Revolution*, Routledge, 1930, chapter 4. There is a graphic description of the effects of population growth in a report from Kovno province, dated 1894: 'Woods and land are here taking the form of thin strips [*shnury*, literally laces]. If a peasant has three sons, he divides each piece into three portions, such that the small plots of land are impossible to work effectively. As a result, they give poor yields.' Quoted in S. M. Dubrovsky, *Stolypinskaya zemelnaya reforma*, Nauka, 1963, p. 67.

9 This is the approach favoured by Pavlovsky, in particular, Gerschenkron tends to emphasize the inability of peasants to finance new investment, because their income was squeezed by taxation; but it may be suggested

that some improvements in technique and organization of production required only modest application of capital.

10 It must be emphasized that this picture is a necessarily aggregated one, and rests largely on the situation in central European Russia. For an attempt at disaggregation, see Chapter Four.

11 Gerschenkron, op. cit., p. 754; idem, 'Problems and patterns of Russian economic development', in C. E. Black, ed., *The Transformation of Russian Society*, Harvard U.P., 1960, pp. 48–9, reprinted in his volume of essays entitled *Economic Backwardness in Historical Perspective*, Harvard U.P., 1962, pp. 119–51.

12 This is a central argument in the work of Gerschenkron, and of von Laue: see T. H. von Laue, *Sergei Witte and the Industrialization of Russia*, Columbia U.P., 1963

13 See Chapter Four for further discussion.

14 For Witte's attitude see the brief remarks in H. T. Willetts, 'The agrarian problem', in G. Katkov et al., eds., *Russia Enters the Twentieth Century*, Temple Smith, 1971, pp. 125–8, and D. Atkinson, *The End of the Russian Land Commune, 1905–1930*, Stanford U.P., 1983, pp. 34–7. The views of some liberal economists, notably A. A. Kaufman, are discussed in L. Volin, *A Century of Russian Agriculture*, Harvard U.P., 1970, pp. 61–2. For a valuable Soviet analysis see M. S. Simonova 'Problema 'oskudeniya' tsentra i ee rol v formirovanii agrarnoi politiki samoderzhaviya v 90kh godakh XIX – nachale XXv.', in *Problemy sotsialno-ekonomicheskoi istorii Rossii*, Nauka, 1971, pp. 236–63.

15 It does not follow that all commentators adhered to a laisser-faire programme, on classical nineteenth-century liberal lines; many businessmen and economists supported tariff protection and government subsidies. But these spokesmen can, none the less, be distinguished as 'liberals', in their support for an industrialization policy designed to absorb a labour surplus. The following works may be considered representative of the contemporary liberal viewpoint: P. P. Migulin, *Russkii gosudarstvennyi kredit*, 3 vols., Kharkov, 1901–3; D. Mendeleev, *K poznaniyu Rossii*, 3rd edition, St. Petersburg, 1906; Litvinov-Falinsky, op. cit.; V. I. Grinevetskii, *Poslevoennyie perspektivy russkoi promyshlennosti*, Vserossiiskii Tsentralnyi Soyuz Potrebitelnykh Obschestv, Kharkov, 1919.

16 T. H. von Laue, 'A secret memorandum of Sergei Witte on the industrialization of Imperial Russia', *Journal of Modern History*, no. 26, 1954, pp. 60–74.

17 ibid., p. 71.

18 For a general introduction to populist economic thought see the following: A. P. Mendel, *Dilemmas of Progress in Tsarist Russia: Legal Populism and Legal Marxism*, Harvard U.P., 1961; A. Walicki, *The Controversy Over Capitalism: Studies in the Social Philosophy of the Russian Populists*, O.U.P., 1969; S. Schwartz, 'Populism and early Russian marxism on ways of economic development in Russia', in E. J. Simmons, ed., *Continuity and Change in Russian and Soviet Thought*, Harvard U.P., 1955, pp. 40–62; M. Bleaney, *Underconsumption Theories*, Lawrence and Wishart, 1976, chapter 7; S. Amato, 'The debate between marxists and legal populists on the problems of the market and industrialization in Russia (1882–1899), and its classical foundations', *J.E.E.H.*, no. 12, 1983,

pp. 119–44; G. Kitching, *Development and Underdevelopment in Historical Perspective*, Methuen, 1982.

19 A. von Haxthausen, *Studies on the Interior of Russia*, ed., S. F. Starr, Chicago U.P., 1972; see also F. Venturi, *Roots of Revolution: A History of Populist and Socialist Movements in Nineteenth-Century Russia*, 1960, reissued by University of Chicago, 1983, chapters 1 and 3.

20 Cited in R. Wortman, *The Crisis of Russian Populism*, C.U.P., 1967, p. 58.

21 The references are to N. F. Danielson, *Ocherki nashego poreformennogo khozyaistva*, St. Petersburg, 1893, partially reprinted in N. K. Karataev, ed., *Narodnicheskaya ekonomicheskaya literatura*, Sotsekgiz, 1958, pp. 482–572; and to V. P. Vorontsov, *Sudba kapitalizma v Rossii*, St. Petersburg, 1882.

22 See the discussion in Mendel, op. cit., pp. 9–24. Mikhailovsky distinguished between 'technical' division of labour (that is, functional specialization, dictated by the requirements of the job in hand), and 'social' division of labour, which was imposed by convention or force.

23 Amato, op. cit.; Mendel, op. cit., p. 276.

24 Vorontsov, in Karataev, op. cit., pp. 529, 539, 553, 563.

25 For Yuzhakov, see Mendel, op. cit., p. 46. See, in addition, Chapter 5, section 5.6b.

26 These are the words of State Controller Lobko, as cited in von Laue, *Sergei Witte*, p. 220.

27 Mendel, op. cit., pp. 49–50; Maslov, op. cit., pp. 18–19, 122–3; I. Kh. Ozerov, *Na temy dnya: k ekonomicheskomu polozheniyu Rossii*, 1912. For the 1920s see A. Erlich, *The Soviet Industrialization Debate, 1924–1928*, Harvard U.P., 1960. The relationship between these ideas and contemporary development economics needs still to be disentangled; for a useful attempt see Kitching, op. cit.

28 A. V. Chayanov, *The Theory of Peasant Economy*, R. D. Irwin, 1966, p. 41. This volume is an English edition of one of Chayanov's major writings, *Organizatsiya krestyanskogo khozyaistva*, first published in 1925.

29 ibid, p. 48.

30 S. G. Solomon, *The Soviet Agrarian Debate: A Controversy in Social Science, 1923–1929*, Westview Press, 1977; M. Harrison, 'Chayanov and the economics of the Russian peasantry', *J.P.S.*, no. 2, 1975, pp. 389–417; idem, 'The peasant mode of production in the work of A. V. Chayanov', *J.P.S.*, no. 4, 1977, pp. 323–36; T. Shanin, *The Awkward Class: Political Sociology of Peasantry in a Developing Society, Russia, 1910–1925*, O.U.P., 1972.

31 S. Pollard, *Peaceful Conquest: The Industrialization of Europe, 1760–1970*, O.U.P., 1981, p. 240.

32 Von Laue, *Sergei Witte*; R. Portal, 'The industrialization of Russia', in *Cambridge Economic History of Europe*, op. cit., pp. 801–72.

33 Shanin, op. cit., pp. 137, 140.

34 K. Marx, *Capital*, 3 volumes, 1867–95; Volume 1, Penguin, 1976. See also K. Marx and F. Engels, *Manifesto of the Communist Party*, 1848, reprinted in Marx and Engels, *Selected Works in One Volume*, Lawrence and Wishart, 1973, pp. 35–63.

35 Marx, 'Preface to the first German edition of *Capital*', in *Selected Works*, op. cit., p. 228.

36 Haruki Wada, 'Marx and revolutionary Russia', in T. Shanin, ed., *Late Marx and the Russian Road*, Routledge, 1983, pp. 40–76. The quotation is from a letter from Marx to Danielson, dated 15 November 1878, cited in ibid., p. 58.

37 ibid, pp. 98–126 for the drafts and the final letter; p. 124 for the quotation in the text, from Marx's final reply. Among the 'poisonous influences' that Marx had in mind were the state, merchants and kulaks. How the state was to be removed was, of course, the key question, and one that Marx did not examine.

38 ibid, pp. 138–9, preface to the second Russian edition of the Communist Manifesto, dated 1882.

39 For further discussion consult Hal Draper, *Karl Marx's Theory of Revolution: State and Bureaucracy*, Monthly Review Press, 1977, chapter 23.

40 Apart from the writings of Lenin, cited below, see Neil Harding, *Lenin's Political Thought: Theory and Practice in the Democratic and Socialist Revolutions*, Macmillan, 1983, part 1, chapter 4.

41 V. I. Lenin, *The Development of Capitalism in Russia*, Progress Publishers, 1977; G. V. Plekhanov, 'Our differences', in *Selected Philosophical Works*, 5 vols., Foreign Languages Publishing House, 1961, vol. 1, pp. 166–399; I. Hourwich, *The Economics of the Russian Village*, 1892, reprinted by AMS Press, 1970.

42 Lenin, op. cit., pp. 68, 175–6, 184. The internal market could also be extended 'in breadth', by colonial expansion into Central Asia and Siberia: ibid., pp. 599–601.

43 V. I. Lenin, *The Agrarian Programme of Russian Social Democracy in the First Russian Revolution, 1905–1907*, written in 1907, published in 1917, Progress Publishers, 1977, p. 190. Lenin noted that the argument about feudal landholding did not apply to the periphery, that is Trans-Volga, New Russia and the North Caucasus: ibid., p. 26.

44 ibid., p. 25.

45 But note the discussion in Lenin, *Development*, pp. 539–42, where he refers to the 'appendage to the factory', that is small-scale, cottage enterprise, to which the factory may give rise. 'The development of forms of industry, like that of social relationships in general, cannot but proceed very gradually, among a mass of interlocking, transitional forms and seeming reversions to the past'.

46 V. I. Lenin, *Imperialism, the Highest Stage of Capitalism*, 1917, Foreign Languages Press, Peking, 1975, p. 96.

47 Among Lenin's writings in 1917, see 'The threatening catastrophe and how to combat it', and 'Can the Bolsheviks retain state power?'.

48 See V. I. Shunkov, ed., *Perekhod ot feodalizma k kapitalizma v Rossii*, Nauka, 1969; P. I. Lyashchenko, *A History of the National Economy of Russia to the 1917 Revolution*, Macmillan, 1949. For an emphasis upon government decision-making, however, see L. G. Zakharova, 'Pravitelstvennaya programma otmeny krepostnogo prava v Rossii', *Istoriya SSSR*, no. 2, 1975, pp. 22–47.

49 I. D. Kovalchenko and L. V. Milov, *Vserossiiskii agrarnyi rynok, XVIII-nachalo XXvv.*, Nauka, 1974.
50 See the discussion in *Ob osobennostyakh agrarnogo stroya Rossii v period imperializma*, Nauka, 1962.
51 *Voprosy istorii kapitalisticheskoi Rossii (problema mnogoukladnosti)*, Nauka, Sverdlovsk, 1972.
52 I. F. Gindin, *Gosudarstvennyi bank i ekonomicheskaya politika tsarskogo pravitelstva, 1861–1892gg.*, Gosfinizdat, 1960; idem, 'Sotsialno-ekonomicheskie itogi razvitiya rossiiskogo kapitalizma i predposylki revolyutsii v nashei strane', in I. I. Mints, ed., *Sverzhenie samoderzhaviya*, Nauka, 1970, pp. 39–88; idem, 'O nekotorykh osobennostyakh ekonomicheskoi i sotsialnoi struktury rossiiskogo kapitalizma v nachale XXv.', *Istoriya SSSR*, no. 3, 1966, pp. 48–66.

Chapter Two (pp. 29–47)

1 A. Gerschenkron, 'Agrarian policies and industrialization, Russia 1861–1917', in M. M. Postan and H. J. Habakkuk, eds., *Cambridge Economic History of Europe*, vol. 6, part 2, C.U.P., 1965, pp. 757–8. See also the remarks in O. Crisp, *Studies in the Russian Economy before 1914*, Macmillan, 1976, pp. 93–4. In 1858, when the Tenth 'Revision' or census of the tax-paying population was conducted, the total number of serfs was put at 21 million. State peasants were thought to number 20 million. Peasants belonging to the Imperial Family (so-called appanage or *udelnyie* peasants) amounted to just over 2 million. The total estimated population was around 59 million in 1858. All these figures refer to 49 provinces of European Russia. Other estimates, however, suggest that state peasants may have outnumbered privately owned serfs. See P. A. Khromov, *Ekonomicheskoe razvitie Rossii v XIX–XX vekakh*, Gospolitizdat, 1950, p. 83, and J. Blum, *Lord and Peasant in Russia from the Ninth to the Nineteenth Centuries*, Princeton, 1961, pp. 476–7 and chapters 21–23 passim.
2 For further details see Chapter Three.
3 This point is discussed further in Chapter Four. Details on migration and employment will be found in Chapter Three.
4 S. N. Prokopovich, *Opyt ischisleniya narodnogo dokhoda 50 gubernii Evropeiskoi Rossii*, Soviet Vserossiiskikh kooperativnykh sezdov, Moscow, 1918; M. E. Falkus, 'Russia's national income, 1913: a revaluation', *Economica*, no. 35, 1968, pp. 52–73. See also A. Kaufman, 'The history and development of the official statistics of Russia', in J. Koren, ed., *The History of Statistics*, Franklin, New York, 1918, pp. 469–534; and A. L. Vainshtein, *Narodnyi dokhod Rossii i SSSR*, Nauka, part one.
5 P. Gregory, *Russian National Income, 1885–1913*, C.U.P., 1982.
6 The growth of population is discussed in Chapter Three.
7 A good general guide to world literacy rates is C. M. Cipolla, *Literacy and development in the west*, Penguin, 1969. See also pp. 161–2 below.
8 A sense of ethnic heterogeneity in imperial Russia may be obtained from H. Rogger, *Russia in the Age of Modernization and Revolution, 1881–1917*, Longman, 1982, chapter 9. For Russian geography, it is best

to turn to the maps in the *Oxford Regional Economic Atlas: USSR and Eastern Europe*, O.U.P., 1956.

9 M. L. de Tengoborsky, *Commentaries on the Productive Forces of Russia*, 2 vols., London, 1856; D. Mackenzie Wallace, *Russia*, London, 1912; *Baedeker's Russia 1914*, repr. Allen and Unwin, 1971.

10 See the table in Falkus, op. cit., p. 55.

11 Some details on educational provision will be found in H. Seton-Watson, *The Russian Empire, 1801–1917*, O.U.P., 1967, pp. 359–60, 477. In 1904, around 5.3 million children between the ages of seven and eleven attended state or church elementary schools; this represented just over one-quarter of the total number of children in this age-range. For details on rural literacy (in 1897, 17 per cent of the juvenile and adult rural population was literate) and urban literacy (the corresponding figure was 45 per cent), see A. G. Rashin, *Naselenie Rossii za 100 let*, Gosstatizdat, 1956, pp. 293, 297.

12 Gregory, op. cit., p. 130. There is some discussion of urban mortality in Chapter Three.

13 R. H. Gorlin, 'Problems of tax reform in imperial Russia', *Journal of Modern History*, no. 49, 1977, pp. 246–65.

14 Gregory, op. cit., pp. 146–7, 175. An article in *Vestnik finansov*, no. 29, 1915, pp. 93–103 ('O podokhodnom naloge'), by N. Pokrovsky, gave the following breakdown of incomes:

Income (rubles)	Number of people with incomes of 1000 rubles and more	Percentage of total number assessed
1,000–2,000	397,000	57
2,000–5,000	216,000	31
5,000–10,000	52,000	8
10,000–20,000	20,000	3
20,000–50,000	9,000	1
>50,000	4,000	<1

15 R. Pipes, *Russia Under The Old Regime*, Penguin, 1974, p. 179.

16 Evidence of the differentiation of the gentry will be found in A. P. Korelin, *Dvoryanstvo v poreformennoi Rossii*, Nauka, 1979, p. 62.

17 See Chapter Three, section 3.

18 Rashin, op. cit. pp. 206–7.

19 See the discussion in A. Kahan, 'Determinants of the incidence of literacy in rural nineteenth-century Russia', in C. A. Anderson and M. J. Bowman, eds., *Education and Economic Development*, Cass, 1965, pp. 298–302.

20 R. E. Zelnik, *Labor and Society in Tsarist Russia: The Factory Workers of St. Petersburg, 1855–1870*, Stanford University Press, 1971, chapter 7; J. H. Bater, *St. Petersburg: Industrialization and Change*, Edward Arnold, 1976, chapter 7.

21 Bater, op. cit.; D. Koenker, *Moscow Workers and the 1917 Revolution*, Princeton U.P., 1981, chapter 1.

22 The Pale of Settlement comprised 15 provinces in south and west Russia, together with 10 provinces in the Kingdom of Poland. See Rogger, op. cit., p. 200.

23 ibid.; and H. Rogger, 'Government, Jews, peasants and land in post-emancipation Russia', *Cahiers du monde russe et soviétique*, no. 17, 1976, pp. 5–25 and 171–211. Between 1881 and 1914, some two million Jews left Russia; to set this in context, the 1897 Census put the total number of Jews in the Empire at five million.

24 N. Stone, *The Eastern Front, 1914–1917*, Hodder and Stoughton, 1975, pp. 18, 37, 40–2. It may be noted that some contemporaries believed that it was the agrarian resources of Russia, rather than Russian industrial capacity, that conferred upon her the likely advantage over other European powers, in the event of war.

25 Vainshtein published the major work on the Russian capital stock in 1913: A. L. Vainshtein, *Narodnoe bogatstvo i narodnokhozyaistvennoe nakoplenie predrevolyutsionnoi Rossii*, Gosstatizdat, 1960; Strumilin undertook several studies of tsarist retail trade, employment and investment (S. G. Strumilin, *Statistiko-ekonomicheskie ocherki*, Gosstatizdat, 1958); and Kondratiev compiled an index of industrial production (amongst his many other activities), which is discussed in Chapter Five, and, in more detail, by Goldsmith (see the following note).

26 R. Goldsmith, 'The economic growth of tsarist Russia, 1860–1913', *Economic Development and Cultural Change*, no. 9, 1961, pp. 441–75. This rate of growth was faster than that of Britain, France and Italy; nearly as fast as Germany; but behind that of Japan and the U.S.A., where output grew by around 4 per cent per annum in roughly the same period. ibid., p. 474.

27 Both scholars put the rate at 2 per cent per annum in 1860–80.

28 Gregory, op. cit., pp. 70, 78.

29 ibid., pp. 72–9, where Gregory explains his estimate of national income by sector of origin. Note that Gregory accepts the Goldsmith estimates of the growth of industrial production.

30 Gregory, op. cit., Appendix H; see also Chapter Four.

31 ibid., pp. 75–6, 83–4; and Chapter Four.

32 Productivity in Russian agriculture is discussed in Chapter Four, section 3; for industry, see Chapter Five, sections 1 and 5.

33 Gregory, op. cit., pp. 134–7, 189–91.

34 ibid., pp. 130–1.

35 T. H. Von Laue, 'The state and the economy', in C. E. Black, ed., *The Transformation of Russian Society*, Harvard U.P., 1960, pp. 209–25; A. Ermansky, 'Krupnaya burzhuaziya do 1905 goda', in L. Martov et al., eds., *Obshchestvennoe dvizhenie v Rossii v nachale XX veka*, St. Petersburg, 1909, vol. 1, pp. 313–48. One must not exaggerate the total assets of the state and the imperial family, relative to private holdings. Vainshtein estimated that the state's share of total capital stock in 1914 did not exceed 10 per cent – this, notwithstanding the fact that most railways were state-owned. The proportion in Germany was closer to 20 per cent, according to J. Kocka, 'Capitalism and bureaucracy in German industrialization before 1914', *Ec.H.R.*, no. 34, 1981, pp. 453–68.

36 The *indirect* role played by the Russian government is another matter: see Chapter Five. For the general point made in this paragraph, see A. Kahan, 'Government policies and the industrialization of Russia', *J.Ec.H.*, no. 27,

1967, pp. 460–77. Similar general points were made by leading liberal economists at the time, including Ozerov and Migulin.
37 Gregory, op. cit., pp. 129, 137; and P. Gregory, '1913 Russian national income: some insights into Russian economic development', *Quarterly Journal of Economics*, no. 90, 1976, pp. 445–60.
38 Cited in A. P. Mendel, *Dilemmas of Progress in Tsarist Russia: Legal Populism and Legal Marxism*, Harvard U.P., 1961, pp. 39–40.

Chapter Three (pp. 48–97)

1 The population of European Russia (50 provinces) grew from 61 million to 122 million in the same period, 1860–4 to 1909–13. Thus, population growth in the periphery, in particular in Siberia and Central Asia, was more rapid than in European Russia. This resulted largely from migration to the periphery. Figures on population change are taken from A. G. Rashin, *Naselenei Rossii za sto let (1811–1913): statisticheskie ocherki*, Gosstatizdat, 1956, p. 25; P. A. Khromov, *Ekonomicheskoe razvitie Rossii v XIX–XX vekakh*, Gospolitizdat, 1950, pp. 452–5. For international comparisons see P. R. Gregory, *Russian National Income, 1885–1913*, C.U.P., 1982, p. 162.
2 For general introductions see H. J. Habakkuk, *Population Growth and Economic Development since 1750*, Leicester U.P., 1974; M. W. Flinn, *The European Demographic System, 1500–1820*, Harvester, 1981; W. R. Lee, ed., *European Demography and Economic Growth*, Croom Helm, 1979.
3 Russian population statistics derive from three main sources. Annual figures on population size and vital rates were issued by the tsarist government from 1867 onwards. They derived from records kept by provincial and municipal authorities. However, these records were incomplete, because the clergy who recorded information did no more than send abstracts from their registers to higher authorities. In any case, not all vital events were solemnized in the Church. The second source is the register of peasant households, kept by the government as a record of the population that was liable for taxes and military service. These so-called 'revisions' began during the reign of Peter the Great, the first being conducted in 1724. The final, Tenth Revision took place in 1859. Thereafter, government officials calculated the net addition to this population, by using information furnished by the police and local administrative bodies. Finally, a comprehensive census of the population of the Russian Empire took place in 1897. For details, see M. M. Kovalevsky, *Modern Customs and Ancient Laws of Russia*, 1891; A. A. Kaufman, 'The history and development of the official Russian statistics', in J. Koren, ed., *The History of Statistics*, Franklin, New York, 1918, pp. 480–4, 491–2.
4 See A. Armengaud, 'Population in Europe, 1700–1914', in C. Cipolla, ed., *The Fontana Economic History of Europe*, vol. 3, Collins-Fontana, 1973; and the editor's introduction in Lee, ed., op. cit.
5 A. J. Coale, B. Anderson and E. Härm, *Human Fertility in Russia since the Nineteenth Century*, Princeton U.P., 1979. See also H. Chojnacka, 'Nuptiality patterns in an agrarian society', *Population Studies*, no. 30, 1976, pp. 203–26; J. Hajnal, 'European marriage patterns in perspective',

n D. V. Glass and D. E. C. Eversley, eds., *Population in History*, Edward Arnold, 1965, pp. 101–43.

6 For the anecdotes about serf marriage see P. A. Kropotkin, *Memoirs of a Revolutionist*, Dover Publications, 1971 (first published 1899), pp. 52–4. For marriage patterns during the sixteenth and seventeenth centuries see R. E. F. Smith, *Peasant Farming in Muscovy*, C.U.P., 1977, pp. 81, 221. Serf marriage patterns are discussed in B. N. Mironov, 'Traditsionnoe demograficheskoe povedenie krestyan v XIX–XX vv.' and in A. G. Vishnevsky, 'Rannie etapy stanovleniya novogo tipa rozhdaemosti v Rossii', both in A. G. Vishnevsky, ed., *Brachnost rozhdaemost i smertnost v Rossii i v SSSR*, Statistika, 1977, pp. 90–1, 113.

7 Cited in Mironov, op. cit., p. 86.

8 The household that lost a daughter through marriage clearly lost her labour at the same time. However, as a wife, she would henceforth be supported by her husband, who would in principle be able to claim a portion of allotment land from the village community on behalf of the conjugal unit. It is also worth noting that many peasant marriages took place in October, suggesting that the bride's parents ensured that they retained her labour until the harvest had been gathered in. For contemporary discussion of the status and role of peasant women see A. Efimenko, *Issledovaniya narodnoi zhizni*, Moscow, 1884, p. 73 ('There is no special respect at all for women, for their dignity as human beings'). Some discussion in English will be found in I. Hourwich, *The Economics of the Russian Village*, New York, 1892, reprinted by AMS Press, 1970, p. 97; and M. Matossian, 'The peasant way of life', in W. Vucinich, ed., *The Peasant in Nineteenth-Century Russia*, Stanford, U.P., 1968, pp. 16–20.

9 Chojnacka, op. cit.; Mironov, op. cit., p. 96; Vishnevsky, op. cit., p. 133; Coale, Anderson and Härm, op. cit., pp. 16, 20–1. Rashin, op. cit., pp. 182–3 gives much lower figures for the average number of births per marriage, suggesting some degree of under-registration in his original data. Furthermore, his data relate to 1910, by which time the 'fertility decline' in Russia was already under way.

10 Chojnacka, op. cit., p. 212fn.; Mironov, op. cit.

11 According to a Russian peasant proverb, 'By keeping my parents I repay my debts'. Cited in T. Shanin, *The Awkward Class: Political Sociology of Peasantry in a Developing Society, Russia 1910–1925*, p. 222fn.

12 G. A. Pavlovsky, *Agricultural Russia on the Eve of the Revolution*, Routledge, 1930, p. 83. See also D. Heer, 'The demographic transition in the Russian Empire and the Soviet Union', *Jl. Social History*, no. 1, 1968, pp. 228–9.

13 D. Atkinson, *The End of the Russian Land Commune, 1905–1930*, Stanford U.P., 1983, pp. 30–2; see also Kovalevsky, op. cit., pp. 93–4. The weakness of the argument linking communal land tenure with high marital fertility is further compounded by the fact that fertility declined in Russia after the turn of the century, while the commune continued to function until the late 1920s. For the history of the commune after 1917, see Atkinson, op. cit., part V, and D. J. Male, *Russian Peasant Organization before Collectivization*, C.U.P., pp. 56ff.

14 Coale, Anderson and Härm, op. cit., pp. 63–6 (but see ibid., pp. 116–17); details on provincial patterns of fertility and infant mortality

derive from Rashin, op. cit., pp. 182–3, 195–6. For a restatement of the importance of infant mortality in determining fertility, see Heer, op. cit., p. 199.

15 Chojnacka, op. cit., pp. 213–5; A. Plakans, 'Peasant farmsteads and households in the Baltic littoral, 1797', *Comparative Studies in Society and History*, no. 17, 1975, pp. 2–35.

16 Vishnevsky, op. cit., p. 122.

17 Chojnacka, op. cit., p. 204.

18 For information on population density, see V. Z. Drobizhev et al., eds., *Istoricheskaya geografiya SSSR*, Vysshaya shkola, 1973, pp. 192–3. The Census of 1897 revealed that the density of population (per square *verst*) was as follows:

European Russia	
(non-black earth)	15.0 (1867 = 10.6)
(black earth)	31.0 (1867 = 20.0)
Western Siberia	1.7 (1867 = 1.0)
Central Asia (1867 territory)	3.0 (1867 = 1.7)

19 As the information in note 18 indicates, the impressive increase in the population of western Siberia (the result of immigration as well as natural growth) had only a modest impact on the density of settlement. By 1914, the population density in Tomsk province was still only one-fifth of the average for European Russia, and this was the most densely settled part of Siberia. For details, see L. M. Goryushkin, *Agrarnyie otnosheniya v Sibiri perioda imperializma, 1900–1917gg.*, Nauka, Novosibirsk, 1976, p. 138.

20 See note 18.

21 This is discussed in M. K. Karakhanov, 'Demograficheskie protsessy v Srednei Azii vo vtoroi polovine XIX stoletiya', in Vishnevsky, ed., op. cit., p. 211, and in Coale, Anderson and Härm, op. cit., chapter 3.

22 Coale has demonstrated that nuptiality in European Russia (in his notation, I_m), fell from 0.70 in 1897 to 0.63 in 1926. This is measured against the Hutterite 'norm' of 1.0 (see p. 52, above). The rate of marital fertility (I_g) fell from 0.76 to 0.67. ibid., pp. 20–3.

23 Evidence on nuptiality is presented in Table 3.2. Overall, the proportion of women in European Russia who married before their 21st birthday fell from 57.4 per cent (1867–70) to 56 per cent (1900) and 54.5 per cent (by 1910). However, this tendency was hardly evident at all in the most populous regions (Central Black-Earth, Lower Volga and New Russia).

24 Heer, op. cit., pp. 228–30; see also Chapter Four, p. 124.

25 Heer, op. cit., pp. 198–9; Mironov, op. cit., p. 103; Coale, Anderson and Härm, op. cit., pp. 116–7.

26 Mironov, op. cit., *passim*; Coale, Anderson and Härm, op. cit., pp. 115–7; Heer, op. cit., *passim*. Trends in literacy in tsarist Russia are best gauged from the statistics on army recruits. In 1875–80, 21 per cent of recruits were able to read or write; by 1909–13 the average had jumped to 66 per cent. Rashin, op. cit., p. 304.

27 Details in R. E. Johnson, *Peasant and Proletarian: The Working Class of Moscow in the Late Nineteenth Century*, Leicester, U.P., 1979, pp. 56–61; D. Koenker, *Moscow Workers and the 1917 Revolution*,

Princeton U.P., 1981, pp. 57–8. See also J. H. Bater, *St. Petersburg: Industrialization and Change*, Edward Arnold, pp. 111–12, 255–6.

28 Rashin, op. cit., pp. 210–11. Even when doctors did penetrate the village, they found suspicion and hostility. After reading some doctors' accounts of their techniques, one can understand why. For one account of the interaction of doctors and peasant patients, see G. Gorer and J. Rickman, *The People of Great Russia: A Psychological Study*, Cresset Press, 1949.

29 Kurkin demonstrated that two-fifths of infant deaths in Moscow province took place in June, July and August. He related this in turn to the frequency of conceptions in the village during the late spring and summer – the result, so he argued, of *otkhodniki* returning to the fields and thus to their wives. Is there, perhaps, a hint here of the populist lament for the older, more stable Russian village? P. I. Kurkin, *Detskaya smertnost v Moskovskoi gubernii i ee uezdakh v 1883–1897gg.*, Moscow, 1902, p. 101. See also V. I. Grebenshchikov and D. A. Sokolov, *Smertnost v Rossii i borba s neyu*, St. Petersburg, 1901; and S. A. Glebovskii and V. I. Grebenshchikov, *Detskaya smertnost v Rossii*, St. Petersburg, 1907, pp. 37ff. The efforts of government and intelligentsia to devise a system of rural midwives are discussed in S. C. Ramer, 'Childbirth and culture: midwifery in the nineteenth-century Russian countryside', in D. Ransel, ed., *The Family in Imperial Russia*, Illinois U.P., 1978, pp. 218–35.

30 P. Gregory, 'Grain marketings and peasant consumption in Russia, 1885–1913', *E.E.H.*, no. 17, 1980, p. 148. Cf. Heer, op. cit., p. 219. S. G. Wheatcroft, 'A re-examination of the population dynamic and factors affecting it in the Soviet Union during the 1920s and 1930s', SIPS Discussion Paper, Centre for Russian and East European Studies, Birmingham University, 1976, pp. 86–101.

31 V. Zaitsev, 'Vliyanie kolebanii urozhaev na estestvennoe dvizhenie naseleniya', in V. G. Groman, ed., *Vliyanie neurozhaev na narodnoe khozyaistvo Rossii*, Priboi, 1927, vol. 1, pp. 3–59.

32 I. D. Kovalchenko and L. V. Milov, *Vserossiiskii agrarnyi rynok, nachalo XVIII–XXvv.*, Nauka, 1974, *passim*.

33 B.Ts. Urlanis, *Wars and Population*, Progress, 1971, pp. 46ff., 198; J. S. Curtiss, *The Russian Army Under Nicholas I*, Duke U.P., 1965, pp. 359–60; Wheatcroft, op. cit., p. 30.

34 F. Lorimer, *The Population of the Soviet Union*, League of Nations, Geneva, 1946, p. 30.

35 For details, consult Drobizhev et al., eds., pp. 167–75, 185–93.

36 ibid., p. 194.

37 For urbanization, see pp. 67–9 below. The best guide to internal migration is B. V. Tikhonov, *Pereseleniya v Rossii vo vtoroi polovine XIXv.*, Nauka, 1978. For the application of a model of 'modernization' to the 1897 Census material, see B. A. Anderson, *Internal Migration during Modernization in Late Nineteenth-Century Russia*, Princeton U.P., 1980.

38 Anderson, op. cit., chapter 4.

39 V. I. Lenin, *The Development of Capitalism in Russia*, Progress, 1977, p. 582.

40 G. T. Robinson, *Rural Russia Under the Old Regime*, University of California Press, 1973, pp. 109–11. But compare this negative appraisal

with the remarks of Lenin, op. cit., pp. 584–5. There is an implicit counterfactual question in the text, namely what fate would have befallen these migrants had they not left the central agricultural provinces?

41 One investigation suggested that Moscow *otkhodniki* in 1914–15 sent back around 50 per cent of their incomes, but this wartime level of repatriation may not be typical of peacetime. A survey conducted in 1907 among Moscow printers suggested that 46 per cent of the total maintained a plot of land, that virtually all of these sent money back home, and that the average sum represented 25 per cent of income. See L. A. Shlykov, 'Vliyanie otkhozhykh promyslov na selskom khozyaistve', *Vestnik selskogo khozyaistva*, nos. 2, 3, 5 and 6, 1915; and Johnson, op. cit., p. 42. There is further evidence on repatriation in Hourwich, op. cit., p. 88.

42 S. M. Dubrovsky, *Stolypinskaya zemelnaya reforma*, Nauka, 1963, pp. 390ff. For other estimates see D. Treadgold, *The Great Siberian Migration*, Princeton U.P., 1957, p. 34.

43 F.–X. Coquin, *La Sibérie: Peuplement et immigration paysanne au XIXe siècle*, Armand Colin, 1969, p. 729, quoting a report by I. Yamzin, written in 1912. The quotation in the text is taken from Tikhonov, op. cit., pp. 150–1. The problem of 'land hunger' is discussed in Chapter Four, pp. 109–12.

44 Treadgold, op. cit., p. 131. For further information on the growth of settlement and railway construction, see R. N. North, *Transport in Western Siberia*, University of British Columbia Press, 1979, chapter 3. North notes, however, that the growth in exports from Siberia outstripped the capacity of the railway.

45 Treadgold, op. cit., pp. 78–9. It is worth noting that the well-known statesman, M. M. Speransky, had – as early as 1821 – expressed concern about 'overpopulation' in European Russia, and had used this as justification for promoting settlement in Siberia (where, at the time, he was Governor-General).

46 Drobizhev et al., pp. 197–9. The 1867 figures are taken from *Statisticheskii vremennik Rossiiskoi imperii*, series 2, no. 1, 1871; those for 1897, from the summary of the Census; and the 1916 figures from *Selskoe khozyaistvo Rossii v XX v.*, ed. N. P. Oganovsky and N. D. Kondratev, 1923. The 1897 Census defined as a town any centre with more than 15,000 inhabitants.

47 Bater, op. cit., pp. 186–9, 342–53; S. A. Novoselskii, *Demografiya i statistika*, Statistika, 1978, p. 108. For high rates of mortality elsewhere, see L. Siegelbaum, 'The Odessa grain trade: a case-study in urban growth and development in tsarist Russia', *J.E.E.H.*, no. 9, 1980, pp. 113–51.

48 Bater, op. cit., p. 304; Johnson, op. cit., pp. 31–2; see also R. H. Rowland, 'Urban in-migration in late nineteenth-century Russia', in M. F. Hamm, ed., *The City in Russian History*, Lexington, 1976, pp. 115–24

49 J. H. Bater, 'Modernization and the municipality: Moscow and St Petersburg on the eve of the great war', in J. H. Bater and R. A. French, eds., *Studies in Russian Historical Geography*, Academic Press, 1983, vol. 2, pp. 305–27; Siegelbaum, op. cit., p. 118.

50 Bater, 'Modernization. .', op. cit., pp. 318–20; Siegelbaum, op. cit.; M. Miller, *The Economic Development of Russia, 1905–1914*, Cass, 1967, pp. 144–6. Miller notes the higher proportion of revenue that was

earmarked for debt repayments. Other scholars have pointed out that the towns also had to assume part of the burden of billeting troops.
51 Bater, 'Modernization. .', op. cit., pp. 316, 321; Siegelbaum, op. cit., *passim*; H. Rogger, *Russia in the Age of Modernization and Revolution, 1881–1917*, Longman, 1983, pp. 61–2. Bater makes a distinction between Moscow, where civic consciousness appears to have been reasonably developed, and St. Petersburg, where it was lacking.
52 R. Sifman, 'Dinamika chislennosti naseleniya Rossii za 1897–1914', in Vishnevsky, ed., *Brachnost*, op. cit., p. 78. These figures refer to total crossings, so there is an element of double-counting involved, in that some people left and re-entered the country more than once in a given year. But this behaviour was certainly uncommon. For a comment upon the economic significance of tourism, see Gregory, op. cit., pp. 325–30.
53 V. V. Obolensky-Osinsky, 'Emigration from and immigration into Russia', in W. F. Willcox, ed., *International Migrations*, National Bureau of Economic Research, 1931, vol. 2, pp. 521–85. Figures on (gross) migration from Europe are given in A. G. Kenwood and A. L. Lougheed, *The Growth of the International Economy, 1820–1960*, Allen and Unwin, 1971, p. 60. It has been pointed out, however, that a large proportion of emigrants (perhaps 30–40 per cent) returned to Europe sooner or later. Assuming, as one may, that the proportion was much lower among Russian emigrants, the contribution of Russia to total permanent emigration would be higher than 10 per cent. See J. D. Gould, 'European inter-continental emigration, 1815–1914: patterns and causes', *J.E.E.H.*, no. 8, 1979, p. 609.
54 Obolensky-Osinsky, op. cit., pp. 529, 543; Rogger, op. cit., chapter 9.
55 Lenin, op. cit., p. 104.
56 *ibid.*, p. 144; R. E. Johnson, 'Liberal professionals and professional liberals: the Zemstvo statisticians and their work', in T. Emmons and W. Vucinich, eds., *The Zemstvo in Russia*, C.U.P., 1983, pp. 343–64; E. Kingston-Mann, 'Marxism and Russian rural development: problems of evidence, experience and culture', *Amer.Hist.Rev.*, no. 86, 1981, pp. 731–52.
57 I. D. Kovalchenko, ed., *Massovyie istochniki po sotsialno-ekonomicheskoi istorii Rossii perioda kapitalizma*, Nauka, 1979, pp. 282–4; Shanin, op. cit., pp. 66–71; Hourwich, op. cit., pp. 15–16; N. N. Koronevskaya, *Byudzhetnyie obsledovaniya krestyanskogo khozyaistva v dorevolyutsionnoi Rossii*, Gosstatizdat, 1954, p. 6.
58 F. A. Shcherbina, *Krestyanskie byudzhety*, Voronezh, 1900, pp. 124ff., 198–9, 237. Cf. Shanin, op. cit., pp. 68–9. See also E. M. Wilbur, 'Was Russian peasant agriculture really that impoverished?', *J.Ec.H.*, no. 43, 1983, pp. 137–44.
59 S. M. Stepniak, *The Russian Peasantry: Their Agrarian Condition, Social Life and Religion*, 1888, p. 271.
60 Lenin, op. cit., pp. 104, 141, 150.
61 A. M. Anfimov, *Krestyanskoe khozyaistvo Evropeiskoi Rossii, 1881–1904*, Nauka, 1980, pp. 94ff. See Chapter Four for further discussion.
62 Lenin, op. cit., pp. 189, 196–7; Hourwich, op. cit., p. 77; Pavlovsky, op. cit., pp. 107, 200; I. D. Kovalchenko and N. B. Selunskaya, 'Labor rental in the manorial economy of European Russia at the end of the

nineteenth and the beginning of the twentieth century', *E. E. H.*, no. 18, 1981, pp. 1–20.

63 Lenin, op. cit., pp. 180, 187–9; see also Chapter Six. I have also benefited from an unpublished paper by P. Reading, Centre for Russian and East European Studies, University of Birmingham.

64 Lenin, op. cit., pp. 187–9, 200; idem, *The Agrarian Programme of Social Democracy in the First Russian Revolution, 1905–1907*, Progress, 1977, p. 36. This work was written in late 1907, but not published until 1917. See also Pavlovsky, op. cit., p. 108.

65 Lenin, *Development*, pp. 96–7; A. M. Anfimov, *Ekonomicheskoe polozhenie i klassovaya borba krestyanstva Evropeiskoi Rossii, 1881–1904*, Nauka, 1984, pp. 168–9; Yu. I. Smykov, *Krestyane Srednego Povolzhya v period kapitalizma*, Nauka, 1984.

66 The 1917 Agricultural Census counted 122,000 landless households in Siberia: Goryushkin, *Agrarnyie otnosheniya*, pp. 155ff., 188, 303–12; D. I. Budaev, *Smolenskaya derevnya v kontse XIX-nachale XXvv.*, Smolensk, 1972; Lenin, *Development*, pp. 108–11, 179–80; Hourwich, op. cit., pp. 101–2; Anfimov, *Krestyanskoe khozyaistvo*, p. 188. Anfimov notes that the middle peasant households devoted the spring crop to rye and potatoes; the rich sowed oats for their own horses or for sale to *izvoshchiki*.

67 See Chapter Six; Anfimov, *Ekonomicheskoe polozhenie*, p. 153 (making the point that agrarian capitalism was restrained in parts of European Russia); Lenin, *Development*, pp. 79, 81, 98.

68 Chapter Four, p. 115; Anfimov, *Krestyanskoe khozyaistvo*, pp. 138, 144–7; Hourwich, op. cit., pp. 65–6. So far as the *upravshchiki* were concerned, some populists drew attention to the remarkable fact that poor peasants 'hired' the labour of their wealthier neighbours – a bizarre conclusion.

69 Anfimov, *Ekonomicheskoe polozhenie*, p. 173.

70 Lenin, *Development*, pp. 73–7, 92, 154–7. The question of capital formation in agriculture is taken up in Chapter Six.

71 M. Sahlins, quoted in P. Worsley, *The Three Worlds: Culture and World Development*, Weidenfeld & Nicolson, 1984; p. 83. Lenin's remarks will be found in *Development*, p. 181.

72 Shanin, op. cit., p. 83.

73 ibid., pp. 73–5.

74 ibid., pp. 85–94. Note that the fission of households was not a characteristic of peasant society under serfdom, because the seigneur strove to keep the household intact and to prevent the formation of potentially weak economic units. See P. Czap, 'A large family, the peasant's greatest wealth', in R. Wall, ed., *Family Forms in Historic Europe*, C.U.P., 1983, pp. 105–51.

75 Shanin, op. cit., pp. 79–80, 97. See the remarks of Stepniak, quoted on p. 72.

76 A. V. Chayanov, *The Theory of Peasant Economy*, R. D. Irwin, 1966, pp. 68, 109–15; Shanin mentions other factors that influenced 'residual mobility', including natural disaster, the impact of the market (changes in the terms of trade) and the role of the state (as in the period of 'war communism' in 1918–20): Shanin, op. cit., pp. 114–15.

77 Shanin, op. cit., pp. 137, 140.

78 There is an important discussion of these issues in M. Harrison, 'Resource allocation and agrarian class formation: the problem of social mobility among Russian peasant households, 1880–1930', *J.P.S.*, no. 4, 1977, pp. 127–61. For western Europe see G. W. Grantham, 'Scale and organization in French farming, 1840–1880', in W. N. Parker and E. L. Jones, eds., *European Peasants and Their Markets*, Princeton U.P., 1975, pp. 293–326.

79 Razumov and Kovalchenko have demonstrated that the ability to rent land correlated closely with the ownership of farm equipment, but weakly with the availibility of household labour: *Massovyie istochniki*, p. 315.

80 A. G. Rashin, *Formirovanie rabochego klassa Rossii: istoriko-ekonomicheskie ocherki*, Sotseklit, 1958, p. 175.

81 ibid., p. 156; O. Crisp, 'Labour and industrialization', in P. Mathias and M. M. Postan, eds, *Cambridge Economic History of Europe*, vol. 7, part 2, C.U.P., 1978, pp. 330–1.

82 Rashin assumed that 50 per cent of the estimated number of rural craftsmen (*kustari*) were wage-earners. To this 2m. he added 1m. urban craftsmen (*remeslenniki*). Rashin, *Formirovanie*, pp. 149–52. For a review of Rashin's study, see G. Rimlinger, 'The expansion of the labor market in capitalist Russia, 1861–1917', *J.Ec.H.*, no. 21, 1961, pp. 208–15.

83 Crisp, 'Labour', pp. 342–3, 347 for further discussion; Rashin, *Formirovanie*, chapter 2. Note that the mining industry was subject to a separate inspectorate.

84 Crisp, 'Labour', pp. 347–9. Further information has been derived from L. E. Mints, *Trudovyie resursy SSSR*, Nauka, 1975, p. 39. The figures in Mints relate to the pre-1939 territory of the USSR, and have to be adjusted to take account of the territory of the Russian Empire.

85 R. E. Zelnik, 'The peasant and the factory', in W. Vucinich, ed., *The Peasant in Nineteenth-Century Russia*, Stanford, U.P., 1968, pp. 158–90. Zelnik notes that the decree issued by Peter was modified in 1752, and that the future attachment of peasants to factories was prohibited in 1762. In 1798 the status quo ante 1762 was restored; finally, in 1816, further acquisition of possessional labour was abolished, except for the metallurgical industry.

86 Quoted in R. E. Zelnik, *Labor and Society in Tsarist Russia; The Factory Workers of St. Petersburg, 1855–1870*, Stanford U.P., 1971, p. 29. See also M. I. Tugan-Baranovsky, *The Russian Factory in the Nineteenth Century*, R. D. Irwin, 1970, part 2, chapter 3.

87 J. S. Curtiss, 'The peasant and the army', in Vucinich, ed., op. cit., pp. 110–25; V. Yu. Krupyanskaya, *Kultura i byt rabochikh gornozavodskogo Urala, konets XIX – nachalo XXv.*, Nauka, 1971, chapter 1.

88 Kablukov is quoted in Lenin, *Development*, p. 542. See, in addition, the critical remarks in Tugan-Baranovsky, op. cit., p. 355.

89 A. Gerschenkron, 'Agrarian policies and industrialization in Russia, 1861–1917', in *Cambridge Economic History of Europe*, vol. 6, part 2, C.U.P., 1965, pp. 706–800; T. H. von Laue, 'Russian peasants in the factory, 1892–1904', *J.Ec.H.*, no. 21, 1961, pp. 61–80; idem, 'Russian labor between field and factory, 1892–1903', *California Slavic Studies*, no. 3, 1964, pp. 33–65.

90 Rashin, *Formirovanie*, pp. 327–8.

91 P. P. Maslov, *Agrarnyi vopros v Rossii*, 3rd edition, St Petersburg, 1906, pp. 413ff.; Robinson, op. cit., p. 107; Lenin, *Development*, chapter 3, part 11.

92 Maslov, op. cit., pp. 416–23; T. Mixter, 'Perceptions of agricultural labor and hiring market disturbances in Saratov, 1872–1905', *Russian History*, no. 7, 1980, pp. 139–68.

93 Maslov, op. cit., pp. 428–31; Lenin, *Development*, pp. 252–4, 554, 582, 592ff.; Tikhonov, op. cit., pp. 6–14.

94 E. M. Dementev, *Fabrika: chto ona daet naseleniyu i chto ona ot nego beret*, 1893. This work is discussed at some length in Tugan-Baranovsky, op. cit.; see, in addition, Rashin, *Formirovanie*, pp. 566, 571.

95 S. N. Prokopovich, 'Krestyanstvo i poreformennaya fabrika', in A. K. Dzhivelegov et al., eds., *Velikaya reforma: russkoe obshchestvo i krestyanskii vopros v proshlom i nastoyashchem*, 1911, vol. 6, pp. 268–76; Rashin, *Formirovanie*, pp. 483–5, 545.

96 S. P. Turin, *From Peter the Great to Lenin: A History of the Russian Labour Movement with Special Reference to Trade Unionism*, Cass, 1935 (repr. 1968), pp. 34, 39, 185–6; Tugan-Baranovsky, op. cit., pp. 357–8; Crisp, 'Labour', pp. 378–80; Johnson, *From Peasant to Proletarian*, pp. 81–2.

97 Tugan-Baranovsky, op. cit., p. 335; Rashin, *Formirovanie*, p. 445; 'A.R'., 'Rabochie Sormovskikh zavodov', *Narodnoe khozyaistvo*, no. 5, 1902, p. 90.

98 Yu. I. Kiryanov, *Zhiznennyi uroven rabochikh Rossii (konets XIX-nachalo XXv.)*, Nauka, 1979, p. 227 and chapter 4, *passim*; Johnson, op. cit., pp. 84–7.

99 Johnson, op. cit., pp. 70–1, 91–2; Crisp, 'Labour', pp. 376–8; Rashin, *Formirovanie*, chapter 16; A. M. Pankratova, 'Proletarizatsiya krestyanstva i ee rol v formirovanii promyshlennogo proletariata Rossii, 60–90e gg. XIXv.', *Ist.zap.*, no. 54, 1955, p. 206. For a comparable pattern of recruitment in nineteenth-century Germany see J. Lee, 'Labour in German industrialization,, in Mathias and Postan, eds., *Cambridge Economic History of Europe*, vol. 7, part 1, p. 452.

100 Johnson, op. cit., p. 83; Rashin, op cit., pp. 496ff.; S. A. Smith, *Red Petrograd: Revolution in the Factories, 1917–1918*, C.U.P., 1983, p. 20; L. M.Ivanov, 'Preemstvennost fabrichno-zavodskogo truda i formirovanie proletariata v Rossii', in idem, ed., *Rabochii klass i rabochee dvizhenie v Rossii, 1861–1917*, Nauka, 1966, pp. 95–6.

101 Rashin, op. cit., pp. 532–44; Smith, op. cit., p. 19; Ivanov, op. cit., referring to a survey of metalworkers, conducted in 1930; for a different view see Crisp, 'Labour', pp. 372–3.

102 Rashin, op. cit., p. 573; Smith, op. cit., pp. 17, 243 (noting other factors that also contributed to the decimation of the Petrograd proletariat in 1917–18).

103 Quoted in V. Bonnell, *Roots of Rebellion; Workers' Politics and Organization in St. Petersburg and Moscow, 1900–1914*, University of California Press, 1983, p. 54; see also Lenin, *Development*, p. 544.

104 Crisp, 'Labour', pp. 366–8; Johnson, op. cit., pp. 37–8; von Laue, 'Russian peasants', *passim*, for a somewhat more sanguine interpretation.

105 Kiryanov, op. cit., p. 117; *Statisticheskii sbornik za 1913–1917*, Trudy TsSu, 1921, part 1, pp. 118–27; Smith, op. cit., pp. 30–2.

106 Rashin, *Formirovanie*, p. 236; Smith, op. cit., pp. 23–7.

107 Tugan-Baranovsky, op. cit., pp. 312–3 (for the quotation); Turin, op. cit., pp. 93, 110; Bonnell, op. cit., *passim*; T. H. von Laue, 'Tsarist labour policy, 1895–1903', *Journal of Modern History*, no. 34, 1967, pp. 135–45.

108 Turin, op. cit., pp. 185–6; T. C. Owen, *Capitalism and Politics in Russia: A Social History of the Moscow Merchants, 1855–1905*, C.U.P., 1981, pp. 126–31; Tugan-Baranovsky, op. cit., pp. 320–32; G. Rimlinger, 'Autocracy and the factory order in early Russian industrialization', *J.Ec.H.*, no. 20, 1960, pp. 67–92.

109 For recent statements of a semi-populist character, see Johnson, op. cit., p. 161, and D. Brower, 'Labor violence in Russia in the late nineteenth century', *S.R.*, no. 41, 1982, pp. 417–31. Trotsky's analysis of the Russian proletariat is contained in *The History of the Russian Revolution*, Gollancz, 1934, chapters 1 and 3.

Chapter Four (pp. 98–140)

1 R. Goldsmith, 'The economic growth of tsarist Russia, 1860–1913' *Economic Development and Cultural Change*, no. 9, 1961, pp. 441–75; P. Gregory, *Russian National Income, 1885–1913*, C.U.P., 1982, pp. 70–77 and appendix H. For a survey of the primary data see I. D. Kovalchenko, ed., *Massovyie istochniki po sotsialno-ekonomicheskoi istorii Rossii perioda kapitalizma*, Nauka, 1979, chapter 7.

2 M. E. Falkus, 'Russia's national income, 1913: a revaluation', *Economica*, no. 35, 1968, pp. 52–73; Goldsmith, op. cit., pp. 444–5.

3 S. G. Wheatcroft, 'Grain production and utilization in Russia and the USSR before collectivization', unpublished Ph.D. thesis, University of Birmingham, 1980, part 1, chapter 4.

4 Details of regional trends in sowings are taken from A. S. Nifontov, *Zernovoe proizvodstvo Rossii vo vtoroi polovine XIX veka*, Nauka, 1974, pp. 157, 229.

5 See V. I. Lenin, *The Development of Capitalism in Russia*, Progress, 1977, pp. 294–5. On a national level, the area sown to potatoes grew fourfold between 1850 and 1900; yields rose by 50 per cent. In the Baltic, South-East and New Russia, sowings of grain and potatoes increased simultaneously, according to Nifontov, op. cit. For the potato as a sign of progressive methods, albeit limited in scope, see G. A. Pavlovsky, *Agricultural Russia on the Eve of the Revolution*, Routledge, 1930, p. 292; J. Pallot, 'Agrarian modernization on peasant farms in the era of capitalism', in J. H. Bater and R. A. French, eds., *Studies in Russian Historical Geography*, 2 vols., Academic Press, 1983, vol. 1, pp. 423–50; A. N. Antsiferov, *Russian Agriculture During the War*, Yale U.P., 1930, p. 51.

6 Lokhtin and Robinson agree on a figure of 36 per cent for the proportion of allotment land that lay fallow in 1880–9; Robinson follows Oganovsky in citing a figure of 32 per cent in 1903. P. Lokhtin, *Sostoyanie selskogo khozyaistva v Rossii sravnitelno s drugimi stranami*, St. Petersburg, 1901, pp. 145–6; G. T. Robinson, *Rural Russia Under the Old Regime*, University of California Press, 1972, p. 98. For the land 'reserve' before 1914, see

Pavlovsky, op. cit., pp. 43–59. Boundary land represented around seven per cent of arable during the 1920s, according to D. J. Male, *Russian Peasant Organization Before Collectivization*, C.U.P., 1971, p. 8. During the late eighteenth century, uncultivated land amounted to between 20 and 40 per cent of the total, according to M. Confino, *Systèmes agraires et progrès agricole: L'assolement triennal en Russie aux XVIIIᵉ–XIXᵉ siècles*, Mouton, 1969, pp. 365–6.

7 V. Z. Drobizhev et al., eds., *Istoricheskaya geografiya SSSR*, Vyshshaya shkola, 1973, pp. 205–11.

8 ibid., pp. 217–22; Pavlovsky, op. cit., chapter 10.

9 Details in Gregory, op. cit., pp. 89–93, and Appendices H, I and J. Compare A. Kahan, 'Capital formation in Russia, 1890–1913', in P. Mathias and M. M. Postan, eds., *Cambridge Economic History of Europe*, vol. 7, part 2, C.U.P., 1978, p. 280. On mechanization, see R. Munting, 'Mechanization and dualism in Russian agriculture', *J.E.E.H.*, no. 8, 1979, pp. 743–60.

10 J. Blum, *Lord and Peasant in Russia from the Ninth to the Nineteenth Century*, Princeton U.P., 1961, p. 477.

11 ibid., pp. 362, 489, 493, and chapter 18, *passim*.

12 ibid, p. 477, and chapter 24, *passim*.

13 Further discussion of cropping procedures will be found in Confino, op. cit.

14 The detailed course of the emancipation deliberations may be gleaned from the following: Blum, op. cit., chapter 26; T. Emmons, *The Russian Landed Gentry and the Peasant Emancipation of 1861*, C.U.P., 1968; idem 'The Peasant and Emancipation', in W. Vucinich, ed., *The Peasant in Nineteenth-Century Russia*, Stanford U.P., 1968, pp. 41–71; D. Field, *The End of Serfdom: Nobility and Bureaucracy in Russia, 1855–1861*, Harvard U.P., 1976; P. A. Zaionchkovsky, *The Abolition of Serfdom in Russia*, Academic International, 1978 (translated from the 3rd Russian edition, 1968).

15 Blum, op. cit., p. 582.

16 ibid., chapter 26. For the Baltic settlement see ibid., pp. 229–30; Field, op. cit., pp. 242, 246–7; Robinson, op. cit., p. 81; B. Kerblay, 'La Réforme de 1861 et ses effets sur la vie rurale dans la province de Smolensk', in R. Portal, ed., *Le Statut des paysans libérés du servage, 1861–1961*, Mouton, 1961, pp. 267–310.

17 This point is made by Daniel Field in *The End of Serfdom*.

18 Blum, op. cit., pp. 596–8 for a clear exposition; Robinson, op. cit., pp. 84–5.

19 Robinson, op. cit., p. 81. On the question of misshapen plots see A. A. Manuilov, 'Arenda zemli v Rossii v ekonomicheskom otnoshenii', in idem, ed., *Ocherki po krestyanskomu voprosu*, 2 vols., 1904–5, vol. 2. This point was brought to my attention by Mark Harrison.

20 Blum, op. cit., pp. 594, 599–600; but see Robinson, op. cit., pp. 89–90 for a slightly different assessment.

21 Zaionchkovsky, op. cit., Russian edition, pp. 223, 229; Robinson, op. cit., pp. 87–8; A. Gerschenkron, 'Agrarian policies and industrialization in Russia, 1861–1917', in M. M. Postan and H. J. Habakkuk, eds.,

Cambridge Economic History of Europe, vol. 6, part 2, C.U.P., 1965, p. 730.

22 Other figures are given in P. I. Lyashchenko, *History of the National Economy of Russia to the 1917 Revolution*, Macmillan, 1949, p. 466. For the suggestion that capitalist farms were found more towards the lower end of the scale, see I. D. Kovalchenko and N. B. Selunskaya, 'Labor ental in the manorial economy of European Russia at the end of the nineteenth and the beginning of the twentieth century', *E.E.H.*, no. 18, 1981, pp. 1–20. For further discussion see Pavlovsky, op. cit., p. 191.

23 Kaufman believed that the amount of land offered for lease fell, because andlords became disillusioned with the ability of peasants to meet their payments. A. A. Kaufman, *Agrarnyi vopros v Rossii*, 1918, pp. 79, 104; A. M. Anfimov, *Zemelnaya arenda v Rossii*, Nauka, 1961, pp. 14–15; for a wide-ranging survey see Lenin, op. cit., chapters 3 and 4.

24 This is one of the chapter headings in Robinson, op. cit.

25 N. P. Oganovsky and N. D. Kondratev, eds., *Selskoe khozyaistvo Rossii v XX veke*, Novaya derevnya, 1923, pp. 60–1; A. M. Anfimov and I. F. Makarov, 'Novyie dannyie o zemlevladenii Evropeiskoi Rossii', *Istoriya SSSR*, no. 1, 1974, pp. 82–97; N. A. Proskuryakova, 'Razmeshchenie i struktura dvoryanskogo zemlevladeniya v Evropeiskoi Rossii v kontse XIX-nachale XX veka', *Istoriya SSSR*, no. 1, 1973, pp. 55–75. In Kherson and Ekaterinoslav, total gentry landholdings fell by almost 50 per cent between 1877 and 1905.

26 A. P. Korelin, *Dvoryanstvo v poreformennoi Rossii, 1861–1904*, Nauka, 1979, p. 66; Anfimov and Makarov, op. cit.

27 Robinson, op. cit., p. 268 (referring to 49 provinces).

28 Details from A. N. Zak, *Krestyanskii pozemelnyi bank, 1882–1910*, 1911, pp. 90–1, 226–7; R. M. Ivanova, 'K izucheniyu materialov krestyanskogo pozemelnogo banka', in *Problemy istorii SSSR*, Nauka, 1973, pp. 273–96

29 For general surveys in English see Robinson, op. cit., chapter 9; M. Perrie, 'The Russian peasant revolution of 1905–1907', *Past and Present*, no. 57, 1972, pp. 123–55; and R. T. Manning, *The Crisis of the Old Order in Russia: Gentry and Government*, Princeton, U.P., 1982, pp. 138–76.

30 Manning, op. cit., Part Four; M. S. Simonova, 'Agrarnaya politika samoderzhaviya v 1905g.', *Ist. zap.*, no. 81, 1968, pp. 199–215; H. T. Willetts, 'The agrarian problem', in G. Katkov et al., eds., *Russia Enters the Twentieth Century*, Temple Smith, 1971, pp. 111–37.

31 I. Fleischauer, 'The agrarian programme of the Russian constitutional democrats', *Cahiers du monde russe et soviétique*, no. 20, 1979, pp. 173–201; V. I. Lenin, *The Agrarian Programme of Social Democracy in the First Russian Revolution, 1905–1907*, Progress, 1977; M. Perrie, *The Agrarian Policy of the Russian Socialist-Revolutionary Party from its Origins through the Revolution of 1905–1907*, C.U.P., 1976.

32 Krivoshein, who had government responsibility for agriculture, is cited in H. D. Mehlinger and J. M. Thompson, *Count Witte and the Tsarist Government in the 1905 Revolution*, Indiana U.P., 1972, p. 203. The process whereby the land reforms came about has been admirably traced by Manning, op. cit.; Robinson, op. cit., chapter 11; Lyashchenko, op. cit., chapter 36; and D. Atkinson, *The End of the Russian Land Commune*,

1905–1930, Stanford U.P., 1983, chapter 4. For an emphasis upon bureaucratic initiatives, see G. L. Yaney, *The Urge to Mobilize: Agrarian Reform in Russia, 1861–1930*, University of Illinois Press, 1982.

33 The standard Soviet account is S. M. Dubrovsky, *Stolypinskaya zemelnaya reforma*, Nauka, 1963, pp. 124ff.

34 For one account of peasant protest during 1917 see J. Keep, *The Russian Revolution: A Study in Mass Mobilization*, Weidenfeld and Nicolson, 1976, Part 3. A full treatment of peasant revolution in 1905 and 1917 still remains to be undertaken.

35 Details in R. A. Pierce, *Russian Central Asia, 1867–1917: A Study in Colonial Rule*, University of California Press, 1960. See also Lyashchenko, op. cit., chapter 27.

36 Lyashchenko, op. cit., p. 588 and chapter 28, *passim*. See also Chapter Three, section 2, above.

37 Gregory, op. cit., pp. 134–7; compare his earlier, and somewhat less favourable assessment, in 'Economic growth and structural change in tsarist Russia: a case of modern economic growth?', *Soviet Studies*, no. 23, 1972, pp. 418–34.

38 Cited in Anfimov, op. cit., p. 19.

39 Lokhtin, op. cit., pp. 145, 224; Robinson, op. cit., p. 100; Kovalchenko and Selunskaya, op. cit., *passim*.

40 Confino, op. cit. No one questions the fact that output could and did increase under serfdom, but the suggestion (made by Struve in 1913) that significant gains in yields were made on manorial land seems dubious. See O. Crisp, *Studies in the Russian Economy before 1914*, Macmillan, 1976, chapter 2; and I. D. Kovalchenko, *Russkoe krepostnoe khozyaistvo v pervoi polovine XIX veka*, Nauka, 1967, p. 377, who also notes that yields on allotments were double those on the demesne.

41 N. M. Druzhinin, 'Pomeshchiche khozyaistvo posle reformy 1861g., po dannym Valuevskoi komissii 1872–1873gg.' *Ist. zap.*, no. 89, 1972, pp. 187–230; for long fallow in the Mid-Volga region, see Yu. I. Smykov, *Krestyane Srednego Povolzhya v period kapitalizma*, Nauka, 1984, p. 131.

42 A description will be found in A. N. Engelhardt, *O khozyaistve v severnoi Rossii*, St. Petersburg, 1888.

43 Munting, op. cit., pp. 743–60.

44 Pavlovsky, op. cit., pp. 218–20; for the 1916 Census see A. M. Anfimov, *Russkaya derevnya v gody pervoi mirovoi voiny*, Nauka, 1962, pp. 293–6.

45 For further elaboration see L. Volin, *A Century of Russian Agriculture*, Harvard U.P., 1970, pp. 61–2, 90–1; Pavlovsky, op. cit., pp. 81–83; Robinson, op. cit., p. 97. For examples of contemporary opinion see Lokhtin, op. cit.; Valuev, cited in Yaney, op. cit., p. 174; and N. K. Brzheskii, *Obshchinnyi byt i khozyaistvennaya neobezpechennost krestyan*, St. Petersburg, 1889.

46 For government legislation in the 1890s see Gerschenkron, op. cit., pp. 772–5, and Atkinson, op. cit., p. 33. The exclusion of improved land from partition is noted in A. M. Anfimov and P. N. Zyryanov, 'Nekotoryie cherty evolyutsii russkoi pozemelnoi obshchiny v poreformennyi period, 1861–1914gg.', *Istoriya SSSR*, no. 4, 1980, pp. 26–41.

47 D. McCloskey, 'The persistence of English common fields', in W. N. Parker and E. L. Jones, eds., *European Peasants and Their Markets*,

Princeton U.P., 1975, pp. 73–119. He argues that no *market* mechanism would have insured peasants against the need to buy grain, in the event of crop failure.

48 Pavlovsky, op. cit., pp. 119, 135–6, 272; Robinson, op. cit., p. 97; Volin, op. cit., p. 62.

49 For detailed discussion in English see Yaney, op. cit., chapter 7. The decrees are reprinted in S. M. Sidelnikov, *Agrarnaya reforma Stolypina*, izdatelstvo Moskovskogo Univ., 1973, pp. 95–128.

50 Atkinson, op. cit., chapter 5; Yaney, op. cit., *passim*. The fact that consolidation was forced upon peasant households tends to be borne out by the reassertion of the communal principle by peasants after 1917.

51 Pavlovsky, op. cit., pp. 118–9; Dubrovsky, op. cit., p. 66. Scope existed under Article 165 of the Emancipation Statute for individual land tenure and land consolidation, provided that the head of the household 'had paid his share of the redemption debt'. Legislation in 1893 imposed the additional requirement of a two-thirds majority of commune members; see Gerschenkron, op. cit., pp. 774–5.

52 Antsiferov, op. cit., p. 55.

53 Pavlovsky, op. cit., p. 275; D. B. Grigg, *Population Growth and Agrarian Change: An Historical Perspective*, C.U.P., 1980, pp. 200–1 and chapters 12 and 14, *passim*; A. S. Milward and S. B. Saul, *The Economic Development of Continental Europe, 1780–1870*, Allen and Unwin, 1973, pp. 75ff.; E. Kingston-Mann, 'Marxism and Russian rural development: problems of evidence, experience and culture', *American Historical Review*, no. 86, 1981, pp. 731–52.

54 Grigg, op. cit.; Milward and Saul, op. cit.; J. A. Perkins, 'The agricultural revolution in Germany, 1850–1914', *J.E.E.H.*, no. 10, 1981, pp. 71–118.

55 Pavlovsky, op. cit., pp. 215–7, 279; Antsiferov, op. cit., p. 84.

56 Pavlovsky, op. cit., pp. 276–8, 280–1, 291–2; Lyashchenko, op. cit., p. 732.

57 Pallot, op. cit., pp. 422–49.

58 Lokhtin, op. cit., p. 211; Pavlovsky, op. cit., chapter 10; Volin, op. cit., pp. 363–5.

59 See E. J. Collins, 'Labour supply and demand in European agriculture, 1800–1880', in E. L. Jones and S. J. Woolf, eds., *Agrarian Change and Economic Development*, Methuen, 1969, pp. 61–94; G. W. Grantham, 'Scale and organization in French farming, 1840–1880', in Parker and Jones, eds., *European Peasants*, op. cit., pp. 293–326.

60 It is also true that deep ploughing in the black-earth provinces could accelerate the evaporation of moisture; in these circumstances, the use of the *sokha* was not irrational.

61 A. M. Anfimov, *Krestyanskoe khozyaistvo Evropeiskoi Rossii, 1881–1904*, Nauka, 1980, pp. 156–62; Crisp, op. cit., p. 31; Munting, op. cit., pp. 744, 748–9; N. M. Druzhinin, *Russkaya derevnya na perelome, 1861–1881*, Nauka, 1978, pp. 151–3; R. W. Davies, *The Socialist Offensive: The Collectivization of Soviet Agriculture, 1929–1930*, Macmillan, 1981, p. 9.

62 A. Fortunatov, *Urozhai rzhi na krestyanskikh zemlyakh Kazanskoi gubernii*, n.p., 1889; E. Boserup, *The Conditions of Agricultural Growth:*

The Economics of Agrarian Change Under Population Pressure, Allen and Unwin, 1965.

63 Volin, op. cit., pp. 61–2; Pavlovsky, op. cit., conclusion; Kingston-Mann, op. cit., pp. 733–37.

64 P. B. Struve, *Krepostnoe khozyaistvo: Issledovaniya po ekonomicheskoi istorii Rossii v XVIII-XIX vv.*, 1913; A. Kahan, 'The costs of 'westernization' in Russia: the gentry and the economy in the eighteenth century', *S.R.*, no. 25, 1966, pp. 40–66; Blum, op. cit., pp. 390–2.

65 Blum, op. cit., pp. 395–400.

66 Kovalchenko, op. cit., p. 78 offers the following estimates of cereal output per head (in *chetvert*): European Russia as a whole, 2.8 (Central Black Earth average, 4.2) in 1802–11; 2.7 (3.8), 1841–50; and 2.6 (3.3) in 1851–60.

67 Some details in Blum, op. cit., pp. 401–4; Struve, op. cit., and Lyashchenko, op. cit., chapters 15, 17 and 20.

68 Lyashchenko, op. cit., p. 360; Blum, op. cit., p. 471 and, in particular, I. D. Kovalchenko, 'Sootnoshenie krestyanskogo i pomeshchichego khozyaistva v zemledelcheskom proizvodstve kapitalisticheskoi Rossii', in *Problemy sotsialno-ekonomicheskoi istorii Rossii*, Nauka, 1971, pp. 171–94

69 C. M. White, 'The impact of railways on the market for grain in the 1860s and 1870s', in L. Symons and C. White, eds., *Russian Transport*, Bell, 1975, pp. 1–45; J. Metzer, 'Railroad development and market integration: the case of tsarist Russia', *J.EcH.*, no. 34, 1974, pp. 529–50, and the debate between Kelly and Metzer in *J.Ec.H.*, no. 36, 1976, pp. 908–18; P. I. Lyashchenko, *Ocherki agrarnoi evolyutsii Rossii*, St. Petersburg, 1908, vol. 1, p. 244.

70 Lyashchenko, *Ocherki*, pp. 254–7.

71 The diagram is based upon data in N. A. Egiazarova, *Agrarnyi krizis kontsa XIX veka v Rossii*, Nauka, 1959, p. 71. The original figures are expressed in rubles/pud and have been converted to index numbers with the base 1883–5. The weights used to derive the composite index are taken from V. M. Obukhov, 'Dvizhenie urozhaev zernovykh kultur v Evropeiskoi Rossii za 1883–1915', in V. G. Groman, ed., *Vliyanie neurozhaev na narodnoe khozyaistvo Rossii*, Priboi, 1927, vol. 1, pp. 2–5. For the period 1884–94 they are given as 53.7 (rye), 28.2 (oats), 11.5 (barley) and 6.5 (winter wheat). Prices were those prevailing at local markets. For further discussion of the agrarian crisis consult M. E. Falkus, 'Russia and the international wheat trade, 1860–1913', *Economica*, no. 33, 1966, pp. 416–29. The European context is provided by S. Pollard, *Peaceful Conquest: the Industrialization of Europe, 1760–1970*, O.U.P., 1981, pp. 264–70.

72 Lyashchenko, *History*, p. 470; Egiazarova, op. cit., pp. 76ff.

73 Volin, op. cit., pp. 61–2.

74 Anfimov, *Krestyanskoe khozyaistvo*, p. 199; Pavlovsky, op. cit., pp. 227–8.

75 Pavlovsky, op. cit., pp. 97–8; Lyashchenko, *Ocherki*, p. 359.

76 Anfimov, *Krestyanskoe khozyaistvo*, pp. 180ff.; Kh. Yu. Beilkin, 'Padenie tsen i sostoyanie khlebnoi torgovli Belorussii v gody agrarnogo krizisa kontsa XIX veka', in *Ezhegodnik po agrarnoi istorii Vostochnoi Evropy, 1968g.*, Nauka, Leningrad, 1972, pp. 255–63. Producers in

Belorussia 'imported' cereals as fodder and as an input to the brewing industry – a clear response to relative prices.

77 Anfimov, *Krestyanskoe khozyaistvo*, op. cit., pp. 212–14; Drobizhev et al., *Istoricheskaya geografiya*, pp. 220–1; Pavlovsky, op. cit., chapter 10.

78 R. North, *Transport in Western Siberia*, University of British Columbia Press, 1979, pp. 74–6; T. M. Kitanina, *Khlebnaya torgovlya Rossii v 1875–1914gg.*, Nauka, Leningrad, 1978, pp. 85ff., 183–4. North doubts that the 'tariff break' was of paramount importance, because transport costs would have anyway reduced the comparative advantage of Siberian farmers. But the political significance of the 1893 decision is not in doubt. Further information on grain shipments will be found in L. M. Goryushkin, *Sibirskoe krestyanstvo na rubezhe dvukh epokh*, Nauka, Novosibirsk, 1967, pp. 356, 358.

79 Goryushkin, op. cit., pp. 143–7, 182. For a glowing verdict see Pavlovsky, op. cit., pp. 171ff.

80 North, op. cit., pp. 76–8, 154, 162. Data on agricultural exports will be found in P. A. Khromov, *Ekonomicheskoe razvitie Rossii v XIX–XX vekakh*, Gospolitizdat, 1950, pp. 486–7.

81 P. R. Gregory, 'Grain marketings and peasant consumption in Russia, 1885–1913', *E.E.H.*, no. 17, 1980, pp. 135–64. Cf. J. Y. Simms, 'The crisis in Russian agriculture at the end of the nineteenth century: a different view', *S.R.*, no. 36, 1977, pp. 377–98.

82 P. B. Struve, ed., *Food Supply in Russia during the World War*, Yale U.P., 1930; this remains the best treatment.

83 Kovalchenko, 'Sootnoshenie. . .'. On average, according to this source, gentry marketed 50 per cent of their output in 1909–13.

84 S. G. Wheatcroft, 'The significance of climatic and weather change on Soviet agriculture', *SIPS*, no. 11 (Centre for Russian and East European Studies, University of Birmingham). For a different approach see J. Y. Simms, 'The crop failure of 1891; soil exhaustion, technological backwardness and Russia's "agrarian crisis" ', *Slavonic and East European Review*, no. 41, 1982, pp. 236–50.

Chapter Five (pp. 141–187)

1 T. H. von Laue, 'A secret memorandum of Sergei Witte on the industrialization of imperial Russia', *Journal of Modern History*, no. 26, 1954, pp. 60–74.

2 A. Gerschenkron, *Economic Backwardness in Historical Perspective*, Harvard U.P., 1962, pp. 119–42; idem, *Europe in the Russian Mirror*, C.U.P., 1970, pp. 122–30.

3 A. Kahan, 'Government policies and the industrialization of Russia', *J.Ec.H.*, no. 27, 1967, p. 461; O. Crisp, *Studies in the Russian Economy before 1914*, Macmillan, 1976, chapter 1. Crisp, too, notes elements of irrationality in aspects of government economic policy. For a recent emphasis upon the alternative view (lack of rural purchasing power and of autonomous industrial growth), see P. Kriedte et al., *Industrialization Before Industrialization: Rural Industry in the Genesis of Capitalism*, C.U.P., 1981, pp. 149–50. The views of Gindin are close to those of Olga Crisp: see I.

F. Gindin, *Gosudarstvennyi bank i ekonomicheskaya politika tsarskogo pravitelstva, 1861–1892gg.*, Gosfinizdat, 1960.

4 Details in R. Goldsmith, 'The economic growth of tsarist Russia, 1860–1913', *Economic Development and Cultural Change*, no. 9, 1961, pp. 441–75.

5 ibid.; A. Gerschenkron, 'The rate of industrial growth in Russia since 1885', *J.Ec.H.*, supplement VII, 1947, pp. 144–74; R. Portal, 'The industrialization of Russia', *Cambridge Economic History of Europe*, vol. 6, part 2, C.U.P., 1965, pp. 801–72; M. E. Falkus, *The Industrialization of Russia, 1700–1914* Macmillan, 1972.

6 P. Gregory, *Russian National Income, 1885–1913*, C.U.P., 1982, p. 134.

7 A. Kahan, 'Capital formation during the early period of industrialization in Russia, 1890–1913', in P. Mathias and M. M. Postan, eds., *Cambridge Economic History of Europe*, vol. 7, part 2, C.U.P., 1978, pp. 270, 290.

8 I. F. Gindin, 'O nekotorykh osobennostyakh ekonomicheskoi i sotsialnoi struktury rossiiskogo kapitalizma v nachale XX v.', *Istoriya SSSR*, no. 3, 1966, pp. 48–66; Crisp, op. cit., pp. 42–3.

9 S. Blanc, 'The economic policy of Peter the Great', in W. L. Blackwell, ed., *Russian Economic Development from Peter the Great to Stalin*, New Viewpoints, 1974, pp. 21–50; E. I. Zaozerskaya, *Razvitie legkoi promyshlennosti v Moskve v pervoi polovine XVIIIv*. Nauka, 1953, p. 84; A. Kahan, 'The costs of "westernization" in Russia: the gentry and the economy in the eighteenth century', *S.R.*, no. 25, 1966, pp. 40–66; P. I. Lyashchenko, *History of the National Economy of Russia to the 1917 Revolution*, Macmillan, 1949, p. 273 (giving the urban population in 1722 as 0.3 m., and 1.3 m. in 1796). On the iron industry, see R. Portal, *L'Oural au XVIII siècle*, Institut d'etudes slaves, 1950; N. I. Pavlenko, *Razvitie metallurgicheskoi promyshlennosti Rossii v pervoi polovine XVIII veka*, Nauka, 1953; E. Koutaisoff, 'Urals metal industry in the eighteenth century', *Ec.H.R.*, no. 4, 1951–2, pp. 252–5.

10 There is evidence on rising labour costs in S. I. Smetanin, 'Nachalo promyshlennogo perevorota na Urale', *Voprosy istorii*, no. 3, 1977, pp. 16–23; and in T. Esper, 'The incomes of Russian serf ironworkers in the eighteenth century', *Past and Present*, no. 93, 1981, pp. 137–59. For general discussion of the iron industry, see V. K. Yatsunsky, 'The geography of the iron market in pre-reform Russia' and 'The industrial revolution in Russia', both in Blackwell, ed., op. cit., pp. 71–136. For the British iron industry see D. S. Landes, *The Unbound Prometheus: Technological Change and Industrial Development in Western Europe from 1750 to the Present*, C.U.P., 1969, pp. 89–93.

11 M.L. de Tengoborsky, *Commentaries on the Productive Forces of Russia*, 2 vols., 1856, vol. 2, p. 81. For uniform costs, see W. M. Pintner, 'The Burden of Defense in Imperial Russia, 1725–1914', in *Russian Review*, no. 43, 1984, p. 239. According to another source, 'soldiers' wool' comprised one-fifth of total woollen output in the 1850s: W. L. Blackwell, *The Beginnings of Russian Industrialization, 1800–1860*, Princeton U.P., 1968, p. 48. For the role of gentry industrialists, see M. I. Tugan-Baranovsky, *The Russian Factory in the Nineteenth Century*, R. D. Irwin, 1970, pp. 24–5.

12 Tugan-Baranovsky, op. cit., pp. 40–3; Blackwell, op. cit., pp. 48–9; G.

von Schulze-Gaevernitz, *Volkswirtschaftliche Studien aus Russland*, Leipzig, 1899, pp. 26, 47–8; Landes, op. cit., p. 44.

13 G. S. Isaev, *Rol tekstilnoi promyshlennosti v genezise i razvitii kapitalizma v Rossii, 1760–1860*, Nauka, Leningrad, 1970, pp. 25, 28, 53.

14 ibid., pp. 162–6; Tengoborsky, op. cit., p. 65. For Britain, Landes, op. cit., chapter 2 is indispensable.

15 Landes, op. cit., p. 148; Blackwell, op. cit.; Tengoborsky, op. cit., p. 68.

16 K. A. Pazhitnov, *Ocherk istorii tekstilnoi promyshlennosti dorevolyutsionnoi Rossii: khlopchatobumazhnaya, lno-penkovaya i shelkovaya promyshlennost*, Nauka, 1958, pp. 16–17; Tengoborsky, op. cit., p. 79; R. Portal, 'Muscovite industrialists: the cotton sector, 1861–1914', in Blackwell, ed., op. cit., pp. 159–96.

17 Figures from P. A. Khromov, *Ekonomicheskoe razvitie Rossii v XIX-XX vekakh*, Gospolitizdat, 1950, pp. 91–2. In 1845 Russian goods traded at Nizhnii-Novgorod represented three-quarters of total turnover at the fair. N. S. Kinyapina, *Politika russkogo samoderzhaviya v oblasti promyshlennosti 20–50e gody XIXv.*, Izdatelstvo Moskovskogo universiteta, 1968, p. 99.

18 Price data are taken from Khromov, op. cit., p. 93. To some extent the upward movement in food prices led to an increase in manufacturing costs, except where (as in the Urals) workers grew food for their own consumption. See Esper, op. cit., pp. 147–8.

19 Blackwell, op. cit., pp. 64, 432; Kinyapina, op. cit., p. 104; M. O. Gately, 'The development of the Russian textile industry in the pre-revolutionary years, 1861–1913', Ph.D., Kansas, 1969, p. 32.

20 Details in Blackwell, op. cit., pp. 170–4; Kinyapina, op. cit., pp. 96, 112–13; W. M. Pintner, *Russian Economic Policy Under Nicholas I*, Cornell U.P., 1967. For a positive assessment of the effect of the tariff on cotton textiles see V. Wittschewsky, *Russlands Handels-, Zoll- und Industriepolitik von Peter dem Grossen bis auf die Gegenwart*, Berlin, 1905, p. 67. The European context is discussed in S. Pollard, *Peaceful Conquest: The Industrialization of Europe, 1760–1970*, O.U.P., 1981, pp. 255–7.

21 Vronchenko is quoted in Kinyapina, op. cit., p. 119. As late as 1847 the Tsar and the Minister both thought that iron should continue to receive protection: ibid., pp. 126–7.

22 Details in Lyashchenko, op. cit., p. 492; Khromov, op. cit., pp. 452–3; and in A. M. Soloveva, *Zheleznodorozhnyi transport Rossii vo vtoroi polovine XIX veka*, Nauka, 1975, pp. 126ff.

23 Soloveva, op. cit., pp. 134–8, 141; Gindin, *Gosudarstvennyi bank*, p. 192. Domestic output of locomotives rose from 2.33 m. rubles (annual average, 1869–75) to 6.76 m. (1876–80); imports fell from 6.86 m. to 4.22 m. rubles. The European background is discussed in P. O'Brien, 'Transport and economic growth in Western Europe, 1830–1914', *J.E.E.H.*, no. 11, 1982, pp. 335–68.

24 Details in A. F. Yakovlev, *Ekonomicheskie krizisy v Rossii*, Gospolitizdat, 1955, pp. 41, 102, 111–14; L. E. Shepelev, *Aktsionernyie kompanii v Rossii*, Nauka, Leningrad, 1973, pp. 82–3. For a different argument: Tugan-Baranovsky, op. cit., pp. 262–4; Lyashchenko, op. cit., p. 493. The first railway-building boom was followed by a fall in investment

during the 1880s and by government acquisition of private company assets: Gindin, *Gosudarstvennyi bank*, pp. 211ff., 235–6, 245–6, 266.

25 R. Fremdling, 'Railroads and German economic growth: a leading sector analysis', *J.Ec.H.*, no. 37, 1977, pp. 583–601. The main source for the argument in this paragraph is Gregory, op. cit., Appendices I, J and L. Compare the remarks of Lyashchenko, op. cit., p. 507, and Kahan, op. cit., pp. 274–5.

26 Kahan, op. cit., pp. 288–9.

27 Details in J. P. McKay, *Pioneers for Profit: Foreign Entrepreneurship and Russian Industrialization, 1885–1913*, University of Chicago Press, 1970, appendix; Soloveva, op. cit., pp. 279–82.

28 Lyashchenko, op. cit., p. 506; Soloveva, op. cit., p. 287.

29 P. G. Ryndzyunskii, *Krestyanskaya promyshlennost poreformennoi Rossii, 60–80e gody XIX v.*, Nauka, 1966, pp. 78–9; V. I. Lenin, *The Development of Capitalism in Russia*, Progress, 1977, chapters 5 and 6; G. Drage, *Russian Affairs*, 1904, pp. 184–6.

30 Ryndzyunskii, op. cit., pp. 91–3; Tugan-Baranovsky, op. cit., pp. 367ff. For a different interpretation of the origins of cottage industry see G. Sinzheimer, 'Les industries kustar: un aspect de la révolution industrielle en Russie', *Cahiers du monde russe et soviétique*, no. 8, 1967, pp. 205–22. For comparative material see R. Samuel, 'The workshop of the world: steam power and hand technology in mid-Victorian Britain', *History Workshop*, no. 3, 1977, pp. 6–72.

31 Tugan-Baranovsky, op. cit.; M. Miller, *The Economic Development of Russia, 1905–1914*, Cass, 1926, p. 229.

32 Tugan-Baranovsky, op. cit., p. 368. For a different view, see A. Baker, 'Deterioration or development: the peasant economy of Moscow province prior to 1914', *Russian History*, no. 6, 1978, pp. 1–23.

33 P. I. Lyashchenko, *Mukomolnaya promyshlennost v Rossii*, St. Petersburg, 1910.

34 Lyashchenko, *History*, pp. 499–500, 512; M. K. Rozhkova, 'Torgovlya', in *Ocherki ekonomicheskoi istorii Rossii pervoi poloviny XIXv.*, Nauka, 1958, p. 251; G. A. Dikhtyar, *Vnutrennyaya torgovlya v dorevolyutsionnoi Rossii*, Nauka, 1960, pp. 91–2, 141.

35 Lenin, op. cit., pp. 535ff.; E. H. Carr and R. W. Davies, *Foundations of a Planned Economy, 1926–1929*, vol. 1, Pelican, 1974, p. 374.

36 D. Layton, 'The tariff of 1891 and the debate on the Russian economy', Ph.D., Indiana, 1965, p. 49; F. Carstensen, *American Enterprise in Foreign Markets: Singer and International Harvester in Imperial Russia*, University of North Carolina Press, 1984.

37 Layton, op. cit., p. 47; Savin is quoted in E. C. Pickering, 'The International Harvester Company in Russia', Ph.D., Princeton, 1974, p. 104. According to Sergeev, it cost between 12 and 15 rubles per spindle to build a cotton mill in England in 1900 (with around 40,000 spindles), but 30 rubles per spindle in Russia: Layton, op. cit.

38 McKay, op. cit., pp. 117–18, 121–6; Landes, op. cit., pp. 262–5.

39 Details in W. J. Kelly and T. Kano, 'Crude oil production in the Russian Empire, 1818–1919', *J.E.E.H.*, no. 6, 1977, pp. 307–38; Khromov, op. cit., p. 205; G. Jones, *The State and the Emergence of the British Oil Industry*, Macmillan, 1981, p. 53; O. Crisp, 'Labour and industrialization

in Russia', in Mathias and Postan, eds., *Cambridge Economic History*, p. 402; P. V. Volobuev, 'Iz istorii monopolizatsii neftyanoi promyshlennosti Rossii, 1903–1914gg.', *Ist. zap.*, no. 52, 1955, pp. 80–111.

40 P. V. Volobuev, 'Iz istorii sindikata "Produgol" ', *Ist. zap.*, no. 58, 1956, pp. 107–44; idem, 'Toplivnyi krizis i monopolii v Rossii nakanune pervoi mirovoi voiny', *Voprosy istorii*, no. 1, 1957, pp. 33–46; Khromov, op. cit., p. 323; Crisp, 'Labour and industrialization', p. 402. On the importance of cheap fuel before 1900 see V. Varzar, 'Factories and workshops', in A. Raffalovich, ed., *Russia: Its Trade and Commerce*, P. S. King, 1918, pp. 122–6.

41 Gately, op. cit., pp. 141–2, 148–50, 193.

42 Lenin, op. cit., pp. 480–1, 484–5; Varzar, op. cit., p. 115.

43 Varzar, op. cit., p. 116.

44 R. E. Zelnik, *Labor and Society in Tsarist Russia: The Factory Workers of St. Petersburg, 1855–1870*, Stanford U.P., 1971, pp. 174ff., 236–8.

45 McKay, op. cit., p. 258; Crisp, 'Labour and industrialization', p. 395.

46 For further discussion see Chapter Three, section 4, and V. I. Grinevetskii, *Poslevoennyie perspektivy russkoi promyshlennosti*, Kharkov, 1919, p. 159.

47 Carstensen, op. cit., pp. 90–1, 394–5; Schulze-Gaevernitz, op. cit.; R. E. Johnson, *Peasant and Proletarian: The Working Class of Moscow in the Late Nineteenth Century*, Leicester U.P., 1979, p. 87.

48 D. I. Mendeleev, *K poznaniyu Rossii*, 3rd edition, St. Petersburg, 1906, pp. 116–18; Crisp, 'Labour and industrialization', pp. 402–4.

49 Examples taken from N. Charnovsky, 'Mashinostroitelnaya promyshlennost v Rossii', *Narodnoe khozyaistvo v 1916 godu*, vol. 4, Petrograd, 1921, p. 52; E. M. Izmailovskaya, *Russkoe selsko-khozyaistvennoe mashinostroenie*, VSNKh, 1920, p. 119; S. N. Vankov, 'O normalizatsii metalloobrabatyvayushchei promyshlennosti', *Nauchno-tekhnicheskii vestnik*, nos. 4–5, 1921. It should be noted, however, that the Nevsky Engineering Works specialized in transport equipment during the 1870s, with disastrous results: Gindin, *Gosudarstvennyi bank*, pp. 208ff.

50 See Tugan-Baranovsky, op. cit., chapter 11; Yu. I. Kiryanov, *Zhiznennyi uroven rabochikh Rossii, konets XIX – nachalo XX v.*, Nauka, 1979, pp. 104–5.

51 Some details in Tugan-Baranovsky, op. cit. chapter 10, and in Chapter Three, section 4.

52 Tugan-Baranovsky, op. cit., p. 338; Kiryanov, op. cit., p. 87.

53 Kiryanov, op. cit., pp. 65–9; Gately, op. cit.; V. E. Bonnell, *Roots of Rebellion: Workers' Politics and Organization in St. Petersburg and Moscow, 1900–1914*, University of California Press, 1983, pp. 66–7; and, above all, H. Hogan, 'The reorganization of work processes in the St. Petersburg metal-working industry, 1901–1914', *Russian Review*, no. 42, 1983, pp. 163–90.

54 Gindin, *Gosudarstvennyi bank*, pp. 60, 190, 268. For Bunge's attitudes see B. V. Ananich, 'The economic policy of the tsarist government and enterprise in Russia', in G. Guroff and F. V. Carstensen, eds.,

Entrepreneurship in Imperial Russia and the Soviet Union, Princeton U.P., 1983, pp. 125–39.

55 Kahan, 'Government policies', pp. 470–1; Lyashchenko, *History*, p. 558; A. Finn-Enotaevskii, *Sovremennoe khozyaistvo v Rossii, 1890–1911*, St. Petersburg, 1911, pp. 138ff.

56 This section draws heavily upon remarks in Crisp, *Studies*, pp. 29–31. Carstensen, op. cit., pp. 161, 174 points out that the tariff increase on iron in 1881 hit the nascent agricultural machinery industry hard, and only an emergency package of protection to the firms themselves helped them to survive. For the situation in Germany, see S. L. Webb, 'Tariffs, cartels, technology and growth in the German steel industry, 1879–1914', *J.Ec.H.*, no. 40, 1980, pp. 309–29.

57 Webb, op. cit.; Crisp, op. cit.; Gindin, *Gosudarstvennyi bank*, pp. 196–7, 207–8; V. P. Litvinov-Falinsky, *Nashe ekonomicheskoe polozhenie*, St. Petersburg, 1908, pp. 60ff.; L. E. Shepelev, *Tsarizm i burzhuaziya vo vtoroi polovine XIX v.*, Nauka, Leningrad, 1981, p. 218.

58 Cited in T. H. von Laue, *Sergei Witte and the Industrialization of Russia*, Columbia U.P., 1963, p. 220.

59 V. P. Vorontsov, *Sudba kapitalisticheskoi Rossii: Ekonomicheskie ocherki Rossii*, St. Petersburg, 1907, pp. 112–13, 132–3; P. P. Migulin, *Russkii gosudarstvennyi kredit*, 3 vols., Kharkov, 1901–3, vol. 3, pp. 360–79, 430; Litvinov-Falinsky, op. cit., pp. 61–2.

60 D. Atkinson, *The End of the Russian Land Commune, 1905–1930*, Stanford U.P., 1983, pp. 33–4; M. S. Simonova, 'Problema "oskudeniya" tsentra i ee rol v formirovanii agrarnoi politiki samoderzhaviya v 90kh godakh XIX-nachale XX v.', *Problemy sotsialno-ekonomicheskoi istorii Rossii*, Nauka, 1971, pp. 236–63.

61 For the official view: B. F. Brandt, *Torgovo-promyshlennyi krizis na zapadnom Evrope i v Rossii*, 2 vols., St. Petersburg, 1902–4; and Wittschewsky, op. cit.

62 Brandt, op. cit., vol. 2, pp. 99–102; Yakovlev, op. cit., p. 251; Khromov, op. cit., p. 543 (official discount rate of the State Bank); and R. Girault, *Emprunts russes et investissements français en Russie, 1887–1914*, Armand Colin, 1973, pp. 331–3, 347.

63 I. F. Gindin, *Russkie kommercheskie banki*, Gosfinizdat, 1948, pp. 116–17, 128, 131–2. Crisp, *Studies*, pp. 135, 146; Migulin, op. cit., pp. 370–1; Finn-Enotaevsky, op. cit., pp. 86–8; Girault, op. cit., pp. 338–9; Shepelev, *Aktsionernyie kompanii*, pp. 151–2.

64 V. I. Bovykin, *Formirovanie finansovogo kapitala v Rossii, konets XIXv.–1908g.*, Nauka, 1984, pp. 121–56; Crisp, *Studies*, p. 32. For a different view see Portal, 'Industrialization', p. 843.

65 Wittschewsky, op. cit., p. 353. This did not prevent him from calling for a reduction in taxes levied on peasant consumption.

66 ibid., pp. 266–7; Girault, op. cit., pp. 331–3; D. Geyer, *Der russische Imperialismus: Studien über den Zusammenhang von innerer und auswärtiger Politik, 1860–1914*, Vandenhoeck und Ruprecht, 1977, p. 114.

67 Shepelev, *Tsarizm*, p. 219. B. H. Sumner, 'Tsardom and imperialism in the Far East and Middle East, 1880–1914', *Proceedings of the British Academy*, no. 27, 1941, pp. 42–3.

68 M. L. Entner, *Russo-Persian Commercial Relations, 1828–1914*,

University of Florida Press, 1965, chapter 2; for the tsar's position see S.
A. Pokrovsky, *Vneshnyaya torgovlya v SSSR*, Gosfinizdat, 1947, p. 337.
Other sources of information include Geyer, op. cit., pp. 144–8; von Laue,
Sergei Witte, pp. 78ff., and A. Malozemoff, *Russian Far Eastern Policy,
1881–1904*, University of California Press, 1958, pp. 39, 47.
69 Entner, op. cit., pp. 22–4, 44–5; A. J. Rieber, *Merchants and
Entrepreneurs in Imperial Russia*, University of North Carolina Press,
1981, p. 118; B. V. Ananich, *Rossiiskoe samoderzhavie i vyvoz kapitalov,
1895–1914*, Nauka, Leningrad, 1975, p. 6; O. Crisp, 'The Russo-Chinese
Bank: an episode in Franco-Russian Relations', *Slavonic and East European
Review*, no. 52, 1974, pp. 197–212.
70 Entner, op. cit., pp. 41, 54–5, 69; Ananich, *Rossiiskoe samoderzhavie*,
pp. 44, 199.
71 B. V. Ananich, *Rossiya i mezhdunarodnyi kapital, 1897–1914*, Nauka,
Leningrad, 1970, p. 25; Malozemoff, op. cit., p. 119; Pokrovsky, op. cit.,
p. 340; Geyer, op. cit., pp. 162–3.
72 Pokrovsky, op. cit., pp. 317, 360; Khromov, op. cit., p. 474; V. I. Lenin,
Imperialism, the Highest Stage of Capitalism, Foreign Languages Press,
Peking, 1973, p. 95; V. I. Bovykin, 'O nekotorykh voprosakh izucheniya
inostrannogo kapitala v Rossii', in *Ob osobennostyakh imperializma v
Rossii*, Nauka, 1963, p. 259. Tsarist Russia did diversify her export product
mix, but only to the extent of substituting a broader range of primary
commodities for grain. In 1883–5, grain accounted for 53 per cent of total
export values; in 1909–13 the share had fallen to 45 per cent. By contrast,
Egypt and Brazil relied more heavily upon a single commodity (cotton and
coffee, respectively) in 1914 than in 1860. See J. R. Hanson III, 'Victorian
Trends in LDC Exports', *E.E.H.*, no. 14, 1977, pp. 44–68.
73 The first quotation is from G. D. Bakulev, *Chernaya metallurgiya Yuga
Rossii*, Sotsekgiz, 1953, p. 106, reporting the Congress of Trade and
Industry in 1908. For the government to become a 'regulator' see M. Ya.
Gefter, 'Tsarizm i monopolisticheskii kapital v metallurgii Yuga Rossii do
pervoi mirovoi voiny', *Ist. zap.*, no. 43, 1953, p. 92. For the suggestion that
the government should plan demand for railway equipment over the long
term, see *Doklad soveta sezdov predstavitelei promyshlennosti o merakh k
razvitiyu proizvoditelnykh sil Rossii*, Petrograd, 1915, p. 155. There are
some further pointers in R. A. Roosa, 'Russian industrialists look to the
future', in J. S. Curtiss, ed., *Essays in Russian and Soviet History*, Columbia
U.P., 1963, pp. 210–11.
74 Lyashchenko, op. cit., chapter 23; Crisp, *Studies*, pp. 175–6; Girault,
op. cit., pp. 354ff.: A. L. Tsukernik, *Sindikat 'Prodamet' 1902–1914gg.,
Istoriko-ekonomicheskii ocherk*, Gosfinizdat, 1959.
75 Lyashchenko, op. cit., p. 675; Crisp, *Studies*, pp. 177–9; *Monopolii v
metallurgicheskoi promyshlennosti Rossii, 1900–1917gg.*, Nauka, 1963,
pp. 22, 25, 122–3; Tsukernik, op. cit., pp. 18–21, 75, 109ff.
76 A. P. Pogrebinsky, 'Komitet po zheleznodorozhnym zakazam i ego
likvidatsiya v 1914g.', *Ist. zap.*, no. 83, 1969, pp. 233–43; Tsukernik, op.
cit.; Crisp, *Studies*, p. 179.
77 A. L. Tsukernik, 'K istorii sindikata "Krovlya" ', *Ist. zap.*, no. 52, 1955,
pp. 112–41; Gefter, op. cit.
78 Girault, op. cit., pp. 549–50; Tsukernik, *Sindikat*, pp. 38, 44, 51.

Bryansk produced 1.3 m. tons of iron ore, but consumed only 50 per cent; the South-Russian Dneprovsk produced 1.1 m., and consumed 80 per cent; the Russo-Belgian produced 0.95 m. and consumed 60 per cent. Details in *Obshchii obzor glavneishikh otraslei gornoi i gornozavodskoi promyshlennosti*, 2 vols., St. Petersburg/Petrograd, 1913–1915, vol. 2, p. 173.

79 *Obshchii obzor*, vol. 1; Gefter, op. cit.; D. I. Shpolyanskii, *Monopolii ugolno-metallurgicheskoi promyshlennosti Yuga Rossii v nachale XX veka*, Nauka, 1953; Tsukernik, *Sindikat*, p. 189. Prices of pig iron rose from 47 kopecks/*pud* in 1908 to 74 kopecks in 1913; merchant iron from 103 to 150 kopecks/*pud*.

80 The case is set out in more detail in P. W. Gatrell, 'Industrial expansion in tsarist Russia, 1908–1914', *Ec.H.R.*, no. 35, 1982, pp. 99–110.

81 A. L. Tsukernik, 'Iz istorii monopolizatsii zheleznogo rynka v Rossii', *Ist. zap.*, no. 42, 1953, pp. 192–3; Gefter, op. cit., p. 119. For Russia as a great power see Geyer, op. cit., *passim*.

82 S. V. Voronkova, 'Statistika promyshlennogo proizvodstva', in *Massovyie istochniki po sotsialno-ekonomicheskoi istorii Rossii perioda kapitalizma*, Nauka, 1979, pp. 73ff.

83 Lyashchenko, op. cit., p. 682; Pazhitnov, op. cit., p. 130. V. Ya. Laverychev, 'Protsess monopolizatsii khlopchatobumazhnoi promyshlennosti Rossii, 1900–1914gg.', *Voprosy istorii*, no. 2, 1960, pp. 137–51. Laverychev exaggerates when he talks of an 'export cartel'.

84 Gately, op. cit., pp. 183, 193, 208; Gindin, 'O nekotorykh'; Pazhitnov, op. cit., p. 130; Lyashchenko, op. cit., p. 616.

85 Gately, op. cit., pp. 205, 211–12; Lyashchenko, op. cit., pp. 612–16.

86 G. A. Pavlovsky, *Agricultural Russia on the Eve of the Revolution*, Routledge, 1930, pp. 292–4; A. M. Anfimov, *Krupnoe pomeshchiche khozyaistvo Evropeiskoi Rossii, konets XIX-nachalo XX veka*, Nauka, 1969, pp. 261ff.; V. Ya. Laverychev, *Gosudarstvo i monopolii v dorevolyutsionnoi Rossii*, Mysl, 1982, p. 102; R. Munting, 'The Russian Beet Sugar Industry in the Nineteenth Century'. *J.E.E.H.*, no. 13, 1984, pp. 291–310.

87 Laverychev, *Gosudarstvo*, pp. 105–6.

88 A. L. Sidorov, *Ekonomicheskoe polozhenie Rossii v gody pervoi mirovoi voiny*, Nauka, 1973; Grinevetsky, op. cit.

89 The administrative and political history of the tsarist war effort is discussed in N. Stone, *The Eastern Front 1914–1917*, Hodder, 1975, and L. Siegelbaum, *The Politics of Industrial Mobilization in Russia, 1914–1917*, Macmillan, 1983.

Chapter Six (pp. 188–230)

1 For a concise and influential modern statement, see A. Kahan, 'Government policies and the industrialization of Russia', *J.Ec.H.*, no. 27, 1967, pp. 460–77. Similar views can be found in the writings of contemporary liberal economists, such as I. Kh. Ozerov.

2 A. Gerschenkron, *Economic Backwardness in Historical Perspective*, Harvard U.P., 1962.

3 N. Danielson, *Ocherki nashego poreformennogo khozyaistva*, St. Petersburg, 1893, Part 1, Conclusion.

4 P. I. Lyashchenko, *The History of the National Economy of Russia to the 1917 Revolution*, Macmillan, New York, 1949, chapter 22; I. F. Gindin, 'Russkaya burzhuaziya v period kapitalizma', *Istoriya SSSR*, no. 2, 1962, pp. 57–80; no. 3, 1963, pp. 37–60; V. I. Bovykin, 'O nekotorykh voprosakh izucheniya inostrannogo kapitala v Rossii', in *Ob osobennostyakh imperializma v Rossii*, Nauka, 1963, pp. 250–313; V. I. Lenin, *Imperialism, the Highest Stage of Capitalism*, Foreign Languages Publishing House, Peking, 1973.

5 A. Kahan, 'Capital formation during the early period of industrialization in Russia, 1890–1913', in P. Mathias and M. M. Postan, eds., *Cambridge Economic History of Europe*, vol. 7, part 2, C.U.P., 1978, pp. 265–307.

6 Ibid., p. 287; F. Carstensen, *American Multinational Corporations in Imperial Russia: Chapters on Foreign Enterprise and Russian Economic Development*, Ph.D., Yale, 1976, p. 311.

7 J. H. Bater, *St. Petersburg: Industrialization and Change*, Edward Arnold, 1976, pp. 328–9.

8 P. R. Gregory, *Russian National Income, 1885–1913*, C.U.P., 1982, Appendix F.

9 J. Blum, *Lord and Peasant in Russia from the Ninth to the Nineteenth Centuries*, Princeton, 1961, pp. 464–5.

10 Ibid., pp. 443–71.

11 Details may be found in the following: G. T. Robinson, *Rural Russia Under the Old Regime*, University of California Press, 1972, pp. 82–5; A. Gerschenkron, 'Agrarian policies and industrialization in Russia, 1861–1917', in *Cambridge Economic History of Europe*, vol. 6, part 2, C.U.P., 1965, pp. 731–2, 735–41; and P. A. Zaionchkovsky, *The Abolition of Serfdom in Russia*, Academic International Press, 1978.

12 Gerschenkron, 'Agrarian policies . . .'; Lyashchenko, op. cit., p. 387; B. Kerblay, 'La Réforme de 1861 et ses effets sur la vie rurale dans la province de Smolensk', in R. Portal, ed., *Le Statut des paysans libérés du servage, 1861–1961*, Mouton, 1961, pp. 267–310. In Smolensk, the redemption value of allotment land was 30 rubles per dessyatin, compared to a 'market' value of 10.4 rubles (1854–9 average) and 9.9 rubles (1863–72).

13 Zaionchkovsky, op. cit., pp. 167–8; N. M. Druzhinin, *Russkaya derevnya na perelome, 1861–1880gg.*, Nauka, 1978, pp. 59–83. In 1881, when redemption became compulsory, the 15 per cent of former serfs who had not yet entered into the redemption arrangements were relieved of the need to find this 20 per cent lump sum.

14 State peasants paid a much smaller redemptions for their allotments, which were relatively larger than those assigned to former serfs. For details of their emancipation (in 1866), see Robinson, op. cit., pp. 89–90. The assessment made by Gerschenkron, 'Agrarian policies. . .', op. cit., pp. 761–2 is less sanguine.

15 The average reduction of 27 per cent in annual payments conceals large regional variations: for example, 90 per cent in Olonets, but only 16 per cent in Kherson. L. V. Khodsky, 'Vykupnyie platezhi', in Brockhaus and Efron, *Entsiklopedicheskii slovar*. See, in addition, Druzhinin, op. cit., pp. 78–9; Robinson, op. cit., pp. 95–6.

16 Ya. E. Yanson, *Opyt statisticheskogo issledovaniya o krestyanskikh nadelakh i platezhakh*, 1877.

17 Druzhinin, op. cit., p. 128; Yanson, op. cit., pp. 48–9; Prince A. Vasilchikov, *Zemlevladenie i zemledelie v Rossii*, 2 vols., 1881, vol. 2, p. 85.

18 Yanson, op. cit., p. 38; Druzhinin, op. cit., pp. 125ff.; Lyashchenko, op. cit., pp. 446–7.

19 A. M. Anfimov, *Ekonomicheskoe polozhenie i klassovaya borba krestyan Evropeiskoi Rossii, 1881–1904gg.*, Nauka, 1984, pp. 135–53; D. I. Budaev, *Smolenskaya derevnya v kontse XIX–nachale XXvv.*, Smolensk, 1972, pp. 350–5.

20 A. M. Anfimov, *Krestyanskoe khozyaistvo Evropeiskoi Rossii, 1881–1904*, Nauka, 1980, chapter 4; Budaev, op. cit., p. 350.

21 T. H. von Laue, *Sergei Witte and the Industrialization of Russia*, Columbia, U.P., 1963, p. 145. Compare J. Y. Simms, 'The crisis in Russian agriculture at the end of the nineteenth century: a different view', *S.R.*, no. 36, 1977, pp. 377–98. Simms overstates the originality of his argument; for some similar observations see O. Crisp, *Studies in the Russian Economy before 1914*, Macmillan, 1976, pp. 26–8.

22 For an analogous case see M. Palairet, 'The peasantry of Serbia and the burden of a fiscal revolution, 1862–1911', *J.Ec.H.*, no. 39, 1979, pp. 719–40.

23 A. L. Vainshtein, *Oblozheniya i platezhi krestyanstva v dorevolyutsionnoe i revolyutsionnoe vremya*, Ekonomist, 1924, pp. 23–4, 47–8.

24 Crisp, op. cit., p. 131. The data quoted here are taken from *Sbornik statistiko-ekonomicheskikh svedenii po selskomu khozyaistvu Rossii i inostrannykh gosudarstv*, vol. 10, 1917, pp. 536–9.

25 A. Baker, 'Community and growth: muddling through with Russian credit cooperatives', *J.Ec.H.*, no. 37, 1977, pp. 139–60; G. A. Pavlovsky, *Agricultural Russia on the Eve of the Revolution*, Routledge, 1930, pp. 230–40; A. N. Antsiferov, 'Credit and agricultural cooperation', in E. M. Kayden and A. N. Antsiferov, eds., *The Cooperative Movement in Russia During the War*, Yale U.P., 1930, pp. 286–7. For the European context, see A. S. Milward and S. B. Saul, *The Development of the Economies of Continental Europe, 1850–1914*, Allen and Unwin, 1977, pp. 58–9.

26 A. M. Anfimov, *Krupnoe pomeshchiche khozyaistvo*, Nauka, 1969, p. 72; Carstensen, op. cit., pp. 115–8.

27 V. I. Lenin, *The Development of Capitalism in Russia*, Progress Publishers, 1977, pp. 222–40, 270; Pavlovsky, op. cit.

28 Polyakov, the Russian peasant, is quoted in S. M. Dubrovsky, *Stolypinskaya zemelnaya reforma*, Nauka, 1963, p. 84. For the distribution of capital equipment among the peasantry, see Anfimov, *Krestyanskoe khozyaistvo*, op. cit., p. 157.

29 Robinson, op. cit., chapter 8.

30 M. Confino, *Domaines et seigneurs en Russie vers la fin du XVIIIᵉ siècle*, Mouton, 1963, *passim*.

31 A. Kahan, 'The costs of "westernization" in Russia', *S.R.*, no. 25, 1966, pp. 40–66; Blum, op. cit., pp. 368–70, 376–85; Brockhaus and Efron, *Entsiklopedicheskii slovar* (entry under 'Banki').

32 Blum, op. cit., pp. 318–21; M. I. Tugan-Baranovsky, *The Russian Factory in the Nineteenth Century*, R. D. Irwin, 1970, pp. 83–8.

33 Khodsky, op. cit. According to a modern Soviet historian, redemption payments in the black-earth region amounted to 180 m. rubles by 1881, of which 64 m. went to pay off debts. V. G. Litvak, *Russkaya derevnya v reforme 1861g.: Chernozemnyi tsentr, 1861–1895gg.*, Nauka, 1972, pp. 402–3.

34 A. A. Kaufman, *Agrarnyi vopros v Rossii*, 1919, pp. 83–5; Budaev, op. cit., p. 352; N. M. Druzhinin, 'Likvidatsiya feodalnoi sistemy v russkoi pomeshchichei derevni', *Voprosy istorii*, no. 12, 1968, pp. 203–4; Anfimov, *Krupnoe . . .*, op. cit., p. 298.

35 Pavlovsky, op. cit., p. 195; Brockhaus and Efron, op. cit., entry under 'Vzaimnyi kredit'; A. P. Korelin, 'Krupnyi selsko-khozyaistvennyi kredit v kapitalisticheskoi Rossii', *Ist.zap.*, no. 106, 1981, pp. 162–204.

36 A. P. Korelin, *Dvoryanstvo v poreformennoi Rossii, 1861–1904gg.*, Nauka, 1979, pp. 110–19; Anfimov, *Krupnoe . . .*, op. cit., p. 305.

37 Katkov is quoted in Yu.B. Solovev, *Samoderzhavie i dvoryanstvo v kontse XIX veka*, Nauka, Leningrad, 1973, p. 167. For the supply of short-term credit, see Korelin, 'Krupnyi . . .', op. cit., and Pavlovsky, op. cit., pp. 196–7. For government support, see T. M. Kitanina, *Khlebnaya torgovlya Rossii v 1875–1914gg.*, Nauka, Leningrad, 1978, pp. 179–201.

38 Anfimov, *Krupnoe . . .*, op. cit., p. 299; note, also, the remarks of Kahan, 'Capital formation', p. 283.

39 T. Esper, 'The incomes of Russian serf ironworkers in the nineteenth century', *Past and Present*, no. 93, 1981, pp. 137–59.

40 T. C. Owen, *Capitalism and Politics in Russia: A Social History of the Moscow Merchants, 1855–1905*, C.U.P., 1981, pp. 3–5, 17ff., 83, 153, 255; A. J. Rieber, *Merchants and Entrepreneurs in Imperial Russia*, University of North Carolina Press, 1982, chapter 1; M. C. Kaser, 'Russian entrepreneurship', in Mathias and Postan, *Cambridge Economic History of Europe*, vol. 7, part 2, C.U.P., 1978, pp. 447–50; W. L. Blackwell, *The Beginnings of Russian Industrialization to 1860*, Princeton U.P., 1968; Gindin, 'Russkaya burzhuaziya . . .', pp. 38–9.

41 Tugan-Baranovsky, op. cit., pp. 76–80; Blum, op. cit., pp. 472–4; H. Rosovsky, 'The serf entrepreneur in Russia', in H. Aitken, ed., *Explorations in Enterprise*, Harvard U.P., 1965, pp. 341–70; G. S. Isaev, *Rol tekstilnoi promyshlennosti v genezise i razvitii kapitalizma v Rossii*, Nauka, Leningrad, 1970.

42 Brockhaus and Efron, op. cit. ('Banki'); Crisp, op. cit., p. 114.

43 Cited in L. E. Shepelev, *Aktsionernyie kompanii v Rossii*, Nauka, Leningrad, 1973, p. 82. For an assessment of Reutern's early career see J. W. Kipp, 'M.Kh. Reutern on the Russian state and economy: a liberal bureaucrat during the Crimean War', *Jl. of Modern History*, no. 47, 1975, pp. 437–59.

44 Shepelev, op. cit.; B. V. Ananich, 'The economic policy of the tsarist government', in G. Guroff and F. Carstensen, eds., *Entrepreneurship in Russia and the Soviet Union*, Princeton U.P., 1982, pp. 125–39.

45 Gindin, 'Russkaya burzhuaziya', *passim*; idem, 'Sotsialno-

ekonomicheskie itogi razvitiya rossiiskogo kapitalizma i predposylki revolyutsii v nashei strany', in I. I. Mints, ed., *Sverzhenie samoderzhaviya*, Nauka, 1970, p. 47.

46 O. Crisp, 'Labour and industrialization in Russia', in Mathias and Postan, eds., *Cambridge Economic History*, op. cit., p. 405.

47 McKay, op. cit., pp. 140, 223–5, 233, 305; G. von Schulze-Gaevernitz, *Volkswirtschaftliche Studien aus Russland*, Leipzig, 1899, pp. 274–304.

48 Details in McKay, op. cit., pp. 221–2 and chapter 6, *passim*; Crisp, *Studies*, chapter 5, esp. pp. 144–5, 151–2; Shepelev, op. cit., pp. 140–2.

49 Crisp, *Studies*, p. 125; I. F. Gindin, *Russkie kommercheskie banki*, Gosfinizdat, 1948, pp. 360ff.; P. A. Khromov, *Ekonomicheskoe razvitie Rossii v XIX-XX vekakh*, Gospolitizdat, 1950, p. 365.

50 Gindin, *Russkie kommercheskie banki*, pp. 371, 378–80; Bovykin, op. cit., pp. 250–313.

51 Lenin, *Imperialism . . .*, *passim*; idem, *Can the Bolsheviks Retain State Power?*, Progress Publishers, 1971 (written in late September 1917).

52 Crisp, *Studies*, pp. 121–2, 155; I. F. Gindin, *Gosudarstvennyi bank i ekonomicheskaya politika tsarskogo pravitelstva, 1861–1892gg.*, Gosfinizdat, 1960, pp. 61, 206 and *passim*; Ananich, op. cit.

53 McKay, op. cit., p. 225; Kahan, 'Capital formation', p. 287; F. Carstensen, 'Numbers and reality: a critique of foreign investment estimates in tsarist Russia', in M. Levy-Leboyer, ed., *La Position Internationale de la France*, Bibliothèque Générale de l'Ecole des Hautes Etudes en Sciences Sociales, Paris, 1977, pp. 275–83.

54 Owen, op. cit.; Gindin, 'Russkaya burzhuaziya', *passim*; I. F. Gindin, 'Moskovskie banki v period imperializma, 1900–1917gg., *Ist.zap.*, no. 58, 1956, pp. 38–106; Gindin, *Russkie kommercheskie banki*, pp. 266–75.

55 McKay, op. cit., pp. 229–32.

56 Kahan, 'Government policies . . .'

57 Yu. A. Hagemeister, 'Gosudarstvennyie finansy Rossii nakanune reformy 1861g', *Istoricheskii arkhiv*, no. 2, 1956. See, in addition. W. M. Pintner, *Russian Economic Policy Under Nicholas I*, Cornell, U.P., 1967; Crisp, *Studies*, p. 115.

58 A. P. Pogrebinsky, 'Stroitelstvo zheleznykh dorog v poreformennoi Rossii i finansovaya politika tsarizma', *Ist.zap.*, no. 47, 1954, pp. 149–80.

59 Pogrebinsky points out that the private railway companies juggled with tariff rates in order to achieve some semblance of profitability. For other points in this paragraph see P. P. Migulin, *Russkii gosudarstvennyi kredit*, 3 vols., Kharkov 1901–3, vol. 3, pp. 1126–7; and A. P. Pogrebinsky, 'Finansovaya politika tsarizma v 70–80kh godakh XIXv.', *Istoricheskii arkhiv*, no. 2, 1960, pp. 130–44. This article reproduces some of Bunge's memoranda on the subject of state finances.

60 Kahan, 'Government Policies . . .', p. 469.

61 B. F. Brandt, *Inostrannyie kapitaly: ikh vliyanie na ekonomicheskoe razvitie strany*, 3 vols., St. Petersburg, 1899–1901, vol. 2, pp. 11–14, 51 and chapter 2, *passim*; Shepelev, op. cit., pp. 143–5; Tugan-Baranovsky, op. cit., p. 277.

62 Yanson, op. cit., *passim*; Ananich, op. cit.; Pogrebinsky, 'Finansovaya politika'.

63 A. Babkov, 'National finances and the economic evolution of Russia', *Russian Review*, no. 3, 1912, p. 180; Crisp, *Studies*, pp. 26–8.

64 M. P. Kashkarov, *Finansovyie itogi poslednego desyatiletiya*, *1892–1901*, 2 vols., 1903, vol. 1, *passim*; E. Müller, 'Der Beitrag der Bauern zur Industrialisierung Russlands, 1885–1930', *Jahrbücher für Geschichte Osteuropas*, no. 27, 1979, pp. 197–219. Compare Simms, 'The crisis in Russian agriculture', op. cit.

65 Kashkarov, op. cit., p. 186; Crisp, *Studies*, p. 28.

66 Kahan, 'Government policies', pp. 465–7; Gregory, op. cit., pp. 249–50. Compare von Laue, op. cit., pp. 100–1. For a brilliant examination of the relationship between the Russian finances and tsarist diplomacy see D. Geyer, *Der russische Imperialismus*, Vandenhoeck and Ruprecht, 1977.

67 J. D. Gould, *Economic Growth in History*, Methuen, 1972, pp. 178ff.; H. Feis, *Europe, the World's Banker*, *1870–1914*, Yale U.P., 1930, pp. 27, 57, 78; A. G. Kenwood and A. L. Lougheed, *The Growth of the International Economy*, *1820–1960*, Allen and Unwin, 1971, pp. 43–5.

68 There is a vast literature on foreign investment in Russia, of which the following items have been particularly useful in preparing this section: McKay, op. cit., pp. 73–4 and *passim*; Crisp, *Studies*, chapters 4, 6, 7 and 8; M. E. Falkus, 'Aspects of foreign investment in tsarist Russia', *J.E.E.H.*, no. 8, 1979, pp. 5–36; P. Gregory, *Russian National Income*, pp. 95–99 and Appendix M; idem, 'The Russian balance of payments, the gold standard and monetary policy', *J.Ec.H.*, no. 39, 1979, pp. 379–99; B. Thomas, 'The historical record of international capital movements to 1913', in J. H. Dunning, ed., *International Investment*, Pelican, 1972, pp. 27–58; J. Viner, 'International finances and balance of power diplomacy, 1880–1914', in his *International Economics*, Glencoe Free Press, 1951; F. Stern, *Gold and Iron: Bismarck, Bleichröder and the Building of the German Empire*, Allen and Unwin, 1977, pp. 346, 429–30, 441; B. V. Ananich, *Rossiya i mezhdunarodnyi kapital*, *1897–1914*, Nauka, Leningrad, 1970; and R. Girault, *Emprunts russes et investissements français en Russie*, *1887–1914*, Armand Colin, 1973.

69 Migulin, op. cit., III, p. 478.

70 This paragraph draws upon material presented in Crisp, *Studies*, chapter 4. See also L. E. Shepelev, *Tsarizm i burzhuaziya vo vtoroi polovine XIX veka*, Nauka, Leningrad, 1981, chapter 4, and B. Bonwetsch, 'Handelspolitik und Industrialisierung: zur aussenwirtschaftlichen Abhängigkeit Russlands', in D. Geyer, ed., *Wirtschaft und Gesellschaft im vorrevolutionären Russland*, Kiepenheuer and Witsch, 1975, pp. 277–99.

71 Shepelev, *Tsarizm*, chapter 5; von Laue, op. cit., for the most detailed treatment in English.

72 Crisp, *Studies*, pp. 100–110; Lyashchenko, op. cit., pp. 561–2.

73 H. Barkai, 'The macroeconomics of tsarist Russia in the industrialization era', *J.Ec.H.*, no. 33, 1973, pp. 339–72; Kahan, 'Government policies'; I. Drummond, 'The Russian gold standard, 1897–1914', *J.Ec.H.*, no. 36, 1976, pp. 663–88; P. Gregory and J. Sailors, 'Russian monetary policy and industrialization, 1861–1913', *J.Ec.H.*, no. 36, 1976, pp. 836–51. Drummond puts the rate of growth of total money supply at between 6.5 and 7.0 per cent (1896–1914).

74 For a colourful statement, see von Laue, op. cit., p. 145.

75 Brandt, op. cit., vol. 2, chapter 4.
76 Geyer, op. cit., pp. 132ff., 187–8; Girault, op. cit., pp. 490–1.
77 McKay, op. cit., chapter 6; Carstensen, 'Numbers and reality', pp. 275–83; P. V. Ol, *Foreign Capital in Russia*, Engl. edn, Garland, 1983.

Conclusion (pp. 231–4)

1 V. I. Lenin, *The Development of Capitalism in Russia*, Progress, 1977, p. 603.
2 ibid., p. 104.
3 The evidence is summarized in P. Gatrell, 'The impact of war on Russian and Soviet development, 1850–1950', *World Development*, no. 9, 1981, pp. 793–802.
4 Recent research on the Soviet economy during the 1920s and early 1930s, is assessed by M. Harrison, 'Why did NEP fail?', *Economics of Planning*, no. 16, 1980, pp. 57–67, and S. G. Wheatcroft, R. W. Davies and J. M. Cooper, 'Soviet industrialization reconsidered', *Ec.H.R.*, 1986, forthcoming.

Select Bibliography

The Bibliography is designed to draw the reader's attention to the most important works in English. Some items in French and German have also been included. More comprehensive lists of books and articles will be found in the two reference books listed at the beginning. The third item is given for the benefit of those with a knowledge of Russian, and is an indispensable guide to official and semi-official publications from the tsarist period.

Reference

ALDCROFT, D. H., and RODGER, R., *Bibliography of European Economic and Social History*, Leicester University Press, 1984.

KAZMER, D., and KAZMER, V., *Russian Economic History: A Guide to Information Sources*, Gale, Detroit, 1977.

ZAIONCHKOVSKY, P. A., ed., *Spravochniki po istorii dorevolyutsionnoi Rossii: bibliograficheskii ukazatel*, 2nd edition, Kniga, 1978.

Major books and articles

AMATO, S., 'The debate between marxists and legal populists on the problems of market and industrialization in Russia (1882–1899) and its classical foundations', *J.E.E.H.*, no. 12, 1983, pp. 119–44.

ANANICH, B. V., 'The economic policy of the tsarist government', in GUROFF, G., and CARSTENSEN, F. V., eds., *Entrepreneurship in Russia and the Soviet Union*, Princeton University Press, 1982, pp. 125–39.

ANDERSON, B. A., *Internal Migration During Modernization in Late Nineteenth-Century Russia*, Princeton University Press, 1980.

ANTSIFEROV, A. N., *Russian Agriculture During the War*, Yale University Press, 1930.

BAKER, A., 'Community and growth: muddling through with Russian credit cooperatives', *J.Ec.H.*, no. 37, 1977, pp. 139–60.

BARKAI, H., 'The macro-economics of tsarist Russia in the industrialization era: monetary developments, the balance of payments and the gold standard', *J.EcH.*, no. 33, 1973, pp. 339–72.

BATER, J. H., *St. Petersburg: Industrialization and Change*, Edward Arnold, 1976.

BATER, J. H., and FRENCH, R. A., eds., *Studies in Russian Historical Geography*, 2 volumes, Academic Press, 1983.

BLACKWELL, W. L., *The Beginnings of Russian Industrialization, 1800–1860*, Princeton University Press, 1968.

——, ed., *Russian Economic Development from Peter the Great to Stalin*, New Viewpoints, New York, 1974.

BLUM, J., *Lord and Peasant in Russia from the Ninth to the Nineteenth Century*, Princeton University Press, 1961.

BONNELL, V. E., *Roots of Rebellion: Workers' Politics and Organisation in St. Petersburg and Moscow, 1900–1914*, University of California Press, 1983.

BONWETSCH, B., 'Handelspolitik und Industrialisierung: zur aussenwirtschaftlichen Abhängigkeit Russland', in GEYER, D., ed., *Wirtschaft und Gesellschaft im vorrevolutionären Russland*, Kiepenheuer und Witsch, Cologne, 1975.

CARSTENSEN, F. V., 'Numbers and reality: a critique of foreign investment estimates in tsarist Russia', in LEVY–LEBOYER, M., ed., *La Position Internationale de la France*, Bibliothèque Générale de l'Ecole des Hautes Etudes en Sciences Sociales, Paris, 1977, pp. 275–83.

——, *American Enterprise in Foreign Markets: Singer and International Harvester in Imperial Russia*, University of North Carolina Press, 1984.

CHAYANOV, A. V., *The Theory of Peasant Economy*, R. D. Irwin, Homewood, Illinois, 1966.

CHOJNACKA, H., 'Nuptiality patterns in an agrarian society', *Population Studies*, no. 30, 1976, pp. 203–26.

COALE, A., ANDERSON, B. A., and HÄRM, E., *Human Fertility in Russia Since the Nineteenth Century*, Princeton University Press, 1979.

CONFINO, M., *Systèmes agraires et progrès agricole: L'assolement triennal en Russie aux XVIIIe-XIXe siècles*, Mouton, Paris, 1969.

CRISP, O., *Studies in the Russian Economy before 1914*, Macmillan, 1976.

——, 'Labour and industrialization in Russia', in MATHIAS, P., and POSTAN, M. M., *Cambridge Economic History of Europe*, vol. 7, part 2, C.U.P., 1978, pp. 308–415.

CZAP, P., ' "A large family: the peasant's greatest wealth": serf households in Mishino, Russia, 1814–1858', IN WALL, R., ed., *Family Forms in Historica Europe*, C.U.P., 1983, pp. 105–51.

DRUMMOND, I. M., 'The Russian gold standard, 1897–1914', *J.Ec.H.*, no. 36, 1976, pp. 663–88.

EMMONS, T., *The Russian Landed Gentry and the Peasant Emancipation of 1861*, C.U.P., 1968.

——, 'The peasant and emancipation', in VUCINICH, W., ed., *The Peasant in Nineteenth-Century Russia*, Stanford University Press, 1968, pp. 41–71.

——, and VUCINICH, W., eds., *The Zemstvo in Russia: An Experiment in Local Self-Government*, C.U.P., 1982.

ENTNER, M. L., *Russo-Persian Commercial Relations, 1828–1914*, University of Florida Press, 1965.

ESPER, T., 'The incomes of Russian serf ironworkers in the nineteenth century', *Past and Present*, no. 93, 1981, pp. 137–59.

FALKUS, M. E., 'Russia's national income, 1913: a revaluation', *Economica*, no. 35, 1968, pp. 52–73.

——, *The Industrialization of Russia, 1700–1914*, Macmillan, 1972.
——, 'Aspects of foreign investment in tsarist Russia', *J.E.E.H.*, no. 8, 1979, pp. 5–36.
FIELD, D., *The End of Serfdom: Nobility and Bureaucracy in Russia, 1855–1861*, Harvard University Press, 1976.
GATELY, M. O., 'The development of the Russian textile industry in the pre-revolutionary years, 1861–1913', unpublished Ph.D. dissertation, Kansas, 1969.
GATRELL, P. W., 'Industrial expansion in tsarist Russia, 1908–1914', *Ec.H.R.*, no. 35, 1982, pp. 99–110.
GERSCHENKRON, A., *Economic Backwardness in Historical Perspective*, Harvard University Press, 1962.
——, *Europe in the Russian Mirror: Four Lectures in Economic History*, C.U.P., 1970.
——, 'Agrarian policies and industrialization in Russia, 1861–1917', in POSTAN, M. M., and HABAKKUK, H. J., eds., *Cambridge Economic History of Europe*, vol. 6, part 2, C.U.P., 1965, pp. 706–800.
GEYER, D., *Der russische Imperialismus: Studien über den Zusammenhang von innerer und aussenwärtiger Politik, 1860–1914*, Vandenhoeck und Ruprecht, Göttingen, 1977.
GIRAULT, R., *Emprunts russes et investissements français en Russie, 1887–1914*, Armand Colin, Paris, 1973.
GOLDSMITH, R. W., 'The economic growth of tsarist Russia, 1860–1913', *Economic Development and Cultural Change*, no. 9, 1961, pp. 441–75.
GORLIN, R. H., 'Problems of tax reform in imperial Russia', *Journal of Modern History*, no. 49, 1977, pp. 246–65.
GREGORY, P. R., 'The Russian balance of payments, the gold standard and monetary policy: a historical example of foreign capital movements', *J.Ec.H.*, no. 39, pp. 379–99.
——, 'Grain marketings and peasant consumption in Russia, 1885–1913', *E.E.H.*, no. 17, 1980, pp. 135–64.
——, *Russian National Income, 1885–1913*, C.U.P., 1982.
—— and SAILORS, J. W., 'Russian monetary policy and industrialization, 1861–1913', *J.Ec.H.*, no. 36, 1976, pp. 836–51.
GUROFF, G., and CARSTENSEN, F. V., eds., *Entrepreneurship in Imperial Russia and the Soviet Union*, Princeton University Press, 1983.
HAIMSON, L., 'The problem of social stability in urban Russia, 1905–1917', *S.R.*, no. 23, 1964, pp. 619–42; no. 24, 1965, pp. 1–23.
HAJNAL, J., 'European marriage patterns in perspective', in GLASS, D. V., and EVERSLEY, D. E. C., eds., *Population in History*, Edward Arnold, 1965, pp. 101–43.
HAMM, M. F., ed., *The City in Russian History*, Kentucky University Press, Lexington, Kentucky, 1976.
HARRISON, M., 'Resource allocation and agrarian class formation: the problem of social mobility among Russian peasant households, 1880–1930', *J.P.S.*, no. 4, 1977, pp. 127–61.
—— 'Chayanov and the economics of the Russian peasantry', *J.P.S.*, no. 2, 1975, pp. 389–417.
HEER, D. M., 'The demographic transition in the Russian Empire and the Soviet Union', *Journal of Social History*, no. 1, 1968, pp. 193–240.

HOGAN, H., 'The reorganization of work processes in the St. Petersburg metal-working industry, 1901–1914', *Russian Review*, no. 42, 1983, pp. 163–90.

HOURVITCH, I., *The Economics of the Russian Village*, 1892, reprinted by AMS Press, New York, 1970.

HUSSAIN, A., and TRIBE, K., *Marxism and the agrarian question*, Macmillan, 1983.

JOHNSON, R. E., *Peasant and Proletarian: The Working Class of Moscow in the Late Nineteenth Century*, Leicester University Press, 1979.

KAHAN, A., 'Determinants of the incidence of literacy in rural nineteenth-century Russia', in ANDERSON, C. A., and BOWMAN, M. J., eds., *Education and Economic Development*, Frank Cass, 1965, pp. 298–302.

——, 'The costs of "westernization" in Russia: the gentry and the economy in the eighteenth century', *S.R.*, no. 25, 1966, pp. 40–66.

——, 'Government policies and the industrialization of Russia', *J.Ec.H.*, no. 27, 1967, pp. 460–77.

——, 'Capital formation during the period of early industrialization in Russia, 1890–1913', in MATHIAS, P., and POSTAN, M. M., eds., *Cambridge Economic History of Europe*, vol. 7, part 2, C.U.P., 1978, pp. 265–307.

KAUFMAN, A., 'The history and development of the official statistics of Russia', in KOREN, J., ed., *The History of Statistics*, Franklin, New York, 1918, pp. 469–534.

KERBLAY, B., 'La Réforme de 1861 et ses effets sur la vie rurale dans la Province de Smolensk', in PORTAL, R., ed., *Le Statut des paysans libérés du servage, 1861–1961*, Mouton, Paris, 1961, pp. 267–310.

KINGSTON-MANN, E., 'Marxism and Russian rural development: problems of evidence, experience and culture', *American Historical Review*, no. 86, 1981, pp. 731–52.

KITCHING, G., *Development and Underdevelopment in Historical Perspective: Populism, Nationalism and Industrialization*, Methuen, 1982.

KOENKER, D., *Moscow Workers and the 1917 Revolution*, Princeton University Press, 1981.

KOVALCHENKO, I. D., and SELUNSKAYA, N. B., 'Labor Rental in the manorial economy of European Russia at the end of the nineteenth and the beginning of the twentieth century', *E.E.H.*, no. 18, 1981, pp. 1–20.

LANDES, D. S., *The Unbound Prometheus: Technological Change and Industrial Development in Western Europe from 1750 to the Present*, C.U.P., 1969.

LAUE, T. H. VON, 'A secret memorandum of Sergei Witte on the industrialization of imperial Russia', *Journal of Modern History*, no. 26, 1954, pp. 60–75.

——, 'The state and the economy', in BLACK, C. E., ed., *The Transformation of Russian Society*, Harvard University Press, 1960, pp. 209–25.

——, 'Russian peasants in the factory, 1892–1904', *J.Ec.H.*, no.21, 1961, pp.61–80.

——, *Sergei Witte and the Industrialization of Russia*, Columbia University Press, 1963.

LAYTON, D., 'The tariff of 1891 and the debate on the Russian economy', unpublished Ph.D. dissertation, Indiana, 1965.

LENIN, V. I., *The Development of Capitalism in Russia*, 1899, 2nd edition 1907, reissued by Progress Publishers, Moscow, 1977.

——, *The Agrarian Programme of Russian Social Democracy in the First Russian Revolution, 1905–1907*, 1917, reissued by Progress Publishers, Moscow, 1977.

——, *Imperialism, the Highest Stage of Capitalism*, 1917, reissued by Foreign Languages Publishing House, Peking, 1975.

LEWIS, W. A., 'Economic development with unlimited supplies of labour', in AGARWALA, A. N., and SINGH, S. P., eds., *The Economics of Underdevelopment*, O.U.P., 1963 pp. 400–49.

LYASHCHENKO, P. I., *History of the National Economy of Russia to the 1917 Revolution*, Macmillan, New York, 1949.

MCKAY, J. P., *Pioneers for Profit: Foreign Entrepreneurship and Russian Industrialization, 1885–1913*, University of Chicago Press, 1970.

MANNING, R. T., *The Crisis of the Old Order in Russia: Gentry and Government*, Princeton U. P., 1982.

MENDEL, A. P., *Dilemmas of Progress in Tsarist Russia; Legal Marxism and Legal Populism*, Harvard University Press, 1961.

METZER, J., 'Railroad development and market integration: the case of tsarist Russia', *J.Ec.H.*, no. 34, 1974, pp. 529–50.

MILLER, M., *The Economic Development of Russia, 1905–1914*, 1926, reprinted, Frank Cass, 1967.

MÜLLER, E., 'Der Beitrag der Bauern zur Industrialisierung Russlands, 1885–1930', *Jahrbücher für Geschichte Osteuropas*, no. 27, 1979, pp. 197–219.

MUNTING, R., 'Mechanization and dualism in Russian agriculture', *J.E.E.H.*, no. 8, 1979, pp. 743–60.

NORTH, R. N., *Transport in Western Siberia: Tsarist and Soviet Development*, University of British Columbia Press, 1979.

OBOLENSKY-OSINSKY, V. V., 'Emigration from and immigration into Russia', in WILLCOX, W. F., ed., *International Migrations*, National Bureau of Economic Research, New York, 1931, vol. II, pp. 521–80.

OL, P. V., *Foreign Capital in Russia*, 1922, translated and edited by G. Jones, Garland Press, New York, 1983.

OWEN, T. C., *Capitalism and Politics in Russia: A Social History of the Moscow Merchants, 1855–1905*, C.U.P., 1981.

PALLOT, J., 'Agrarian modernization on peasant farms in the era of capitalism', in BATER, J. H., and FRENCH, R. A., eds., *Studies in Russian Historical Geography*, Academic Press, 1983, vol. I, pp. 423–50.

PARKER, W. N., and JONES, E. L., eds., *European Peasants and Their Markets* Princeton University Press, 1975.

PAVLOVSKY, G. A., *Agricultural Russia on the Eve of the Revolution*, Routledge, 1930.

PICKERING, E. C., 'The International Harvester Company in Russia, 1860s to 1930s', unpublished Ph.D. dissertation, Princeton, 1974.

PIERCE, R. A., *Russian Central Asia, 1867–1917: A Study in Colonial Rule*, University of California Press, 1960.

PINTNER, W. M., *Russian Economic Policy Under Nicholas I*, Cornell University Press, 1967.

POLLARD, S., *Peaceful Conquest: The Industrialization of Europe,*
1760–1970, O.U.P., 1981.

PORTAL, R., 'The industrialization of Russia', in POSTAN, M. M., and
HABAKKUK, H. J., eds., *Cambridge Economic History of Europe*, vol. 6,
part 2, C.U.P., 1965, pp. 801–72.

RAFFALOVICH, A., ed., *Russia: Its Trade and Commerce*, P. S. King, London,
1918.

RANSEL, D. L., ed., *The Family in Imperial Russia: New Lines of Historical*
Research, Illinois University Press, 1978.

RIEBER, A. J., *Merchants and Entrepreneurs in Imperial Russia*, University
of North Carolina Press, 1982.

RIMLINGER, G., 'Autocracy and the factory order in early Russian
industrialization', *J.Ec.H.*, no. 20, 1960, pp. 67–92.

——, 'The expansion of the labor market in capitalist Russia, 1861–1917',
J.Ec.H., no. 21, 1961, pp. 208–15.

ROBINSON, G. T., *Rural Russia Under the Old Regime*, 1932, reprinted by
University of California Press, 1973.

ROGGER, H., *Russia in the Age of Modernization and Revolution,*
1881–1917, Longman, 1983.

SCHULZE-GAEVERNITZ, G. VON, *Volkswirtschaftliche Studien aus Russland*,
Leipzig, 1899.

SETON-WATSON, H., *The Russian Empire, 1801–1917*, O.U.P., 1967.

SHANIN, T., *The Awkward Class: Political Sociology of Peasantry in a*
Developing Society, Russia 1905–1930, O.U.P., 1972.

——, ed., *Late Marx and the Russian Road*, Routledge, 1983.

——, *Russia as a 'Developing Society'*, Macmillan, 1985.

SIEGELBAUM, L., 'The Odessa grain trade: a case-study in urban growth and
development in tsarist Russia', *J.E.E.H.*, no. 9, 1980, pp. 113–52.

SIMMS, J. Y., 'The crisis in Russian agriculture at the end of the nineteenth
century: a different view', *S.R.*, no. 36, 1977, pp. 377–98.

——, 'The crop failure of 1891: soil exhaustion, technological backwardness
and Russia's "Agrarian crisis" ', *Slavonic and East European Review*,
no. 41, 1982, pp. 236–50.

SMITH, R. E. F., and CHRISTIAN, D., *Bread and Salt: A Social History of*
Food and Drink in Russia, C.U.P., 1984.

SMITH, S. A., *Red Petrograd: Revolution in the Factories, 1917–1918*,
C.U.P., 1983.

TENGOBORSKY, M. L. DE, *Commentaries on the Productive Forces of Russia*,
2 volumes, 1856.

TREADGOLD, D. W., *The Great Siberian Migration*, Princeton University
Press, 1957.

TUGAN-BARANOVSKY, M. I., *The Russian Factory in the Nineteenth Century*,
3rd Russian edition, 1907, translated by A. and C. Levin, R. D. Irwin,
Homewood, Illinois, 1970.

TURIN, S. P., *From Peter the Great to Lenin: A History of the Russian*
Labour Movement with Special Reference to Trade Unionism, 1935,
reprinted by Frank Cass, 1968.

VOLIN, L., *A Century of Russian Agriculture*, Harvard University Press,
1970.

VUCINICH, W., ed., *The Peasant in Nineteenth-Century Russia*, Stanford University Press, 1968.

WALICKI, A., *The Controversy Over Capitalism: Studies in the Social Philosophy of the Russian Populists*, O.U.P., 1969.

WHEATCROFT, S. G., 'Grain production and utilization in Russia and the USSR before collectivization', unpublished Ph.D. dissertation, Birmingham, 1980.

WHITE, C. M., 'The impact of Russian railway construction on the market for grain in the 1860s and 1870s', in SYMONS, L., and WHITE, C. M., eds., *Russian Transport*, Bell, 1975, pp. 1–41.

WILLETTS, H. T., 'The agrarian problem', in KATKOV, G., et al., eds., *Russia Enters the Twentieth Century*, Temple Smith, 1971, pp. 111–37.

YANEY, G. L., *The Urge to Mobilize: Agrarian Reform in Russia, 1861–1930*, University of Illinois Press, 1982.

ZELNIK, R. E., *Labor and Society in Tsarist Russia: The Factory Workers of St. Petersburg, 1855–1870*, Stanford University Press, 1971.

——, 'The peasant and the factory', in VUCINICH, W., ed., *The Peasant in Nineteenth-Century Russia*, Stanford University Press, 1968, pp. 158–90.

Index